C. S. Lewis—The Work
of Christ Revealed

C. S. Lewis—The Work of Christ Revealed

P. H. Brazier

Foreword by Justyn Terry

SERIES: C. S. LEWIS: REVELATION AND THE CHRIST
www.cslewisandthechrist.net

◆PICKWICK *Publications* • Eugene, Oregon

C. S. LEWIS—THE WORK OF CHRIST REVEALED

Series: C. S. Lewis: Revelation and the Christ 2

Copyright © 2012 Paul H. Brazier. All rights reserved. Except for brief quotations in critical publications or reviews, no part of this book may be reproduced in any manner without prior written permission from the publisher. Write: Permissions, Wipf and Stock Publishers, 199 W. 8th Ave., Suite 3, Eugene, OR 97401.

Pickwick Publications
An Imprint of Wipf and Stock Publishers
199 W. 8th Ave., Suite 3
Eugene, OR 97401

www.wipfandstock.com

ISBN 13: 978-1-61097-719-7

Cataloging-in-Publication data:

Brazier, Paul.

C. S. Lewis—the work of Christ revealed / P. H. Brazier.

Series: C. S. Lewis: Revelation and the Christ 2

xx + 300 p. ; 23 cm. Includes bibliographical references and index.

ISBN 13: 978-1-61097-719-7

1. Lewis, C. S. (Clive Staples), 1898–1963—Religion. 2. Lewis, C. S. (Clive Staples), 1898–1963—Theology. 3. Apologetics. I. Title. II. Series.

BX5199.L53 B639 2012

Manufactured in the U.S.A.

All royalties from this series are donated to the University of Oxford C. S. Lewis Society

Typeset by P. H. Brazier, Ash Design
Minion Pro 10.75pt on 14pt

SERIES PREFACE
C. S. LEWIS: REVELATION AND THE CHRIST

This is a series of books that have a common theme: the understanding of Christ, and therefore the revelation of God, in the work of C. S. Lewis. These books are a systematic study of Lewis's theology, Christology, and doctrine of revelation; as such they draw on his life and work. They are written for academics and students, but also, crucially, for those people, ordinary Christians, without a theology degree who enjoy and gain sustenance from reading Lewis's work.

Book One
Revelation, Conversion, and Apologetics

Book Two
The Work of Christ Revealed

Book Three
The Christ of a Religious Economy

A fourth volume, consisting of an in-depth bibliography, plus an introductory essay on Christology as the study of Christ, and a glossary, completes the series:

C. S. Lewis—An Annotated Bibliography and Resource

There is a website to accompany (www.cslewisandthechrist.net) that provides material and downloads to complement these books. Those who feel somewhat bemused by the concepts in Christology (the study of Christ) may gain understanding from browsing the site, which will give an introduction to the series. In addition a full detailed contents, including all sections can be downloaded and printed as an aide-memoire and guide to each book in the series.

This series has been many years in the making. The serious writing of it started in 2007; however, sketches relating to some of the topics go back much further. With writing the work grew. Lewis was not a systematic theologian, nor did he attempt to write a systematic theology (though the aim of *Mere Christianity* gets close to it). What this work attempts is to present a systematic study of what Lewis understood about Jesus Christ, and the revelation of God, who is at the heart of orthodox, traditional, theology.

For Hilary

Contents

List of Illustrations / xi

Foreword / xiii

Acknowledgements / xvii

Introduction: C. S. Lewis—The Work of Christ Revealed / 1

Part One
Scripture—Revelation Transposed

1. Scripture, Revelation, and Reason I: Skepticism and Suspicion / 21
2. Scripture, Revelation, and Reason II: Mediation and the Bible / 45
3. Scripture, Revelation, and Reason III: Idealism and Transposition / 71

Part Two
The Revelation of Christ—God, Or a Bad Man

4. *aut Deus aut malus homo* I: What did Lewis Say? / 89
5. *aut Deus aut malus homo* II: The Theological Tradition / 103
6. *aut Deus aut malus homo* III: Divine Self-Disclosure / 127
7. *aut Deus aut malus homo* IV: Arguments For and Against / 151
8. *aut Deus aut malus homo* V: Lewis's Trilemma / 165

Part Three
Christ Prefigured—Intimations to the Pagans

9. Christ as the Light of the World I: A Doctrine of Christological Prefigurement / 191
10. Christ as the Light of the World II: Revelation and Meaning—Imagination, Illumination, and Prevenience / 217
11. Christ as the Light of the World III: Refractions—Splintered Fragments of the True Light / 245

Conclusion. The Work of Christ—Revealed / 265

Select Bibliography / 269

Indexes / 279

Sectional Contents / 293

List of Illustrations

Figure 1 (Chapter 1)
C. S. Lewis's Classification of Genre in the Old Testament / 29

Figure 2 (Chapter 2)
Four Models on the Relationship of Scripture and Inspiration / 47

Figure 3 (Chapter 2)
C. S. Lewis and Karl Barth—The Word of God in a Threefold Form / 55

Figure 4 (Chapter 2)
C. S. Lewis and Revelation: A Hierarchy of Modes of Revelation / 67

Figure 5 (Chapter 4)
C. S. Lewis—*aut Deus aut malus homo*, sources / 91

Figure 6 (Chapter 4)
C. S. Lewis—The Lucy Triumvirate / 99

Figure 7 (Chapter 5)
The Johannine Trilemma / 125

Figure 8 (Chapter 6)
John's Gospel—The "I Am" Sayings / 137

Figure 9 (Chapter 7)
C. S. Lewis—Summary of His Position on *aut Deus aut malus homo* / 153

Figure 10 (Chapter 8)
C. S. Lewis—A 1+2 Trilemma / 167

Figure 11 (Chapter 8)
Stephen T. Davis—The Logical Form of C. S. Lewis's Trilemma / 171

Figure 12 (Chapter 8)
Peter Kreeft—The Logical Form of C. S. Lewis's Trilemma 1 / 175

Figure 13 (Chapter 8)
Peter Kreeft—The Logical Form of C. S. Lewis's Trilemma 2 / 175

Figure 14 (Chapter 8)
Anselm of Canterbury and C. S. Lewis—Faith and Understanding / 179

Figure 15 (Chapter 8)
"But Who do you Say that I Am?"—Answers / 183

Figure 16 (Chapter 9)
A Doctrine of Christological Prefigurement / 193

Figure 17 (Chapter 9)
C. Stephen Evans—Four Definitions of Myth / 195

Figure 18 (Chapter 9)
C. S. Lewis—Six Elements towards a Definition of Myth / 197

Figure 19 (Chapter 9)
Sources for C. S. Lewis's Christological Prefigurement / 205

Figure 20 (Chapter 10)
The Young and Mature Lewis, with George MacDonald in the Centre, pen-and-ink drawing by P. H. Brazier / 233

Figure 21 (Chapter 10)
A General and a Specific Theory of Illumination / 239

Figure 22 (Chapter 11)
Illumination–Inspiration in Pagan Mythopoeia / 249

Figure 23 (Chapter 11)
The Death–Descent/Rebirth-Reascent Paradigm, in C. S. Lewis's Work / 261

Foreword

Naturalism, the view that nothing of any importance exists beyond the natural universe, has become one of the greatest challenges the church has faced since the Reformation. With the rise of modern science and its success in providing explanations for natural events that make no reference to divine agency, naturalism has become a powerful alternative to theistic religion. It has made it difficult, some would say impossible, to speak about the heavenly realm, which is so vital to understanding the Christian faith. If it really is the case, as naturalism claims, that there are scientific explanations for all things, whether we currently know those explanations or not, we can see why many people who have been influenced by this teaching have lost their faith in God or thought twice before taking seriously the gospel proclamation. The fear of being seen as ignorant of scientific progress or naively superstitious has proved a stumbling block for many believers and would-be believers.

The challenge is most especially acute when the subject of our inquiry is Jesus Christ. If we have to shave away all references to divine revelations or miraculous powers, it is amazing how little we have left of the Jesus of the New Testament. He can hardly be acknowledged to speak for God or act as God when the claims that God speaks or acts in the world are so firmly ruled out. To meet the stringent demands of naturalism, the traditional Chalcedonian claim that Jesus is fully God and fully man has to be set aside in favour of a much diminished view of a very limited and purely human Jesus. He may remain perhaps as one of the great religious teachers of human history, to be held up as an example of rare insight into our life on earth, but his claims to being the Son of God or bearing salvation for the sins of the world have to be withdrawn.

The question arises: can Christianity meet the demands of naturalism? One way of understanding the painfully public rifts in the major Christian denominations in the West today is by seeing them as the result of two very different answers to that question. There are those who would wish to provide an affirmative answer, and regard shedding those teachings of the Bible or Christian tradition that are incompatible with naturalism as a necessity for the future of Christianity. On the other hand, there are those who say that such a reconfiguration of the Christian faith is not only unnecessary but also unsustainable, since it is naturalism that needs to bend before the revelation of the risen Jesus Christ, and any such scaling down of the faith renders it impotent.

Of all the Christian apologists who have sought to directly confront the challenge of naturalism, one of the most effective and enduring has been C. S. Lewis. He was unusually well prepared for such a task by his background and education. He could understand the thinking of a naturalist, having become an atheist in adolescence after losing the Protestant faith in which he had grown up in Belfast, Northern Ireland. He also knew of the world of the imagination from his study of literature and poetry and could see how stifling to such thinking naturalism could become. In addition, he was well versed in philosophy, which gave him important tools to engage the ideas of naturalists. He was especially aided by the writings of George MacDonald and G. K. Chesterton, and his colleague in the English Department at Oxford University, J. R. R. Tolkien. They not only assisted him in overcoming his objections to the Christian faith, but also introduced him to concepts that would supply him for his future work. They prepared him to engage the naturalists on their own ground with unusual clarity and effectiveness.

Paul Brazier's book, the second in a series, brings out Lewis's great contribution to this challenge with clarity and depth. Following the introductory work, which considers Lewis on revelation, conversion, and apologetics, Brazier here moves into Lewis's Christology and expounds it in relation to theologians like Anselm of Canterbury, Augustine of Hippo, Samuel Taylor Coleridge, and Karl Barth, and philosophers like Stephen T. Davis, Peter Kreeft, and C. Stephen Evans. This allows us not only to understand Lewis's own views more thoroughly, but also to locate them in the wider scholarly scene.

Brazier has three main foci in this work. The first is Lewis's views of Scripture, his primary source for knowledge about Jesus. Lewis was highly critical of the prevailing "higher critical methods" of the naturalistic biblical scholars of his day, bringing his skills in the analysis of literature to bear on their methods. Brazier also investigates Lewis's trilemma, which poses the alternative conclusions about Jesus in terms of him being bad, mad, or God. He investigates how this kind of argument has been used in the Christian tradition and finds it to be well-supported, if rarely used by academic theologians. Finally, he examines how the revelation of Christ is pre-figured in the pagan world, using Lewis's idea of the myths becoming reality in the incarnation of Jesus Christ.

This book is not intended to promote any one particular expression of Christianity. It follows Lewis's vision of, "Mere Christianity," which was largely free from the demands of championing one denominational position or another, but rather fully committed to showing the truth of the traditional claims of the church against its cultured despisers. He was also mindful that his own teachers included Roman Catholics like G. K. Chesterton, who taught him to seek "Mere Christianity," and J. R. R. Tolkien, and Congregationalists like George MacDonald. He became a committed member of the Church of England, whose broad-based reformed catholicism gave him room to embrace members of other denominations and allowed a truly ecumenical spirit to permeate his many works.

Like Lewis, Brazier has endeavoured to provide a text that can at the same time help enquirers into the Christian faith, lay Christians who are wrestling with questions about their faith, and academics in the theological college and university who are engaging these issues in the public sphere. There is that combination of clarity and depth that so characterises Lewis and makes him not only a communicator of the faith but also a model of how to communicate it.

There are many shorter works on Lewis that touch on his theological positions but what Brazier offers here is an in-depth analysis that is an invitation to treat Lewis as one of the major figures in Christian philosophy and theology. This is a further sign that what Lewis has to say about methodological naturalism continues to be important. As secularism advances around the world, the naturalism that is so endemic to its modern aspects continues to present difficulties for the church even as the postmodern turn blunts its earlier sharpness. Those who are wondering about becoming Christians themselves, Christians who are wondering about how to respond to the secular challenge, and academics looking to advance our understanding of the faith in the light of the current challenges can all benefit from this book. The teaching of C. S. Lewis remains timely today and Brazier has helped lay out his theology in a way that is both systematic and accessible. It will be a help to all who read it.

The Very Rev. Dr. Justyn Terry,
Dean/President and Associate Professor of Systematic Theology,
Trinity School for Ministry, Ambridge PA, USA

Acknowledgements

My initial interest in C. S. Lewis started with a Sunday afternoon TV serialization of *The Lion, the Witch and the Wardrobe* in, I think, 1967. Crude by today's CGI standards, and in black-and-white, I only saw the first episode amidst a chaotic time of my life, yet a seed was sown, thoughts which I could not get out of my mind. Credit should also be given to a fellow student, Debbie Gould, when I was at art college, who commented pointedly to me that I should read Lewis's works. Something I started to do seriously when I became a Christian in 1980. Acknowledgement must be accorded to Dr. Murray Rae and Dr. Brian Horne (both formerly of King's College London) for engendering in me a serious study of Lewis from 1999, which culminated in this work. Thanks must also be given to Dr. Pat Madigan S. J. (Editor of *The Heythrop Journal*), for encouragement—and for publishing articles generated by this research), Judith and Brendan Wolfe (The University of Oxford C. S. Lewis Society), and also to John Field, a well-read Christian, for advice in reading early drafts. My thanks go to N. T. (Tom) Wright, for discussions (conducted by e-mailed message) on the nature of *the Christ* as presented in this work. My deepest thanks must go to Robin Parry (editor, Wipf and Stock) for countless ideas and advice, and his unrivaled expertise as a biblical scholar, particularly in his editing of this series. But ultimately acknowledgement and thanks must go to Hilary, my wife, without whom I would not be the person I am, and this work would never have existed.

Acknowledgement and thanks is given to the C. S. Lewis Co. Pte., for permission to quote from the following works.

Correspondence
C. S. Lewis, *Collected Letters, Vol. I: Family Letters 1905–1931* (2004). Extracts by C. S. Lewis, copyright © C. S. Lewis Co. Pte. Reprinted by permission.

C. S. Lewis, *Collected Letters, Vol. II: Books, Broadcasts and War 1931–1949* (2004). Extracts by C. S. Lewis, copyright © C. S. Lewis Co. Pte. Reprinted by permission.

C. S. Lewis, *Collected Letters, Vol. III: Narnia, Cambridge and Joy 1950–1963* (2007). Extracts by C. S. Lewis, copyright © C. S. Lewis Co. Pte. Reprinted by permission.

Single Volumes

C. S. Lewis, *Beyond Personality: the Christian Idea of God* (1944). Extracts by C. S. Lewis, copyright © C. S. Lewis Co. Pte. Reprinted by permission.

C. S. Lewis, *Broadcast Talks. Reprinted with some alterations from two series of Broadcast Talks "Right and Wrong: A Clue to the Meaning of the Universe" and "What Christians Believe" given in 1941 and 1942* (1942). Extracts by C. S. Lewis, copyright © C. S. Lewis Co. Pte. Reprinted by permission.

C. S. Lewis, *Mere Christianity. A revised and amplified edition, with a new introduction, of the three books Broadcast Talks, Christian Behaviour and Beyond Personality (based on radio talks of 1941–1944; 1952)*. Extracts by C. S. Lewis, copyright © C. S. Lewis Co. Pte. Reprinted by permission.

C. S. Lewis, *Miracles* (1st Edition, 1947). Extracts by C. S. Lewis, copyright © C. S. Lewis Co. Pte. Reprinted by permission.

C. S. Lewis, *Miracles* (2nd Edition, 1960). Extracts by C. S. Lewis, copyright © C. S. Lewis Co. Pte. Reprinted by permission.

C. S. Lewis, *Reflections on the Psalms* (1958). Extracts by C. S. Lewis, copyright © C. S. Lewis Co. Pte. Reprinted by permission.

C. S. Lewis, *Surprised by Joy. The Shape of my Early Life* (1955). Extracts by C. S. Lewis, copyright © C. S. Lewis Co. Pte. Reprinted by permission.

C. S. Lewis, *That Hideous Strength. A Modern Fairytale for Grown-Ups* (1945). Extracts by C. S. Lewis, copyright © C. S. Lewis Co. Pte. Reprinted by permission.

C. S. Lewis, *The Pilgrim's Regress: An Allegorical Apology for Christianity, Reason and Romanticism* (third edition, 1944). Extracts by C. S. Lewis, copyright © C. S. Lewis Co. Pte. Reprinted by permission.

C. S. Lewis, *The Problem of Pain* (1940). Extracts by C. S. Lewis, copyright © C. S. Lewis Co. Pte. Reprinted by permission.

The Chronicles of Narnia

C. S. Lewis, *The Chronicles of Narnia. The Last Battle* (1956). Extracts by C. S. Lewis, copyright © C. S. Lewis Co. Pte. Reprinted by permission.

C. S. Lewis, *The Chronicles of Narnia. The Lion, the Witch and the Wardrobe* (1950). Extracts by C. S. Lewis, copyright © C. S. Lewis Co. Pte. Reprinted by permission.

C. S. Lewis, *The Chronicles of Narnia: The Silver Chair* (1953). Extracts by C. S. Lewis, copyright © C. S. Lewis Co. Pte. Reprinted by permission.

C. S. Lewis, *The Chronicles of Narnia: The Voyage of the Dawn Treader* (1952). Extracts by C. S. Lewis, copyright © C. S. Lewis Co. Pte. Reprinted by permission.

Volumes of Essays

C. S. Lewis, *Christian Reflections* (ed. Walter Hooper; 1967). Extracts by C. S. Lewis, copyright © C. S. Lewis Co. Pte. Reprinted by permission.

C. S. Lewis, *God in the Dock: Essays on Theology* (1979). Extracts by C. S. Lewis, copyright © C. S. Lewis Co. Pte. Reprinted by permission.

C. S. Lewis, *The World's Last Night and Other Essays.* New York, NY: Harcourt, Brace, 1960. Extracts by C. S. Lewis, copyright © C. S. Lewis Co. Pte. Reprinted by permission.

C. S. Lewis, *They Asked for a Paper* (1962). Extracts by C. S. Lewis, copyright © C. S. Lewis Co. Pte. Reprinted by permission.

C. S. Lewis, *Transposition and Other Addresses* (1949). Extracts by C. S. Lewis, copyright © C. S. Lewis Co. Pte. Reprinted by permission.

C. S. Lewis, *Undeceptions: Essays on Theology and Ethics* (1971). Extracts by C. S. Lewis, copyright © C. S. Lewis Co. Pte. Reprinted by permission.

Single Papers in Journals or as Guest Writer
C. S. Lewis, "Introduction." In *English Literature in the Sixteenth Century* (1954). Extracts by C. S. Lewis, copyright © C. S. Lewis Co. Pte. Reprinted by permission.

C. S. Lewis, "Introduction." In, J. B. Phillips, *Letters to Young Churches: A Translation of the New Testament Epistles* (1947). Extracts by C. S. Lewis, copyright © C. S. Lewis Co. Pte. Reprinted by permission.

C. S. Lewis, "Socrates was a Realist." In *The Socratic Digest*, No. 1 (1943). Extracts by C. S. Lewis, copyright © C. S. Lewis Co. Pte. Reprinted by permission.

C. S. Lewis, "Will we lose God in Outer Space." In, *The Christian Herald* (1958). Extracts by C. S. Lewis, copyright © C. S. Lewis Co. Pte. Reprinted by permission.

Acknowledgement and thanks is given to Houghton Mifflin Harcourt for the U.S. right for permission to quote from the following works:

Excerpts from REFLECTIONS ON THE PSALMS, copyright © 1958 by C. S. Lewis, renewed 1986 by Arthur Owen Barfield, reprinted by permission of Harcourt, Inc.

Excerpts from SURPRISED BY JOY: THE SHAPE OF MY EARLY LIFE, by C. S. Lewis, copyright © 1956 by C. S. Lewis and renewed 1984 by Arthur Owen Barfield, reprinted by permission of Harcourt, Inc.

Extracts from the Bible used with permission:

Revised Standard Version of the Bible, copyright 1952 [2nd edition, 1971] by the Division of Christian Education of the National Council of the Churches of Christ in the United States of America. Used by permission. All rights reserved.

New Revised Standard Version Bible, copyright 1989, Division of Christian Education of the National Council of the Churches of Christ in the United States of America. Used by permission. All rights reserved.

New Revised Standard Version Bible: Anglicized Edition, copyright 1989, 1995, Division of Christian Education of the National Council of the Churches of Christ in the United States of America. Used by permission. All rights reserved.

THE HOLY BIBLE, NEW INTERNATIONAL VERSION®, NIV® Copyright © 1973, 1978, 1984, 2011 by Biblica, Inc.™ Used by permission. All rights reserved worldwide.

Nestle-Aland, Novum Testamentum Graece, 27th Revised Edition, edited by Barbara Aland, Kurt Aland, Johannes Karavidopoulos, Carlo M. Martini, and Bruce M. Metzger in cooperation with the Institute for New Testament Textual Research, Münster/Westphalia, © 1993 by Deutsche Bibelgesellschaft, Stuttgart. Used by permission.

Introduction
C. S. Lewis—The Work of Christ Revealed

This is a book about Jesus Christ.

Jesus of Nazareth, the Christ, is of central importance to humanity.

Jesus Christ is considered by orthodox Christians to be the unique revelation of God, the God above all gods, the God beyond all gods.

These are strong, dynamic, and assertive claims. There are various ideas and interpretations of who or what this Jesus of Nazareth, the Christ, was and is; these theories vary across the churches. However, down the centuries there has been a constant and steady seam of knowledge and understanding as to who Jesus Christ is, how he is God, and how this affects all of humanity.

To talk about Jesus Christ is to speak of revelation—God's self-revelation, God's revealedness to humanity. Therefore, God is the one who initiates both in our knowledge and understanding about these most important of matters, but also, crucially, in our salvation.

1. WHO OR WHAT IS *THE* CHRIST

This is one of a series of books entitled *C. S. Lewis: Revelation and the Christ*. Like many ancient names that had cultural or religious meanings, the name Jesus—in Hebrew, *Yeshua*, given to Mary by Gabriel, the angel at the annunciation—was known to those who heard it as signifying "God is savior," or "Jehovah is savior"; Christ means "anointed one," messiah. The word Messiah was commonly used in the era between the two testaments, Old and New (i.e., the intertestamental period), the concept of messiahship having developed in later Judaism (from the early Hebrew *Mashiach*, the anointed one, derived from the ancient Hebrew tradition of anointing the king with oil). Messiah was not necessarily a name, but a label, an attribution, an office, a role, essentially a title. By the time of Jesus of Nazareth the title "Messiah" was often attributed to someone the people liked, whom they believed could fulfill, they hoped, a role for them. However, *the* Messiah was to be the one anointed at the end of days. Jesus is therefore taken by those around him to be *the* Messiah; hence the early attribution that he is the Christ. The word Christ is simply a translation from the Greek (χριστός, *Christos*) and the Latin (*Christus*) for messiah. Therefore Jesus Christ, in name and title, was God's salvation, the anointed one. This did not necessarily imply that he was the second person of the Trinity. The trinitarian perception is part of the dawning realization in the early church, with ample pointers and examples of Jesus's trinitarian nature in the books that became the New Testament (texts produced by the earliest church in the years after the resurrection and ascension).

Around the time of Jesus's birth messiahship carried expectations. Some saw the coming messiah as a political leader who would expel the Romans; others expected a messiah who would be a partisan revolutionary whose aims were unclear; to yet more the messiah would return the Temple religion back to a happier time, he would oversee the restoration of Israel. To an extent these can be seen as purely human offices. During the intertestamental period there were many false messiahs, men raised up to realize a revolutionary, political, or religious role supported by a group or sect to save Israel in some way or other. However, false messiahs lapsed, disappeared, or were killed by the Romans or the Jewish religious authorities. The Jews were left still hoping.

The idea of redemption, salvation, was part of these multitudinous expectations of a messiah figure during the intertestamental period—but saved *from what*, redeemed *to what*? The answers to those questions were as varied as the messianic expectations of these false messiahs. As a redeemer figure, expected and foretold, Jesus does not necessarily live up to the expectations of his fellow Jews. However, on reflection, the clues were there all along in Jesus's life and ministry, and crucially in the Old Testament. The ancient Hebrews priests and kings were anointed, they were messiahs (Exod 30:22–25); later, this messiahship entitled one anointed by God as a leader, a king from the line of David. Therefore, Jesus of Nazareth was perceived by many who saw and heard him to be *the* long awaited Messiah, with different and often subjective expectations as to his role. What is important is that *a posteriori*, after the event, the proto early church interpreted this messiahship in the context of Jesus's role as God descended to earth to judge and forgive humanity, hence the use of the Greek word χριστός (*Christos*), Christ, by the writers of the New Testament. Jesus is then *the* final Messiah of messiahs.

Messiah, Christ, is then revealed to be trinitarian: God anoints God to descend to save his chosen people, in potential, along with all humanity, reascending with them into the divine life. Only in the fullness of the incarnation-cross-resurrection and the ascension is messiahship finally defined by Jesus. Then his life and ministry, his sayings and actions, take on new meaning, a significance and understanding veiled to many during his lifetime. Whatever the expectations of messiahship, Jesus of Nazareth is *the* Messiah (therefore, *the* Christ), not *a* messiah, political or otherwise. It is fair to say that some of the Hebrew expectations were blown away by God's revelation; whatever people expected, it fell short of what was given by God in this Jesus. People couldn't see or fully understand what Messiah was to be, even though the evidence was there in the Old Testament.

The witness of the apostles, disciples, and the early church is then a form of revelation equal to Scripture. The early church tradition replaces the old Hebrew categories of messiahship; the expectations of Jesus's contemporaries were fulfilled by God's revelation, but not necessarily in accordance with what they desired or expected. This divergence also extended to the interpretation of messiahship that the Jewish religious authorities held to in Jerusalem. For many years the Western church concentrated only on the early church tradition and the conclusions of the church councils in the fourth and fifth centuries, often, in effect, ignoring the Hebrew tradition that Jesus of Nazareth was born into. In recent years many theologians and Bible scholars, for example the orthodox Christian N. T. Wright, derive most of their conclusions about Jesus of Nazareth from an understanding of the New Testament's Jewish background, a setting in the life of the times in some ways. Perhaps the answer is to hold in balance the Hebrew tradition and categories, the perceptions of the earliest church, and also the conclusions of the later church councils, about the person and nature of Jesus. This is how to see and understand the term Messiah, *the Christ*.

This is a work, in many ways, of Christology; that is, the work and person of Christ, Jesus of Nazareth. Christology is thinking about Christ; explaining using the faculty of reason, mostly in written form, so as to explicate who and what Jesus Christ was and is. Lewis's work was very much in the context of the developed understanding of who and what Christ was; an understanding that took shape in the first seven centuries of the Christian era. As with the Bible, this understanding became something of a compass as to what counts as sound doctrine about Christ and what does not. This body of understanding of what is a traditional and orthodox understanding of Jesus Christ developed gradually during the early church, and then through the following centuries, and was complete by around the year 750 AD. Christology is therefore seen to be the study of the person and work of Christ, fully human and fully divine, historical and universal, and his significance for humanity: this systematic study is therefore the doctrine of Christ, but it must always understand the Hebrew roots into which Jesus of Nazareth was born and lived.

2. WHY C. S. LEWIS

This is a book about one man's understanding of, and his encounter with, Jesus Christ. That man is Clive Staples Lewis—C. S. Lewis, Jack, at his insistence, to all he knew—who wrote many, many books to defend Christianity and the witness of the churches. Lewis's aim was to defend Christianity itself, not Anglican or Roman Catholic, not Methodist or Baptist, not Presbyterian or Evangelical. Why? He sought to defend what he famously called "Mere Christianity," which was not his own personal religion, or his own personal selection from Christian theology and church history, but the faith set out in the creeds and explained by the church fathers living more than fifteen hundred years ago, the faith that originated with the apostles who knew this Jesus of Nazareth. Lewis sought to defend the faith that the martyrs died for. Being a "Mere Christian" for him represented the distilled basics of the faith rooted in the God-man Jesus Christ. This was to be distinguished, for Lewis, from watered-down Christianity, from human-centered religion.

Lewis's "Mere Christianity" was, therefore, polemical in its assertiveness. This "Mere Christianity" was there to a greater or lesser degree in all the churches of Lewis's day, but had been compromised by disputes between the churches; indeed the very fragmentation of the church into so many denominations or groupings weakened the basic core of the faith. Games of one-upmanship and power politics between bishops from competing denominations, or arguments over the finer points of worship, or in some instances a wholesale rejection of the beliefs set out in the creed, this all weakened the gospel: that God became incarnate as a human being in Jesus of Nazareth and died for our sins to open up a way for us into heaven. This was at the heart of the Christian faith. This Jesus of Nazareth, the Christ, did not simply live two thousand years ago leaving us alone in the world: the Holy Spirit of this Christ is active, alive, presses on us, seeks to convert us, to save us.

Lewis believed strongly in a basic core to the faith, a "mere" Christian core. All else could be considered to be an embellishment, details that are to a greater or lesser degree important to individual denominations, and are valid to a greater or lesser extent before God, but nonetheless these details and differences are culturally relative, they are in many ways subjective religion. Lewis therefore distinguished what he called "Mere Christianity" from this subjective religion. Lewis was an Anglican; he saw this "Mere Christianity" in the Church of England of his day, that it was at its strongest in the Catholic and Evangelical wings, as distinct from the liberal, modernist, central ground, which he believed marginalized this core of "Mere Christianity": Lewis could therefore be fairly described as a Catholic-Evangelical, indeed he described himself as such.

This book then is written for students and theologians, but also general readers familiar with Lewis's works. Because Lewis was an Anglican this is a work written to be appreciated by Anglicans; however, it can also be appreciated by Roman Catholics who in recent years have developed an interest more and more in the writings of C. S. Lewis; it is also aimed at Evangelicals who have long had a love of Lewis's work, but have been selective about what they agree with and disagree with in Lewis's presentation of the basic core of the Christian faith. Evangelicals may not like the way Lewis subscribed to what can be considered a traditional Catholic position on the sacraments and on purgatory, but he held these beliefs for good reason. And Evangelical readers would do well to think why he did. Likewise Roman Catholic readers would do well to see how Lewis could get beyond the external structure of religion to appreciate the immediacy of relationship any believer can have with the Lord Jesus, which in some ways by-passes the structures and authority of the church(es).

3. AIMS AND OBJECTIVES

This series, *C. S. Lewis: Revelation and the Christ*, is a study of C. S. Lewis's Christology, and his doctrine as such of revelation: that is, his understanding of the person and the work of Jesus Christ, and how this is God's self-revelation. This study includes Lewis conversion, his acceptance of what Jesus Christ had done for him, but also his understanding of the church, which is to be seen as the body of Christ. Therefore this book is about how he put that understanding into words, but it is also about his encounter with Jesus Christ, how Christ revealed of Christ's person, Christ's self, to Lewis, and therefore brought him to the one true trinitarian God. This is, in effect, what this book is about: who and what Jesus Christ is, and what *he* does.

The aim of this book is to show what C. S. Lewis understood about Jesus Christ. The objective is to examine what he then wrote, but also how he came to know and to believe in the God behind and in the Christ. This book is–

- A systematic study of the person and work of Christ Jesus in the writings of C. S. Lewis, and the place this understanding has in the wider church, contemporary and historical.

- A systematic study of Lewis's understanding of revelation—God's self-revelation to humanity—and with it humanity's salvation.

- This is therefore a work about Lewis's doctrine of Christ (including his understanding of the church—the body of Christ), his doctrine of salvation, and his doctrine of revelation (including the respectful criticism he had for "religion").

- A presentation of the personal God in Christ, which is central to understanding C. S. Lewis himself, both child and adult, public and private, and how this relates to his work as a philosopher and theologian, and his personal salvation.

- A work that presents an understanding for thinking Christians and professional academics, which ranks Lewis amongst the more important theologians and philosophers of the twentieth century.

- An analysis of Lewis's method and technique (both theological and philosophical) in the way he re-presented the basic non-negotiable core of the faith in his apologetic, his analogical stories, and in his theological narrative.

- A study of Lewis's Christology that acknowledges the Catholic (for example, a high sacramental theology, a belief in purgatory) and the Evangelical (his acknowledgement of the need for personal conversion in the form of a direct relationship with the Lord) within his faith as a Catholic-Evangelical.

Many books relating to C. S. Lewis's theology assume that he was an amateur theologian who simply summarized Christian doctrine and ethics for his audience, that he was not an original thinker or a systematician on the scale of more noted professionals. This series of books, *C. S. Lewis: Revelation and the Christ*, demonstrates that this is *not* so, that such conclusions are spurious. Lewis may not have been employed as a religious professional but the same can be said for many theologians and apologists in church history. Lewis's work is original, underlyingly systematic, and orthodox (i.e., traditional).

Lewis excelled at a cohesive expounding of the essentials at the heart of the Christian belief, nonetheless he held to an understanding of the wider logical sweep of the faith, without becoming embroiled in the more controversial details that have bedevilled the churches, individual denominations, for centuries. Lewis's understanding of Christ was grounded in his conversion. This was a conversion that paralleled, in many ways, that of Augustine in his acceptance of what God had done for him in the incarnation and in his invocation of Christ as the light of the world, and was given its systematic edge by his daily reading of key works of theology and related philosophy from before the modern era (that is, works written prior to the Age of Reason and the Enlightenment in the eighteenth and nineteenth centuries, and the modernism-postmodernism of the twentieth century).

Revelation and salvation are all intertwined with what we know of and understand about Jesus Christ. Therefore we are dealing with three doctrines (that is, doctrine as a set of beliefs or principles held and taught by a group, whether the church, a political party, or academics, from the Latin *doctrina* "teaching, learning"). Those three doctrines are closely related: a doctrine of *revelation*, a doctrine of *Christ*, and a doctrine of *salvation*. We cannot separate who and what Jesus is from what he came to achieve, and what this person reveals to us about God. This work is a systematic study of Lewis's presentation and understanding of Jesus Christ that, following his conversion, underpinned his work. It assesses the implications of what he wrote and how Lewis the philosopher/theologian—when writing on Christ—is to be seen in relation to the church. This is in regard to his reputation as a Christian theologian, but also how the person and work of Christ Jesus is central to the human that he was.

4. EXPLANATIONS, QUALIFICATIONS

Despite often being classified as an amateur, Lewis was a highly educated man. Although he had no formal training in theology, his intellect was confirmed in that he received, within four years of study, two BA Hons degrees from the University of Oxford, having passed all three required public examinations with first class honors. These degrees were in Greats (Greek and Roman Literature and Classical Philosophy) and in English. Despite the astute sharpness and strength of his intellect, Lewis tried to avoid specialized theological language (jargon). However, a few terms do need to explained before we proceed. Some readers familiar with Lewis's books may not appreciate the full meaning and use of the terms used here. Professionals familiar with these terms may still gain some understanding of the context in which they are used in this book. Many Catholics and Evangelicals are familiar with these terms derived from New Testament Greek, and from *ecclesial* (i.e., church) Latin—ironically it is often Lewis's Anglicans who are ignorant of them.

i. Revelation and Reason

Revelation is personal, as in the realization of perception and understanding many people will have—a eureka moment when one finds something, or when something is

Introduction

revealed to one. But it is also more than that, more than the personal and subjective. Revelation is about God's *self-disclosure* to humanity. Lewis understood and accepted how God had revealed of God's self to humanity in multifarious and diverse ways down the millennia and across vast geographical and cultural eons, but as an orthodox Christian he knew, both as fact and from personal encounter, that Christ was the unique, the highest, form of self-revelation of the one true living God. So to talk about Christ is to talk about God; to speak of Christ is to speak of revelation. Over recent centuries revelation has often been pitted against reason. Because of the confidence emanating from the Age of Reason and the Enlightenment, a confidence issuing from the belief that the human capacity to reason things out for ourselves was all that was needed, revelation became, in certain quarters, obsolete.[1] Lewis seeks to try to hold both revelation and reason in balance; as a trained philosopher he knew and understood the background against which he was writing.

ii. Patristic

The patristic era is from the time of Christ's resurrection through to the mid-eighth century. The church leaders and theologians of this period of over 700 years are called "patristic"—from the Greek for Fathers, *patēr*, *patros*—hence the theology of these centuries is patristic, formed by the early church fathers. The immediate years after Christ's resurrection is called the apostolic era—the era or period of the apostles, essentially the people who knew Jesus of Nazareth or were of his generation, all of whom had died by around the year 100 AD. We then have the sub-apostolic era, which is essentially the second century, then fully the patristic era.

iii. Platonism

Platonism is the name given to the philosophy of Plato (c.424/423BC–348/347BC), and his writings. The term also applies to systems of philosophy derived from Plato's work and ideas, for example, Neo-Platonism or Platonic Realism. Central to Platonism is the theory of forms. The forms are transcendent archetypes; what we take for reality is in some way a pale imitation of the forms—reality relates to the forms as an imperfect copy does to an original. The forms tell us that what we take for reality is *perceivable* but not *intelligible*, but that there is another higher reality that is *intelligible* but not *perceivable*. Lewis was a trained philosopher; indeed early in his career he taught philosophy. Platonism is a type of philosophy that he not only subscribed to but which characterized his work throughout his life. Most patristic theologians were Platonists, to varying degrees; Neo-Platonism was in many ways part of patristic theology. Many Protestant, Reformed, or Evangelical supporters of Lewis's work today object strongly to his Platonism, not realizing that it is fundamental to Lewis's interpretation of the gospel and is at the heart of his understanding of revelation. The precise nature of Lewis's Platonism will be fully explained at the appropriate point in this work.

---

1. For an understanding of the relationship between revelation and reason in terms of the disciplines of theology and philosophy, see: Gunton, *Revelation and Reason*.

iv. Apologist/Apologetics

C. S. Lewis is an apologist. Apologetics are defined by the Oxford English Dictionary as, *reasoned arguments in justification of a theory or doctrine*. An apologist is one who argues, who confronts the disagreements and divergences that are evident between different belief systems. The term comes from the Greek word, ἀπολογία, *apologia*, meaning *to speak in defense*. Christian apologetics are written to defend the truth of the gospel against attack from atheists, scientists, philosophers, exponents of non-Christian religions, indeed anyone that denies the heart of the Christian faith. Christian apologetics are considered different to theology *per se*, because in apologetics the truth of the gospel is represented in such a way as possibly to change the content in reaction to a perceived threat, indeed the apologetic content may be defined by the threat. Academic theology is considered by some to be impartial, disinterested, and neutral—in theory—and therefore in some ways superior. Yet if the gospel is true we cannot hold to an impartial multi-faith position that regards all religions and philosophies as equal, more pertinently that regards the content of all world religions as equally valid. Lewis did not: he understood that the gospel stands in contrast to the world, was *against* the world in many ways. Most of the theological writings in the early church are considered to be apologetics because they were written against the background of pagan Roman religion and politics, and were therefore written under persecution.

v. Creation, Fall, Incarnation, Resurrection, Second Coming, and the Four Last Things

The heart of the Christian faith, the basics, are in some ways summarized by the creation and the fall into original sin set out in the Book of Genesis; by the incarnation, crucifixion, resurrection, and second coming of God in Christ, in the New Testament; but also the four "last things" from the Book of Revelation as well as the Gospels. This is Lewis's basic summary of the faith. Lewis believed in the traditional faith, set out by the apostles, the early church, and the early church fathers, which was biblical. At the centre of the Bible story, in some ways summarized by the creeds, is, as Lewis asserted "the Creation, the Fall, the Incarnation, the Resurrection, the Second Coming, and the Four Last Things."[2] Some of this may be obvious but it separates Lewis from many modern theologians and churchmen who have watered down the faith. First, whatever we may learn about evolution and the origin of the world and the universe, God created everything out of nothing and sustains it. Second, that humanity, through its own fault, disobeyed God and was infected by original sin; furthermore we brought this on ourselves, and the predicament we find ourselves in is perilous. Third, God became incarnated as a human being, Jesus Christ, who was crucified for our sins and was resurrected, all to atone for our fall into original sin and restore us to a right relationship with God. Fourth, that this same Jesus Christ will return to judge all at the end of the world, which will be, as Lewis terms it, the four last things: death, judgment, heaven, and hell. This is the *eschaton* (from the Greek for last or final things).

2. Lewis writing to *The Church Times*, Feb. 8, 1952. Lewis, *Collected Letters Vol. III*, 164.

Introduction

vi. Liberal/liberal, Modernism

C. S. Lewis's writings are set against the background of liberal culture and society in Britain specifically, and the United States and Europe generally. "Liberalism" is often seen as a contentious and problematic word—often it appears to generate an emotional response, may be considered pejorative, and may also be invoked in an equally subjective manner. In this work the words "Liberal" and "Liberalism" with an initial capital letter are used strictly in the context of theological Liberalism in the church: this is a position that more often than not denies the incarnation and resurrection, seeking to promote Jesus of Nazareth as an ordinary human being, furthermore, a Liberal theological position may not believe in God (with a capital "G") but happily allow people to believe in "gods" of their own making, their own invention. Lewis often referred to this as a modernist tendency. Theological Liberalism since the eighteenth-century has claimed freedom not only from traditional dogmas and creeds but also in the analysis of and value accorded to Scripture. Such theology was to a large degree formulated in the light of what were considered advances in the natural sciences and philosophy—the spirit of the Age of Reason and the Enlightenment. In this work, when cited with a lower case initial letter ("liberal"), the term refers to liberalism in society and culture generally, in ethics and morality in the twentieth-century. This has often been to do with sexual behavior, but is also seen in culture, the media, entertainment, etc. Therefore a distinction needs to be drawn between Liberalism as a *theological* movement or belief system and what is often euphemistically called a liberal perspective in Western society generally. Today those who subscribe to ethical liberalism (particularly in the area of sexuality and marriage) may or may not to a greater or lesser degree subscribe to theological Liberalism. For example, there are East Coast American Episcopalians today who support the legitimization of homosexual behavior within Christian ethics yet who are strongly orthodox and creedal in their doctrinal beliefs; but then there are also those who subscribe to this ethical liberalism whilst simultaneously denying Christ's divinity and regarding him as just another ordinary man, therefore these two liberals (differentiated by an upper or lower case initial letter) cannot be seen as identical, or as completely separate from each other. Lewis uses the term "Modernism"/"Modernist" very much in the same context as Liberalism—he was often scathing about Modernist tendencies in the Church of England, tendencies that essentially were theological Liberalism, which argued that all our ideas about God were wrong, that there was no supernatural God beyond the ideas in our minds, our deepest desires, and wishes.

vii. Pagan

Lewis's theological writings, as indeed with his conversion, are played out against the backdrop of what is termed pagan religion or paganism. A pagan is essentially someone holding beliefs from outside of the world's main religions. "Pagan" therefore refers to this form of religion and religious myths from outside of, in our instance, the Jewish and Christian traditions. It is important to remember that the term "pagan" was used by Lewis, and is likewise used here, with no derogatory intent, nor as a term of abuse. Lewis used the term simply to refer to those peoples and cultures outside of the Jewish and Christian traditions: that is, Oriental, Middle Eastern, Indian, and European tribes and nations, but particularly in the ancient world (Greek and Roman philosophy and literature, religion, and mythology) and especially the religion and mythology of the North European tribes (Celtic, Norse, etc.), with whom the name pagan is most often associated. In comparison to the post-Christian world in the West today (Lewis was amongst the first to coin the term "post-Christian" at a time when Britain still perceived its civic pageantry and public religion, and its people as Christian, first using the term "post-Christian" publically in an address on November 29, 1954[3]), where it often being asserted that Britain is "slipping," "descending," "regressing" into paganism, Lewis was quite adamant.

> When grave persons express their fear that England is relapsing into Paganism, I am tempted to reply, "Would that she were." For I do not think it at all likely that we shall ever see Parliament opened by the slaughtering of a garlanded white bull in the House of Lords or Cabinet Ministers leaving sandwiches in Hyde Park as an offering for the Dryads. If such a state of affairs came about, then the Christian apologist would have something to work on. For a Pagan, as history shows, is a man eminently convertible to Christianity. He is essentially, the pre-Christian, or sub-Christian, religious man. The Post-Christian man of our own day differs from him as much as a divorcée differs from a virgin. The Christian and the Pagan have much more in common with one another than either has with the writers of the *New Statesman*; and those writers would of course agree with me.[4]

When Lewis is talking about Paganism he is therefore speaking of the pre-Christian world of peoples and cultures diverse from the Christian but moving towards the fulfillment of some sort of understanding of the revelation of Jesus Christ. Essentially the difference between a pre-Christian pagan and the contemporary post-Christian pagan is one of movement: the pre was moving *towards* in his/her theistic beliefs, the post is moving *away* in his/her atheistic beliefs.

viii. Romantic

The term Romantic, with an initial capital letter, has nothing to do with cheap romantic novels or magazines, or romance! The term Romantic represents a movement in art and culture—poets such as Longfellow, Wordsworth, and Keats were considered Romantics, as were painters such as Constable and Turner, and composers such as Beethoven and, to a degree, Wagner. As an artistic and cultural term Romantic is to do with feeling, with expressing oneself, with responding to the innate beauty in landscape and the natural world. Romanticism was in some ways a reaction against the scientific rationalism of the Age of Reason. The Romantic Movement was often

---

3. Lewis's inaugural lecture at Cambridge, Nov. 29, 1954. C. S. Lewis, "De Descriptione Temporum," 9–25.
4. Lewis, "Is Theism Important?," 138.

associated with the cult of the individual—of emaciated, troubled artists starving in garrets and producing works of genius entirely by themselves without any input and involvement from anyone else.

5. "... AND THE COLLECTED WORKS OF C. S. LEWIS"

Many people over the last one hundred and fifty years have tried to encapsulate the intellectual rigor, the cogency, and veracity of the gospel, while communicating it to an audience of ordinary people, often interested skeptics. The Bible scholar and bishop N. T. Wright, commenting on Lewis's writings, notes how "millions around the world have been introduced to, and nurtured within, the Christian faith through his work where their own preachers and teachers were not giving them what they needed."[5] Wright was a case in point; he notes how his tutors, when an undergraduate at the University of Oxford, "looked down their noses if you so much as mentioned him [Lewis] in a tutorial. This was, we may suppose, mere jealousy: He sold and they didn't. It may also have been the frustration of the professional who, busy about his footnotes, sees the amateur effortlessly sailing past to the winning post." But Wright, like other academics, raises questions about just how universal Lewis's work was—it was about the gospel, was a defense of the gospel, but it was not *the* gospel: "the Christianity offered by Lewis both was and wasn't the 'mere' thing he made it out to be... But above all it worked; a lot of people have become Christians through reading Lewis." There is, therefore, a universal appeal to Lewis's work that is lacking in many other apologists and academic theologians, whose work is often soon forgotten, being relative to and emerging from particular cultural, human, subjective positions. This has not been the case with Lewis's defense of the gospel. For example, the writer Joseph Pearce has noted how Joseph Fessio SJ cited this universal appeal in comments at a theological conference in the mid-1990s. Quoting from an address given by the philosopher Peter Kreeft, Pearce notes Fessio's comments, initially given somewhat tongue-in-cheek, which were roundly endorsed across all denominational divisions:

> Father Fessio made these remarks during a theological conference in the mid-1990s, which Peter Kreeft recalled in 1998 as "the most memorable moment of the most memorable conference I ever attended." Attending the meeting, says Kreeft, were "dozens of high-octane Roman Catholics, Anglicans, Eastern Orthodox and Protestant Evangelicals," who, despite their noted theological differences, converged near the end of the conference in a crescendo of agreement. Kreeft continues: "In the concluding session Father Fessio got up and proposed that we issue a joint statement of theological agreement among all the historic, orthodox branches of Christendom saying that what united us was 'Scripture, the Apostles' Creed, the first six ecumenical councils and the collected works of C. S. Lewis.' The proposal was universally cheered."[6]

---

5. This and the following quotations are from, Wright, "Simply Lewis," 39–40. Online: http://www.touchstonemag.com/archives/article.php?id=20-02-028-f.

6. Pearce, *C. S. Lewis and the Catholic Church*, xiii–xiv. Joseph Pearce quotes from, Peter Kreeft, "The Achievement of C. S. Lewis: A Millennial Assessment," unpublished address given at Boston College, 1998.

Pearce notes how Protestants, Catholics, and Eastern Orthodox have managed to find areas of substantial agreement in Lewis's works. For example, Pearce notes, the centrality to salvation history of Christ's atoning death on the cross, the historical event of the resurrection, the authority of Scripture, and the unchanging reality of moral law. So despite flaws, despite Lewis's humanity, there is categorically, objectively, something to Lewis's work that transcends the relative, the fashionable and transient, the subjective, the slanted, prejudiced, and blatantly one-sided (i.e., denominational), in ways that other apologists and theologians have failed in.

6. LEWIS ON THE CHRIST: GOD AND REDEEMER

As the second book in the series, *C. S. Lewis—the Work of Christ Revealed*, consists of three parts, eleven chapters in all; each chapter opens with a synopsis (of between 200 and 500 words) of the content and argument contained therein. Some chapters are quite long, but nonetheless are a coherent thematic whole despite their length. All chapters are divided into multiple sections and sub-sections to allow for ease of access to the material contained in these long chapters. (A full, detailed, sectional contents can be found at the end of this volume.)

i. Part One: Scripture—Revelation Transposed

Part One (chapters 1–3) is an assessment of C. S. Lewis on the Bible; his doctrine of Scripture will tell us much about the basis of his understanding of revelation and the Christ: person, act, event. Lewis connects revelation with illumination, how the writers of Scripture were inspired. Lewis lays great stress on the humanity of Scripture—infinite wisdom, which comes down and is beyond complete human comprehension. How reliable is the picture we have of Christ from Scripture? What value did Lewis accord to Scripture? Lewis was highly critical of modern biblical criticism where it attempted to reduce and explain away and where it sought to demythologize. Lewis questioned the expertise of "modern" critics in understanding genre and literary types, where this understanding was based on the mistaken notion of historical superiority, and a denial of the miraculous.

Can we deduce a doctrine of Scripture in Lewis's work? Did Lewis regard the Bible as inerrant? What authority does Scripture hold? Does it have special status over all other books? What does it mean to say it is the word of God? For Lewis, God was infallible, yet God also allowed for the freedom of creation to be. Hence, the writers of Scripture were divinely inspired, but were fallen and fallible: God breathed; the Holy Spirit imparted intimations to the human mind, though the mind is free to make of these intimations what it will. For Lewis the very act of reading is revelatory. Lewis, like Karl Barth, distinguishes between the word of God (Scripture) and the Word of God (Christ). We can consider what other theologians have written on Lewis's understanding of how God reveals of God's self to humanity, and how they identify and categorize modes of revelation: the numinous (God's holiness); the universal ought (moral responsibility); *Sehnsucht* (wistful longings); election (Israel and the law); good

Introduction

dreams (pagan premonitions of Christ), even, for Lewis, the natural world. However, these categories exclude Scripture and the developing church tradition that constituted Lewis's "mere" core; therefore, these categories need to be ranked hierarchically in relation to the concrete, perfect, and particular revelation that is the incarnation: the Word of God revealed. All revelation must be seen as related to Christ the mediator. Lewis therefore saw all revelation perceivable by humanity as coming from Christ who is the true Word of God.

We need to consider something of Lewis's background as a philosopher, and how his thought is formed through his reading of the seventeenth-century Cambridge Platonists, and the eighteenth-century Irish philosopher George Berkeley, which drew him yet again back to Plato. Lewis proposed what he called a doctrine of transposition, which was heavily reliant upon Platonic concepts, but also on the patristic theologian and philosopher Augustine. Revelation is transposed, changed, altered, without one-to-one correspondence. Lewis's doctrine of transposition is designed to explain how revelation works, how revelation is communicated, or, more pertinently, how revelation can never be fully imparted; this we conclude relates to the *communicatio idiomatum* (the communication of attributes), the knowability of God (which is both a veiling and an unveiling), and how human fallibility can lead us to misread what is communicated to us. Lewis referred to his doctrine of transposition as his contribution to the philosophy of the incarnation.

ii. Part Two: The Revelation of Christ—God, or a Bad Man

Part Two (chapters 4–8) is based on the proposition that Jesus was "Bad, Mad, or God." This is central to C. S. Lewis's popular apologetics, and he used it often to argue for the truth of the gospel. It is fêted by American Evangelicals, cautiously endorsed by Roman Catholics and Protestants, but often scorned by philosophers of religion. Most, mistakenly, regard Lewis's trilemma as unique. However, we can trace its origin to Jesus's question to Peter—"But who do you say that I am?" (Matt 16:15, cf. Mark 8:27–30 and Luke 9:20–21)—and thereby we can examine the roots of this proposition in a two thousand year old theological and philosophical tradition (that is, *aut Deus aut malus homo*—"either god, or a bad man"): for example in the fourth-century writings of Gaius Marius Victorinus, in his apologetic arguments to counter Julian the Apostate. We can also find reference to it in medieval scholasticism and in the writings of Sir Thomas More. However, its use is essentially post-Reformation, in response to the skepticism of the Age of Reason and the Enlightenment: "What do we say about Jesus if he was not God incarnate?" The work of the Victorian churchman and theologian H. P. Liddon (*Christus, si non Deus, non bonus*—"Christ, if not God, is not good") is important here, along with the nineteenth-century American preacher and theologian Mark Hopkins. The immediate origin of Lewis's use is found in the influence of G. K. Chesterton.

This tradition is ultimately grounded in the Johannine trilemma (that Jesus was taken to be an "unbalanced liar," or he was castigated as "demonically possessed," or he was perceived to be "the God of Israel come amongst his people"). Thus Jesus can only be understood in the context of the Jewish religious categories he was born into; therefore, for Lewis, Jesus is who he reveals himself to be. Jesus's self-understanding reflects his identity, his triune salvific role; this is, for Lewis, the transposed reality of divine Sonship. Reason and logic are paramount here, reflected in the structure of Lewis's argument.

What is the structure of Lewis's argument? Is it bipartite or tripartite? As popular apologetics Lewis presents the argument as a 1+2 trilemma specifically using simplistic language: a) mad, b) bad, or c) God (MBG or BMG). How does this compare with other examples of trilemmas—both religious and secular? Many have attempted to analyze Lewis's trilemma—chief among them are Peter Kreeft and Stephen T. Davis. Lewis's trilemma is not so much a proof of God's existence, but a question, a dilemma, where each and every person must come to a decision. For all its perceived faults and its simplistic language, Lewis's trilemma still is a very successful piece of Christian apologetic, grounded in a serious philosophical and theological tradition.

iii. Part Three: Christ Prefigured—Intimations to the Pagans

Part Three (chapters 9–11) is an examination of the Christology that C. S. Lewis read from the apparent prefiguring of elements of the incarnation-resurrection narrative in non-Christian religious myths. This is, in effect, what we may term a doctrine of christological prefigurement. Such a doctrine is summarized in two propositions: first, the actuality of the historic event of the incarnation-cross-resurrection was previsioned in pagan religion and myth (i.e., in non-Judaic-Christian religious stories and myths); second, the Gospel account, the incarnation-cross-resurrection narrative, acts on us, whether spoken or read, both as fact and myth. From his teenage years on Lewis the apostate atheist held the North European pagan myths in very high regard. This was related to his love of Wagner's music, which is rooted in such myths; but he also valued Middle Eastern and Asiatic-Indian-Oceanic myths—in particular ancient Hindu. However, with his conversion he chose not to reject these pagan myths out-of-hand but try to understand how they related to the Christ event: an event that was an actuality that he had come to realize was central to human history.

Initially we need to examine what we mean by myth and reality, by fact and fiction. Lewis's writings on the myth that became reality (the incarnation-resurrection) are discussed along with examples of prefigurement (in particular the myth of Balder the Beautiful). By examining the relationship between religion and human creativity we can establish a paradigm—that revelation precedes religion. In contrast to his earlier deference for the conclusions of the Victorian colonial religionist and social anthropologist Sir James George Frazer (conclusions rooted, as they were, in a Feuerbachian-Freudian interpretation of a Darwinian model of human evolution, which classified religion as a tribal human construct to a hostile world), Lewis came to regard these prefigurements as the work of the Holy Spirit—intimations of God's salvific action in Christ.

Some may consider there to be a problem with a doctrine of christological prefigurement because it appears to do an injustice to the original aims and intentions of the author of the myth in asserting a second, a subsequent, christological level of meaning. Lewis thought not, and could defend such an interpretation. Through his understanding of natural theology, revelation, and human imagination (proximate to that of Augustine, but also to the English Romantics, especially the poet, theologian, and philosopher Samuel Taylor Coleridge), Lewis's esteem, prior to his conversion, for pagan myths relating to the appearing (incarnation?) and reviving from death (resurrection?) of pagan gods, avatars, and spirits, led him after his conversion to analyze why and how these religious myths/stories related to the actual Christ event. Lewis's understanding in this is contiguous to Coleridge and George MacDonald, but also J. R. R. Tolkien (from whom he learns and uses many concepts—for example, sub-creation, mythopoeic/mythopoeia, refractions and splinters of the true light, also eucatastrophe). His cautious respect for these intimations of prefigurement was as a mode of revelation rooted in Augustine's doctrine of illumination and the proposition that there is no un-aided true knowledge of God.

Following on from what we have established with regard to the prefigurement of the incarnation-resurrection narrative, and in the light of what we have concluded on meaning and revelation, imagination, illumination, and prevenience, Lewis's doctrine of christological prefigurement leads us to ask three groups of questions. First, how do these prefigured ideas come to be in these myths and how do these intimations, splintered fragments of the true light, relate to Lewis's understanding of Christ as the light of the world? Are these intimations the product of mythopoeia or of demonic mimicry? The second group of questions centers on how the incarnation-resurrection narrative acts and operates on us as a myth, whether spoken or read (a baptized imagination is crucial here, for Lewis, in both the creation and receiving/hearing of such narratives). The third group of questions relate to the internal evidence for a mythopoeic interpretation within the incarnation-resurrection narrative? Lewis asserted that the incarnation-resurrection narrative operates on us both as fact *and* myth—was he right? Do these prevision narratives—and the gospel story—act on us in a perlocutionary manner? Why does the incarnation-resurrection narrative appear to resonate with agrarian corn myths the world over? Lewis concluded that "the pattern is there in nature because it was first there in God," that there is a death descent/rebirth-reascent paradigm written into creation. Jesus Christ is not another *example* of this paradigm; he is the Lord of creation, nature's creator, the *author* of the paradigm.

7. LEWIS'S CHRIST

We can ask what do we make of Lewis's understanding of Jesus Christ, the incarnation of the one true living God? How do we assess the rare accusations by some professional theologians/writers that there are elements of christological heresy in some of Lewis's writings? How do we define/categorize Lewis's objective understanding of Christ, and likewise his subjective appropriation? What christological model does Lewis draw?

Lewis's Christ, that is the picture he gives us in his Christology, is essentially a picture in words, a Christ from below, not primarily from above because it starts with Immanuel, God with us. This is balanced, initiated, by a shift (a Platonic shift for Lewis) from eternity into our reality: the Christ descends to raise us up; in doing so we are drawn into the divine life. However, humanity is not overwhelmed by Christ: Christ is the loving servant, but authoritative in *his* divine claim on all creation, a creation that, for Lewis, Christ sang into being, into existence, *ex nihilo* (out of nothing). Lewis's Christology is therefore high—this is God incarnate, not a wandering preacher/healer who was super-religious, or a Palestinian carpenter who was a good moral teacher.

The key to Lewis's Christology is in the authority of Christ in majesty, in the Last Judgment. This was represented in Patristic art by the Pantocrator, the risen and ascended Christ enthroned in majesty, surveying, sustaining and judging creation: Christ as the ruler of the universe. This was seen especially in Byzantine art (for example, The Christ Pantocrator, a mosaic in the apse of Monreale Cathedral in Sicily, see: www.cslewisandthechrist.net). Christ, the second person of the Trinity was always shown in paintings and mosaics of the Pantocrator in the form of a Jewish man, God descended to be the humble servant, though reigning in the future, on high. Lewis's understanding of Christ is grounded in many ways in the future, the pure transcendent action of the loving God, the God of love, manifested in and with humanity that comes to us: Immanuel (this is essentially, the timeless breaking into space-time rather than an anticipation). We will see this in Lewis's own personal relationship with God in Christ. For Lewis, the conscious start of this relationship is in his conversion, which was both emotional and reasoned. The reasoning was very much pressed on him by J. R. R. Tolkien, the Roman Catholic Oxford Professor of Anglo-Saxon, in bringing Lewis to accept the truth of what is stated in the creed: that Jesus Christ is God incarnate and that this Christ died because of our sins and for our redemption. Though he could then reason this out, for Lewis acceptance was very much through the Holy Spirit, which pressed upon him, possessed and converted him. We must also consider as part of this relationship his deeper conversion after the death of his wife, Joy Davidman, in 1960.

Therefore Lewis reads his Christology initially from below in the light of the evidence of the self-revelation of the one true living God in Jesus of Nazareth: this is the ground, the reality behind his conversion experience and his assertive apologetics. This points repeatedly to Christ from above, the Universal Christ of the Trinity, uncreated, eternally begotten with the Father, the universal light of the world that comes down to redeem in, as Lewis termed our world, "the shadowlands." Reasoning comes after this has happened, after the event, but is revealed to a degree in our minds because God has put this knowledge, this understanding, in our hearts and minds: it is, in effect, retained as a fragment of the *imago dei* (the image of God) despite our Fallen state, our willfulness to deny God and God's claims on our lives. Christ is within as well as without. Lewis's understanding/knowledge is after the event, after the incarnation, cross, and resurrection reveals the absolute—God—drawing us all towards eternity from above. This is Immanuel's descent to raise us up, to draw us into God, to bring us home; therefore it is the potential salvation of all, subject to our appropriation of Christ's atonement. Holiness/sanctification, for Lewis, is the key here: we are to be perfect—whatever it takes (even a purifying after death, if needed). We will see how this is often presented by Lewis using nature metaphors and therefore is in many ways an organic Christology. Because there is a dialectical balance between the humanity and humility of Jesus Christ as compared to the authority and freedom of the Father from above we are not overwhelmed—despite the direction of God's actions. This is shown in Lewis's writings and his Christian symbolic narratives (for example, *The Chronicles of Narnia*). In Lewis's writings Christ is characterized often by beauty, a beauty that comes to us from the future. This is a beauty that simultaneously judges and forgives, that is, if the human accepts in repentance this judgment and forgiveness. Despite the religious upbringing and education, even religious prejudices, of many of the characters in these Christian symbolic narratives (for example, Narnia) each and every individual must at some point meet with the Christ-Aslan, the embodiment of the love and salvation of the Father; these meetings represent a crisis in each individual's life: they must choose one way or the other. Subject to the vagaries and vicissitudes of the Narnian reality (i.e., he can be killed by the White Witch on the stone table), the Christ-Aslan changes not as we do, our perception changes as we grow spiritually in Christ.

Lewis's picture of Christ in his writings is not simply a restatement of orthodox, classic or high Christology in the form of apologetic writings and symbolic narratives; Lewis's Christology is important in its vibrant balance between the humanity of Immanuel and the power and authority of the shift from the above, the timeless, to here below, into to the world of shadows. Lewis's Christ is significant and important and has often been overlooked in the history of twentieth-century theology.

Part One

Scripture—

Revelation Transposed

> "Then comes the real shock.
> Among these Jews there suddenly turns up a man
> who goes about talking as if he was God. He claims to forgive sins.
> He says he has always existed.
> He says he is coming to judge the world at the end of time."
>
> C. S. Lewis, *Mere Christianity* (1952), 50–51.

1

Scripture, Revelation, and Reason I: Skepticism and Suspicion

SYNOPSIS:
An assessment of C. S. Lewis on the Bible, his doctrine of Scripture, will tell us much about the basis of his understanding of revelation and the Christ: person, act, event. Importantly Lewis connects revelation with illumination, how the writers of Scripture were inspired; therefore, how do we assess apparently mythological narratives, such as the creation story in Genesis? What is the historicity of the Old Testament, of Scripture generally? Lewis lays great stress on the humanity of Scripture—infinite wisdom, which comes down and is beyond complete human comprehension, presenting Scripture as "an untidy and leaky vehicle." Lewis's understanding of Scripture can be gleaned from his multitudinous letters as well as his apologetics: for example, the Clyde S. Kilby letter (1959), and *Reflections on the Psalms*, (1958), where he identifies certain general propositions: we must distinguish between divine word and human comment; we must note that inconsistencies and historical discrepancies point to different levels of historicity even within the Gospels. The humanity of Scripture in relation to the historicity-unhistoricity (as distinct from falsity) must not be understated—Lewis dismisses the proposition that *all* statements in Scripture must be seen as historical truth, or that *all* are unhistorical. For Lewis, Scripture shows that inspiration operates regardless of moral probity (likewise, inspiration is not always of the same mode and to the same degree); we cannot take a passage in isolation, and ignore contradictions, we cannot assume that if one event written in the Bible is true, all events are without flaw. This will lead us to an examination of Lewis on the reliability of the witnesses—the Gospel writers—and the trial of the witnesses (here Lewis's work "God in the Dock" (1948) is highly pertinent). How reliable is the picture we have of Christ from Scripture?

What value did Lewis accord to Scripture? Lewis was highly critical of modern biblical criticism where it attempted to reduce and explain away, where it sought to demythologize. His acerbic criticisms are set out in "Modern Theology and Biblical Criticism" (1959). He was particularly critical of this approach in scholars and clerics such as the German New Testament scholar Rudolf Bultmann, and the Anglican clerics Revd. Dr. Alec R. Vidler and Revd. Dr. Walter Lock, especially in their classification of John's Gospel as myth, their classification of the miracles as metaphorical signs, but pertinently in their use of literary categories: Lewis questioned their expertise in understanding genre and literary types, where this understanding was based on the mistaken notion of historical superiority, a denial of the miraculous, and an attempt to place the text in the context of the life and times in which they were written (*Sitz im Leben*). Lewis was therefore skeptical of a modernist hermeneutic of suspicion (i.e., an analysis and interpretation of the biblical text where it was grounded in suspicion, doubt, and mistrust). This was, for Lewis, an approach that was rooted in the Enlightenment, and the claim to "know" the texts better than the authors did. For Lewis, we should be "agnostic" towards such modern scholarship, which was to be classified as transitory, relative, and ultimately unprovable in its reductionism.

1. PERSON, ACT, EVENT

When asked by the eminent logician and mathematician Heinrich Scholz (originally trained in theology), what was the basis on which theology operated as an intellectual discipline in the university, the Swiss theologian Karl Barth is reported to have answered, assertively, that it is the resurrection of Jesus Christ from the dead. Barth was not embarrassed by an act and event that most academics, particularly scientists and philosophers, repudiated; he did not beat about the bush, he did not obfuscate, there was no hedging around religious emotionalism, no putting any notion of a "god" into a box to be analyzed from the safe secure position of the absolute certainty of a seemingly enlightened human intellect. To Barth the resurrection was the only basis on which you could do theology as a distinctive *Wissenschaft*—that is, a science rooted in reason, objectivity, and knowledge. For Barth, and for C. S. Lewis, all was related to this single event, which had cosmic implications: herein lies the intellectual responsibility that underpinned Lewis's commission and vocation as a Christian apologist—the person, act, and event of God in Jesus of Nazareth, and the resurrection of Jesus Christ. Lewis knew that some of the worst sins were intellectual—they were ideas. So what we believe, or don't believe, has a profound effect upon us, and thereby on other people. Doctrines are sets of beliefs or principles held by the church, taught by the church. We do not as individuals make up what we want to believe to suit our individual needs: truth is *given*. This is what C. S. Lewis had to accept in that momentous conversation with Hugo Dyson and J. R. R. Tolkien in 1931, which triggered his final acceptance and conversion.

When speaking of a doctrine of the Trinity in *Mere Christianity* Lewis addresses the distinction between religion and theology; more pertinently he asserts the importance of doctrine. Lewis regarded theology as a science: "Theology means 'the science of God', and I think any man who wants to think about God at all would like to have the clearest and most accurate ideas about him which are available. You are not children why should you be treated like children?"[1] Lewis acknowledges that there is for some people a distinction between an experience of God on the one hand and the dry almost clinical statements that are the creeds and the doctrines. For someone who has had a genuine experience of God a consideration of doctrine may seem like, for Lewis, turning from something real to something less real. Lewis uses picture and analogy to explain. He compares a map of the Atlantic Ocean with the real thing: observing the ocean from the coast, then looking at a map of the Atlantic is to turn from the real to the less real:

---

1. Lewis, *Mere Christianity*, 127.

1. Scripture, Revelation, and Reason I: Skepticism and Suspicion

> But here comes the point. The map is admittedly only coloured paper, but there are two things you have to remember about it. In the first place, it is based on what hundreds and thousands of people have found out by sailing the real Atlantic. In that way it has behind it masses of experience just as real as the one you could have from the beach; only, while yours would be a single glimpse, the map fits all those different experiences together. In the second place, if you want to go anywhere, the map is absolutely necessary. Now, Theology is like the map. Merely learning and thinking about the Christian doctrines, if you stop there, is less real and less exciting. Doctrines are not God: they are only a kind of map. But that map is based on the experience of hundreds of people who really were in touch with God—experiences compared with which any thrills or pious feelings you and I are likely to get on our own are very elementary and very confused.[2]

This is important because through using narrative and pictures (the map and the ocean) Lewis communicates as an apologist just how important theological doctrines are. The creeds are based on, and grew out of, the *witness* of the apostles. The early Christians did not just come up with ideas about a holy man named Jesus. They had seen with their own eyes, touched and were touched. The witnesses run to hundreds from the start of Jesus's ministry to the Ascension and the Day of Pentecost. Many of these witnesses were women, and if the early Christians were simply making it all up they would not have used women for key witnesses because, according to the Greek and Roman social traditions of the day, a woman's testimony counted for nothing in a court of law. Furthermore, by witnessing to the Christ-event they were putting their lives on the line—Stephen was stoned to death for his testimony. The witness of the many men and woman and children who saw what happened, the events recounted in the Gospels, are, for Lewis, to be considered as more reliable than whatever religious experience we may have today—though such intimations must not be dismissed, they are, as Lewis had seen personally, pointers and allusions, suggestions and intimations, of God's love and expectations for us: "Everyone reads, everyone hears things discussed. Consequently, if you do not listen to theology that will not mean that you have no ideas about God. It will mean that you have a lot of wrong ones—bad, muddled, out-of-date ideas. For a great many of the ideas about God which are trotted out as novelties today are simply the ones which real theologians tried centuries ago and rejected. To believe in the popular religion of modern England is retrogression—like believing the earth is flat."[3] Contrary to the spirit of the age of "modernism," and contrary to the fashionable watered down Christianity that Lewis identified as his opponent, we can see Lewis's content-led method here: his appeal to the testimony of the witnesses who wrote and compiled Scripture, and the developing patristic church tradition. He also refers obliquely to the early church heresies about Jesus Christ that resurface now and again, and for Lewis were evident among some of the Anglican clerics of his day. And popular religion? Popular contemporary religion can be seen as in effect a regression into a neo-paganism. But, as Lewis noted, a pagan, history shows, is a one convertible to Christianity. A pagan is, in religious terms, *pre*-Christian, or *sub*-Christian. Today's

2. Ibid., 127–28.
3. Ibid., 155.

pagans are *post*-Christian.⁴ The difference is essentially that the pagans before Christ were, certainly for Lewis, moving *towards* Christ, whereas today's Western neo-pagans are moving *away* from the Christ-event (arguably to an even greater extent today than in the 1950s, when Lewis commented).

2. C. S. LEWIS ON SCRIPTURE

i. Illumination and Revelation

People have understood the nature of the Bible in subtly different ways down the centuries; likewise any understanding of the authority of the Bible has varied along with its use. The Bible is generally accepted as a mode of special revelation—therefore, if we say the Bible is inspired what exactly do we mean? In these three chapters we will come to see what exactly Lewis believed to be meant by inerrancy, inspiration, and infallibility in relation to revelation and the human faculties of reason and imagination, specifically in two forms of revelation: Scripture, and the Christ-event. When the writers of the New Testament asserted that Scripture was inspired by God, they used the word *theopneustos* (θεόπνευστος): God-breathed. The initiative lay with God: God breathed and the writers received. But in what way? Scripture is a form of revelation caused by the activity of God: Scripture reveals God. Inspiration is taken to be the influence of the Holy Spirit acting on the human mind. Something that is fundamental to Lewis's understanding of Scripture is that myth and sacred fiction can explain the human condition better than historical fact. He wrote, "Myth can be truer than historical fact."⁵ Michael J. Christensen, writing here, who produced an important study of C. S. Lewis and Scripture, written in the late 1970s, explains,

> The Adam and Eve tale, for instance, may express poetically the reality of man's fall from perfection better than any strictly historical account possibly could. Was the forbidden fruit symbolic, then? "For all I can see, it might have concerned the literal eating of a fruit," says Lewis, "but the question is of no consequence." Clyde S. Kilby, an acknowledged authority on C. S. Lewis, states that "Lewis's frequent discussions of the Garden of Eden make it apparent that it means a hundred times more to him as myth than it does to most Christians as history."⁶

Our understanding of God is conditioned and established by the images that God gives us, therefore Lewis talks of divine illumination. So what did Lewis have to say as a theologian and philosopher about Scripture, and on the questions of authority, the nature of Scripture, and related topics?

Lewis's early pre-conversion letters (circa 1914–28) have a surprising number of references to Scripture, even allusions and quotations. This is surprising considering

---

4. C. S. Lewis, "Is Theism Important? A Reply," 138.
5. Christensen, *C. S. Lewis on Scripture*, 35.
6. Ibid., 34–35. Christensen is quoting from Lewis, *The Problem of Pain*, 68; also Kilby, *The Christian World of C. S. Lewis*, 153.

1. Scripture, Revelation, and Reason I: Skepticism and Suspicion

Lewis's anti-Christian position as a young man.[7] These references indicate that Lewis had read his Bible as a child and teenager and key phrases were remembered, apart from which he was living in a cultural milieu that was steeped in what was considered to be Christian culture. For example, he writes, "There is no wind, so where the snow 'falleth, there shall it lie'"[8] an explicit reference to the King James Bible of his schooling and Churchmanship at Wynyard ("In the place where the tree falleth, there shall it be" Ecclesiastes 11:3). In relationship to *Sehnsucht*, "Joy," writing at the time of the horrors of the First World War, Lewis wrote, again to Arthur Greeves, of how, "When the morning stars sang together and all the sons of God shouted for joy" (Job 38:7).[9]

Initially we can see Lewis's approach to Scripture through his voluminous correspondence. Lewis was a dedicated letter writer who answered all correspondence sent to him by readers; he replied in hand written letters; he did not employ a secretary for this task or an amanuensis. In a letter to *The Spectator*, in 1942, Lewis commented, in the context of contradicting a published assumption that it was only clergy who were interested in doctrine, that while he was undertaking the lecture tour for the RAF, an airman exclaimed that it was the first time he'd heard anyone advance a reason for believing that the Bible might contain truth! Lewis commented further that, "we layman are often more easily shocked than our clergy by clerical disbelief or neglect of doctrine."[10] When speaking on modern biblical criticism, Lewis commented that "Probably the best single book of modern comment on the Bible is *A New Commentary on Holy Scripture* edited by Gore, Goudge and Guillaume, and published by SPCK," therefore he was not averse to all modern Bible studies.[11] On the spiritual use of Scripture, he wrote prayerfully, "give me grace so to live that by daily obedience I daily increase in faith and in understanding of thy Holy Word . . ."[12] On the relationship of modern philosophy to Scripture, more pertinently where the seventeenth-century mathematician and philosopher Blaise Pascal contradicts Scripture, Lewis wrote, "Yes Pascal does directly contradict several passages in Scripture and must be wrong."[13] However, he does stress that God speaks not only through Scripture, but other sources as well: "I don't doubt that the Holy Spirit guides your decisions from within when you make them with the intention of pleasing God. The error would be to think that he speaks only within whereas, in reality, he speaks also through Scripture, the Church, Christian friends, books, etc."[14] On the question of hard sayings in Scripture, Lewis commented that when we come across, to use his term, "the dark places" in the Bible, our reaction must not be to dismiss the saying but to believe we have missed the point: God is never evil; but we must never dismiss any passage that seems to imply he is not good: "Behind that apparently shocking passage, be sure, there lurks some great truth

---

7. Lewis, *Collected Letters, Vol. I*, see, 60, 83, 101, 108, 121, 136, 167, 204, 214, 253, 277, 312, 331, 333, 397, 442, 444, 447, 498, 503, 538, 540, 608, 611, 626, 665, 668, 677, 749, and 776.
8. Lewis to Arthur Greeves, Feb. 28, 1916. *Collected Letters, Vol. I*, 167.
9. Lewis to Arthur Greeves, Aug. 4, 1917. *Collected Letters, Vol. I*, 333.
10. Lewis to the editor of *The Spectator*, Dec. 11, 1942. *Collected Letters, Vol. II*, 540.
11. Lewis to Arthur Greeves, Jan. 30, 1944. *Collected Letters, Vol. III*, 1548.
12. Lewis to Genia Goelz, Mar. 18, 1952. *Collected Letters, Vol. III*, 172.
13. Lewis to Dom Bede Griffiths, May, 28, 1952. *Collected Letters, Vol. III*, 195.
14. Lewis to Genia Goelz, Jun. 20, 1952. *Collected Letters, Vol. III*, 204

which you don't understand. If one ever does come to understand it, one will see that *he* is good and just and gracious in ways we never dreamed of."[15]

On the relationship between Scripture and church doctrine, indeed in support of the method and principle we outlined earlier, Lewis asserted in writing to a Mrs. Allcock in 1955, that only what is clearly stated in Scripture and the early creeds can be seen as doctrinal.[16] On fundamentalism and the nature of Scripture Lewis admits he is ill acquainted with modern theological literature, but asserts, writing again in 1955, that he "is not a fundamentalist, if fundamentalism means accepting as a point of faith at the outset the proposition 'Every statement in the Bible is completely true in the literal, historic sense.'"[17]

ii. Genre

As the style or category of art and literature, that is, the style or type of writing that is represented by a biblical book, genre is to be seen as closely related to the aims and objectives of the writer. Genre raises questions: Is a particular text intended to be factual, historic, or scientific? Is it meant to teach something spiritual or moral through story, allegory or parable? Is it to be seen as simply entertaining or an amusing insight into the superstitions and magic of primitive people as some atheists would assert? For Lewis genre is of vital importance; he clearly distinguishes genre: that is, between parables, sacred fiction and history where such books as the Acts of the Apostles are concerned; likewise with the accounts of David's reign in the Old Testament—they are "everywhere dovetailed into a known history and genealogies." By comparison, books like Ester and Jonah, even Job, "proclaim themselves to be sacred fiction."[18] Lewis here is responding to a Mrs. Janet Wise who wrote from the Middle East concerned by some letters in *The Times*, which claimed that there was now a widespread disbelief in the authority of the Bible, especially the Gospels. She wrote that, "it appeared that the unforgivable sin to these clerics was to be a fundamentalist. I regard myself, and still do, as an intelligent fundamentalist."[19] Fundamentalism is, in effect, pressing the Bible too much, pushing it too far. Lewis commented (writing in 1960) that "The Bible seems scrupulously to avoid any descriptions of the other world, or worlds, except in terms of parable or allegory."[20] Another form of Fundamentalism, another misuse of the Bible for Lewis, which is related to genre is in proof texting, that is, taking sayings or verses or a few words out of context, quoting it as a proof for some personal belief or ethic: "The habit of taking isolated texts from the Bible and treating the effect which they have on one in a particular mood at a particular moment as direct messages from God, is very misleading."[21] Lewis commented that this leads to presumptions. However,

15. Lewis to Emily McLay, Aug. 8, 1953. *Collected Letters, Vol. III*, 356–57.
16. Lewis to Mr Allcock, Mar. 24, 1955. *Collected Letters, Vol. III*, 587–89.
17. Lewis to Janet Wise, Oct. 5, 1955. *Collected Letters, Vol. III*, 652–53.
18. Ibid., 652.
19. Ibid., 652, n.284.
20. Lewis to Vera Gebbert, Oct. 16, 1960. *Collected Letters, Vol. III*, 1198.
21. Lewis to Mrs Green, Jun. 18, 1962. *Collected Letters, Vol. III*, 1353.

at the other extreme Lewis saw the emphasis on treating the Bible as an intellectual curiosity as highly questionable; he was not against the academic dissecting of the Bible but saw little value in such antiquarianism when the Bible was clearly addressed to our conscience, to our Fallen will, and was concerned with our salvation.[22] Nor, we may say, building on what Lewis wrote, is Scripture primarily for our intellectual curiosity or for career development in academia.

iii. Language

In the introduction to a translation of the New Testament Epistles by the Bible scholar J. B. Phillips published in 1947,[23] Lewis comments that it is not necessarily good to be lulled by the beauty, majesty, and cadence of the Authorized translation (the King James Bible). Lewis was writing in the context of new translations in contemporary English, which were being criticized because of their newness and their difference from the Authorized. Lewis asserts that if we are shocked by contemporary translations then they ought to shock us. He then explains that it is no bad thing if it does shock us because the incarnation itself ought to shock us.

> The same divine humility which decreed that God should become a baby at a peasant-woman's breast, and later an arrested field-preacher in the hands of the Roman police, decreed also that he should be preached in a vulgar, prosaic and unliterary language. If you can stomach the one, you can stomach the other. The incarnation is in that sense an irreverent doctrine: Christianity, in that sense, an incurably irreverent religion. The real sanctity, the real beauty and sublimity of the New Testament (as of Christ's life) are of a different sort: miles deeper or further in.[24]

Lewis continues by explaining how the Authorized Version has ceased to be an accurate translation; neither is the Latin (Jerome's early fifth century Vulgate) to be praised simply for itself. The original language was Common Greek (*koine Helene*) that had come to dominate the Eastern Mediterranean at the time when the books of the New Testament were written, and this form of Greek was in itself not as beautiful as Classical Greek, and was certainly not "sacred" or "comforting."

3. THE HISTORICITY OF SCRIPTURE

The nature of Scripture and its relationship to humanity was addressed by Lewis in an essay entitled, "The World's Last Night."[25] This essay illustrates much of what we can understand of Lewis's approach to Scripture, focused as it is on what he has to say with regard to what is called the doctrine of the second coming. This essay raises questions about a literal interpretation of the Bible. For example, the ultra-early church expected Jesus's return—the *parousia*—within their lifetime. But it did not happen. The second coming did not happen according to what we can read from the New Testament—

---

22. Lewis, *The Problem of Pain*, see ch. 8.
23. Lewis, "Introduction." *Letters to Young Churches*, vii–x.
24. Ibid., viii.
25. Lewis, "The World's Last Night," 93–113.

or pertinently, it has not happened yet, it is delayed. We await Christ's presence, which according to the New Testament, recorded in the sayings of Jesus, should have happened within the lifetime of the disciples and first apostles. Lewis notes:

> The apocalyptic beliefs of the first Christians have been proved to be false. It is clear from the New Testament that they all expected the Second Coming in their own lifetime. And, worse still, they had a reason, and one which you will find very embarrassing. Their Master had told them so. He shared, and indeed created, their delusion. He said in so many words, "this generation shall not pass till all these things be done." And he was wrong. He clearly knew no more about the end of the world than anyone else. It is certainly the most embarrassing verse in the Bible. Yet how teasing, also, that within fourteen words of it should come the statement "But of that day and that hour knoweth no man, no, not the angels which are in heaven, neither the Son, but the Father."[26]

So do we have error and ignorance in the Sayings of Jesus? Such a conclusion points to the nature of the historicity of the New Testament. The confusion and contradiction in these comments (Mark 13:30–32) and Christ's cry of dereliction from the cross ("My God, my God, why have you forsaken me?" Mark 15:34) are seen by Lewis as proof of the historicity of the Gospels, that the writers and copyists of the Gospels made no effort to mask, erase or spin-doctor anything that was embarrassing: "The evangelists have the first great characteristic of honest witnesses: they mention facts which are, at first sight, damaging to their main contention."[27] Therefore, if Jesus owned ignorance both in error and in admittance, is he still God? Yes: if he is truly incarnated in human form he will display ignorance, in keeping with human limitation. Lewis comments that a generation that has accepted the curvature of space-time must surely be able to accept the paradox of the consciousness of God-incarnate where the temporal and the timeless were united, therefore Christ could at the same moment be ignorant and omniscient.[28]

What does this tell us about the Bible? What does this tell us about Lewis's understanding of what we may term the historicity of Scripture? First, as Lewis asserts, we can read from Scripture, endorsed by the doctrine of the second coming, that we do not and cannot know when the world will end: "The curtain may be rung down at any moment."[29] The historicity of Scripture tells us that the end will come, that we do not live in a steady state world, that it will be sudden and catastrophic and unpredictable in its nature and timing, but the end *will* come. This has, Lewis admits, led to some embarrassing moments in the life of the churches—people that were convinced the end was going to happen on such-and-such a date, usually backed-up by quoting an obscure verse of Scripture out of context. There is, therefore, a general level of historicity to Scripture, but not necessarily in the detail when it comes to predicting how and when the end of the world will come. The lesson for Lewis is that we must

26. Ibid., 97–98.
27. Ibid., 98–99.
28. Ibid., 99.
29. Ibid., 105.

1. Scripture, Revelation, and Reason I: Skepticism and Suspicion

C. S. LEWIS GENRE IN THE OLD TESTAMENT	
Chronicle	Romances and Myths
Poetry	Material unclassifiable by contemporary models/genres
Moral and political diatribe	of literature

Figure 1: C. S. Lewis's Classification of Genre in the Old Testament

watch and wait, attentively; for God will come, be assured, but like a thief in the night: the parables are replete with this—watching and waiting for a burglar, making sure we have enough oil for our lamps as we wait, etc.[30] Michael J. Christensen, writing on Lewis's understanding of Scripture, notes how many people press Scripture to give more of itself than there is. Such Christians demand a divine infallible authority, universal and absolute, eternal yet manifest and controllable by us in this reality.[31] We err if we desire to replace the freedom of God with a book. This also raises questions about the dangers of theology—if theology attempts to tie-up all systematically in neatly defined propositions: "To demand this of Scripture is to fail to recognize that God's infinite wisdom exceeds man's ability to conceptualize it . . . the divine light is obscured by the medium through which it shines."[32] We therefore make demands on the historicity of Scripture that it will not sustain, precisely because it is not the product of an ordinary academic discipline: it is both human and divine in origin.

The historicity of Scripture is a pertinent question when dealing with the Old Testament. Lewis commented that some of his critics argued that he was a fundamentalist for not dismissing *per se* the miraculous and the historic in the Old Testament; others criticized him if he did not accept every event recorded, every sentence in the Hebrew Bible, as historic and as scientific truth: "The reason why I can accept as historical a story in which a miracle occurs is that I have never found any philosophical grounds for the universal negative proposition that miracles do not happen."[33] For Lewis, the Book of Job appears unhistorical simply because the events recorded do not fit in with the historical tradition of ancient Israel. The story of the fall meant more to Lewis as the truth about humanity's fall from perfection presented as myth than if it is argued as historical and scientific fact. Therefore, Lewis classifies the material in the Old Testament as chronicle (essentially historical, though perhaps different to concepts of historicity today), poetry (Song of Solomon, Job, and the book

---

30. For example, Matt 24:43 and 25:1–13.
31. Christensen, *C. S. Lewis on Scripture*, 94–95.
32. Ibid., 94.
33. Lewis, *Reflections on the Psalms*, 94–95.

of Psalms—but the Psalms also represent other genre), moral and political diatribe (pietistic and spiritual teaching), romances and myths (the creation stories—for example, Genesis and Psalm 104), however, there is also material which is essentially unclassifiable according to twentieth-century conceptions of genre, model, and type of literature.[34] He explains that the poet who wrote the Song of Songs did not, in all probability, conceive the work for anything other than what he terms a secular and natural purpose.

4. THE HUMANITY OF SCRIPTURE

i. Reflections on the Psalms

The books that make up the Bible come from a variety of widely disparate sources, but broadly from the Hebrew tribes and nation, then from the early church. As the years passed the church preserved them and then formed the canon of Scripture (the Tetramorph—the four gospels—was endorsed by the mid-second century; the New Testament *per se*, by the mid-fourth century). Many of the books are not just composed, written, by a single person. Then there is the work of editors and redactors who change and rearrange the material, but—and this is important considering the criticisms of the Bible by Modern and Liberal theologians, philosophers, and Bible scholars, criticisms that Lewis rejects—overall is the hand of God in the influence of the Holy Spirit, or as Lewis terms it, a divine presence.[35]

Therefore, Lewis, in the context specifically of the book of the Psalms, speaks of the human qualities—naivety, error, contradiction, cursing, and wickedness—these are, for Lewis, not excluded.[36] This represents what we can term *the humanity of Scripture*. This presents us with a Bible that is—as Lewis terms it—an untidy and leaky vehicle: "To a human mind this working up (in a sense imperfectly), this sublimation (incomplete) of human material, seems, no doubt, an untidy and leaky vehicle."[37] We no doubt would have preferred absolute truth systematically presented, unrefracted light that we could have contained and quantified in an encyclopedic fashion. But this is not what God has given to us, and it is important to remember that there is a *givenness* about the Bible. Lewis does not approach the Bible with the fundamentalist mind-set. The humanity that shines through in the Old Testament, and indeed in Paul's Epistles, is also there in the sayings of Jesus. Jesus Christ wrote and published no book in his earthly life, he preached rather than lecturing in an academically impartial manner; what he says is in response to question and demands placed on him, then he answers in paradox, proverb, exaggeration, parable, irony. The sayings of Jesus exude his humanity. This, Lewis asserts strongly, is what God has given us, what God has done, and it is for the best: Scripture is steeped in humanness, with all the failings of

---

34. Ibid., 96.
35. Ibid., 96.
36. Ibid., 96.
37. Ibid., 100.

humanity, but it is good, indeed it is very good, and it is what was best for us. In the context of the sayings of Jesus, and remembering that it is the universal Christ who is behind all Scripture, Lewis concludes, "Yet it is, perhaps, idle to speak here of spirit and letter. There is almost no 'letter' in the words of Jesus. Taken by a literalist, he will always prove the most elusive of teachers. Systems cannot keep up with that darting illumination. No net less wide than a man's whole heart, nor less fine of mesh than love, will hold the sacred Fish."[38]

ii. The Clyde S. Kilby Letter

By 1959 Lewis's fame, if we may call it that, was quite considerable. An American scholar, Clyde S. Kilby, wrote to Lewis asking his opinion of the *Wheaton College Statement concerning Inspiration of the Bible*. Wheaton College was at the time reputed to subscribe to a relatively strict evangelical approach to Scripture, believing the Bible to be inerrant; that is, without flaw or fault or contradiction. Lewis's response, a letter dated May 7, 1959, is valuable because he deals head on with the issues that underpin Fundamentalism, and he deals in a small but systematic way with questions raised in relation to Scripture, in particular the nature and value of the Bible.[39] Lewis gets right to the heart of the question: that is the relationship between scriptural text and history, and between what is written—flaws and contradictions included—and the nature of Scripture: "To me the curious thing is that neither in my own Bible-reading nor in my religious life as a whole does the question in fact even assume that importance which it always gets in theological controversy. The difference between reading the story of Ruth and that of Antigone—both first class as literature—is to me unmistakable and even overwhelming. But the question 'Is Ruth historical?' (I've no reason to suppose it is not) doesn't really seem to arise till afterwards."[40] Therefore the pertinent question is, what exactly is it that Scripture teaches us? What are we supposed to be learning? Here Lewis asserts that some stories/events can—indeed must—be taken as non-historical, while others as historical. Not all of Scripture is the same genre. The resurrection is *fundamentally* an historic event; the precise fate of Lot's wife is not. Lewis then goes on to cite several examples of questions/difficulties that mitigate a Fundamentalist approach to inerrancy: the key being the genre or type of text—some texts are to be seen as sacred fiction. Lewis cautiously rejected the concept of biblical inerrancy. Given the different genres and function, given the various writings in the Bible, given the aims of the authors, inerrancy for the whole is not possible. He comments that we should "rule out the view that every statement in Scripture must be historical truth . . . [also] rule out the view that any one passage taken in isolation can be assumed to be inerrant

---

38. Ibid., 102–3.
39. Lewis to Clyde S. Kilby, May 7, 1959. *Collected Letters, Vol. III*, 1044–46. Clyde Samuel Kilby (1902–86) was writer and Professor of English at Wheaton College, and founder of the Marion E. Wade Centre at Wheaton; he met C. S. Lewis in 1953, and exchanged correspondence with him until Lewis's death ten years later.
40. Ibid., 1044–45.

in exactly the same sense as any other."[41] One is reminded here of Karl Barth. For Barth biblical inerrancy is a basis or ground other than Jesus Christ—*Christ* is the foundation of faith, not a perfect flawless Bible.[42] The Bible's primary value is as *witness to* the Word of God; that is, as testimony, witness, bystander, and onlooker, to Jesus of Nazareth, the second person of the Trinity incarnate, crucified, and resurrected as atonement realized.

In the context of inerrancy Lewis states that, "Whatever view we hold on the divine authority of Scripture must make room for the following facts."[43] He then proceeds to outline six categories that must be considered.

Divine and Human Origin

First, that we must distinguish between divine word and human comment; for Lewis this is where the apostle Paul draws a distinction in 1 Corinthians between what he says is from the Lord, while other sayings are *his* and *not from the Lord* (1 Cor 7:10 and 12). This is the difference between the *Deus dixit* (God spoke), and *paulus dixit* (Paul spoke); therefore, some words in the Bible are, to a greater extent, of human origin.

Levels of Historicity

Second, that there are inconsistencies between the lineage and descent of Jesus listed in Matthew's Gospel and Luke's; likewise there are historical discrepancies between the account of Judas's death in Matthew and Act. Therefore, there are different levels of historicity even within the Gospels.

A Human Element

Third, that Luke, in the preface to his Gospel, acknowledges that he was instrumental in being the historian—gathering together records of events, personal accounts, and testimony from witnesses. Therefore, there is an important human element in what Luke has selected, compiled (Luke 1:1–4).

Mythological Narratives

Fourth, the, as Lewis terms it, "universally admitted unhistoricity (I do not say, of course, falsity) of at least some narratives in Scripture (the parables), which may well extend also to Jonah and Job."[44] Whether they are historically true or false is not relevant for the characters within Jesus's parables have a profound effect on us whether they existed or not as real people.

Divinely Inspired Writings

Fifth, Lewis, quoting James, asserts that if every good and perfect gift comes from the Father of Lights then all Scripture must be accorded the value of *inspired*. However, he

---

41. Ibid., 1046.
42. Barth, *Der Römerbrief*, Zweite Fassung, 6.
43. Lewis to Clyde S. Kilby, May 7, 1959, 1045.
44. Ibid., 1045.

1. Scripture, Revelation, and Reason I: Skepticism and Suspicion

then continues by asserting a proposition we will come across again and again in his work, that if this is so then all true and edifying writings, whether in Scripture or not, must be in some sense inspired. God's action through the Holy Spirit may not stop at inspiring the writers of Scripture.

Inspiration and the Purposes of God

Sixth, therefore, writes Lewis, "inspiration may operate in a wicked man without his knowing it, and he can then utter the untruth he intends (propriety of making an innocent man a political scapegoat) as well as the truth he does not intend (the divine sacrifice)."[45] Lewis is here referring to John 11:49–53; Caiaphas's comment about how one man should die for the people was quite ironic, he stated truth but for the wrong reasons. Therefore, there is a human element in the writing of Scripture as well as the events recorded: the humanity of Scripture.

For Lewis these examples dismiss the proposition that all statements in Scripture must be seen as historical truth; also the view that inspiration is always of the same mode and to the same degree. The problem is compounded when a passage is taken in isolation, any contradictions are then ignored: we cannot assume that if one event written in the Bible is true, all events are without flaw—"that the numbers of Old Testament armies (which in view of the size of the country, if true, involves continuous miracle) are statistically correct because the story of the Resurrection is historically correct."[46] For Lewis, the aim of Scripture is to convey the Word of God: therefore both writer and reader are inspired, but not necessarily to the same degree and in the same mode (Lewis's understanding of the Word of God will be examined in the next chapter). Lewis concludes his comments to Clyde S. Kilby by pointing out that "the very kind of truth we are often demanding was, in my opinion, never even envisaged by the Ancients," that is, those who were inspired to write and to construct the Bible.[47]

5. THE GOSPEL ACCORDING TO JOHN

i. Skepticism and Suspicion

The Bishop of Bangor, the Right Revd. Thomas Sherlock, wrote, in 1729, an apologetic defense of the Gospel writers entitled, *The Trial of the Witnesses of the Resurrection of Jesus*.[48] More pertinently his work was a defense of the apostles, those who witnessed Jesus's resurrection. The work was set in a courtroom where the apostles were on trial for faking the resurrection. Sherlock sets the powerful arguments of the apostles against the skepticism of Thomas Woolston, whereby Woolston had argued that the apostles had fabricated their story. Thomas Woolston (1668–1733) was a theologian, cleric, and English Deist, who asserted that all Scripture was allegorical. In keeping

---

45. Ibid., 1046.
46. Ibid., 1046.
47. Ibid., 1046.
48. Sherlock, *The Trial of the Witnesses of the Resurrection of Jesus*. First published in 1729 by SPCK.

with the Deistic belief that denied miracles as an interference with the self-governing nature of the universe, Woolston had published a work in 1727 entitled, *A Discourse on the Miracles of our Saviour, in View of the Present Controversy between Infidels and Apostates*, which effectively dismissed the miraculous in the Gospels, arguing for an allegorical interpretation.[49] Writing in reply, Sherlock was conscious of the skepticism of the Age of Reason. Along with Woolston, Sherlock's opponents were the English Deists—rational atheists and scientists who repudiated the witness of those who had seen Jesus Christ after his resurrection. A characteristic of the Age of Reason, and the Enlightenment that followed, and the Modernism that Lewis was so critical of, was the principle, adhered to by many, but not all, that a respectable intellectual must be suspicious of any religious truth claims—especially when dealing with, in this case, the Bible—and only allow to exist as truth that which could be measured, quantified, and controlled in principle by the human intellect. Thus the argument by the skeptics against the witness of the apostles recorded in the Gospels was that it all happened too long ago for there to be any reliability in the accounts. This was an approach championed by two European philosophers and Bible scholars: Hermann Samuel Reimarus and Gotthold Ephraim Lessing. Lessing coined the phrase "ugly broad ditch," which was applied to the time elapsed since the New Testament era. Lessing argued that we could not trust the contingency of history because there was this ugly broad ditch between then and now; therefore we could not accept the New Testament accounts as fact or truth, further, this ditch lay between the contingent truth of history and what Lessing claimed to be the universal truth of reason.[50] Lessing was convinced that rationalism was the universal mode of understanding available to humanity for comprehending the world. Lessing concluded that the Bible was not a source of truth, let alone the truth of God, also that the church's account of Jesus was flawed with what was called the scandal of particularity: only the *universal* was true, the universal available to all humanity through reason, not the particular enacted in the contingency of history. His argument was that if God was to come and reveal God's-self to humanity it would be through the universal—everybody would "know." By the mid-twentieth century the approach by Reimarus and Lessing dominated debate in the West; the church was on the defense in justifying the Gospel accounts, not only in the face of rational scientific skepticism but also, as we have seen, in the light of skepticism and religious atheism in some quarters of the Church of England. Lessing invented the concept of the contingency of history (as a "broad ugly ditch") to repudiate the church's story of Jesus; however, for two centuries the followers of Lessing have ignored this contingency of history in attempting to proclaim their story of Jesus as the one true version, grounded in an overinflated concept of reason and universalism, which postmodernism has now done away with?

49. Revd. Thomas Woolston published what he called "a discourse on the miracles of our saviour, in view of the present controversy between infidels and apostates," as a private publication in 1727. Woolston's work ran to many editions, but resulted in his imprisonment for criminal blasphemy. See: Woolston, *Six Discourses on the Miracles of Our Saviour and Defences of his Discourses*.

50. See: Lessing, *Theological Writings*.

1. Scripture, Revelation, and Reason I: Skepticism and Suspicion

This approach by the skeptics was driven by what was termed a hermeneutic of suspicion. As a method of analysis and interpretation of texts, especially of the Bible or literary texts, a hermeneutic of suspicion was considered by many as especially critical and destructive (the term was coined in the seventeenth century, at the time of the skepticism of the Age of Reason, derived from the Greek, *hermēneutikos*, *hermēneuein*: interpret). The driving element of this hermeneutic, particularly when applied to the New Testament, was suspicion: whatever was read and analyzed, one was to be suspicious of it, assume it to be false until it could be proved otherwise. Lewis knew of this approach among the scholars and clergy of his day, and formulated his own criticism of the hermeneutic of suspicion, his own skepticism of the investigative techniques of the academics of his day.

Lewis summed up the approach of humanity generally, academics specifically, in dismissing the veracity of the New Testament in a brief essay entitled "Difficulties in Presenting the Christian Faith to Modern Unbelievers" (later renamed, "God in the Dock," for obvious reasons), first published in 1948:

> The ancient man approached God (or even the gods) as the accused before his judge. For the modern man the roles are reversed. He is the judge: God is in the dock. He is quite a kindly judge: if God should have a reasonable defence for being the God who permits war, poverty and disease, he is ready to listen to it. The trial may even end in God's acquittal. But the important thing is that Man is on the bench and God is in the dock.[51]

This is very much in the mould of Sherlock's apologetics. Lewis understood that the danger here is that since the Age of Reason humanity has made itself the measure of all things: God, if *he* is to be allowed to exist, must be measured, quantified, by and in comparison to humanity. The watchword, so to speak, of the Age of Reason in its full confidence, echoing the ancient Greek pre-Socratic philosopher Protagoras, was that man was the measure of all.[52] God must justify *himself* where humanity sets the criteria. This convoluted, inverted, thinking, characterized Lewis's *The Screwtape Letters*: good becomes evil; evil is lauded as the good. Therefore, we have Lewis's suspicion of suspicion, if we may call it that, or skepticism of the hermeneutic of suspicion.

ii. Lock, Vidler, and Bultmann

Lewis was aware of contemporary biblical scholarship—particularly in the Church of England—which applied this hermeneutic of suspicion to the Gospel of John; often the work was dismissed as a fantasy written by the faithful nearly a century after the events it

---

51. Lewis, "Difficulties in Presenting the Christian Faith to Modern Unbelievers," 426.
52. "Man is the measure of all things: of things which are, that they are, and of things which are not, that they are not." See, Hermann Alexander Diels (1848–1922), a German classical scholar known for his work compiling a collection of quotations from and about Pre-Socratic philosophers. Protagoras' statement that humanity (ἄνθρωπος) is the measure of all is summarized and reiterated by Plato in his *Theaetetus*, §152a, however, a full quotation is given by Sextus Empiricus (c. 2nd–3rd C. BC) in *Adversus Mathematicos* (*Against the Mathematicians*), §7.60: πάντων χρημάτων μέτρον ἐστὶν ἄνθρωπος, τῶν μὲν ὄντων ὡς ἔστιν, τῶν δὲ ὄντων ὡς οὐκ ἔστιν. See Plato, *Theaetetus*, §152a, 169.

purported to present. Lewis criticizes this approach to John's Gospel in the work of two Anglican clerics, Revd. Dr. Alec Vidler (1899–1991) and Revd. Dr. Walter Lock (1846–1933), and also in the German Lutheran theologian and New Testament scholar, Rudolf Bultmann. Bultmann is attributed with inventing the concept of demythologizing; that is, identifying anything that he considered to be a myth, a fictional embellishment, in the Gospels, and excluding it.[53] Bultmann's demythologizing agenda was typical of the dominant spirit of the age amongst intellectuals in the twentieth century. His attempt to identify how the Gospels had been constructed was through form criticism; the aim being to try to get back in time to how the Gospel had been written. This approach was controversial but popular in academic circles. Bultmann was at his most controversial when he applied this technique to John's Gospel claiming that it was simply theology in story form.[54] Bultmann believed the Gospels had to be reduced so as to present and explain them to his intellectual contemporaries, which meant identifying that which did not fit in with a modern mind-set. Bultmann's technique is driven by skepticism, but with an unquestioning acceptance of a modern scientific worldview. He asserted that it is not possible to use electric light and the radio and to avail ourselves of modern medical and surgical discoveries and at the same time believe in the New Testament world of demons and spirits.[55] It has often been asserted that Bultmann carried form criticism to such an extreme that the veracity and the historical value of the Gospels is done away with. Bultmann is the culmination in many ways of 150 years of biblical analysis driven by a hermeneutic of suspicion, which had started with Reimarus and Lessing.

The Revd. Dr. Alec R. Vidler and Revd. Dr. Walter Lock[56] represented this "modern" approach to John's Gospel, which in Liberal Anglican terms simply dismissed it as spiritual writing, an elaboration on what had happened. In a sermon delivered in St Paul's Cathedral, London, Walter Lock commented that: "There are very many critical doubts raised about the fourth Gospel—doubts as to its authorship, its date, its literary method—but of one thing there is no doubt at all, that when at any

---

53. Rudolf Karl Bultmann (1884–1976) was a German theologian, Professor of New Testament Studies, University of Marburg, and a Lutheran, who invented the technique of demythologizing arguing for a separation between history and faith, reducing the gospels to the crucifixion and little else.

54. Bultmann, *Das Evangelium des Johannes*. For what is probably the most important work establishing the demythologizing, reductionist, form criticism see *Die Geschichte der synoptischen Tradition*, first published by Bultmann in 1921: Bultmann, *History of the Synoptic Tradition*. See also, Bultmann, *Jesus Christ and Mythology*; also Bultmann, T*he New Testament and Mythology and Other Basic Writings*.

55. Bultmann, *Existence and Faith: Shorter Writings of Rudolf Bultmann*, 69.

56. Fr. Alexander Roper Vidler, (1899–1991) was a noted Anglican Liberal theologian; he was Professor and later Dean of King's College, Cambridge. In 1958 he published *The Windsor Sermons* arguing against a traditional interpretation of miracles, reclassifying then as signs and parables, propositions discussed at a symposium entitled *Soundings* later published by Vidler. Further Liberal biblical studies were published in 1963—*Objections to Christian Belief*. Walter Lock (1846–1933) was educated at Marlborough College and Corpus Christi College, Oxford. A Fellow of Magdalen College, Oxford and tutor at Keble College, Oxford in the 1870s and 1880s, he later was Dean Ireland's Professor of Exegesis of Holy Scripture at Oxford University (1895 and 1919) and Lady Margaret Professor of Divinity (1919 to 1927).

crisis, at any hour of individual need, men turn to it, it always rises to the occasion; and whether they be educated or simple they find a response for their need and a solace for their grief."[57] Lock was therefore prepared to dismiss the historical veracity of John's Gospel, criticize its authorship, genre, date, even its literary method, while in the same sentence laud it as what is, in effect, a piece of pietistic religious therapy. What is more Lock then proceeds to assert that, "It is uncertain whether its narrative is to be taken literally or spiritually"; where "spiritually" is to be taken as vaguely defined, as not real, presumably that the events recorded did not happen.[58]

iii. Modern Theology and Biblical Criticism

This approach was also to be found in the work of Alec Vidler, who dismissed the miracle at Cana (John 2:1–11) as a sign in an essay in a volume published in the late 1950s which Lewis knew and reacted to. Lewis read many of these works, and responded to Lock and Vidler's criticism of John's Gospel in an essay entitled, "Modern Theology and Biblical Criticism."[59] Alec Vidler's "The Sign at Cana"[60] is a short essay, the aim of which is to argue that the story of the wedding at Cana (John 2:1–11) probably was a true and real account of a memory of Jesus attending a wedding, but the miracle of turning water into wine was simply a literary embellishment, a story invented by the writer of the Gospel to act as a sign, a pointer, to God's generosity compared to the rigid formality of the Jewish law: "In the case of the wedding at Cana the evangelist has taken hold of a story he had heard somewhere about Jesus at a wedding feast and has re-told it and refashioned it in his own way, so as to illustrate or enforce the theme of his book."[61] Vidler mistakenly considers the use of the term "woman" by Jesus as derogatory, whereas simply for a man and a teacher to talk to a woman, as Jesus did, was breaking through social taboos—in talking to women Jesus was regarding them as equals, he was not talking down to them. Vidler is writing in the tradition of the German theologian and Bible scholar David Friedrich Strauss, whom he cites in support of his arguments. Strauss' attempt to write a secular history of the life of Jesus—Jesus as simply and only human—was seen as a model by Vidler; though for many, this portrait of Strauss's was simply Jesus the Jew repackaged as an enlightened, educated, and cultivated member of the nineteenth-century European bourgeoisie.[62] Therefore the miracle at Cana should, to Vidler, be seen not as a miracle

---

57. Lock, *The Raising of Lazarus. The Message of the Fourth Gospel for Mourners*, 3.
58. Ibid., 4. See also: W. Lock, "History and Character of the Fourth Gospel"; also, Lock, "The Gospel according to St John," 240–76.
59. Lewis, "Modern Theology and Biblical Criticism."
60. Vidler, "The Sign at Cana," 66–71.
61. Ibid., 67.
62. David Friedrich Strauss (1808–74), German theologian who shocked European intellectuals and the church with his *Leben Jesu* (*The Life of Jesus*, 1835) in which he denied Jesus' divine nature; later he published a follow-up volume, *Das Leben Jesu für das deutsche Volk* (*The Life of Jesus for the German People*, 1864), written in a similar vein, to extend his thesis. He revolutionized the study of the New Testament and early Christianity and pioneered the investigations into the so-called "historical Jesus". See: Strauss *The Life of Jesus Critically Examined*.

but as a sign—"It should be read more as a parable than as a miracle."[63] The statement by Mary that they have no wine simply ushers in the metaphorical "story" of the new wine of the new covenant for Vidler. Therefore, the difficulty that he perceives—what to a modern mind-set is the absurdity and the impossibility of miracles—is overcome: "This is no longer a difficulty; for it represents, it symbolizes the glorious abundance of the new life which the Christ brings and gives. 'I am come,' he says, 'that they may have life, and may have it abundantly.'"[64] In many ways this is Jesus the enlightened and cultivated nineteenth-century European of Straussian invention who is a good teacher, a super religious person, but not the miracle working Son of God.

In "Modern Theology and Biblical Criticism" C. S. Lewis takes to task this modern reductionist form criticism characterized by a hermeneutic of suspicion. He acknowledges how this approach has come to dominate many theological colleges training priests for the Church of England, further that the undermining of the old orthodoxy has been mainly the work of divines, as he terms them, engaged in New Testament criticism. Therefore, Lewis asserts that,

> A theology which denies the historicity of nearly everything in the Gospels to which Christian life and affections and thought have been fastened for nearly two millennia—which either denies the miraculous altogether or, more strangely, after swallowing the camel of the Resurrection strains at such gnats as the feeding of the multitudes—if offered to the uneducated man can produce only one or other of two effects. It will make him a Roman Catholic or an atheist.[65]

Lewis believes that this approach leads to elitism. This elitism is essentially Gnostic in that it defends itself behind secret knowledge. Lewis recounts how a mature clergyman informed him that such "Modern Liberals" faced with the problem of divergent beliefs in relation to Scripture held by their congregations recalled a late medieval conception of two truths. The first truth was a picture-truth to be presented to the ordinary laity (replete with stories of miracles, etc.); however, the clergy hid behind the second form of truth, which was characterized by superior knowledge—an "esoteric" (to use Lewis's word) truth that came about through special understanding that was only available to clergy, bishops, and theologians.[66] Lewis's piercing critique of this reductionist demythologizing agenda is in four broad categories, followed by some concluding propositions about knowledge and the nature of Scripture

Genre and Types of Literature: Expertise

First, these biblical scholars may be experts in knowing the object of their study—in many instances, John's Gospel—but Lewis distrusts them as critics: "They seem to me to lack literary judgement, to be imperceptive about the very quality of the texts they are reading."[67] Lewis is not interested in how many years such a critic has been

---

63. Vidler, "The Sign at Cana," 68.
64. Ibid., 67.
65. Lewis, "Modern Theology and Biblical Criticism," 153
66. Ibid., 153
67. Ibid., 154.

1. Scripture, Revelation, and Reason I: Skepticism and Suspicion

analyzing the books of the New Testament. They may have spent years studying the minutiae of the New Testament text they have built successful careers out of but they lack any appreciation of what literature is. Lewis writes that if one of them argues that the genre of a particular Gospel text is a legend or a romance then he wants to know how many legends and romances the critic has read, knows, and understands. Lewis cites Walter Lock's article "The Gospel according to John" as evidence of this.[68] Lock asserts that John's Gospel is a spiritual romance, a poem, not history. Lewis comments,

> I have been reading poems, romances, vision-literature, legends, myths all my life. I know what they are like. I know that not one of them is like this. Of this text there are only two possible views. Either this is reportage—though it may no doubt contain errors—pretty close up to the facts; nearly as close as Boswell. Or else, some unknown writer in the second century, without known predecessors or successors, suddenly anticipated the whole technique of modern, novelistic, realistic narrative.[69]

Lewis then proceeds to apply his skepticism of the hermeneutic of suspicion to Bultmann—specifically, his *Theology of the New Testament*.[70] This is where Bultmann claims that certain passages were written/invented after the events they purport to depict—in effect spin-doctoring in the later centuries. There is, of course, no limit to how far such a hermeneutic of suspicion goes: nothing can be accepted or believed; the critic's ego is paramount. In addition Lewis rejects Bultmann's claim that there is no evidence of or use for the personality of Jesus in John's Gospel—or in the epistles of Paul for that matter. Lewis refutes this by astutely comparing the portrait of Jesus and the sayings of Jesus in John's Gospel with the picture we get in the apocryphal Gospels, to show how we do begin to detect a vein of genuineness. Lewis concludes that these critics ask him to believe they can read between the lines to reveal something that was unknown to the original readers/listeners. Regarding these critics Lewis commented that, "the evidence is their obvious inability to read (in any sense worth discussing) the lines themselves. They claim to see fern-seed and can't see an elephant ten yards away in broad daylight."[71]

Historical Superiority

Second, Lewis points out that a central tenet of "Modern" or "Liberal" theology is the claim that the behavior and teaching, the mission and purpose, of Jesus Christ was misunderstood and misrepresented by the disciples and apostles. The true meaning can only be recovered by modem scholars. Lewis had met this type of historical arrogance elsewhere: in English literature and in Classical studies. Lewis knew this as an undergraduate: that critical studies were ephemeral, fashionable, and fleeting—the "must have" garment of one year became very rapidly yesterday's fashion to be scorned. There is, of course, an element of self-interest at play here: careers are built, publishing

68. Lock, "The Gospel according to St John," 241.
69. Lewis, "Modern Theology and Biblical Criticism," 155.
70. Bultmann, *Theology of the New Testament*.
71. Lewis, "Modern Theology and Biblical Criticism," 157.

success achieved, from claiming to have discovered what was not known before. Lewis commented that, "every week a clever undergraduate, every quarter a dull American don, discovers for the first time what some Shakespearian play really meant."[72] The assumption is that when applied to John's Gospel a writer's contemporaries who spoke the same language shared the same mental imagery and assumptions, maybe even knew the writer and the events recounted, failed utterly to grasp what the writer was saying. For Lewis this is preposterous: "There is an *a priori* improbability in it which almost no argument and no evidence could counterbalance."[73] There is an historical arrogance in this approach which asserts that humanity can only get better and better, that intellectuals today are superior to those who lived two thousand years ago; there is even a form of implicit racism in this, especially when such demythologizing reductionism assumes Jesus to be a white liberal Westerner, and not a Jew.

The Non-Miraculous

Third, there is a fundamental—almost a foundational—principle that underpins the hermeneutic of suspicion as evident in Lewis's opponents: the miraculous cannot happen and never did exist. Any prophetic statement or miraculous action by Christ Jesus in the Gospel is to be seen as a fabrication by his followers: predictions of the future and miracles as an interference with the laws of nature are not allowed to be. Lewis notes how this principle is not learned from the texts but is brought to the text, and is the product of the spirit of the age these men have grown up in.

Sitz im Leben

Fourth, Lewis invokes a concept common amongst twentieth-century Bible scholars: *Sitz im Leben* (broadly meaning, "setting in life"). As a German concept central to form criticism and a reductionist demythologizing agenda, it aims to try to ascertain what the original context and purpose was for a particular text. This revolves around such questions as, how do we classify the material, who wrote the text, who heard it? The objective is to attempt to recapture the original setting, meaning, and context of a text, passage, or book. Lewis is at his most philosophically astute and logical when he acknowledges that this work is done with great ingenuity and immense erudition, but he fears that in the end it does not work. It is an attempt to reconstruct the genesis of texts, what unknown vanished sources/documents were used, when and where composition took place, for what purpose, with what influence; but, asserts Lewis, it does not work with twentieth-century texts, so there is even less chance for it to work with ancient texts. Why? First, Lewis comments that he has observed reviewers/critics of his own books (and those of his colleague, Tolkien) attempting to reconstruct the genesis, as he puts it, and failing miserably. When the text is ancient (classical or biblical) this analysis may appear convincing, but, as Lewis notes, "one is after all sailing by dead reckoning; the results cannot be checked by fact . . . The 'assured results of modern scholarship', as to the way in which an old book was written, are 'assured', we

72. Ibid., 157.
73. Ibid., 158.

1. Scripture, Revelation, and Reason I: Skepticism and Suspicion

may conclude, only because the men who knew the facts are dead and can't blow the gaff."[74] In *De Descriptione Temporum*, an inaugural lecture Lewis gave at Cambridge University in 1954 when he was appointed Professor of Medieval and Renaissance Literature, Lewis commented on this state of affairs in Classical Studies: "I would give a great deal to hear any ancient Athenian, even a stupid one, talking about Greek tragedy. He would know in his bones so much that we seek in vain. At any moment some chance phrase might, unknown to him, show us where modern scholarship had been on the wrong track for years."[75] Lewis notes that although he respects the skill and learning of these Bible scholars, their judgment is not to be respected. If contemporary critics who share the same language and culture as the author they are criticizing cannot get the *Sitz im Leben* right then how can they hope to when the language, mind-set, and culture is ancient and utterly strange and different. Twentieth-century biblical criticism may have generated the concept of *Sitz im Leben*, the attempt to understand and thereby classify the material in its original context, however, if the objective is to attempt to recapture the original setting, meaning, and context of a text, passage, or book, it has generally proved impossible for such Bible scholars to separate out their personal preferences, beliefs, and even prejudices, from such an interpretation: *Sitz im Leben* was still a viewpoint from the distance of two thousand or more years. This is a fairly controversial point; it may be justifiable to advance such a criticism against those who seek to denigrate Scripture and deny the miraculous as recorded in the Bible (for example, Bultmann), but are all scholars who use this approach so bad? As an orthodox Christian N. T. Wright derives most of his conclusions from an understanding of the New Testament's Jewish *Sitz im Leben*—though the question remains, "To what extent is this still a personal, perhaps prejudiced, viewpoint?":

> The superiority in judgment and diligence which you are going to attribute to the Biblical critics will have to be almost superhuman if it is to offset the fact that they are everywhere faced with customs, language, race-characteristics, class-characteristics, a religious background, habits of composition, and basic assumptions, which no scholarship will ever enable any man now alive to know as surely and intimately and instinctively as the reviewer can know mine. And for the very same reason, remember, the Biblical critics, whatever reconstructions they devise, can never be crudely proved wrong. St Mark is dead.[76]

Lewis then questions whether Bultmann has ever written a Gospel—if he had then he might have had a better idea of how to understand an ancient one written by people who were caught up in what Lewis terms the central religious experience of the whole human race. Not surprisingly W. Norman Pittenger criticized Lewis for believing the Gospel of John to be broadly historical; Lewis, in his rejoinder to Pittenger, revealed the lack of coherence and consistency in Pittenger's argument and repeats much that we have seen in "Modern Theology and Biblical Criticism."[77]

74. Ibid., 160–61.
75. Lewis, "De Descriptione Temporum," 24.
76. Lewis, "Modern Theology and Biblical Criticism," 161.
77. Lewis, "Rejoinder to Dr Pittenger," 1370-1.

6. MODERN SCHOLARSHIP AND AGNOSTICISM

Therefore, such scholarship is assured only of how transitory, relative, and unprovable it is. For Lewis the "Liberal" or "Modern" equates with the short-lived and ephemeral, the fleetingly passing; modern biblical criticism appeared to him to be skeptical of all but skepticism itself. Hence, Lewis asserts, *multa renascentur quae iam cecidere*: of all that fell before much will rise again, much will rise again that has long been buried![78] Therefore, we can only take the text for what it is, and what it is, is what the authors/compilers meant it to be: Lessing's ugly broad ditch now works against the modern mind in attempting to understand the *Sitz im Leben*. This did not apply only to biblical criticism; Lewis reminds his readers how the English Idealist philosophers (T. H. Green, Bradley, *et al*) dominated thinking in early twentieth-century Britain, as though they would reign for all time, yet their thought disappeared as quickly as yesterday's fashions: "For agnosticism is, in a sense, what I am preaching. I do not wish to reduce the sceptical element in your minds. I am only suggesting that it need not be reserved exclusively for the New Testament and the Creeds. Try doubting something else. Such scepticism might, I think, begin at the very beginning with the thought which underlies the whole demythology of our time."[79] Therefore, if scholars are embarrassed by such events as the ascension, the resurrection, the second coming they need to see that this does not deny the truth of the account, rather that the expression, the actual account, falls short of their expectations, or for that matter, falls short of what happened. We cannot know all, and we can only write-off the representation of an event as symbolic if we have independent access to the event and can compare it with the representation: the actual with the account. We need to take our ignorance seriously, writes Lewis; many of these critics write-off as mythological an account of a transcendent objective reality recorded in the New Testament because they measure the account against their own religious, philosophical, and scientific ideas, therefore they define as inadequate what is the sole access they have to an event of a transcendent objective reality breaking-in—that is, accounts witnessed, attested to, by the writers of the New Testament books.[80]

This sort of skepticism is not limited to academic Bible studies, it has happened in recent times to an event well known, an event still in human memory: the holocaust, the Nazi's final solution. The historian David Irving produced a detailed account as to why the holocaust did not happen; his argument (like that of the Bible critics with regard to the Gospels) relied upon the assumption that the Jewish witnesses were innately wrong, they could not know the truth, and in some cases fabricated the truth. Irving was, thankfully, proved wrong, yet the skepticism of his argument was persuasive to people who wanted to believe that the holocaust had not happened: they were inventing the truth they wanted to hear and feel comfortable with. In 1969

---

78. Lewis, "Modern Theology and Biblical Criticism," 162.
79. Ibid., 164.
80. Ibid., 164–66.

1. Scripture, Revelation, and Reason I: Skepticism and Suspicion

when America landed men on the moon the Soviet Union (who throughout the 1960s had been racing the Americans to get to the moon first) argued that America had fabricated the moon landing in a Hollywood studio. Many in the Soviet Empire were taken in by and believed the propaganda.

2

Scripture, Revelation, and Reason II: Mediation and the Bible

SYNOPSIS:
This assessment of C. S. Lewis on Scripture leads us now to examine revelation and reason in terms of mediation and the Bible. First, can we deduce a doctrine of Scripture in Lewis's work? Did Lewis regard the Bible as inerrant? What authority does Scripture hold? Does it have special status over all other books? What does it mean to say it is the Word of God? In so doing we must consider questions about truth and reason, the problem of inerrancy and infallibility, which will leads us to consider the place of inspiration and interpretation. For Lewis, God was infallible, yet God also allowed for the freedom of creation to be; hence, the writers of Scripture were divinely inspired, but were fallen and fallible—this leads to the concept of Scripture as *theopneustos*—God breathed: that is, the dove whispering into the ear, the Holy Spirit imparting intimations to the human mind, though the mind is free to make of these intimations what it will. Second, what was the relationship, for Lewis, between revelation and the Bible? For Lewis the very act of reading is revelatory. Third, what is the relationship between Scripture and Christ? Lewis wrote that, "It is Christ himself, not the Bible, who is the true Word of God." Therefore Lewis, like Karl Barth, distinguishes between the word of God (Scripture) and the Word of God (Christ). What did Lewis write about our interpretation of Scripture in relation to genre? Lewis emphasized the wholeness of Scripture: interpretation should not lead to contradiction. This will lead us to consider what other theologians have written on Lewis's understanding of how God reveals of God's self to humanity, and how they identify and categorize modes of revelation: the numinous (God's holiness); the universal ought (moral responsibility); *Sehnsucht* (wistful longings); election (Israel and the law); good dreams (pagan premonitions of Christ), even, for Lewis, the natural world. However, these categories exclude Scripture and the developing church tradition that constituted Lewis's "mere" core (epitomised by Baxter and Vincentius of Lérins's work). Therefore, these categories need to be ranked hierarchically in relation to the concrete, perfect, and particular revelation that is the incarnation: the Word of God revealed. *Mediation* is the key word here; all revelation must be seen as related to Christ the mediator. Lewis does not have a conventionally theological understanding of God's revelation; his approach is in the form of what we may call supra-theological categories, which acknowledge and allow for the freedom of God revealed through the humanity of Scripture. Lewis therefore saw all revelation perceivable by humanity as coming from Christ who is the true Word of God; if we exclude certain categories (the numinous, *Sehnsucht*, pagan dreams/myths) then we exclude the work of God in Christ speaking in a hidden mode, through the veil, to humanity.

1. C. S. LEWIS: A DOCTRINE OF SCRIPTURE?

i. Doctrine

Did C. S. Lewis have a doctrine of Scripture? Lewis did not lay out a doctrine of Scripture in a coherent written whole; however, by examining what he wrote about the Bible we can begin to get a picture of his doctrine of Scripture. All people hold views about Scripture—from Evangelicals to atheists. Only if these views cohere, gel together, have a logicality to them, can we say that such-and-such a person holds to a particular *doctrine* of Scripture. In the case of Lewis, what value does he accord to Scripture? What is the nature of these texts? Are the books of the Bible all the same type of writings for him? Is the Bible the revelation of God? Is the Bible inspired? Is it inerrant? What authority does it hold? Does it have special status over all other books? What does it mean to say it is the word of God? How can we invoke the phrase, the w/Word of God in relation to Scripture and the Christ-event? Lewis addressed these and many other issues. Therefore, Lewis' understanding of Scripture did cohere; did hold logically together. When it comes to the question of Scripture Lewis was neither a fundamentalist, nor a "Modernist"/"Liberal." He took the text seriously, did not attempt to reduce it, water it down, and exclude whatever failed to comply with a "Modern" mind-set, but neither did he overburden it with a fundamentalist desire to regard it all as factual in a simplistic way. The key was genre: identifying and knowing the types of text in the Bible. Here his expertise in teaching English literature and medieval literature gave him an edge over the "Modern"/"Liberal" New Testament scholars who thought they knew and understood a variety of texts but, it is fair to assert, they did not.

ii. Inerrancy and Infallibility

To say that the Bible is inerrant is to claim that there are no errors, contradictions, or mistakes; that the text is guaranteed solely as a reflection of God's speech-act towards humanity. Inerrancy relates closely to how Scripture was written down: how were the writers of the books of the Bible inspired to create the texts they wrote? There are broadly four approaches/models to the question of the inspiration and creation of Scripture, and hence its authority and its relationship to God.

The Freedom Model

First, there is what we may term the freedom model. God creates in freedom, loves creation in freedom, and allows humanity to exercise freedom. Here the infallible God inspires a fallible human to write. As we noted earlier, God breathes (θεόπνευστος—*theopneustos*), therefore the individual is inspired, God does not necessarily dictate words. God's speech-act cannot be seen in anthropomorphic terms. The writer of Scripture is inspired by God's Holy Spirit to write; the content is inspired through the faculty of the imagination, though it is important that reason is exercised. Therefore, the human element will, to a degree, filter because the human is

2. Scripture, Revelation, and Reason II: Mediation and the Bible

The Freedom Model
God inspires the faithful through the faculties of the imagination and reason: the human element will filter and make independent decisions as to the genre, form, and detail of the text, consciously or subconsciously, because the human is egotistical, flawed and fallen. This leads to scriptural inconsistencies.

The Amanuensis Model
God inspires the faithful through the faculties of the imagination and reason. However, the fallibility of the human mind is suspended at the point of revelation. There are no scriptural inconsistencies because of a one-to-one correspondence between God's speech-act and the words on the page.

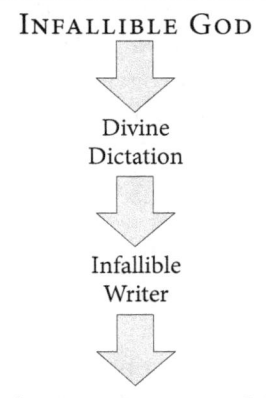

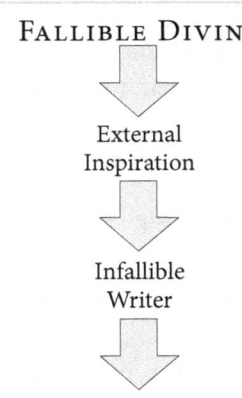

The Automaton Model
God dictates: the conscious mind (including ego, and Fallenness) of the writer of Scripture is suspended, and the exact words are written down unfiltered. There are no scriptural inconsistencies because of a one-to-one correspondence between God's speech-act and the words written down.

The Humanist Model
The conscious mind of the writer of Scripture perceives what he or she calls the divine, is inspired to write, acknowledging that the source appears to be outside the mind of the writer; however, the author's decisions are paramount and therefore infallible. The question of inconsistency does not apply.

Figure 2: Four Models on the Relationship of Scripture and Inspiration

egotistical, flawed and fallen through original sin: the writer will make independent decisions over form, precise content, detail, and genre (though a baptized imagination will influence these decisions). However, it must be acknowledged that because of the corruption of original sin the writer's free will is impaired, as is his or her relationship with God. This leads to inconsistencies in the work but this does not detract from the overall meaning and authority of the text. In addition, the inspiration, the action of the Holy Spirit, will be active in the Christian when reading or hearing the text—it becomes alive to a baptized imagination.

The Amanuensis Model

Second, is what we can term the Amanuensis Model—the biblical authors as God's secretaries. A writer of Scripture was inspired; through the faculties of imagination and reason he or she wrote. The writer was still a fallen human being; however, the fallibility of the human mind was suspended by God at the point of revelation. Therefore, there are no scriptural inconsistencies because of a one-to-one correspondence between God's speech-act and the words on the page (this model fails to explain any actual or real inconsistencies, contradictions or mistakes in the Bible). Further, when Evangelicals, or Catholic mystics for that matter, invoke this one-to-one correspondence they fail to see how, in claiming that the fallen status of the writer is suspended, they are marginalizing the perfect and complete sacrifice of Christ on the cross—the only cure, so to speak, for original sin. For example, if Catholics assert that the fallenness in Mary was at some point suspended in her life, even at her point of conception, then does this still mean she is a complete human being, fully human and at one with all of us? If not then does this separate her Son Jesus from us? We often pay God too many compliments, which actually harm our true understanding of revelation: is inerrancy in this model an example of paying God a compliment too far?

The Automaton Model

Third, is the automaton model—what is often called control writing. The conscious mind of the writer of Scripture is suspended, any human desire or ego or interference is removed, and the exact words are written down unfiltered. This is as if God had spoken into a tape recorder, the recording then being transcribed with no mistakes. Therefore, there is a perfect one-to-one correlation between God's words and the human script, with no inconsistencies. This is the model of Scripture claimed by Muslims—that the prophet Mohammed received exact and unfiltered the text of the Qur'an from God, whereby the Qur'an existed in perfection in eternity and was "given" to the Prophet Mohammed.

The Humanist Model

Fourth, is what we may term the humanist model. Here the conscious mind of the writer of Scripture is believed to have perceived what he or she calls, from a personal perception, "the divine," and is inspired to write. There is acknowledgment that the source "appears" to be outside the mind of the writer, that there is a givenness

2. Scripture, Revelation, and Reason II: Mediation and the Bible

(though from precisely what party, source, or person is unclear). However, the author's decisions are central and paramount and therefore "infallible." After all, all such utterances are often simply expressions of personal feelings and such feelings are rarely questioned because there appears to be no external "objective" basis for such inspiration.[1] The question of inconsistency does not apply. Any inconsistencies that appear on reflection, after the creation of the text, can be explained away as fiction, or artistic style, or postmodern relativism: each text in a humanist model should, therefore, be seen in isolation from other texts.

There are, of course, many other models created from a combination of elements from one or more of these four approaches—Evangelicals will broadly subscribe to the second model, but with differences, subtle distinctions of approach, from one group to another. Some Evangelicals might even subscribe to the third model, but this is rare. Many Roman Catholics will subscribe to the first model, though some cultural Catholics may even subscribe to the fourth model. Most liberals would subscribe to the fourth view, which emphasizes the human ability to be inspired and create, where inspiration is essentially self-referential and ideas are solely the result of our sense perception of the physical world—often the "other" is deemed not to exist—and hence the fourth model can be seen as marginalizing God's inspiration.

What was Lewis's approach to Scripture? Lewis subscribed to the first model: that God was infallible, yet God also allowed for the freedom of creation to be. Hence, the writers of Scripture were divinely inspired, but each writer was a fallen and fallible human being characterized by free will, admittedly a corrupted free will. Both Lewis's approach, and the first model outlined above, is essentially characterized by the concept of the dove whispering into the ear, the Holy Spirit imparting intimations to the human mind, though the mind is free to make of these intimations what it will. This is where Lewis's understanding of the humanity of Scripture comes to play. This also invokes a proposition Lewis shared with Tolkien, that God creates in freedom enabling the world and humanity to be sub-creators: creation creates, it brings forth. A baptized imagination in the mind of a faithful writer would seek to be as true to the revelation as possible, though here Lewis's Platonism wields in: any revelation from on high given to these fallen shadowlands will be a diminution, will be in effect watered-down, changed in form, but not in truth. Therefore, for Lewis, the writer of Scripture is inspired to write; the content is given through the faculty of the imagination and reflected on through reason. Therefore, the human element will filter because the human is egotistical, flawed, and fallen. There is something of a dialectic in Lewis's understanding of Scripture between the God-given freedom to make of the inspiration what the writer will, and the emphasis he places on the importance of a baptized imagination. We are created in freedom yet the Holy Spirit presses on us,

---

1. Although Philip Pullman claimed some sort of external inspiration for the trilogy, *His Dark Material* (which can fairly be described as humanist) in that the ideas came to him, as though pre-existing, this approach has been described by some as "pseudo-Platonic." Pullman often talks about stories in this way. On another occasion he speaks about story-telling in mystical terms: "As I write I find myself drifting into a sort of Platonism, as if the story is there already . . ." Quoted in Rayment-Pickard, *The Devil's Account: Philip Pullman and Christianity*, 24.

and influences our decisions—but God does not force this influence onto people; he stands at the door, knocking, awaiting permission (Rev 3:20). Therefore, by grace the resulting work will have importance and authority—God-given authority—but there will be inconsistencies; often on extraneous details. In addition, all the books and chapters of the Bible are not the same type of genre (Lewis, as we have seen, regarded Jonah as sacred fiction) and the contradictions over the historicity of details in the books of the Old Testament do not necessarily undermine the veracity of the claims of the Gospels. We may attempt to form propositions and ethics from reading the Bible but these will often be human constructs relative to the will of God in Christ: "What we can say with some certainty about Lewis is that he did not subscribe to the view—still widely held in the American Bible-belt—that Scripture is itself God's revelation to humankind. I know of nowhere that Lewis denies that the Bible in some sense reveals something of God's intentions for the world, but neither do I know of anywhere where he talks of revelation in terms of propositional truth, or of isomorphic pairings between biblical words and God's utterances."[2] Andrew Walker, writing here on Lewis's understanding of revelation and Scripture, understands how Lewis refused to subscribe to a Fundamentalist view of Scripture, which ignored the contradictions and inconsistencies self-evident in the books of the Bible, while the philosopher Lewis could see that there was not a direct isomorphic (i.e., corresponding or similar in form or relations) coupling, one-to-one, between God's speech-act and what is written down.

We noted earlier how Lewis was not an inerrantist, how he cited several examples of inconsistencies which worked against a Fundamentalist approach to inerrancy. The key is therefore the types of material that make up the Bible, but also how the Bible is inspired and composed. Therefore, it is fair to say that Lewis cautiously rejects the concept of biblical inerrancy: given genre and function, the aims and objectives of the authors of individual books, also compilers of the Bible itself, inerrancy for the whole is not possible. Therefore, we noted his comments to Clyde S. Kilby, that we should "rule out the view that every statement in Scripture must be historical truth . . . [also] rule out the view that any one passage taken in isolation can be assumed to be inerrant in exactly the same sense as any other."[3]

iii. Inspiration

What is it to be inspired? The verb "to inspire" means to fill with the urge to do or feel something, to animate someone to create. The word comes from the Latin, *inspirare*, to breathe or to blow into. Immediately, therefore, there is a distinction—as we saw in the first model above—between the source of the inspiration (God) and the object (the writer): if a mother inspires a child to go out into the garden to play with its friends, the child is not following a step-by-step instruction guide on how to play, though there will be some common ground rules, and out of love for its mother the child

---

2. Walker, "Scripture, Revelation and Platonism in C. S. Lewis," 19.
3. Lewis to Clyde S. Kilby, May 7, 1959. *Collected Letters Vol. III*, 1046.

2. Scripture, Revelation, and Reason II: Mediation and the Bible

will not want to do anything to contradict or harm the mother: there is freedom, but this freedom is relational. There is God-given space between God's inspiration on the one hand and our reception and transmission of the content, as such, of revelation through words on a page. The books of Scripture are therefore not inerrant; there will be inconsistencies and flaws because they have been written by people who were flawed and fallen, and this was in the context of the freedom God has given humanity. Therefore, for Lewis, the knowledge of God given in Scripture is partial and incomplete: there is as much withheld as there is revealed of God. But also we do injury to Scripture to believe we can press it unremittingly for right knowledge about creation and science, or mathematics and logic: "Lewis may not have had any kind of worked-out doctrine of biblical inspiration; he undoubtedly believed that the Scriptures were a sacred text that did not need defending, simply because they were acknowledged by all the mainline churches as their authoritative teachings. I know of nowhere in his writings, however, where Lewis advocates the *sola scriptura* of the Reformers."[4] In many ways this relativizes the Bible—it is still through its status as an inspired sacred text superior to other books of human creation. Lewis often asserted that the Holy Spirit may also be behind the inspiration of many other works—including myths and works of great literature from a variety of cultures and civilizations. In the context of the Clyde S. Kilby letter it is important to remember his comment, quoting Jas 1:17, that, "If every good and perfect gift comes from the Father of Lights then all true and edifying writings, whether in Scripture or not, must be in some sense inspired."[5]

Writing to a Mr. Lee Turner in 1958 on the question of inspiration in relation to genre, Lewis went straight to the heart of the matter by asserting that the main problem is what exactly we mean by saying something is inspired. He notes how many people in the past believed that "the Holy Spirit either just replaced the minds of the authors (like the supposed "control" in automatic writing) or at least dictated to them as to secretaries."[6] Lewis cites Paul's comments in writing to the church in Corinth that refute such an idea (1 Cor 7:8–10): "Scripture itself refutes these ideas. St Paul distinguishes between what 'the Lord' says and what he says 'of himself'—yet both are 'Scripture'"; in addition much that is now Scripture was not necessarily written with the sort of audience in mind which it is now exposed to: "in Scripture, a mass of human legend, history, moral teaching, etc., are taken up and made the vehicle of God's Word. Errors of minor fact are permitted to remain. (Was Our Lord himself incapable, *qua* Man, of such errors? Would it be a real human incarnation if he was?)"[7] Therefore, to be human is to err; despite our flawed reception Scripture still has an authority that means it is a sacred text that transcends other all books. This is clear, in many ways, because we have four Gospels: four portraits of Jesus, so that the human authorship of each portrait is clear—this again reveals the humanity of Scripture.[8]

4. Walker, "Scripture, Revelation and Platonism," 23.
5. Lewis to Clyde S. Kilby, May 7, 1959. *Collected Letters Vol. III.* 1045.
6. Lewis to Lee Turner Jul. 19, 1958. *Collected Letters, Vol. III,* 960.
7. Ibid., 960–61.
8. For example, Burridge, *Four Gospels, One Jesus?*

iv. Interpretation: Local and Universal Genre

What did Lewis have to say on how to interpret Scripture? To interpret is to explain the meaning of something (from the Latin, *interpretari*, to interpret, to expound, explain, translate). First, Lewis believed in the wholeness of Scripture. The books that constitute the Bible may have been created over many hundreds of years within culturally diverse situations but with the fixing of the canon of Scripture in the fourth century there is then a givenness about the whole of the Bible—we should not pick and choose which bits complement our lifestyle, or not, and so on. Lewis commented:

> I take it as a first principle that we must not interpret any one part of Scripture so that it contradicts other parts: and especially we must not use an Apostle's teaching to contradict that of Our Lord. Whatever St Paul may have meant, we must not reject the parable of the sheep and the goats (Matt 25:30–46). There, you see there is nothing about Predestination or even about Faith—all depends on works. But how this is to be reconciled with St Paul's teaching, or with other sayings of Our Lord, I frankly confess I don't know. Even St Peter you know admits that he was stumped by the Pauline epistles (2 Pet 3:16–17)[9]

In many ways this is about understanding the context of the Bible—the context within which the books/epistles were written, and then the context in which they are read by subsequent generations. Most passages/books were composed in isolation from others and without the intention of the author for them to be read in the context that they are used in today. This may explain some of the inconsistencies: all scriptural passages/books have a local genre and context for which they were created, but also such passages/books have a universal genre and context in the form of the Bible and its use today by people. Hence Lewis, writing to Janet Wise in 1955 asserted that, "The basis of our faith is not the Bible taken by itself but the agreed affirmation of all Christendom: to which we owe the Bible itself."[10] The basis, the foundation or ground, of our faith is Jesus Christ.

2. THE "WORD" OF GOD AND THE "WORD" OF GOD

i. Scripture (word) in Relation to the Christ (Word)

The key to the interpretation of Scripture for Lewis lies in the precise nature of its being in relation to God, or more precisely, in relation to the Word of God. What is the Bible? What is its place as revealing God and God's purposes for humankind? This is about the priority of the *Word* above all else, including the church and the Bible: Lewis commented, "We have no abiding city even in philosophy: all passes except

---

9. Lewis to Emily McLay, Aug. 3, 1953. *Collected Letters, Vol. III*, 355. Lewis refers to Peter's comments: "So also our beloved brother Paul wrote to you according to the wisdom given him, speaking of this as he does in all his letters. There are some things in them hard to understand, which the ignorant and unstable twist to their own destruction, as they do the other Scriptures. You therefore, beloved, since you are forewarned, beware that you are not carried away with the error of the lawless and lose your own stability." 3 Pet 3:15–17.

10. Lewis to Janet Wise Oct. 5, 1955. *Collected Letters, Vol. III*, 653.

2. Scripture, Revelation, and Reason II: Mediation and the Bible

the Word."[11] If it is the Word of God, what does this mean, when the prologue to John's Gospel declares that Jesus Christ is the Word of God? Lewis uses the phrase the w/Word of God in relation to Scripture and Jesus Christ. Exactly what does Lewis mean when invoking the concept of the w/Word of God? This is, in some ways, a key to his understanding of Scripture and revelation. Lewis makes a distinction between the Word of God (the universal Christ of all eternity, incarnated in Jesus of Nazareth) and the word of God (Scripture). There is therefore God-given space between divine inspiration, on the one hand, and our reception and transmission of the content of revelation through words on a page. The Bible, therefore, is ordered to God's revelation to humankind in Jesus Christ: it is Christ who is the Word of God, as the prologue to John's Gospel puts it. Lewis is quite explicit on this: the Word became flesh, it did not become a book—Christ is the Word of God, not the Bible. Lewis, writing to a Mrs. Johnson in 1952 commented:

> It is Christ himself, not the Bible, who is the true word of God. The Bible, read in the right spirit and with the guidance of good teachers, will bring us to him. When it becomes really necessary (i.e., for our spiritual life, not for controversy or curiosity) to know whether a particular passage is rightly translated or is myth (but of course myth specially chosen by God from among countless myths to carry a spiritual truth) or history, we shall no doubt be guided to the right answer. But we must not use the Bible (our fathers too often did) as a sort of Encyclopaedia out of which texts (isolated from their context and not read with attention to the whole nature and purport of the books in which they occur) can be taken for use as weapons.[12]

Lewis is therefore establishing the basic structure of a hierarchy of revelation: Christ first, who is revelation; then the Bible, which is *about* revelation. Jesus Christ is the self-revelation of God. This is a high Christology; he makes no compromise here—God in the form of the universal Christ of all eternity, the unbegotten second person of the Trinity, the Son in relation to the Father, descended to be incarnated human. *This is* revelation. All other revelation is in relation to the incarnation-cross-resurrection; all other revelation is relative to, hierarchically, the Christ-event. The Bible is, therefore, *about* revelation. But is this all there is to the Bible for Lewis? No. There is much more.

For Lewis the graceful inspiration of the Holy Spirit operates on and changes the reader of Scripture (*theopneustos*)—the dove whispering into the mind in a manner similar to how the Holy Spirit inspired and illumined the author of Scripture. This graceful action of the Holy Spirit will raise the level of the physical object that is a book, which is the Bible, to a higher level; it will form revelation second only to Christ himself. Because of the action of the Holy Spirit the reader will elevate the value and meaning of the words on the page; as these words are read the text is imbued with an authority above mere common books and words. Therefore, for Lewis, the act of reading is in itself revelatory; knowledge and understanding of God is given. But this

---

11. From a letter quoted by Alan Bede Griffiths, "The Adventure of Faith," in, Como, *Remembering C. S. Lewis*, 91.
12. Lewis to Mrs Johnson, Nov. 8, 1952. *Collected Letters, Vol. III*, 246.

knowledge and understanding is not for idle curiosity (i.e., "Modern" and "Liberal" Bible studies); it is for our well-being and ultimately relates to our salvation. However, the distinction between the Word of God (Christ) and the word of God (the book about God's self-revelation) remains. Therefore, the Bible, for Lewis, relates to and is validated by Christ himself: "The total result is not 'the Word of God' in the sense that every passage, in itself, gives impeccable science or history. It *carries* the Word of God; and we (under grace, with attention to tradition and to interpreters wiser than ourselves, and with the use of such intelligence and learning as we may have) *receive* that Word from it not by using it as an encyclopaedia or an encyclical but by steeping ourselves in its tone or temper and so learning its overall message."[13] Using the Bible in an encyclopaedic or encyclical fashion is therefore dangerous, it forms an abuse and misuse of Scripture; it may even form a type of idolatry—bibliolatry. If Lewis is repudiating a simplistic fundamentalist use of the Bible then we must acknowledge, as we have seen, that there are a variety of different genres to scriptural books, written with different aims and for widely differing audiences. This does presents us with a Bible that is—as Lewis terms it—an untidy and leaky vehicle;[14] we no doubt would have preferred absolute truth systematically presented, unrefracted light which we could have contained, quantified, in an encyclopaedic fashion. As a word of God (note the indefinite article, and lower case "w"), the Bible as a book will be beyond our human categories, to a degree, and will be a puzzle for those (on the one hand fundamentalists, on the other hand "Modern"/"Liberal" Bible scholars) who wish to misuse it; however, the inspiration of Christ's Holy Spirit will allow it to become for us the Word of God (note the definite article, and upper case "W"). As we noted above, we must "not use the Bible (our fathers too often did) as a sort of encyclopaedia out of which texts (isolated from their context and not read with attention to the whole nature and purport of the books in which they occur) can be taken for use as weapons."[15] Therefore, the question of historicity and inerrancy is, for Lewis, marginalized, to a degree, by the manner in which Scripture is elevated by the Holy Spirit as it carries *a* "word" of God, to act on us as *a* "word" of God, drawing us to *the* "Word" of God (Christ): our reading and learning is integral to our sanctification and salvation, not to our idle curiosity, to our antiquarian studies:

> To me the curious thing is that neither in my own Bible-reading nor in my religious life as a whole does the question in fact even assume that importance which it always gets in theological controversy. The difference between reading the story of Ruth and that of Antigone—both first class as literature—is to me unmistakable and even overwhelming. But the question "Is Ruth historical?" (I've no reason to suppose it is not) doesn't really seem to arise till afterwards. *It would still act on me as the word of God if it weren't, so far as I can see.* All Holy Scripture is written for our learning.[16] (My emphasis.)

13. Lewis, *Reflections on the Psalms*, 96. My emphasis.
14. "To a human mind this working up (in a sense imperfectly), this sublimation (incomplete) of human material, seems, no doubt, an untidy and leaky vehicle." Ibid., 96–97, see also 100.
15. Lewis to Mrs Johnson, Nov. 8, 1952. *Collected Letters, Vol. III*, 246.
16. Lewis to Clyde S. Kilby, May 7, 1959. *Collected Letters Vol. III*, 1044–45.

2. Scripture, Revelation, and Reason II: Mediation and the Bible

---

C.S. Lewis and Karl Barth: The Threefold Forms of the Word of God

C. S. Lewis
Jesus Christ is the primary revelation of God and therefore "It is Christ himself, not the Bible, who is the true Word of God".

⬇

Scripture written is inspired by the Holy Spirit and becomes a word of God; the Bible is a word of God in relation to Jesus Christ, and is a record of revelation produced by the Church.

⬇

Scripture read, illumined by the Holy Spirit, becomes a word of God, drawing us to *the* Word of God (Christ): "Scripture, read in the right spirit (small 's') and with the guidance of good teachers (the church?), draws us to *the* Word of God (Christ)."

Karl Barth
§ 4.1 The Word of God Preached: revelation is explicitly and implicitly in and through the proclamation of the church.

⬇

§ 4.2 The Word of God Written: revelation is disclosed as Scripture is read, inspired by the Holy Spirit, read individually and through the Church.

⬇

§ 4.3 The Word of God Revealed: revelation is primarily Jesus Christ the Son of God who reveals the one true God.

Figure 3: C. S. Lewis and Karl Barth—The Word of God in a Threefold Form

The graceful inspiration of the Holy Spirit in the reader will elevate the value and meaning of the words of Scripture; as these words are read silently or aloud the text is imbued with an authority above mere common books and words. Therefore, for Lewis the act of reading is in itself revelatory.

ii. C. S. Lewis and Karl Barth—The Word of God in a Threefold Form

The Swiss theologian Karl Barth asserts that Scripture preached, Scripture written, and Jesus Christ are forms of the Word of God. There is, therefore, a close intimate link between Scripture and the Christ and, as with Lewis, Barth does differentiate. For Barth—like Lewis—the Bible is not the foundation for the Christian faith: Christ Jesus is. Christ, both particular (Jesus) and universal (the second person of the eternal Trinity) is the ground and foundation of theological truth. Lewis clearly rejected the concept of biblical inerrancy. For Barth biblical inerrancy is a basis or ground other than Jesus Christ. The Bible's primary value is as witness to the Word of God, that is, as testimony, witness, bystander and onlooker, to Jesus of Nazareth, the second person of the Trinity incarnate, crucified and resurrected as atonement realized; this is the only connection: "The Resurrection from the dead is the transformation: the establishing or declaration of that point from above, and the corresponding discerning of it from below. The Resurrection is the revelation: the disclosing of Jesus as the Christ, the appearing of God, and the apprehending of God in Jesus."[17] Lewis is not alone in his use of the w/Word of God in relation to a doctrine of Scripture. Barth exhibited an approach to Scripture that was very similar to Lewis's. To the mature Barth the concept of the Word of God was categorical, fundamental, and all pervasive in his work—God's Word was the sole power and authority in eternity, in this world, and in relation to people, "the Son of God who has come to us or the Word of God that has been spoken to us, is because he is so antecedently in himself as the Son or Word of God the Father."[18] The Word is the sole ground of any knowledge that humanity has, or any understanding humanity claims. Being a systematic theologian Barth's understanding is methodically laid-out across several thousand words; Lewis's, as we have seen, can be gleaned from his multitudinous letters, essays, and apologetics, but nonetheless there is evidence in Lewis's thinking of a systematic structure (see figure 3). Barth's doctrine of the Word of God in relation to Scripture is set out in the first volume of *The Church Dogmatics*—"The Word of God in its Threefold Form"[19] This systematization is then indicative, symptomatic and the foundational ground, to a degree, of his mature work and can be found explicated in detail throughout the remaining volumes of *The Church Dogmatics*. For example, the Word as incarnation, "God's revelation takes place in the fact that God's Word became a man and that this man has become God's Word" (§.13),[20] whereby the eternal Word of God chose, sanctified and assumed human nature, and is thereby the Word of reconciliation (§.15).[21] The relationship between Scripture and the Church is shown whereby "the Word of God is God himself in Holy Scripture . . . and now through their written word he speaks as the same Lord to his Church" (§.19), therefore Scripture is "to the Church a witness to divine revelation" (§.19).[22] Therefore, "The Church does not claim direct and absolute and material authority for itself but for Holy Scripture as the Word of God" (§§.20 & 21).[23] The Word is God in the proclamation of Jesus Christ by the church (§.22);[24] as doctrine this points the church to the Word (§.23),[25] because the Word of God is in the revelation attested to in Scripture, "It can do this only as it accepts itself the position of the teaching Church and is therefore claimed by the Word of God as the object to which the teaching Church as such has devoted itself" (§.24).[26] Epistemologically knowledge of God is in the realization of the revelation of the Word

---

17. Barth, *Der Römerbrief*, Zweite Fassung, 6.
18. Barth, *Church Dogmatics*, I/1, §.11 "God the Son," 399.
19. Ibid., I/1, see, §.4. "The Word of God in its Threefold Form," 88–124, and, §.5 "The Nature of the Word of God" I/1, 125–86; see also, §.6 "The Knowability of the Word of God" I/1, 187–247.
20. Ibid., I/2, §.13 "God's Freedom for man," 1f., see also, 18–24.
21. Ibid., I/2, §.15 "The mystery of Revelation," 122f., specifically 126, and 2. "Very God and Very Man," 132f.
22. Ibid., I/2, §.19 "The Word of God for the Church," 1. "Scripture as a Witness to Divine Revelation," 459–72, quote 457.
23. Ibid., I/2, §.20 "Authority in the Church," 538, and, I/2, §.21 "Freedom in the Church," 661.
24. Ibid., I/2, §.22 "The Mission of the Church," 743, also, generally, 754.
25. Ibid., I/2, §.23 "Dogmatics as a Function of the Hearing Church," 797. For the relationship between the Word and God and the Church's reception of it, see, 799f.
26. Ibid., I/2, §.24 "Dogmatics as a Function of the Teaching Church," 844.

2. Scripture, Revelation, and Reason II: Mediation and the Bible

by the Holy Spirit (§.25);[27] the Church lives through the grace of the Word (§.25),[28] therefore the only possibility of divine knowledge issues from God, because God is the truth given in the Word by the Holy Spirit (§.26).[29] This knowledge of the Word of God is, therefore, true knowledge (§.16).[30] Such understanding is electoral—and is grounded in and issues from the knowledge of Jesus Christ who is the electing God and the elected man (§.32).[31] Humanity's existence under heaven is revealed by and in relation to the Word of God (§.43).[32] This is because God determines the sphere, the manner, the measure and the subordinate relationship of the Word towards and in relation to the world and specifically to humanity (§.50).[33] This is so because, "Jesus Christ as attested to us in Holy Scripture is the one Word of God whom we must hear and whom we must trust and obey in life and in death" (§.69).[34] This is revealed in that the Word as and of Jesus Christ is the creative call by which God awakens humanity to vigorous knowledge of the truth (§.71),[35] and is unified in that the Holy Spirit is the enlightening power of "the Lord Jesus Christ through the prophetic Word" (§.72).[36]

The crucial concept for Barth (and implicitly in Lewis's writings) is that the Word of God is presented to humanity in a threefold form. Barth's three concepts are different in category from Lewis's. Barth distinguishes between the Word of God preached (§4.1), the Word of God written (§4.2), and then the Word of God revealed (§4.3) (see figure 3, right-hand column); Lewis identifies Jesus Christ as the Word of God, the primary revelation of God; then there is Scripture written, and then Scripture read—both Scripture written and Scripture read become a "word" of God through and in Christ who is *the* "Word" of God (see figure 3, left-hand column).

Barth: The Word of God Preached

Barth's exposition of the threefold form opens with "The Word of God Preached":[37] proclamation, that is, the proclamation of the gospel by the church. Yes, this is priests and ministers preaching the Word of God, but also the witness generally of the church. This proclamation (*Verkündung*—the act of proclaiming—a term Barth lays great emphasis on) is often caused by the church's existence—the Word of God may, "simply and visibly be there, but then they are not simply and visibly there either, and then we see the dialectic. Because they may be obvious to us, they may be obvious to believers in the Church as proclamation-bearers but not to everybody."[38] The Word

---

27. Ibid., II/I, §.25 "The Fulfilment of the Knowledge of God," 3.
28. Ibid., II/I, §.25 "The Fulfilment of the Knowledge of God," 5.
29. Ibid., II/1, §.26 "The Knowability of God," 63.
30. Ibid., I/2, §.16 "The Freedom of man for God," 203.
31. Ibid., II/2, §.32 "The Problem of a Correct Doctrine of the Election of Grace," 3.
32. Ibid., III/2, §.43 "Man as a Problem of Dogmatics," 3 and 11.
33. Ibid., III/3, §.50 "God and Nothingness," 289.
34. Ibid., IV/3,i, §.69 "The Glory of the Mediator," 3.
35. Ibid., IV/3,ii, §.71 "The Vocation of Man," 481.
36. Ibid., IV/3ii, §.72 "The Holy Spirit and the Sending of the Christian Community," 729.
37. Ibid., I/1, §.4.1, 88–99.
38. Gunton, *The Barth Lectures*, 72.

as proclamation may not be clear and obvious to people outside the church, but the church's existence does, should, point to the Word of God:

> The presupposition which makes proclamation proclamation, and therewith makes the Church the Church is the Word of God. This attests itself in Holy Scripture in the word of the prophets and apostles to whom it was originally and once and for all spoken by God's revelation . . . The Word of God in all its three forms is God's speech to humanity. For this reason it occurs, applies and works in God's act on man. But as such it occurs in God's way which differs from all other occurrence, i.e., in the mystery of God . . . The reality of the Word of God in all its three forms is grounded only in itself. So, too, the knowledge of it by people can consist only in its acknowledgment, and this acknowledgment can become real only through itself and become intelligible only in terms of itself.[39]

Such proclamation assumes the pre-existence of the gospel, the reality of the Christ-event, but ultimately the prior reality of God. "The Word of God Preached" issues from a commission by God: it is important to remember that the preacher's words—or non-verbal actions—only become God's Word by grace.

Barth: The Word of God Written

Barth's exposition of the threefold form continues with "The Word of God Written."[40] This form is at the heart of Barth's doctrine of Scripture. This is about the mediation of God's Word. *Verkündung*—preaching, the act of proclaiming—is dependent upon the "Word of God Written": this is the "recollection of past revelation . . . recollection of God's enacted revelation."[41] This is essentially the canon of Scripture formulated by the church; but Scripture also governs the church. Like Lewis, Barth is highly critical of "modern" Bible studies: "In certain respects Scripture is just like any other ordinary book, but this is only the beginning—theology takes over from this starting-point. In Scripture God's event becomes God's Word through human words."[42] Like Lewis, Barth is highly critical of "modern" Bible studies. On one level Scripture is an ordinary book but, like with Lewis, this is the starting point—Scripture becomes, eschatologically, God's Word through human words. The Bible is, in this context, human words until God re-makes it as a divine word: "The Church must mean it is guided by the Canon [of Scripture], that is, the prophetic and apostolic word as necessary rule of every word that is valid in the Church."[43] The Bible (almost echoing Lewis's comments writing to Mrs. Johnson in 1952) is not primarily the Word of God, but it is enabled to become the Word of God.[44] Scripture therefore becomes the Word of God when it is preached (explicitly, and implicitly as silent church witness), but also when it is read—God's grace declares it to be so. But, this does raise the question for Barth, is Scripture the Word of God when written? is it inspired? and what is the ontic relationship between

---

39. Barth, *Church Dogmatics*, I/1, §.4, 88; I/1, §.5, 125; and I/1, §.6., 187.
40. Ibid., I/1, §.4.2, 99–111.
41. Ibid., I/1, §.4.2, 99, also 108.
42. Gunton, *The Barth Lectures*, 74.
43. Barth, *Church Dogmatics*, I/1, §.4.2, 104.
44. Ibid., I/1, §.4.2, 108.

inspiration and God? The oft-citied criticism of Barth is that he places too little stress on how Scripture becomes God's Word when it is written, he underplays—often quite severely for many orthodox critics—the place and role of inspiration in authorship.

Barth: The Word of God Revealed

Barth's exposition of the threefold form concludes with Christ.[45] As such, Scripture is not God's revelation but it bears witness to it. This is the characteristically Barthian position. Like Lewis, he asserts Jesus Christ as God's self-revelation: "The Bible is the concrete means by which the church recollects God's past revelation, is called to expectation of his future revelation, and is thus summoned and guided to proclamation and empowered for it. The Bible, then, is not in itself and as such God's past revelation, just as church proclamation is not in itself and as such the expected future revelation. The Bible, speaking to us and heard by us as God's Word, bears witness to past revelation."[46] Jesus Christ is revelation; Scripture is revelation in so far as it reflects, it bears witness to, the Christ-event; Barth notes that the Gospel writers point beyond themselves.[47] In Christ, Scripture may become, the Word of God. Like Lewis, Barth does distinguish between the *Deus dixit* (God spoke), and *paulus dixit* (Paul spoke), therefore some words in the Bible are of human origin—a distinction the apostle Paul himself makes.[48] Essentially, for Barth, revelation is the presence of the Word of God to the humanity, Jesus Christ in the world (which is why the proclamation of the church is revelation because it brings the resurrected Christ to humanity). This is the Word of God revealed; therefore the other two forms of the Word of God are derivative: "the direct identification between revelation and the Bible . . . takes place as an event when and where the biblical word becomes God's Word."[49] Revelation is the Word of God in Christ (John 1), from which issues, by God's grace, Scripture, and the church's witness and proclamation: Jesus Christ as revelation is then the criteria for theology.

Lewis: The Threefold Form of the w/Word of God

Lewis does not explicitly spell-out and name the Word of God as three forms, but he nonetheless identifies three forms, which are similar to Barth's. Barth may systematise the Word of God as three-fold in the context of the economic Trinity, but in keeping with Lewis's approach, he stresses the unity of the forms of the Word of God:

> We have been speaking of three different forms of the Word of God and not of three different Words of God. In this threefold form and not otherwise—but also as the one Word only in this threefold form—the Word of God is given to us and we must try to understand it conceptually. It is one and the same whether we understand it as revelation, Bible, or proclamation. There is no distinction of degree or value between the three forms. For to the extent that proclamation

---

45. Ibid., I/1, §.4.2, 111–20.
46. Ibid., I/1, §.4.3, 111.
47. Ibid., I/1, §.4.3, 112.
48. See, Lewis Letter to Clyde S. Kilby, May 7, 1959. *Collected Letters, Vol. III*, 1044–46. Barth and Lewis are referring to 1 Cor 7:10 and 12.
49. Barth, *Church Dogmatics*, I/1, §.4.3, 113.

> really rests on recollection of the revelation attested in the Bible and is thus obedient reception of the biblical witness, it is no less the Word of God than the Bible . . . Nor should we ever try to understand the three forms of God's Word in isolation.[50]

But there are key differences: Barth starts with the human, he in effect starts with the human in existential *krisis*, proclaiming, preaching; this witness—as recollection—becomes the Word of God through graceful adoption; the progression is then to the Word of God read, again pneumatologically enabled; only then, finally, does he move to Christ, the Word of God that is revelation. By contrast Lewis, ever the Platonist, starts in eternity, with the universal Christ, progressing, descending, first to the event (the incarnation-cross-resurrection); he then moves to the record of the event written (Scripture illumined pneumatologically), which grace raises above the level of mere words. Only then does he progress to the reception, the reading (and hearing—as in an oral tradition) of Scripture, where the mind of the reader is illumined pneumatologically; this act informs about salvation, but also works on the human, raises up, draws the human up to salvation. Progression is the touchstone to Lewis's schemata, progression that echoes the movement of the Incarnation, the descending to reascend. Barth's schemata, though systematically categorized, can appear random in its ordering and in its incompleteness. Both quite correctly identify Jesus Christ as the primary revelation of God (though ironically Barth lists this last of all). This is Barth's position in the first volume of *The Church Dogmatics*; by comparison, in volume 4—written twenty-five to thirty years later—Barth's position is a more eternity-down progression, redolent of an implicitly Platonic position like Lewis's. However, Barth establishes this basis of his doctrine of the Word of God in the first volume of the *Church Dogmatics*, in the mid-1930s, and it is taken and accepted to be the ground of his entire work. Lewis's system, it can be argued, does represent a more logical *procession*, where logic is at the heart of the Logos, the Word.[51] One point of convergence for both of them is the centring of pneumatology, the work of the Holy Spirit, primarily (but not exclusively) in the second form, in relation to the church. For both Barth and Lewis, if the total result of the Bible is not necessarily, in every sense, the "Word of God" (because every passage is not necessarily, as Lewis termed it, impeccable science or history), yet it *carries* the "Word of God" (whereby we "under grace, with attention to tradition and to interpreters wiser than ourselves,"[52] receive the "Word of God") then this raises a question: is Lewis asserting that Scripture only then becomes the word of God for us if and when we give attention to tradition and interpreters wiser than ourselves, when we steep ourselves in its tone or temper and so learn its overall message? The answer is, to a degree, yes. Does not this point to the importance of considering the Bible in the context of the church?

---

50. Ibid., I/1, §.4.4, 121.
51. "Reason is our starting point . . . reason is given before nature." Reason is given, issuing from the Logos, but it is corrupted by our wills. Lewis, *Miracles*, 2nd ed., 21 and 23.
52. Lewis, *Reflections on the Psalms*, 96.

2. Scripture, Revelation, and Reason II: Mediation and the Bible

iii. Lewis and Barth: Convergence and Divergence

Does Lewis's theology of the church give some indication as to the differences here between Barth and Lewis? Why the difference between the threefold forms in Lewis's work as compared to Barth's? Lewis commented that, "The Church exists for nothing else than to draw men into Christ, to make them little Christs. If they are not doing that, all the cathedrals, clergy, missions, sermons, even the Bible itself, are simply a waste of time. God became man for no other purpose."[53] Barth would certainly have agreed with this—Lewis's heavy and exclusive Christ-centred emphasis, the priority of the "Word of God" over everything "religious." Why the difference between the threefold form in Lewis's work as compared to Barth's? Perhaps because Barth, as a Reformed Church minister steeped in Calvinism and the Reformed tradition, laid greater emphasis on preaching—human words proclaiming Jesus. Lewis, as a more private and reticent person without official church status, whose conversion was from within his aloneness before God, could appreciate the solitude that is writing and reading. Hence, Lewis's emphasis on how the words and sentences read from the Bible become the Word of God. Barth was primarily a minister—standing before his congregation, preaching; Lewis allowed for the Word of God to communicate revelation to people through their Bible reading and study; but unlike Barth, Lewis emphatically asserts the divine inspiration of Scripture, through an Augustinian doctrine of illumination, thereby asserting a categorical receptive connection between the human and God. The primary cause of the difference between Barth and Lewis on the threefold forms of the Word of God is essentially ecclesiological. Barth's ecclesiology is a strong, assertive, and eschatologically realised; Lewis's is more nuanced, subtle and hidden, awaiting the completion of the *eschaton*. Lewis denies the possibility, since the Reformation, of any of the churches claiming the concrete and visible authority that once was held by the apostolic and patristic church; therefore Lewis gives credibility to the implicitly Augustinian dialectic between the *ecclesia visibilis* and the *ecclesia invisibilis* (the visible church of earth and the invisible church of all eternity—often seen as the church militant and the church triumphant),[54] which the mature Barth categorically denies.[55] For Lewis the act of reading the Bible, whereby it becomes pneumatologically re-authored as the Word of God, bears witness to this divine act and disclosure. It *may* become the church, though for that matter it may not—the

---

53. Lewis, *Beyond Personality*, 43; also, see, *Mere Christianity*, ch. 8, 164.

54. Lewis, "Introduction." In *English Literature in the Sixteenth Century Excluding Drama*, 2–65. See also, Lewis, *The Screwtape Letters*, 1, 5–8, 16, 26, 35, 39, 45–46, 61–64, 97–100; Screwtape comments, "One of our great allies at present is the Church itself. Do not misunderstand me. I do not mean the Church as we see her spread out through all time and space and rooted in eternity ... that, I confess, is a spectacle which makes our boldest temper uneasy. But fortunately it is quite invisible to these humans. All your patient sees is the half-finished, sham Gothic erection on the new building estate." 5.

55. For Barth's comments see, Barth, *Dogmatics in Outline*, 141–48: "It is best not to apply the idea of invisibility to the Church; we are all inclined to slip away with that in the direction of a *civitas platonica* in which Christians are united inwardly and invisibly while the visible church is undervalued." This does then raise questions about Lewis's explicit Platonism as compared to the implicit, or persistent, Platonism in Barth's theology, therefore see, Gunton, *The Barth Lectures*, specifically ch. 13 "Platonism And Exemplarism in Barth's Christology," 187–200.

dialectic here which complements the *ecclesia visibilis-ecclesia invisibilis* is between grace-dis-grace. Therefore, we may ask, an apostate or atheistic priest or bishop might stand before a congregation and read the Gospel, but is he or she the church? This, in many ways, accounts for the absence of an explicitly visible or institutionalized form of the Word of God as the church's proclamation in Lewis's scheme. Given the flawed and corrupted nature of the church(es) and their history, characterized by a predilection to sin and authoritarian egotism, Lewis is correct to play down the church as a word of God and to lay emphasis on the *ecclesia visibilis-ecclesia invisibilis*, where the church as *the* Word of God consists of individuals raised up by grace independent of humanely conferred status, power, and authority, forming an unseen community, a church community often obscured, abstruse, or indeterminate according to the criteria of this world. The key, as we have established, is, as Lewis explicitly states, that: it is *Christ himself*, not the Bible, who is the true Word of God, therefore we must read the Bible in the right Spirit.[56] So revelation proceeds from eternity, from the Trinity to Jesus of Nazareth, the Christ; Scripture, for Lewis, read within the graceful influence of the Holy Spirit will bring Jesus to us. Scripture is enabled to be the Word of God, and the actual reading becomes a form of the Word of God similar to Barth's form of the Word of God preached. We may say that for Bath and Lewis Scripture is pneumatologically enabled to be the Word of God in direct relation to Jesus Christ the Word of God whereby it simultaneously bears witness to Christ, while embodying the Holy Spirit to draw us into salvation.

3. REVELATION AND THE CHRIST-EVENT

i. Revelation and the Bible

The Bible is revelatory; it reveals something about God to us. It is revelation that is at the heart of the Christian faith and what makes it unique before other world religions. The Bible itself is not the primary form of God's revelation because it is Jesus Christ, the Word of God, a person, who is the primary mode of God's unique self-revelation. It is important that we understand, as Lewis asserted when writing to Mrs. Johnson that the Bible is not the Word of God (note, the capital "W"), Jesus Christ is the Word of God. This does not necessarily deny or repudiate the Bible, or the importance of Scripture as inspired and revealed. The Bible has a unique place in the world, especially in relation to human affairs. However, this sets the priorities: the revelation of God is a person, a unique act in history—God incarnated as a human being, Jesus of Nazareth, the Christ, fully human and fully divine—therefore this has universal and cosmic implications. Scripture recognizes and bears witness to Jesus Christ; this is from God, it is borne by and from the Trinity: the Bible is from God and therefore it is self-referential, it reveals to us something, as much as we can know, of God, and how this triune God has dealt with humanity. However, it is not simply an instruction manual on how to be religious, or a moral code with which we can be judgmental. Scripture, as we have seen, consists

---

56. Lewis to Mrs Johnson, Nov. 8, 1952. *Collected Letters, Vol. III*, 246.

of many types and genres of writing: history, biography, myth, sacred texts, etc. Lewis recognized the givenness of the Bible but he was not a Fundamentalist: Lewis does not deny that the Bible reveals something of God to humanity, but we do injury to Scripture if we claim an exact correlation between God's speech and what we find in the Bible. This was Lewis's view. In its own way this is dogmatic and assertive: in *Mere Christianity*, Lewis asserts that he did not create Christianity, it is not his personal religious view of humanity and reality, therefore there is a givenness to the Christian faith—"I am telling you what Christianity is. I did not invent it," he asserted.[57] This is about revelation, something is given, it is revealed; but how we receive that revelation and what value we place on it is where imagination and reason come in.

Since the Age of Reason and the Enlightenment, and carried through into Modernism, liberalism, and paradoxically postmodernism, is the belief amongst many theologians and philosophers (a belief grounded in itself), that unaided human reason could give all the truth that was necessary—revelation was not needed. Reason becomes paramount; revelation is marginalized. Therefore, the Bible is marginalized and is seen merely as one religious book among many. Likewise church tradition and authority, and religious truth claims generally, are seen as irrelevant to humanity's advancement and enlightenment. It is this mind-set that Lewis works against. Lewis could see how God had worked through the concrete and particular, this single event. Revelation is located in this single event (the Christ-event) but the Spirit of God in Christ works ceaselessly to draw people into the salvation wrought through this event. Therefore, there is not a sharp division between the Christ-event and the sort of personal revelatory experience people may have: all are related to the work of Christ. These experiences of God are general and incomplete compared to the concrete and particular; and they need to be measured, questioned, against the unique revelation of God in Christ. Reason is important in coming to a sound judgment about such mystical experiences as the numinous, or *Sehnsucht*: revelation and reason are therefore to be seen—certainly for Lewis—as symbiotic, and not separate, or divorced from each other, as so many Enlightenment philosophers decided. Revelation is not pitted against reason. Lewis seeks to try to hold both revelation and reason in balance; but how does he classify revelation?

ii. Christensen-Walker on Revelation in Lewis

It will help us to consider the conclusions of two theologians on how to understand and classify Lewis's understanding and categorization of revelation. Michael J. Christensen[58] and Andrew Walker[59] identified six modes of revelation. Andrew Walker takes this a step further by separating them into two groups: five, which are general and incomplete, partial and relative, and a sixth, which is particular and perfect. The Bible, for Lewis, is revelatory but not exclusively—"Lewis saw the Scriptures as

---

57. Lewis, *Mere Christianity*, 115.
58. See Christensen, *C. S. Lewis on Scripture*, ch. 4, 57–80, specifically 68–77.
59. See Walker, "Scripture, Revelation and Platonism in C. S. Lewis," 29–35. Walker extends Christensen's classification 33–35.

pointing to revelation rather than embodying it."[60] Lewis acknowledges that there are different modes to God's revealedness, different ways in which God communicates to humankind. This communication is possible because of the relationship between our reality and the supernatural realm—eternity. The ordering here is from Michael J. Christensen's work on C. S. Lewis and Scripture.[61]

The Experience of the Numinous, God's Holiness

For Lewis this is the human ability to experience awe or wonder, or fear, but it is also more than these intimations; the numinous (from the Latin, *numen, numin-*, meaning divine will) is a brush with the holiness of God and it instills in us a right understanding, a right relationship with God. We encountered something of this in the various stages of Lewis's protracted conversion. Critics will argue that there is nothing specifically Christian in these mystical intimations, that they are not unique to self-confessed Christians. But this is precisely the point: they emanate from Christ; they are part of the work of Christ and should not be thought of solely in terms of human-centered religiosity.

The Universal Ought: Cosmic Bluff or Moral Responsibility

Conscience here is a precursor to and manifestation of the revelation of God, conscience is a universal given. Some people may deny their conscience, smoother it and create their own morality—history is replete with such individuals who raze whole cities, slaughter millions, then sleep soundly at night—but there are universal moral laws that can be known in our minds and our hearts and are from God. The universal is seen by Lewis in that however different morals and ethics are in different cultures and civilizations, "they all have a moral sense that we ought to do some things rather than others."[62] This universal "ought" reveals God's will and his good desire for our welfare and salvation.

Sehnsucht: the Hound of Heaven

In volume 1 we examined *Sehnsucht* in the context of Lewis's conversion, more pertinently the troubling conscience-like stab, which after his conversion could be seen as intimations of the Holy Spirit, encounters with the divine will, that unnamed desire, that longing for heaven, which only God can satisfy. Andrew Walker terms Lewis's conception of *Sehnsucht* as a God-given revelation of longing, unrequited love, a non-rational yearning for ultimate reality, it is an echo of joy from "Joy."[63]

Election: Israel and the Law

In Israel revelation takes the form of covenant and law; God progressively reveals himself and simultaneously his desire and will for humanity, through a chosen people.

---

60. Ibid., 25.
61. Christensen, *C. S. Lewis on Scripture*, 68–77.
62. Walker, "Scripture, Revelation and Platonism in C. S. Lewis," 31, referring to Lewis, *The Problem of Pain*, 4–13, specifically 10; and Lewis, *Mere Christianity*, 3–9.
63. Walker, "Scripture, Revelation and Platonism in C. S. Lewis," 30.

Law is important here but in the context of the creation of the Jews as the chosen people of God (though Lewis is quite reticent to talk in terms of a doctrine of election). As he writes in *Mere Christianity*, God "selected one group of people and spent several centuries hammering into their heads the sort of God he was—that there was only one of him and that he cared about right conduct."[64] However, this process of revealing to a chosen group of people is not an end in itself, it lays the groundwork, and it prepares for the concrete, particular and perfect revelation: the God thus revealed to the ancient Hebrews, the God of Abraham, Isaac and Jacob, reaches it fullest revelation in Jesus Christ.

Good Dreams: Pagan Premonitions of Christ

But outside of Israel humanity is not bereft of revelation. Lewis makes much in his theological apologetics and in his symbolic narratives of premonitions and intimations of Christ to pagan people. This, of course, reflects a deep love Lewis had all his life of such myths—especially North European in origin. Lewis actually balances almost dialectically the rules and election of the Jews with the pictures infused into the minds of the pagans. Both are modes of imperfect revelation, general and incomplete. Pagan premonitions of Christ's incarnation and resurrection relate to the numinous and also to *Sehnsucht* but they contained pictures given to the imagination, which generated words/stories/myths, and hence give meaning and intent whereas the numinous and *Sehnsucht* is more of an instantaneous encounter with the Holy Spirit, leaving the person to try to make out what has happened. The revelation of pagan premonitions relates directly to inspiration and imagination. In *The Pilgrim's Regress*, he explains how both the pagans and the Shepherds (i.e., Israel) pointed towards the full and complete revelation in Christ.

Incarnation: The Word of God Revealed

The fullest revelation possible for humanity to comprehend comes with the incarnation of the Universal Christ in human form: Jesus of Nazareth, Son of God, and Son of Man. The revelation of the incarnation is concrete and real, no nebulous intimation, no lawgiver—except for the law of love and forgiveness. In a comment that reflects Lewis's understanding of the concrete reality of the incarnation (and echoes also with that of Karl Barth's) Andrew Walker comments that "the veil of myth is parted and God steps into the full glare of historical reality, and yet, being God, remains forever veiled and mysterious—always unknown, even in his revealedness."[65]

---

64. See Lewis. *Mere Christianity*, 47–52, specifically, 50–51.
65. Walker, "Scripture, Revelation and Platonism in C. S. Lewis," 30.

4. A HIERARCHY OF REVELATION

i. Mediation

Revelation is communication: God communicates, imparts, conveys. But this is not simply knowledge. Revelation is about mediation and a mediator. Jesus Christ is God's self-revelation and the mediator. A mediator conveys, yes, but intervenes and conciliates: Christ's mediation intervenes in the rent between God and humanity brought about by the fall to bring about a reconciliation: revelation and atonement are intimately intertwined. The word "mediator" is from the Middle English, where it was used as an adjective in the sense of interposed (from late Latin *mediatus*, *mediare*, to place in the middle, from Latin *medius* middle). Christ interposes, steps-in; Christ simultaneously reveals God and appeases, reconciles, makes peace—atones between humanity and God. Initially God revealed the law to Israel through a mediator—Moses; but true mediation is seen in the person of Jesus Christ. This is the true and real covenant. Atonement-reconciliation is achieved through the cross: God is incarnated; God dies to God in our place, and reconciles us to God. Therefore, at the centre of revelation is mediation: all revelation must in some way relate to and issue from Christ the mediator.

Andrew Walker quite correctly separates the mode of revelation that is the incarnation as belonging to a different realm—as particular and perfect, as distinct from the partial, incomplete, and general nature of Lewis's other modes of revelation. However, these categories exclude Scripture and Lewis's respect for the way the natural world reveals God's beauty. Therefore we need three categories, not two:

- The particular and perfect: Christ incarnate

- The general and particular: Scripture, and also church tradition

- The general and incomplete: Israel, pagan premonitions, ethics, the numinous, *Sehnsucht*, and the natural world, etc.

In addition, we must acknowledge a degree of hierarchy: there is an implied hierarchy—the general-incomplete is superseded by the particular and perfect. That is, to a degree. Lewis was wise enough not to deny the ongoing validity of the revelation to and election of the Jews. So if we are to integrate Scripture and church tradition into these modes, and look at them hierarchically we must elevate the incarnation as the final fullest revelation. Scripture, as we have established, is ambiguous because on the one hand it is a human product, but it is divinely inspired, it lays witness to revelation but is not the Word of God (Christ), yet it becomes a word of God when read by a baptized imagination: Christ is in and with the reader. Therefore, we must acknowledge three levels of revelation in Lewis's theology and apologetics. Primarily there is the full self-revelation of God in Christ incarnate, remembering that the second (Scripture and

2. Scripture, Revelation, and Reason II: Mediation and the Bible

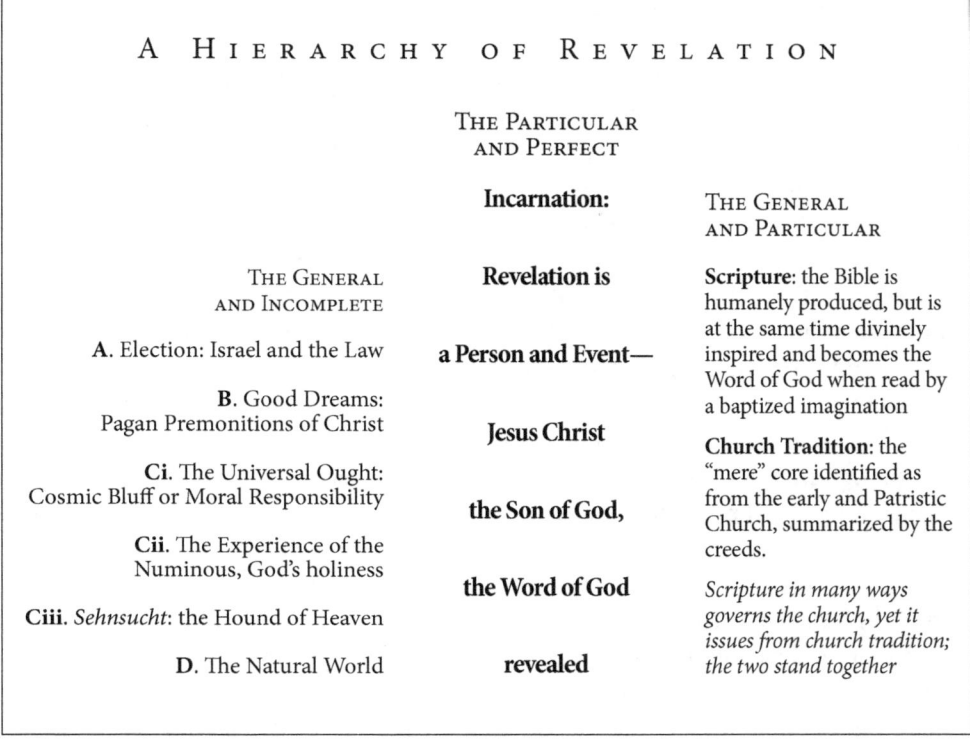

Figure 4: C. S. Lewis and Revelation: A Hierarchy of Modes of Revelation

church tradition) and third (general and incomplete intimations) issue from and bear witness to Christ, whether explicitly or implicitly.

Why elevate Scripture above the general modes of revelation, but hierarchically below the incarnation? Because, as Lewis asserted when writing to Mrs. Johnson in 1952, we must regard Christ himself as the Word of God and not elevate Scripture up into Christ's place.[66] Therefore, though generated by people, it is sourced through divine inspiration, and so the Bible for Lewis becomes for us Christ, the Word of God, through the grace of the Holy Spirit. Lewis's "mere" core, church tradition in many ways, also imparts understanding of God and God's purposes for humanity, authored and authorized as it is by the Holy Spirit. However, unlike Barth who, as we saw earlier, elevated the church as proclamation to be the Word of God, Lewis does not explicitly raise the church to be the w/Word of God. Writing to Clyde S. Kilby in 1959, Lewis commenting on whether or not a passage of Scripture was historical or not, asserted that, "it would still act on me as the word of God if it weren't, so far as I can see. All holy Scripture is written for our learning."[67] (Hence the relative position of the general

---

66. Lewis to Mrs Johnson, Nov. 8, 1952. *Collected Letters, Vol. III*, 246.
67. Lewis to Clyde S. Kilby, May 7, 1959. *Collected Letters, Vol. III*, 1044–45.

and particular—Scripture—just below the particular and perfect—Christ—in figure 4 above.)

Within the five modes of general and incomplete revelation, we must add a sixth—the natural world which, for Lewis, imparts knowledge that there is a God; more than that, often the sense of the numinous and *Sehnsucht* is related to, triggered by, the beauty inherent in creation that sings of the glory of God. Of these six modes of general and incomplete revelation, we must surely rank them in relation to the incarnation (as in figure 4, above, the left column). Therefore, we must rank (A) the election of Israel and the revelation to the Jews as superior to the other general modes—simply because they were the preparation for the incarnation and Jesus the Jew was from the chosen people of God. We may rank the (B) pagan premonitions of Christ's incarnation, cross, and resurrection next because though not concrete and particular, these intimations communicate to a degree what is at the heart of revelation even though most of these visions-myths were misinterpreted. The next three are in the form of general religious modes imparting little in the way of explicit knowledge directly related to the incarnation, but the ability to move the creature towards God: (Ci), the sense of a universal moral impulse; (Cii), the experience of the numinous, and (Ciii) *Sehnsucht*. These are then finally followed by (D) the natural world because the sense of the numinous and *Sehnsucht* is prior to the perception of God as creator; indeed without the numinous and *Sehnsucht* it is perfectly feasible to conclude that creation is an accident, that there is no God: the natural world can impart atheism as much as theism. These general and incomplete modes may convince people that there is a God, that there are demands on them, and these modes are important in moving people towards the love of Christ, but equally they may not. They are relatively minor modes of revelation compared to the others.

ii. Revelation as Supra-Theological Categories

How do all these modes of revelation come together for Lewis? In *Mere Christianity*, he comments about humanity's apparent perception of such intimations as were available through the numinous or *Sehnsucht*, but also of the failure of humanity to really turn to God.

> And what did God do? First of all he left us conscience, the sense of right and wrong: and all through history there have been people trying (some of them very hard) to obey it. None of them ever quite succeeded. Secondly, he sent the human race what I call good dreams: I mean those queer stories scattered all through the heathen religions about a god who dies and comes to life again and, by his death, has somehow given new life to men. Thirdly, he selected one particular people and spent several centuries hammering into their heads the sort of God he was—that there was only one of him and that he cared about right conduct. Those people were the Jews, and the Old Testament gives an account of the hammering process. Then comes the real shock. Among these Jews there

suddenly turns up a man who goes about talking as if he was God. He claims to forgive sins. He says he has always existed. He says he is coming to judge the world at the end of time.[68]

According to traditional theological categorization some of the modes listed above would not be regarded as revelation. Not so, says Lewis; some may be stronger, more temporal and actual, than others but they are still revelation from God (the sense of the numinous is less concrete than the incarnation but has its place in God's plan of salvation, and through the numinous God reveals intimations of God's self, engendering fear, awe, in the presence of holiness). Lewis's understanding of revelation is not confined to conventional "modern" theological categories—his understanding is in effect supra-theological. Most professional theologians will argue that Lewis did not have a systematic doctrine of revelation. It can be argued that no theologian has ever managed to produce a fully worked out and tightly contained doctrine of revelation—for if they did, it would exclude God's freedom to act in the world and towards humanity as God saw fit. For Lewis these modes of revelation are not comprehensive or exclusive. In effect, the general and incomplete modes are all related to and manifestations of the particular and perfect because they all emanate from God in Christ: they are intimations from the second person of the Trinity, the universal Christ, who is incarnated in the man Jesus of Nazareth—the, to our perceptions, nebulous becomes the concrete and particular. Therefore, all revelation perceivable by humanity comes from Christ who is God, the second person of the Trinity. If we exclude the numinous, *Sehnsucht*, pagan dreams/myths, we exclude the work of God in Christ speaking in a hidden mode, through the veil, to humanity.

---

68. C. S. Lewis, *Mere Christianity* (1952), Bk 2, ch. 3, 50–51.

3

Scripture, Revelation, and Reason III: Idealism and Transposition

SYNOPSIS:

This assessment of C. S. Lewis on mediation and the Bible leads us now to draw on the nature of revelation, the manner in which revelation is imparted, but also, how we perceive of what is revealed. We need to consider something of Lewis's background as a philosopher, and how his thought is formed through his reading of the seventeenth-century Cambridge Platonists, and the eighteenth-century Irish philosopher George Berkeley, Bishop of Cloyne, which drew him yet again back to Plato. Lewis proposed what he called "a doctrine of transposition," which was heavily reliant upon Platonic concepts, but also on the patristic theologian and philosopher Augustine. Just how far will reason take us in our understanding of God and eternity, rooted as we are in the shadowlands? Reason must acknowledge transposition. This is how Lewis saw revelation mediated to humanity by Christ: transposed, changed, altered, it was a diminution without one-to-one correspondence (this relates closely to his understanding of the humanity of Scripture). Is the incarnation subject to transposition? Lewis referred to his doctrine of transposition as his contribution to the philosophy of the incarnation. Lewis's doctrine of transposition is designed to explain how revelation works, how revelation is communicated, or, more pertinently, how revelation can never be fully imparted; this we conclude relates to the *communicatio idiomatum* (the communication of attributes), the knowability of God (which is both a veiling and an unveiling), and how human fallibility can lead us to misread what is communicated to us. Therefore we may conclude that the key to Lewis's work is in a doctrine of "flawed" transposition (a doctrine whereby revelation is itself transposed; likewise our codified understanding that we may label doctrinal is also incomplete and flawed). How does Lewis's "flawed" doctrine of transposed revelation come together? The value he accords to reason, indeed the symbiotic relation between revelation and reason he subscribes to, his understanding of the witness that Scripture gives to and as revelation, likewise the importance he gives to church tradition (the role of and for the "mere" core), also his philosophy of the incarnation, this is all epitomised by the transposed *movement* of God towards humanity, descending into the incarnation to draw humanity out of sin and up into the divine life. Therefore the modes of revelation in Lewis's doctrine of transposition move teleologically, lead ever towards eternity; this movement is dialectical, but a supplementary dialectic, in the sense that creation will be subsumed into eternity.

C. S. LEWIS—THE WORK OF CHRIST REVEALED

1. INTRODUCTION

If we assert that the entire Bible is true, we must ask the question, in what sense is it all true—or not? Lewis clearly saw that the Bible contained books and writings of different types; how they all cohered was a difficult question. Lewis asserted that we must spend time feeding on the truth the Bible gives as well as defining and defending it because ultimate truth is part of ultimate reality.[1] If we are to know something of God, to truly know, it will not be because of our capacity to speculate but because God chooses to reveal God's self to us. Truth always comes to us from God—whatever the mode.[2] If we blithely accept everything in the Bible to be the same sort of text and the same sort of truth we will soon—through reason—come to realize that some parts don't make sense, and that there appear to be contradictions. Therefore, for Lewis, a belief in the validity and the objectivity of reason and of truth was central to his understanding of Scripture.

2. TRANSPOSITION

i. Platonic Idealism

This assessment of Lewis on mediation and inerrancy, inspiration and the Bible—Lewis's doctrine of Scripture—leads us now to draw on some of the philosophical background to Lewis. We need to consider something of Lewis's background as a philosopher. Lewis's understanding is informed by his philosophical idealism, specifically the Cambridge Platonism of the seventeenth century and the philosophical idealism of Bishop George Berkeley. Lewis may have been something of a loner but his philosophical development was that of Oxford immediately after the First World War: a brutal logical positivism, a self-asserted atheism, that overlaid the English Idealism of T. H. Green, and English Hegelianism, which had dominated Oxford before the war. It was in many ways through reading the seventeenth-century English philosopher Henry More that began to draw Lewis out of this logical positivism into an older philosophical ground, and assisted Lewis in his own intellectual development. Lewis moved away from "modern" philosophy, returning to Plato, and after his conversion, to the Patristic theologians (essentially Augustine) and the neo-Platonists, and then medieval Scholasticism. Through his post-graduate studies Lewis fell under the influence of the thought of the Irish philosopher George Berkeley, Bishop of Cloyne, which drew him yet again back to Plato. Therefore, the *truly real* lay beyond what we take for reality in the shadowlands, as Tolkien and Lewis referred to our world, the world that we take for reality. By drawing on Berkeley's theory of subjective idealism or immaterialism Lewis began to formulate his understanding of the relationship between eternity and our world; therefore the truly real will translate into our reality as a result of God's love in freedom for humanity, to redeem them, through the movement of the incarnation, the descending to reascend. There is much more to

---

1. Lewis, *Reflections on the Psalms*, 7.
2. Ibid., 86.

3. Scripture, Revelation, and Reason III: Idealism and Transposition

Lewis's philosophical background and formation, which will be analyzed in depth in relation to the Anscombe-Lewis debate, and his philosophical technique (*reductio ad absurdum*, and, the law of the excluded middle); this will all be dealt with in the third book in this series.[3]

How does Lewis's Platonic idealism relate to his understanding of revelation and reason generally, his doctrine of Scripture specifically? Lewis proposed what he called a "doctrine of transposition," which was heavily reliant upon Plato, but was also derived from his reading of the patristic theologian and philosopher Augustine—specifically a doctrine of illumination whereby the faculties of reason and imagination give rise to an understanding through illumination by the divine light. Like Augustine, Lewis knew that we cannot perceive and understand truth from our senses alone. Therefore, just how far will unaided reason take us in our understanding of God and eternity, rooted as we are in the shadowlands? Reason must acknowledge transposition. This is how Lewis saw revelation mediated to humanity by Christ: transposed, changed, altered, a diminution without exact one-to-one correspondence.

Lewis shares an understanding that the Christian faith is essentially supernatural or preternatural with many, but not all, "modern" theologians and philosophers; where he departs from them is in the relation between these two realities. For Lewis we are not closed-off from eternity. Lewis's Christology is clearly framed in such terms: Christ is not Christ because of a value we accord him, he is not the product of human-conferred status, Christ is human but equally more than human: ontologically he is of the Trinity and therefore God incarnate—God descending, entering into our reality in human form to raise us up. Therefore revelation proceeds from eternity and into our reality; this is primarily in the form of the incarnation, but secondarily in the modes of general and incomplete revelation, through the Holy Spirit. Reality, for Lewis, all that we take for the world we inhabit, was simply a veil through which we might glimpse the source of this greater reality: eternity, heaven. But this is on God's terms and proceeds from eternity, drawing our gaze back to eternity. Eternity initiates, the grace of God initiates, always: the fall means we can initiate none of this for ourselves; we cannot pull ourselves up by our boot laces. And that greater reality will affect us, press on us, and influence us; grace draws us up. This other reality is at the heart of Lewis's Platonic idealism. But how does he see the two realities relating?

ii. Revelation Transposed

Lewis is, in many ways, at his most philosophically theological in invoking the concept of transposition to explain how revelation operates, how God mediates truth and God's salvific intentions to us through these various modes—from the general and incomplete to the particular and perfect. A doctrine of transposition is initially set out in a sermon given before an invited congregation of academics at Mansfield College, Oxford, in 1944, which was then published after the war; the sermon was then

---

3. Entitled, *The Christ of a Religious Economy*. See, for details: www.cslewisandthechrist.net

reworked and extended into an academic paper thirteen years later.[4] Transposition is inevitably framed in Platonic terms. Lewis, like the idealists and Platonists, could see that we can only understand the world around us because of its relation to a higher spiritual reality. The key words here are higher, superior, and richer; but this is not to denigrate the inherent biblically asserted goodness of creation. Intimations from the higher realm—eternity—will inevitably be diluted and watered-down, translated, transposed, hence Lewis's term. The Holy Spirit will act on us: revelation will give us intimations; reason will help us understand, the imagination then will conjure up images which help explain and draw us up to where we should be—eternity. The Bible, particularly the New Testament and specifically the parables of Jesus, are therefore couched in analogical and symbolic—transpositional—language. There is no one-to-one correlation because this is simply not possible, in the same way that lines drawn on paper are a diminution because they cannot be the real thing: they represent for us a three-dimensional reality in two-dimensions. Lewis cites many examples in his essay entitled "Transposition" to try to explain this. He gives us the idea of a drawing, also the complexity of a composition for full orchestra in the form of musical notation (especially a piece for full orchestra rescored on paper for a piano alone). In *The Last Battle*, book 7 of *The Chronicles of Narnia*, he waxed Platonic. After the apocalyptically-charged end of the world in Narnia, Digory, having died and been raised in eternity, comments that, "'Of course it is different; as different as a real thing is from a shadow or as waking life is from a dream.' His voice stirred everyone like a trumpet as he spoke these words: but when he added under his breath 'It's all in Plato, all in Plato: bless me, what do they teach them at these schools!', the older ones laughed."[5] In the same book Lewis explains further by using an image, a picture—

> You may have been in a room in which there was a window that looked out on a lovely bay of the sea or a green valley that wound away among mountains. And in the wall of that room opposite to the window there may have been a mirror. And as you turned away from the window you suddenly caught sight of that sea or that valley, all over again, in the looking glass. And the sea in the mirror, or the valley in the mirror, were in one sense just the same as the real ones: yet at the same time they were somehow different—deeper, more wonderful, more like places in a story: in a story you have never heard but very much want to know.[6]

These two realities are intimately connected and inform each other, but our reality, the world, will be drawn up into the spiritual, eternal, realm, and will be subsumed. Lewis establishes two principles for the relationship between the higher realm and the lower realm: first, that the lower can only be understood in terms of the higher (a proposition derived essentially from Berkeley); second, that the word symbolism

---

4. Lewis, "Transposition," a sermon given in Mansfield College, Oxford on Whit Sunday, May 28, 1944, published (1st ed.) 1949. A reworked and extended 2nd edition of the sermon as an academic paper was published in 1962: Lewis, "Transposition," 2nd ed. All subsequent references are to this second edition.
5. Lewis, *The Chronicles of Narnia: The Last Battle*, 159–60.
6. Ibid., 160.

3. Scripture, Revelation, and Reason III: Idealism and Transposition

is inadequate to explain the relationship between the higher and lower realms, the transposition of the higher into the lower.

The problem that Lewis identifies is that all the time we are using images and concepts from this world to try to explain the world to come, the truly real world. In the case of the drawing analogy, Lewis comments that all drawn images of another world and its unimaginable shapes are three-dimensional and solid, but are offered as two-dimensional shapes recognizable as belonging to this world. Therefore, skeptics could deny the existence of a three-dimensional world in much the same way that flat-earthers refused to believe the world was fairly spherical: "your vaunted other world, so far from being the archetype, is a dream which borrows all its elements from this one," writes Lewis.[7] This is the problem with transposition when applied to revelation. In *The Silver Chair*, book 6 in *The Chronicles of Narnia*, he presents such skepticism in symbolic narrative. Jill and Eustace are trapped deep underground among people who have always lived deep underground, people who have never seen the sun or the sky. A witch has ensnared them along with Prince Rilian whom they have come to save. The witch beguiles them with sweet music and perfume and charms in an attempt to convince them that the world above, with the sky and the sun, does not exist. Prince Rilian fighting off the soporific effects of the magic tries to explain that the sun is real, he likens it to a lamp, only greater, much greater, that it hangs in the sky. The witch answers:

> "Hangeth from what, my lord?" asked the Witch; and then, while they were all still thinking how to answer her, she added, with another of her soft, silver laughs: "You see? When you try to think out clearly what this sun must be, you cannot tell me. You can only tell me it is like the lamp. Your sun is a dream; and there is nothing in that dream that was not copied from the lamp. The lamp is the real thing; the sun is but a tale, a children's story."[8]

When Jill and Eustace try to explain who Aslan is her argument and logic is the same—they say he is like a cat because he is just a large cat in their imaginations

> The Witch shook her head. "I see," she said, "that we should do no better with your lion, as you call it, than we did with your sun. You have seen lamps, and so you imagined a bigger and better lamp and called it the sun. You've seen cats, and now you want a bigger and better cat, and it's to be called a lion. Well, 'tis a pretty make believe, though, to say truth, it would suit you all better if you were younger. And look how you can put nothing into your make-believe without copying it from the real world, this world of mine, which is the only world."[9]

They are almost beguiled by the witch's arguments because she is inverting all that they know to conform to her own personal kingdom, which is her own personal hell. This is reminiscent of the arguments of skeptical atheists who turn around the images that have been transposed by the will of God from eternity, transposed into our minds, the

---

7. Lewis, "Transposition." 2nd ed., 172.
8. Lewis, *The Chronicles of Narnia: The Silver Chair*, 142–43.
9. Ibid.

skeptics then claim they are imaginings from below (i.e., of human generation) not from above (from God).

There will inevitably be a diminution. This is why Lewis invokes the term "transposition." Can we see an example of this independent of Lewis? In the Acts of the Apostles Peter has a vision of something like a large sheet being lowered by its four corners; in it were all kinds of creatures, reptiles and birds. Peter is commanded to get up, kill, and eat. This happens three times. Only when Peter receives a visit from three men whom the Spirit commands him to go with does the vision make sense. Peter had been on the roof, hungry, dozing off. His vision is in the imagery of this world, affected by his hunger. The vision was really a reassurance and a command to go with the men and convert the gentile Centurion who had sent the men. Therefore, Peter exclaims, "I truly understand that God shows no partiality, but in every nation anyone who fears him and does what is right is acceptable to him. You know the message he sent to the people of Israel, preaching peace by Jesus Christ—he is Lord of all" (Acts 10:34b–36). Therefore, the nature of the image Peter has in his vision is a transposition, a diminution, effected by his tiredness and, yes, his hunger, only in the context of the visit of the Centurion's men shortly after the vision does it make sense: preach the gospel to the Gentiles, baptize them, not only the Jews.

Such transposed visions have happened throughout history and continue to happen today, but they may not always be part of a divine commissioning as Peter's clearly was; they may simply be part of the dynamics of the relationship between the two realities—heaven and earth—the persistent and consistent consubstantial illumination, as Augustine would have phrased it. It is very easy for contemporary skeptics to dismiss prophetic dreams transposed from eternity and recorded in Scripture simply because they are from long ago and are recorded in a religious context (the Bible). My wife, Hilary, has severe epilepsy. For a period of nearly a week she kept having the same dream at night, the memory of which occupied her during the day: a powerful dream-vision of two jet airliners flying nose vertically in the air next to each other, their engines were on full-power but this meant both planes stayed still, the thrust merely countering gravity. People on board the two planes were contacting loved ones by mobile phone to say farewell because they knew they would die—when the fuel ran out each plane in turn crashed slowly to the ground consumed in dust and fire. This dream was during the first week of September 2001, the week before 9/11. The image she had of what was to happen was transposed, altered; there were not two planes stood vertically in the air, in reality there were two vertical skyscrapers which two planes deliberately crashed in to, yet the transposed image was more real, more than what actually happened to the twin towers on 9/11. The vision encapsulated the action that took place and the suffering experienced all rolled up into a single image. 9/11 had enormous significance eschatologically—that is, in relationship to the judgment of God echoing back from the end of time. In the absence of a commissioning, this vision was not like Peter's dream—in Hilary's case we did not receive a knock at the front door in the days prior to 9/11 from American agents to enquire if we had any intimation of trouble to come! Like Peter's dream-vision any commissioning will be clear and concrete—the men who came to his door. There are people who have no intimation of any connection between the two realities. This is essentially because an epileptic brain is by definition more open to intimation, to influence (angelic or demonic—though we are all open to such influence, it is a question of degree, and of recognition), to acceptance of visions than is the brain of Lewis's "modern" skeptical man.

3. INCARNATIONAL TRANSPOSITION

Transposition does not only occur as revelation between eternity and the human mind; Lewis is not a Gnostic dualist in this sense, he does not believe that the world of matter is corrupt and evil and to be repudiated. No, transposition occurs between spirit and nature, and, importantly for our salvation, between God and humanity. Here the mediation of Christ is essential: "I am not going to maintain that what I call Transposition is the only possible mode whereby a poorer medium can respond to a richer: but I claim that it is very hard to imagine any other. It is therefore, at the very least, not improbable that Transposition occurs whenever the higher reproduces itself in the lower."[10] Therefore, the lower, because of its diminution, can only with meaning exist in relation to the higher. But what is this meaning? It is sacramental. Lewis explains how the sun and the sunlight in a picture only make sense as signs because the real sun shines on them and in the context of the real sun the picture makes sense: "It is a sign, but also something more than a sign: and only a sign because it is also more than a sign, because in it the thing signified is really in a certain mode present. If I had to name the relation I should call it not symbolical but sacramental . . . we are even further beyond mere symbolism."[11] The spiritual can be known within the natural world as sacrament. Symbolism and allegory may help but they are subject to the problem cited above—symbols and allegory borrow all their elements from this world. By contrast a sacrament is a religious ceremony or ritual imparting divine grace, such as baptism or the Eucharist, but a sacrament is also a thing of mysterious or sacred significance. It is a religious symbol; the symbol or sign is sacramental because it is the real participation between the two realms, the higher and lower, but emanating from the higher to draw up the lower. As such these signs are sacramental because they are in reality the coinherence, the participation, of the natural and supra-natural realms: this participation makes of them something that is more than signs or symbols. The revelation is changed, transposed, within the sacrament: there is something in the here and now which was not before. If grace is the action of God imparting a mysterious communion with God though Christ, then the signs/images intimated through this general revelation are the mode whereby grace draws us up. Baptism and the Eucharist are an outward sign from Christ conveying an inward grace. For Lewis these revelatory signs are as much sacramental as baptism and the Eucharist, though he probably would have placed them hierarchically below the sacraments of the church. The Eucharist is

10. Lewis, "Transposition." 2nd ed., 172–73.
11. Ibid., 173.

experiential: it is the highest form of this spiritual drawing-up, the transformation of the material into the eternal. For Lewis the material world is too insubstantial; the material world is therefore a diminution of the spiritual world but is not to be regarded as debased: eternity is not thin and ethereal, wisp-like—eternity, heaven, is supra-real, as in the book of Revelation. The reality we occupy may appear to us as real—often because of the effect of pain—but heaven, eternity, is infinitely more real. Lewis extrapolates this well in *The Great Divorce*, in his treatment of heaven and hell, and purgatory as a fringe area between the two. Hell exists, but it is so close to nothingness that it barely exists in what we take for time and space, and the redeemed cannot enter hell because they are too substantial, the condemned may draw close to the fringes of heaven, but this is too painful for their nihilistic insubstantial pseudo-corporeality, teetering as they are on the abyss of nothingness.[12] Therefore, the spiritual resurrected people who populate heaven are more "real," more "physical/corporeal," than the near-to-nothingness, the vague, ethereal-ghostlike apparitions of those condemned to hell. This reflects a paradox—the nature of reality in hell-(purgatory)-heaven, in *The Great Divorce*, reflects a paradox in terms of space and time. Therefore, only heaven is truly real and our reality can only exist in relation to heaven-eternity; and, logically, humanity (flawed and fallen, teetering close to nothingness through original sin) can only truly exist in relation to Christ because of the incarnation. Through Christ's incarnation, this reality is drawn up into eternity, or begins to be drawn up following Christ's resurrection. This is what is at the heart of the incarnation: the spiritual in the form of Christ, the Logos, descends to rise up again, to draw up humanity into eternity, a humanity rendered insubstantial through sin. Transposition is, therefore, at its most profound, at its most complete and highest in the incarnation. Andrew Walker comments, "Transposition of nature into higher reality works not by bringing the higher down to earth, as it were, but by allowing spiritual life to draw nature into itself."[13] Walker goes on to note how Lewis invokes the Athanasian Creed: "Perfect God and perfect man, of a reasonable soul and human flesh subsisting. Equal to the Father as touching his Godhead, and inferior to the Father as touching his manhood. Who, although he is God and man, yet he is not two, but one Christ. One, *not by conversion of the Godhead into flesh, but by taking of that manhood into God*" (The Creed of Athanasius, lines 30–35. My emphasis). Athanasius of Alexandria (293–373 AD) in his treatise on the incarnation, echoing Ignatius of Antioch (c.35–107) and Irenaeus of Lyons (c.110–c.190), states this explicitly that God became man so we might become God: "He, indeed, assumed humanity that we might become God. He manifested himself by means of a body in order that we might perceive the Mind of the unseen Father. He endured shame from men that we might inherit immortality. He himself was unhurt by this, for he is impassable and incorruptible; but by his

---

12. Lewis, *The Great Divorce*. For the nature and relationship between heaven-(purgatory)-hell, and the substantiality-insubstantiality of humanity post mortem, see, ch. 13, specifically 103–4; in addition, Lewis explicitly invokes Paul on the nature of spiritual bodies and the general resurrection in ch. 11, 87.

13. Walker, "Scripture, Revelation and Platonism in C. S. Lewis," 29.

3. Scripture, Revelation, and Reason III: Idealism and Transposition

own impassability he kept and healed the suffering men on whose account he thus endured."[14] Lewis also notes this:

> I venture to suggest, though with great doubt and in the most provisional way, that the concept of Transposition may have some contribution to make to the theology—or at least to the philosophy—of the incarnation. For we are told in one of the creeds that the incarnation worked not by conversion of the Godhead into flesh, but by taking of the Manhood into God. And it seems to me that there is a real analogy between this and what I have called Transposition: that humanity, still remaining itself, is not merely counted as, but veritably drawn into, Deity.[15]

For Irenaeus God is incorruptible and immortal; the incarnation is essential for atonement, the uniting of God with humanity whereby we are drawn into God through God's graceful action in Christ. The patristic theologian Augustine states this explicitly, in particular the kenotic humiliation involved in this drawing up of humanity through the Son of Man: "For what greater grace could have dawned upon us from God, than that he, who had only one Son, made him the son of man, and so in turn made the son of man a son of God. Ask yourself whether this involved any merit, any motivation, any right on your part; and see whether you find anything but grace!"[16]

The incarnation is therefore the most concrete and complete of God's self-revelation. In relation to Lewis's doctrine of transposition we may ask, is the incarnation a transpositional diminution? Well, cautiously, the answer must be yes, for three reasons: the *communicatio idiomatum*; a veiling-unveiling; and human epistemic limitation.

i. communicatio idiomatum

First, the *communicatio idiomatum* (the communication of attributes or idioms). Within an attempt to account for the relationship between the divine and human natures in the one person of Christ, how do the properties of the Word of God and the human nature coexist? Through revelation we are given to know that God is love, further that God is trinitarian, transcendent, eternal, uncreated, that, according to Greek concepts, God is omnipotent, omniscient, or omnipresent. Furthermore, when we see Jesus Christ we see God; but is not God more than Jesus Christ because God is triune? What is revealed is therefore *mediated through* Jesus Christ—but not everything of God is communicated in Jesus Christ. In the incarnation we have a transposition into human flesh of the second person of the Trinity: God divested of God's self some of his attributes. Jesus of Nazareth was not all-powerful, all-knowing, or simultaneously everywhere, because he was human. This was a diminution but was voluntarily enacted by God out of love for humanity, but not out of any need or weakness in God.

---

14. Athanasius, *The Incarnation of the Word*, ch. 8, §. 54, 93.
15. Lewis, "Transposition." 2nd ed., 178.
16. Sermon CLXXXV, Christmas #2. Augustine of Hippo, "Sermon No. 185 (Homily 3)," 76–79. See, also, Henry William Griffen, *Augustine of Hippo Sermons to the People: Advent, Christmas, New year, Epiphany*, 61–65.

Jesus was the humble servant, lowly, submitting himself to his destiny: therefore the communication of attributes is characterized by restraint and self-denial by God (we see this in particular in the figure of the Aslan-Christ). In terms of the *communicatio idiomatum* there is a self-emptying, a restraint of the divine attributes for the sake of incarnation. This leads us to a kenotic Christology (Phil 2:5–8), characterized by self-restraint by God in taking on human flesh; God is not reduced, God takes this on voluntarily.

ii. Veiling-Unveiling: The Knowability of God

Second, all revealings are in some form a veiling. Many writers, including Andrew Walker, note this in Lewis's work; and it is, of course, a common proposition to be found in Karl Barth's theology. Colin Gunton summarizes this well from Barth's understanding:

> The point here is that in Jesus Christ we see the limits, the possibilities of the knowability of God. God the Father represents the limits of this. The Holy Spirit imparts this to human beings: veiling-unveiling, knowability-unknowability, revelation-hiddenness. God is revealed but at the same time he is a hidden God. Even as he reveals himself he is hidden . . . God is revealed but at the same time it is the hidden God that is revealed, no not even that, even as he reveals himself he is hidden. After all, when you see Jesus Christ it is a hidden God, it is not obviously God is it, it's just a man wandering around teaching. God is hidden and unless the Spirit reveals him then he remains hidden. God is revealed but also remains in himself unknowable. In the end you have only got paradox. For example, Irenaeus says that the impassable becomes passable, the eternal becomes temporal.[17]

This is so even within relations between people: however long we live with and know someone there will always be something of them we don't know, and how that person chooses to reveal themselves to us is personal and subjective, and our perception of them may vary. There will always be something unknown; we can never fully "know" another person. We can never fully know Christ.

iii. Human Fallibility: the Misreading of the Transposition

Third, all "Ideas" transposed from eternity will inevitably be framed in concepts, imaginings, and reasonings from our experience. How is it possible to explain frost, ice, and snow to children living in equatorial Africa? It is not really possible without transposing the idea into language and concepts the children will be familiar with, which may not help. In science fiction films and TV shows (which Lewis would surely have enjoyed) aliens, which are supposed to be beyond our imagining and different from anything we perceive of reality in our world, are always presented in terms of reference from what we perceive of reality *in* our world: therefore they are not truly *alien* for they are only imaginings from our perceptions. But are they not intimations

---

17. Gunton, *The Barth Lectures*, 80.

of the possibility of the truly alien, of the wonders of creation? They should be. Or is there more to science fiction? Is there an element of revelatory disclosure from God in science fiction stories, unknown to the authors, most of whom are not Christian?

Applied to revelation this merely confirms human epistemic limitation. For example, in the essay "Transposition" Lewis uses a picture, a story to explain our flawed perception of transposition. He imagines a woman incarcerated in a dungeon that gives birth to a son; she raises this child as best she can, but the son can never see the outside world. The mother draws pictures—pencil lines on paper—good pictures, artistic representations, to try to explain the real outside world to her son. However there comes a point where the transposition of the real countryside, sky, sun, and world, fails because of the limits in the son's perception and the concepts he uses in his mind. The son appears to be getting on well with his education until he says something that causes his mother to realize she has failed:

> Finally it dawns on her that he has, all these years, lived under a misconception. "But," she gasps, "you didn't think that the real world was full of lines drawn in lead pencil?" "What?" says the boy, "No pencil-marks there?" And instantly his whole notion of the outer world becomes a blank. For the lines, by which alone he was imagining it, have now been denied of it. He has no idea of that which will exclude and dispense with the lines, that of which the lines were merely a transposition—the waving tree-tops, the light dancing on the weir, the coloured three-dimensional realities which are not enclosed in lines but define their own shapes at every moment with a delicacy and multiplicity which no drawing could ever achieve.[18]

In Lewis's picture/story the child is convinced that the outside world is therefore less than the visible world of the prison cell in which they are incarcerated. The real world is without "lines" because it is more visible, more real, but the child, like all of us humans, falls for the realism of the pictures, the drawn lines, and takes it for all there is (which in psychological terms is idolatrous, which is why the second commandment warns us against trying to root our ideas about God utterly in this world). This ability in humanity to constantly hang on to what we can feel and see and hear, and touch, and know, is a form of control that issues from the fall. Are we not blind to what God truly wants for us, blinded by our desire for immediate satisfaction?

The passable and finite, the temporality of the incarnation with all the suffering involved, is in a sense a diminution, yes, voluntarily taken on by God, but it is nonetheless a transposition. But herein lies our salvation—primarily on the cross, but then in the work of the Holy Spirit drawing us upwards and onwards through intimations transposed. At his most profound and Platonic, Lewis commented in a sermon given in St. Mary the Virgin Church in Oxford in 1941, "We discern the freshness and purity of morning, but they do not make us fresh and pure. We cannot mingle with the splendours we see. But all the leaves of the New Testament are rustling with the rumour that it will not always be so. Someday, God willing, we

---

18. Lewis, "Transposition." 2nd ed., 180.

shall get in."[19] The New Testament specifically, the Bible generally, becomes revelation when we read it, though a baptized imagination is paramount here; thereby the New Testament becomes *sacramental* in revelatory terms when we read it. There are intimations, transpositions, from eternity in our perception of the freshness and purity of morning, we perceive but cannot fully be with the splendours we perceive, but the New Testament is crucial here and is therefore superior to the general revelation, the numinous, *Sehnsucht, et al*, for within its pages there is the rumor, as Lewis terms it, more pertinently the promise, that we shall get in, we will be fully drawn into eternity, resulting from Christ's sacrifice on the cross.

4. THE KEY TO LEWIS'S WORK: A "FLAWED" DOCTRINE OF TRANSPOSITION

What value is there to Lewis's doctrine of transposition? Transposition is the key to Lewis's theology and apologetics: it permeates all of his work—theological, philosophical, and apologetic, especially the symbolic narratives. To start with, Lewis knew his vocation was primarily to the Church of England—as he put it, a missionary to the priests of his own church,[20] reasserting a mere orthodox core, developed through the patristic era. Straight away this meant that there was a core of belief and faith that existed outside of human perception: doctrine, belief and faith were not humanely created—truth was revealed and given. This is to evoke a Platonic otherness: eternally created truth that we can perceive; truth that we can realize the veracity of with the human faculty of reason and can intimate meaning through the imagination. This, in many ways, relates to idealism: the ideas are truer than the reality of the shadowlands. Transposition allows us to glean intimations of eternity and loving purposes of God for us but we will invariably get it wrong: we will misconstrue what is being mediated to us; our human sinful desires and needs will get in the way. Peter's hunger affected the vision of the vocation to extend the gospel to Gentiles; the boy in Lewis's story wants to hold on to the idea of drawn lines rather than use his imagination to intimate what the real world is really like. It is always possible to regard these revelatory intimations as nothing more than something of this world because they are transposed in the language and concepts of this world. In *The Voyage of the Dawn Treader*, book 5 in *The Chronicles of Narnia*, Eustace is in conversation with a resting star, who in appearance has the verisimilitude of a human being, he foolishly gets into conversation about what a star is in our reality: "'In our world,' said Eustace, 'a star is a huge ball of flaming gas.' 'Even in your world, my son, that is not what a star is but only what it is made of.'"[21] What lies behind all reality is, therefore, more than we perceive of reality. What we perceive is a transposition. Reductionalist, nominalistic, scientific concepts will only tell us what things are made of, not what they *are*. What is important is what Jesus Christ is, not only what we take him to be.

---

19. Lewis, "The Weight of Glory," 31.
20. Lewis, "Modern Theology and Biblical Criticism," 166.
21. Lewis, *The Chronicles of Narnia: The Voyage of the Dawn Treader*, 159.

3. Scripture, Revelation, and Reason III: Idealism and Transposition

A doctrine of transposition, transposed eternal truth, will inevitably be an inadequate doctrine of how revelation is mediated/communicated to humanity. If we truly understand what Lewis is asserting then the doctrine itself will be inadequate because the idea of the doctrine comes from eternity and is transposed for our understanding, but will inevitably be incomplete, a diminution, a translation. It is incomplete in our perception, not in eternity. This is perhaps one of the reasons why Lewis did not go down the path of attempting a systematic theology: Barth tried it, wrote six million words across fourteen vast volumes of *Church Dogmatics*, and failed—it was incomplete upon his death and he had written himself into a corner which marginalized the work of the Holy Spirit. Many Barthians will acknowledge that he left no room for the work of the Holy Spirit in the later volumes. St Thomas Aquinas wrote a vast *Summa*, which was supposed to be all there was to theology, but near his death he uttered that it was all straw.[22] Lewis's understanding was profound, he knew that our knowledge and understanding would be incomplete this side of eternity. A doctrine of transposition asserts this to be so, even as the doctrine of transposition *in itself* was flawed and incomplete, inadequate, and partial: our heavenward gaze must in humility be characterized by a degree of apophatic agnosticism with regard to the human ability to know, but neither is it impossible for us to know, to accept something of God's revealedness.

A "flawed" doctrine of transposition may therefore be said to apply to Lewis's understanding of Scripture. This is why there are no hard-and-fast systematic propositional truths in every passage of Scripture. The Bible, for Lewis, was an untidy and leaky vehicle, transpositional diminution meant we do not have the absolute truth systematically presented from an unrefracted light that we could contain, quantify, in an encyclopedic fashion. In *Reflections on the Psalms* Lewis notes how there is nothing self-evident, our hold on revelation is precarious, as through the incarnation we are drawn up into God's eternity:

> Because the lower nature, in being taken up and loaded with a new burden and advanced to a new privilege remains, and is not annihilated, it will always be possible to ignore the up-grading and see nothing but the lower. Thus men can read the life of Our Lord (because it is a human life) as nothing but a human life. Many, perhaps most, modern philosophies read human life merely as an animal life of unusual complexity. The Cartesians read animal life as mechanism. Just in the same way Scripture can be read as merely human literature. No new discovery, no new method, will ever give a final victory to either interpretation.[23]

What Scripture gives us, albeit dimmed through transposition, is a certain insight, how to get the focus right. We can ignore that focus, that insight, we can concentrate only on the lower level: Peter could have interpreted his vision recorded in Acts as a

---

22. Shortly before his unexpected death church officials asked Thomas Aquinas why he had stopped writing. He is reputed to have commented to a Brother Reginald, "I cannot, for all that I have written seems like straw to me." This was following what is reported to have been a mystical experience, followed by what was probably a stroke. See: Davies, *The Thought of Thomas Aquinas*, 9.
23. Lewis, *Reflections on the Psalms*, 100.

license to hold a feast, a party, for the other disciples and apostles, with no dietary laws or limitations. But he did not, and was not meant to: it was with the visit of the men to Peter, a concrete event—or as concrete an event as is possible in our reality—that the meaning of the vision and the resulting vocation became clear. (The proximity in time and space of the calling in relation to the dream-vision is important—it would not necessarily have been significant if the visit occurred two years after the vision, two hundred miles away). It is in this context that our reading of the Bible will be taken up by the Holy Spirit to be more than it is on its own—hence Lewis's belief that Scripture becomes revelatory when we read it with a baptized imagination.[24] Therefore Lewis asserts that the Old Testament as literature is taken up to be the medium of something that is more than merely human; so can we set any limit on the multiplicity of meanings, the gravity of the text, which is laid upon it by God?

There are many contemporary Christians who criticize Lewis for his respect for and use of Platonism, and some of their criticisms are valid. But in a wholesale rejection what are they omitting? Lewis, in effect, through his Platonic doctrine of transposition defined (in the limited manner in which we flawed and mortal humans can know) how the Holy Spirit acts and operates between eternity and the reality we inhabit. At the opening of the Bible we are told how the Spirit hovered over the waters, the breath of God swept over the formless earth and the waters. The relationship between Platonism and the gospel (which in effect defined in limited terms the mechanism whereby the Holy Spirit relates to and acts in our world, our reality) is set out by Lewis, in a limited and intentionally incomplete and flawed manner, in his doctrine of transposition.

5. MODES OF REVELATION SUBSUMED INTO ETERNITY

To summarize: an intentionally "flawed" doctrine of transposition, itself platonically transposed, is formulated to explain how revelation works, how revelation is communicated, or, more pertinently, how revelation is never fully imparted. Therefore, as we have established, we can conclude that this relates to the *communicatio idiomatum*, the limits to the knowability of God, and human epistemic limitation. This transpositional key applies to how God is revealed, but it also extrapolates how Lewis's mind was illuminated and inspired to write, to construct his apologetic and his stories. It could be argued that there is an element of circularity to the argument here: that claiming the flaw at the heart of transposition simply covers a badly worked out philosophy; but there is also the "virtuous" circle of consistency, and the deeper criterion of completeness or adequacy to the data. We are the object, not the subject; God is the verb; God initiates; God is the source and origin; the author of all revelation, and thus sets the terms. Moses knew it was impossible to approach God face to face in this reality because of our fallen nature. The triune consubstantial light, though refracted through the shadows of this world, allows us to perceive this world along with

---

24. "It is Christ himself, not the Bible, who is the true word of God. The Bible, read in the right spirit and with the guidance of good teachers, will bring us to him." Lewis to Mrs Johnson, Nov. 8, 1952, *Collected Letters, Vol. III*, 246.

3. Scripture, Revelation, and Reason III: Idealism and Transposition

the supra-real, the intimations of eternity—intimations which by their very nature will be different from the natural world, the mundane; it is inevitable that revelation will be communicated in diminuted, translated, transposed modes. Reason is at the heart of this doctrine for Lewis, but he knows the limits: reason is not simply an abstract faculty presiding over an indeterminate field, analyzing at its will. We are not God; and our kingdom of reason is not God.

We may surmise that there is a greater degree of transposition in the general and incomplete modes of revelation than in the concrete and complete, but diminution and transposition there will be, and there will be a multiplicity of interpretations by humanity because of the freedom given to creation. There will therefore be a translation more than a dilution. Ironically the more concrete revelation is (i.e., the incarnation), the greater the risk of misinterpretation; but this is balanced by the perfection of the incarnate Christ as the fullest self-revelation. The balance that Lewis held to between the freedom of God to inspire yet allow creation to be, while intimating to humanity the truth of eternity as our final home, built on and from the mediation of Christ, is what lies at the heart of his doctrine of transposition, which in turn makes sense of his understanding of Scripture, revelation and reason: this balance between aseity and creation moves all the modes of revelation in Lewis's work teleologically (i.e., there is purpose and that purpose leads ever towards eternity)—there is an end-game to all of this and that is the movement towards the final and full revelation in the incarnation and eventually in the second coming. This is to be seen as dialectical, but a supplementary dialectic, in the sense that creation will be subsumed into eternity. In conclusion, what value is there to Lewis's doctrine of transposition? Does it cohere with his understanding of Scripture and revelation? Yes, but if it is deemed inadequate and flawed, it should be, because only in eternity will we know as we are known (1 Cor 13:12b).

We have seen how Lewis's understanding of Scripture was intrinsically tied in with God's revealedness, but how the Word of God was essentially the Christ-event, witnessed to then by Scripture as the word of God. Scripture, revelation, and reason came together, for Lewis, in a doctrine of transposition: revelation transposed hierarchically and explained in terms of Platonic Idealism.

Part Two

The Revelation of Christ—

God, or a Bad Man

> "But who do you say that I am?"
>
> > Jesus, to his disciples,
> > Matthew 16:15

4

aut Deus aut malus homo I: What did Lewis Say?

SYNOPSIS:
The proposition that Jesus was "Bad, Mad, or God" is central to C. S. Lewis's popular apologetics. It is fêted by American Evangelicals, cautiously endorsed by Roman Catholics and Protestants, but often scorned by philosophers of religion. Most, mistakenly, regard Lewis's trilemma as unique. The roots of this proposition are in a two thousand year old theological and philosophical tradition: *aut Deus aut malus homo* (either God, or a bad man), is a proposition relating to the nature of Jesus of Nazareth; that is, the question of the divinity of Christ. Either he was God incarnate, or he was an ordinary human. Considering the manner of his speech and actions we cannot ignore Jesus: therefore we are faced with a dilemma—if he was a mere human then we cannot consider him to be good but *malus*, bad or wicked, or deluded. These five chapters open with a discursive analysis of what Lewis wrote. This is followed by an examination of the theological tradition over the last two thousand years: this proposition is not unique to Lewis. We then need to examine the proposition in its contemporary context. Did Jesus actually make such claims for himself? If not the argument collapses. A review of the scriptural evidence is important, as is the biblical scholarship. Likewise we will examine contemporary philosophical objections to Lewis's proposition. This digression is necessary given the academic opposition to Lewis.

Initially, in this chapter, we can examine what Lewis actually said: *aut Deus aut malus homo* is a central proposition of Lewis's apologetics. It is a form of philosophical theology used by him on at least thirteen occasions (from 1939 to 1963) in several works, and brought to its fullest extrapolation in *Mere Christianity* (1952). Lewis's concern is evident in his correspondence, not long after his conversion, and also in his first work of apologetics: *The Problem of Pain* (1940). He states the proposition as a provocative apologetic argument in *The Broadcast Talks* in 1942, thereafter in several essays of philosophical theology sometimes using the popular trilemma form, at others the either-or assertion in *aut Deus aut malus homo*, drawing on the law of excluded middle. Lewis adapts the structure of the proposition for *The Lion, The Witch and the Wardrobe*, which confronts the confidence we daily exercise in our ability to "know," and near the end of his life reasserts the inherent logic of this question to humanity in an interview. At the heart of the proposition is the question that is addressed by God to all of humanity (what do we make of Jesus Christ?), though pertinently, Lewis also reverses the question: what does Jesus Christ make of us? In terms of the popular reception of Lewis's works this proposition is often presented as "Mad, Bad, or God" (MBG, or BMG): in this form it is often referred to as Lewis's trilemma. This proposition opens up an immense debate and analysis about Jesus' divinity: what did this man say and do that intimated divine self-disclosure?

C. S. LEWIS—THE WORK OF CHRIST REVEALED

1. INTRODUCTION

We now move into something that is at the very heart of Christianity. A proposition that is central to C. S. Lewis's work as an apologist, as a theologian and philosopher, but pertinently to him as a Christian. This is a proposition that is central to the creed, to the witness of the churches and to humanity's salvation: the divinity of Christ. The creed states that Jesus of Nazareth was both equally God and equally man—he was God incarnated. Following on from this he is the Christ, the anointed one, the Messiah, and is Son of God and Son of Man (terms that will be defined when we deal with the question of identity subsequent chapters). This brings in doctrinal questions about the Trinity, and about salvation. Lewis did not shy away from difficult issues. Since the Age of Reason and the Enlightenment the churches have been on the back heel, so to speak, on the defensive. It may be argued that the consensus of opinion—certainly in academia, and amongst "Modern" and "Liberal" churchmen and theologians—is that Jesus was not divine, that he was an ordinary man. Lewis tackles the skeptics head-on; but also the hermeneutic of suspicion, that we encountered earlier, which drove the dismissal of Scripture amongst such skeptics. In defending Christ's divinity Lewis used reason and logic—he sought to prove the case for Jesus of Nazareth as God incarnate. However, Lewis's defense is in a very specialized argument: we must make a choice for either this man is the Son of God, or mad, or something worse.[1] Essentially Lewis is pointing towards important christological questions—"What or who is this Jesus if he was not God incarnate?" "What can we say about this man if he was not divine?" For Lewis what we are to say about Jesus of Nazareth, the carpenter who lived two millennia ago, is not simply a matter of opinion. Whatever viewpoint or belief system we come from this man won't settle into the background as just an ordinary human being. Jesus's identity has been at the heart of questions of Christology and the church's witness for two thousand years. Lewis's defense is called a trilemma, that is, the proposition that Jesus was "Mad, Bad, or God" (the so-called MBG or BMG argument), which is fundamental to his popular apologetics. It is fêted by American Evangelicals, cautiously endorsed by Roman Catholics and Anglicans, and scorned by most philosophers of religion. Whether endorsed or repudiated, most, mistakenly, regard Lewis's trilemma as unique. For example, the American Christian philosopher Stephen T. Davis, notes, "I have been unable to locate any published uses of the argument prior to the twentieth century."[2] In fact, Lewis's trilemma is rooted in a two thousand year theological tradition, a proposition that asserts that Jesus is, *aut Deus aut malus homo*—either God, or a bad man. This old Latin proposition can be traced back to the medieval church, and earlier to the patristic era. This is about identity and character, personhood: *aut Deus aut malus homo*—if Jesus was not God incarnate then in the light of his sayings and actions what can we conclude about his character? If Jesus was not divine and was merely human then we must conclude that, at the very least, he was not a good person, that he was bad, wicked, perhaps even evil.

---

1. Lewis, *Broadcast Talks*, 50–51.
2. Davis, "Was Jesus Mad, Bad or God?" 2nd ed., 149, n.1.

4. aut Deus aut malus homo I: What did Lewis Say?

> **C.S. LEWIS, *AUT DEUS AUT MALUS HOMO* – SOURCES**
>
> **1939**
> — Correspondence – August 1939
> **1940**
> — Correspondence – 26 March 1940
> **1940**
> — *The Problem of Pain*
> **1942**
> — *Broadcast Talks*
> **1944**
> — "Is Theology Poetry?"
> **1945**
> — "Christian Apologetics"
> **1947**
> — *Miracles*
>
> **1950**
> — "What Are We to Make of Jesus Christ?"
> **1950**
> — *The Lion, the Witch and the Wardrobe*
> **1952**
> — *Mere Christianity*
> **1958**
> — *Reflections on the Psalms*
> **1960**
> — "The Language of Religion"
> **1963**
> — "Cross-Examination"

Figure 5: C. S. Lewis—*aut Deus aut malus homo*—sources

He is *either* God, *or* a bad man. For the purposes of this study we will identify three periods bounded by Lewis's conversion in 1931, and his death in 1963: the early works 1931 to 1944; the middle works 1942 to 1947 (a deliberate overlap is implied in these two periods); and the later works 1948 to 1963. The division between early and middle works is essentially defined by the wartime *Broadcast Talks* (1942–44); the middle from the later works by the Anscombe-Lewis debate (1948).

2. LEWIS: "GOD . . . OR A BAD MAN": THE EARLY WORKS

Aut Deus aut malus homo is a central proposition of Lewis's apologetics. This proposition preoccupies his developing understanding of Jesus Christ and therefore his apologetics, and is crucial to his theory of revelation. *Aut Deus aut malus homo* is a form of philosophical theology that issues from his reading and studying in the 1930s. The source is almost certainly from his reading of G. K. Chesterton's work.[3] It is first alluded to in his correspondence from 1939, then stated in simple bipartite form in *The Problem of Pain*, in 1940. It is brought to its fullest extrapolation in *Mere Christianity* (1952). *Aut Deus aut malus homo* is central to Lewis's understanding of the relationship between faith and reason. However, Lewis develops the proposition from a dilemma to a trilemma; it is in effect a *triumvirate*. The MBG/BMG argument (Jesus was Bad, Mad, or he was God) simplifies the proposition and can distract from the essence of the argument, which is a choice: either-or. But what exactly did Lewis say and write? There are thirteen key references to *aut Deus aut malus homo* in Lewis's broadcasts and writings from 1940 to 1963 (These are representative rather than exhaustive). These vary from references in letters and recorded interviews to systematic explorations of the proposition in major books.

3. Chesterton, *The Everlasting Man*.

C. S. LEWIS—THE WORK OF CHRIST REVEALED

i. Correspondence—August 1939

Lewis's first implicit reference is in correspondence from August 1939. His writings and correspondence from the 1930s exhibit an implicit understanding of the dialectical nature of Christ's ontology (that is, what is he?—man or God incarnate). Writing to Owen Barfield in August 1939,[4] Lewis questions some of the assumptions evident from their correspondence. He questions the orthodoxy of elements in Barfield's view of Christ (Barfield was a committed follower of Anthroposophy[5]). Lewis comments on Barfield's idea that Christ suffered inherently because he was in the flesh—incarnated—and was therefore tempted to rush to his death, to bring on his crucifixion. This, for Lewis, contradicts orthodoxy in the form of the Athanasian Creed, and would suggest that Christ "was not (as the Christian mystery runs) 'perfect God and perfect man' but a kind of composite being, a δαιμον (daemon) or archangel imprisoned in a vehicle unsuitable to it."[6] This demonstrates Lewis's developing christological orthodoxy. However, what is important is that he then comments, "I need not say that on my view, the doctrine (do you hold it) that what was incarnated was 'One of the hierarchies' (or 'one of' the 'anythings') appears to me quite incompatible with the position given to Christ by his own words and by his followers."[7] And in a footnote marked by an asterisk, Lewis comments, "*Aut Deus aut malus angelus* is as true as the old *aut Deus aut malus homo*."[8] Lewis is, therefore, aware even at this early stage of the proposition and all that it implies; only here he replaces bad/evil human (*malus homo*) with bad/evil angel (*malus angelus*) in refuting Barfield's confused christological theorizing.

ii. Correspondence—March 26, 1940

Lewis's first explicit reference is in a long letter to a Mrs. Mary Neylan written from The Kilns on March 26, 1940, in it he addresses a number of questions relating to Christian doctrine.[9] Lewis addresses the problem of reading the character of Jesus from the Gospels and finding it difficult to see a paradigm of moral perfection:

> Now the truth is, I think, that the sweetly-attractive-human-Jesus is a product of 19th century scepticism, produced by people who were ceasing to believe in his divinity but wanted to keep as much of Christianity as they could. It is not what an unbeliever coming to the records with an open mind will (at first) find there. The first thing you really find is that we are simply not invited, so to speak, to pass any moral judgement on him, however favourable: it is only too clear he is going to do whatever judging there is: it is we who are being judged, sometimes tenderly, sometimes with stunning severity, but always *de haut en bas*.* . . . The first real work of the Gospels on a fresh reader is, and ought to be,

---

4. Lewis to Owen Barfield, Aug. 1939. *Collected Letters, Vol. II*, 266–69.
5. Anthroposophy is a philosophical system grounded in and derived from the work of Rudolf Steiner (1861–1925), which speculates on the concept of an objective reality, a spiritual world, accessible to the intellect, a form of thinking independent of sensory experience
6. Lewis to Owen Barfield, Aug. 1939. *Collected Letters, Vol. II*, 268.
7. Ibid., 269.
8. Ibid.
9. Lewis to Mrs Mary Neylan, Mar. 26, 1940. *Collected Letters, Vol. II*, 371–76.

4. aut Deus aut malus homo I: What did Lewis Say?

> to raise v. acutely the question, "Who-or-What is This?" For there is a good deal in the character which, unless he really is what he says he is—is not lovable or even tolerable.[10] (* : From high to low.)

Lewis is stating the dilemma that we are faced with, the question, "Who is this?," or, "What is this person?" Essentially the question is, "What do we say about Jesus if he was not God incarnate?" The attempt to de-Christianize Jesus, to present him as an ordinary human being is at the heart of this dialectic: is he God or merely human. And if human then there is much about him that is the sort of behavior we would not normally expect from someone, indeed it would make us raise serious questions about the person's goodness and/or sanity. Furthermore whatever we decide about this person Jesus, the record shows that we are not in a position to moralize, to pass judgment on him. This man Jesus, who—or—whatever he is, does the judging.

Lewis is clearly aware of his theological history. The nineteenth-century movement, or quest, for the historical Jesus was where scholars spent an inordinate amount of time trying to find who the real Jesus had been if they were to reject the Christ of faith, the Christ of church dogma. Having rejected Jesus' divinity they were prepared to laud him as a good moral teacher, an upright citizen, but not as God incarnate. But what to do with the embarrassing sayings he came out with?

iii. *The Problem of Pain (1940)*

This dialectical dilemma, which Lewis outlined in the above letter to Mary Neylan, was clearly a preoccupation of his in the late 1930s, for while writing *The Problem of Pain*—a work that was published seven months later[11]—Lewis comments how among the Jews a man was born who declared he was the Son of, or was at one with the God YHWH, the creator of all, the one that "haunted" his chosen people, and the giver of the moral law. Lewis acknowledges the dialectic in using the word paradox—Jesus is, but what he asserts appears impossible? What are we to make of him?-

> The claim is so shocking—a paradox, and even a horror, which we may easily be lulled into taking too lightly—that only two views of this man are possible. Either he was a raving lunatic of an unusually abominable type, or else he was, and is, precisely what he said. There is no middle way. If the records make the first hypothesis unacceptable, you must submit to the second . . . Christianity is not the conclusion of a philosophical debate on the origins of the universe: it is a catastrophic historical event following on the long spiritual preparation of humanity.[12]

Lewis does not assert the trilemma (the three elements or components), what we have is the either-or dialectic, and yes, a paradox. What appears abnormal and even impossible must be acknowledged because it is the only path that logically makes sense. In asserting *aut Deus aut malus homo*, the dialectic is between God incarnate

---

10. Ibid., 374–75.
11. Lewis, *The Problem of Pain*. (Published on, 18 October 1940 in the UK; 26 October 1943 in the USA.)
12. Ibid., 10–11.

and a merely human who is *malus* (bad, evil, or wicked). Later *malus* is taken to be evil or wicked, as distinct from delusions or questionable sanity. If we are forced to accept his claims to divine status then the Christian story begins to make sense, in particular the resurrection, However incomprehensible much of the story is to human thought, the Christ-event has changed our relation to YHWH, the righteous Lord. This hinges on *aut Deus aut malus homo*.

iv. Broadcast Talks (1942)

In the Second Series of *The Broadcast Talks*, entitled "What Christians Believe," Lewis again extends this proposition. In the third talk, "The Shocking Alternative," delivered on February 1, 1942,[13] Lewis opens from the same premise as two years earlier in *The Problem of Pain*, by asserting how "among the Jews there suddenly turns up a man who goes about talking as if he was God."[14] Only on this occasion he extends by qualifying the messianic divine claims: Jesus claims to forgive sins; he claims to have always existed; he announces that he is coming to judge all at the end of the world. This man is a Jew; Lewis notes how God for Jesus the Jew is not a pantheistic Indian or Oceanic "god": this is the God of the Jews, the one true living God outside and beyond all other gods—the Being outside the world, the creator, the God who was and is infinitely different from anything else. Lewis comments, "And when you've grasped that, you will see that what this man said was, quite simply, the most shocking thing that has ever been uttered by human lips."[15] We then have the essence of Lewis's presentation of *aut Deus aut malus homo*, the much quoted passage, phrased as apologetic, not as a dilemma, but as a "Mad, Bad, or God" trilemma:

> I'm trying here to prevent anyone from saying the really silly thing that people often say about him: "I'm ready to accept Jesus as a great moral teacher, but I don't accept his claim to be God." That's the one thing we mustn't say. A man who was merely a man and said the sort of things Jesus said wouldn't be a great moral teacher. He'd either be a lunatic—on a level with the man who says he's a poached egg—or else he'd be the Devil of Hell. You must make your choice. Either this man was, and is, the Son of God: or else a madman or something worse. You can shut him up for a fool, you can spit at him and kill him as a demon; or you can fall at his feet and call him Lord and God. But don't let us come with any patronising nonsense about his being a great human teacher. He hasn't left that open to us. He didn't intend to.[16]

Therefore, if it is clear from all who knew him and from the record that he was not deluded, insane, or possessed then the only just and rational decision is that he was and is God. We can choose to reject him; construct belief systems to say it was not so, but we cannot escape the logic, the either-or dialectic. This passage is one of the two

---

13. Lewis, *Broadcast Talks*. (The Second Series, *What Christians Believe*, Third Talk, 3. "The Shocking Alternative," BBC Home Service, London, Feb. 1, 1942, 4:45 to 5:00 pm.)
14. Ibid., 50.
15. Ibid.
16. Ibid., 50–51.

key examples of Lewis's primary exposition of *aut Deus aut malus homo*—the second being a reiteration essentially of this version from The *Broadcast Talks* ten years later in *Mere Christianity* (an extended edition of all of the broadcasts).

3. LEWIS: "GOD . . . OR A BAD MAN": THE MIDDLE WORKS

i. "Is Theology Poetry?" (1944)

Two years later, in a paper read to The Oxford Socratic Club, Lewis proposes this dialectic as proof of the veracity of the Christian gospel, only this time, echoing his conversion, he approaches it from the progression of idealism to theism, then to examining the truth claims of the gospel above and beyond all religions:

> On these grounds and others like them one is driven to think that whatever else may be true, the popular scientific cosmology at any rate is certainly not . . . Something like philosophical Idealism or Theism must, at the very worst, be less untrue than that. And Idealism turned out, when you took it seriously, to be disguised Theism. And once you accepted Theism you could not ignore the claims of Christ. And when you examined them it appeared to me that you could adopt no middle position. Either he was a lunatic, or God. And He was not a lunatic.[17]

So again if one is faced with the claims of Jesus of Nazareth and if you choose to reject what he says and does then you have no option but to regard him as deluded at best, insane at worst. In stating that we cannot adopt a middle position Lewis is not saying that this is unfeasible, impossible. It is perfectly possible to do as many have done and reject Christ's claims to divinity but we cannot argue that our position has been thought through and argued out logically in a reasonable manner. If we are to follow reasoned logic then Jesus is either-or. And if he was and is not *malus* (bad or deluded) then we must take his claims to divinity seriously.

ii. "Christian Apologetics" (1945)

In an address to the Church of England Carmarthen Conference for Youth Leaders and Junior Clergy held at Easter 1945, Lewis extolled the nature and value of Christian apologetics.[18] Lewis assumes that he is talking to theologians and Bible scholars (or at the very least people not entirely theologically illiterate or biblically ignorant). He spoke of approaching doctrinal question from the perspective of what he terms determined atheists, who immediately dismiss the unique claims of Christ upon which the whole Christian worldview is grounded. Lewis considers the number of such determined atheists as to be relatively small; the question of Jesus Christ's status (human or divine) and the difficulties of the incarnation-resurrection seemed to be more characteristic

---

17. Lewis, "Is Theology Poetry?" (a paper read to the Socratic Club in Oxford 1944), 164.
18. Lewis, "Christian Apologetics," (An address to the Church of England Carmarthen Conference for Youth Leaders and Junior Clergy, Easter 1945), 64–76.

of people's interests and puzzlement. Therefore he spells out the heart of the question explicitly:

> When we come to the incarnation itself, I usually find that some form of the *aut Deus aut malus homo* can be used. The majority of them started with the idea of the "great human teacher" who was deified by his superstitious followers. It must be pointed out how very improbable this is among Jews and how different to anything that happened with Plato, Confucius, Buddha, Mohammed. The Lord's own words and claims (of which many are quite ignorant) must be forced home. (The whole case, on a popular level, is very well put indeed in Chesterton's *The Everlasting Man*.) Something will usually have to be said about the historicity of the Gospels. You who are trained theologians will be able to do this in ways which I could not.[19]

Lewis comments on the importance of accepting the veracity and authenticity of the biblical record, explaining how he as a professional literary critic knew the difference between historical writing and legend, and the non-existence of realistic prose fiction before the eighteenth century.

Therefore, before the "professionals" Lewis focuses on the bipartite proposition—the two parts or elements being that Jesus is *Deus*, God, or *malus homo*, a bad man (he does not invoke a tripartite distinction between divinity, insanity, or demonry). However, this bipartite distinction that is behind or underpins the dilemma humanity is faced with is at the heart of Christology and revelation.

iii. Miracles (1947)

Lewis does extend this understanding of *aut Deus aut malus homo* into the more familiar tripartite distinction we know from his apologetics in *Miracles*, two years later. He explores the difficulties underlying the proposition, for example, the historical questions: why should his followers—knowing full well the penalties under the Jewish law for what they were asserting—claim Christ's divinity, and why are these claims, encapsulated in the sayings and actions of Jesus, presented so unsystematically? If we are to dismiss the New Testament account, what other explanation is there? In attempting to explain away the Gospel account Lewis notes how the range of alternatives has proliferated particularly in recent centuries (especially related to "modern" and/or "liberal" philosophies); however, none stand the test of time. Likewise attempts to "find" the historical Jesus (therefore the truly and only human Jesus) have not worked.

> The historical difficulty of giving for the life, sayings and influence of Jesus any explanation that is not harder than the Christian explanation is very great. The discrepancy between the depth and sanity and (let me add) shrewdness of his moral teaching and the rampant megalomania which must lie behind his theological teaching unless he is indeed God, has never been satisfactorily got over. Hence the non-Christian hypotheses succeed one another with the restless fertility of bewilderment. To-day we are asked to regard all the theological

---

19. Ibid., 74–75.

elements as later accretions to the story of a "historical" and merely human Jesus . . .[20]

Lewis is therefore focusing on the alternative—*malus homo*. In so doing he lays emphasis on the sanity and wisdom of this man's teaching as God incarnate. The "rampant megalomania" which is betrayed by his actions and the statements about forgiveness cannot be explained away if we proclaim him as a mere mortal, yet laud his wisdom and apparent sanity.

4. LEWIS: "GOD . . . OR A BAD MAN": THE LATER WORKS

i. "What Are We to Make of Jesus Christ?" (1950)

Despite the popularity of Lewis's tripartite statement ("Mad, Bad or God") in *The Broadcast Talks*, the finest analysis of the proposition, *aut Deus malus homo*, is in a little known paper from 1950—"What Are We to Make of Jesus Christ?"[21] In essence the paper addresses critical issues: how are we to solve the historical problem set us by the recorded sayings and acts of this man? If, as it is, we accept the generally acknowledged depth and sanity of Jesus's moral teaching (as evidenced by the scriptural record), which even the anti-God detractors accept (indeed this is often the only thing they like or agree with in the life and work of this man), then how do we balance the wisdom, profundity, and sanity of Jesus with the nature of his theological assertions—which Lewis asserts would normally be considered the utterances of an appalling megalomaniac with messianic pretensions. Lewis reiterates a central theme, the idea of a great moral teacher saying the things Jesus said is untenable—only God or someone suffering delusions would say such things.[22] What is more, those around Jesus who knew him did not regard him as a moral teacher in the way anti-theistic critics or secular liberal humanists might have done in Lewis's day, or today. On the contrary: "We may note in passing that he was never regarded as a mere moral teacher. He did not produce that effect on any of the people who actually met him. He produced mainly three effects: hatred, terror, or adoration. There was no trace of people expressing mild approval."[23] The only hypothesis, asserts Lewis, that covers the facts is that God has come down into the created universe, down into incarnation—and has come up again, drawing humanity up with him.[24]

---

20. Lewis, *Miracles*, 1st ed., 132.
21. Lewis, "What Are We to Make of Jesus Christ?," 48–53.
22. Ibid., 49–50.
23. Ibid., 50.
24. Ibid., 52.

ii. *The Lion, the Witch and the Wardrobe* (1950)

The Lucy *triumvirate*

Lewis uses the tripartite structure of his trilemma in *The Lion, the Witch and the Wardrobe*, re-phrasing and re-situating.[25] Lucy, an eight-year-old girl, one of four children, has visited Narnia—a country in what can only be described as a parallel universe. Her brothers and sisters don't believe her, so they discuss her strange behavior and beliefs with the professor they are staying with. They are surprised that the professor does not dismiss Lucy's claims immediately as a fantasy. The discussion—relatively long for a children's story—incorporates the essentials of a trilemma, only in this case it is between truth on the one hand, falsehood and/or delusion on the other.

The Structure of the Professor's Argument

Because of the implications of what Lucy proposes, because of the importance of what is implied in the existence of a parallel world (as incredulous as a human being claiming divinity), the question of "badness" or "madness" is raised. A lack of truthfulness implies that the person is "not good." Edmund, Lucy's brother, has been to Narnia also but lies; he pretends the visit never happened. This contributes to the question of doubt over Lucy's sanity. Therefore Professor Kirk asks which of the two is the most likely to be truthful—"does your experience lead you to regard your brother or your sister as the more reliable? I mean, which is the more truthful?"[26] Peter and Susan have to concede that Lucy would always be the honest one; Edmund has always been somewhat troublesome. Susan then questions that something might be wrong with Lucy—yet all agree that Lucy is sane, that she shows no sign of what might be termed "madness." Here we have the structure of Lewis-Professor Kirk's argument, the Lucy *triumvirate*: "'Logic!', said the Professor half to himself. 'Why don't they teach logic at these schools? There are only three possibilities. Either your sister is telling lies, or she is mad, or she is telling the truth. You know she doesn't tell lies and it is obvious that she is not mad. For the moment then and unless any further evidence turns up, we must assume that she is telling the truth.'"[27] The professor is using a tripartite structure to his argument; he is appealing to an understanding of logic in the children (particularly as Susan and Peter are teenagers). Peter then raises an ontological argument: that is, he questions whether Lucy's world is real, he asserts that if this parallel world is real then it should be self-evident to all people all the time (similar to the universalist argument that is often used to deny the divinity of Jesus). Peter therefore comments that, "If things are real, they're there all the time."[28] Professor Kirk's answer is simple: are they? Susan then raises the question of time, commenting that Lucy was gone for no time in our world but she claims she had been in Narnia for

---

25. Lewis, *The Chronicles of Narnia. The Lion, the Witch and the Wardrobe*, ch. 5 "Back on this side of the door," 44–52.
26. Ibid., 47.
27. Ibid., 47–48.
28. Ibid., 48.

4. *aut Deus aut malus homo I: What did Lewis Say?*

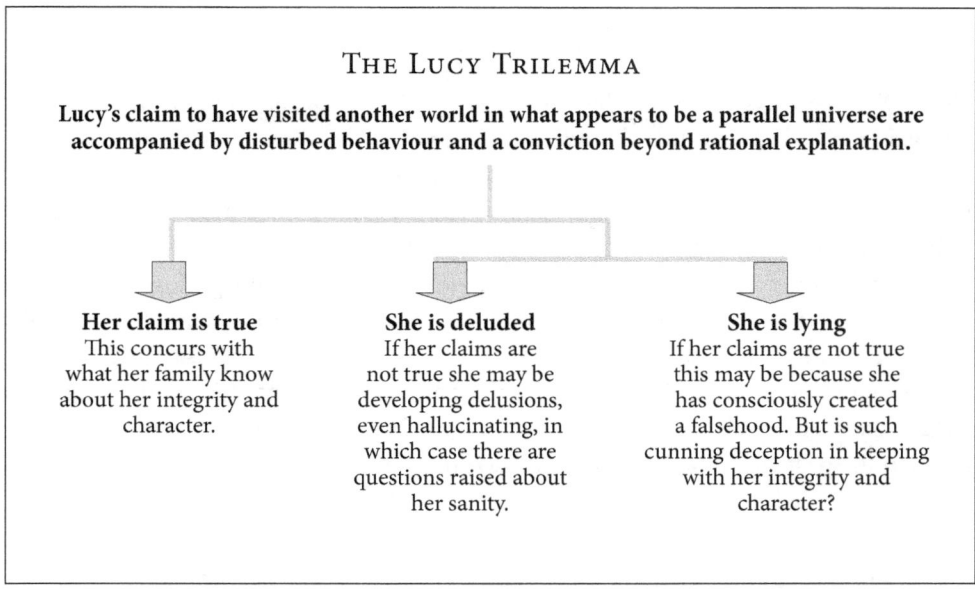

Figure 6: C. S. Lewis—The Lucy *triumvirate*

hours. The professor comments "That is the very thing that makes her story so likely to be true."[29] An eight year old girl, uninhibited by questions of rationality, order, and logic can make the leap of faith when Peter and Susan remain puzzled and doubting: "'But do you really mean, sir,' said Peter, 'that there could be other worlds—all over the place, just round the corner—like that?' 'Nothing is more probable,' said the Professor, taking off his spectacles and beginning to polish them, while he muttered to himself, 'I wonder what they do teach them at these schools.'"[30] The question is then one of probability. Because of the lack of direct personal evidence and experience (i.e., Peter and Susan have not been to Narnia by the time of this conversation, remembering that most of the decisions we make in life are not primarily informed by direct one-to-one evidence and experience), then they must weigh up the options and decide on the grounds of probability. This is characterized by two dialectics first, between credibility and incredibility, and second between belief and disbelief. If they disbelieve her claims, then they must contradict her credible personality, which would be an untruth; if they accept her claim to have visited another world, and they considered her an untrustworthy and discredited character, then this too would be a falsehood. The only option as she is an honest, credible, person and shows no sign of delusion or pretence is to regard her story as true, even though their lack of personal evidence and experience makes then wary. Probability will often contradict our skepticism.

29   Ibid.
30   Ibid., 49.

iii. Mere Christianity (1952)

Mere Christianity is a revised and amplified edition of the three volumes of the BBC Home Service talks broadcast between 1941 and 1944. It is probably Lewis's most famous work of apologetic; as such the material is more nuanced, and the scripts presented a decade earlier are organized as a coherent whole. Throughout the book Lewis has added sentences and paragraphs to answer questions raised by the talks and to address theological and philosophical issues that had emerged in the intervening years—systematic queries raised by clergy, and theologians and philosophers.[31] The text for Lewis's tripartite interpretation of *aut Deus aut malus homo* remains essentially the same as the broadcast version; however, a significant paragraph is added.

The additional material develops a theme that was omitted from the originally 1942 broadcast. This is the question of sin. Lewis comments how one part of the claim tends to slip past us probably because we have been over exposed to it. That is, the claim to forgive sins, all sins, indeed any sins. We tend to forget that this is the prerogative of God; therefore, this is essentially, to use Lewis's term, preposterous. What is more Jesus is either forgiving in place of another to whom the offence has been committed, or the offence has not been made against him—

> Asinine fatuity is the kindest description we should give of his conduct. Yet this is what Jesus did. He told people that their sins were forgiven, and never waited to consult all the other people whom their sins had undoubtedly injured. He unhesitatingly behaved as if he was the party chiefly concerned, the person chiefly offended in all offences. This makes sense only if he really was the God whose laws are broken and whose love is wounded in every sin . . . Christ says that he is "humble and meek" and we believe him; not noticing that, if he were merely a man, humility and meekness are the very last characteristics we could attribute to some of his sayings.[32]

Therefore, the ontological status of Jesus is not simply affirmed by the either-or dialectic we have discussed but by everything the man said and how he approached everyone he came into contact with. Either side of this passage, the bipartite proposition of *aut Deus aut malus homo*, is presented as a tripartite proposition, identical (but for some small grammatical changes) to *The Broadcast Talks*.

iv. Reflections on the Psalms (1958)

Lewis remains preoccupied with question of sin-sinlessness as the key to the ontological nature of this man Jesus of Nazareth. If the detractors are to continue in their classification of him as an ordinary human then they cannot persist in regarding him as wise, gentle and humble considering his relationship to sinners (the absolute forgiver) and the arrogance of his spoken assertions and attitude to all around him.

---

31. Lewis, *Mere Christianity*, Bk. 2, "What Christians Believe," ch. 3 "The Shocking Alternative," and opening of Ch. 4 "The Perfect Penitent," 51–53.

32. Ibid., 51–52.

4. aut Deus aut malus homo I: What did Lewis Say?

> For he denied all sin of himself. That, indeed; is no small argument of his Deity. For he has not often made even on the enemies of Christianity the impression of arrogance; many of them do not seem as shocked as we should expect at his claim to be "meek and lowly of heart." Yet he said such things as, on any hypothesis but one, would be the arrogance of a paranoiac. It is as if, even where the hypothesis is rejected, some of the reality which implies its truth "got across."[33]

This passage from *Reflections on the Psalms* is in the context of the second meanings we can derive from Scripture—second meaning that are fuller than the original aims and intention of the writers, and are inspired by the Holy Spirit.

v. "The Language of Religion" (1960)

Lewis examines the ontology (the very nature of being) between Jesus and God, which makes him the Christ—*aut Deus aut malus homo*—in a late paper, written in 1960 for a conference.[34] Lewis is examining the necessity for poetic expressions in trinitarian language, which is closely connected to the grounds of faith for orthodox Christians. These grounds are authority and religious experience. Authority consists of the declaration, "Jesus is the Son of God." If Christians believe and assert that Jesus Christ is the Son of God, this is, for Lewis, primarily because Jesus demonstrated it to be so through his actions and words: this is an authoritative and dogmatic statement, which we should subscribe to. Such evidence convinces Christians that Jesus was neither, to use Lewis's language, a lunatic nor a quack: *malus homo*. Lewis explains that such statements cannot mean that Jesus stands to God "in the very same physical and temporal relation which exists between offspring and male parent in the animal world."[35] We must see such a statement as poetic: "The theologian will describe it as 'analogical', drawing our minds at once away from the subtle and sensitive exploitations of imagination and emotion with which poetry works to the clear-cut but clumsy analogies of the lecture-room. He will even explain in what respects the father-son relationship is not analogical to the reality, hoping by elimination to reach the respects in which it is. He may even supply other analogies of his own—the lamp and the light which flows from it, or the like."[36] But this does not reduce the ontological reality between Jesus and God the Father, in the Holy Spirit, to something metaphorical, characterized by humanely conferred status. Jesus is not *malus homo* just because there is difference in personhood between the Christ we meet in Scripture and the God of eternity. Lewis continues, "The sentence 'Jesus Christ is the Son of God' cannot be all got into the form 'There is between Jesus and God an asymmetrical, social, harmonious relation involving homogeneity.'"[37] This is because we are best at understanding the relationships within the Trinity—that is we are best at "receiving

33. Lewis, *Reflections on the Psalms*, 117.
34. An address written for the Twelfth Symposium of the Colston Research Society, held at the University of Bristol, March 1960, which Lewis was unable to attend due to ill-health, the address was published posthumously in 1967. Lewis, "The Language of Religion," 129–41.
35. Ibid., 137.
36. Ibid.
37. Ibid.

revelation"—if we continue to see human sonship and fatherhood are still merely analogical themselves.[38] Jesus is divine; the human analogy (the relationship between a father and son) is analogical but it does not deny the nature of being—that Jesus is the Son of God. Lewis asserts that the logic of *aut Deus aut malus homo* should convince us that this is so.

vi. "Cross-Examination" (1963)

Interviewed by a representative of the Billy Graham Evangelistic Association, Sherwood E. Wirt, only months before his death, Lewis spoke candidly about his conversion.[39] In the recorded and transcribed interview Wirt restated the basis proposition from *The Broadcast Talks*, that Jesus was either "Mad, Bad, or was God (incarnate)" to Lewis with the question, "Would you say that your view on the matter has changed since then?" Lewis's answer was straightforward: "I would say there is no substantial change."[40]

---

38 Ibid.

39 Conducted in Lewis's rooms in Magdalene College, Cambridge, on Tuesday, May 7, 1963, the interview was initially published in two parts, (Sherwood E. Wirt. and C. S. Lewis, "Heaven, Earth and Outer Space" and "I was Decided Upon") in the American periodical *Decision*, later to be combined posthumously. See, Lewis, "Cross Examination," 215–21.

40 Lewis, "Cross-Examination," 217–18.

5

aut Deus aut malus homo II:
The Theological Tradition

SYNOPSIS:
Aut Deus aut malus homo—either Jesus of Nazareth was God incarnate, or he was an ordinary human. If human, like the rest of us, then we cannot, in the light of what he said and did, consider him good: his actions and words disclose this. What is the origin of this argument? We can trace it to Jesus' question to Peter: "But who do you say that I Am?" (Matt 16:15; cf. Mark 8:27–30; and Luke 9:20–21). There is evidence of the use of *aut Deus aut malus homo* in the patristic church—for example, in the work of Gaius Marius Victorinus, in his apologetic arguments to counter Julian the Apostate; we can also find reference to it in medieval scholasticism and in the writings of Sir Thomas More. However, its use is essentially post-Reformation, in response to the skepticism of the Age of Reason and the Enlightenment: What do we say about Jesus if he was not God incarnate? The work of the Victorian churchman and theologian H. P. Liddon ("*Christus, si non Deus, non bonus*"—Christ, if not God, is not good) is important here, along with the nineteenth-century American preacher and theologian Mark Hopkins. Both Liddon and Hopkins are working against the background of nineteenth-century Liberal theologians and Bible scholars who claimed that Jesus was not divine, but was a good moral teacher, a high and laudable example of humanity. We can trace Lewis's source directly to G. K. Chesterton, a crucial influence in the period leading to Lewis's conversion. Lewis's trilemma, like the theological tradition of *aut Deus aut malus homo*, is rooted in Jesus's question to all of us: who do we say that he is? However, the tripartite nature of the Chesterton-Lewis proposition can be found in John's Gospel (identified by the Roman Catholic theologian Gerald O'Collins): the Johannine trilemma is where those representing the Jewish religious authorities were forced to conclude, because Jesus could not be ignored, that he was an "unbalanced liar," or he was "demonically possessed," or he really was "The God of Israel come amongst them."

1. "GOD . . . OR A BAD MAN": THE PATRISTIC AND MEDIEVAL THEOLOGICAL TRADITION

Lewis's proposition that Jesus was either, "Mad, Bad, or God" issues from a long theological tradition. This tradition is rooted in Scripture; on most occasions what we term "Lewis's trilemma" is presented as an either/or decision: *aut Deus aut malus homo*. The proposition *aut Deus aut malus homo* is christological; it is essentially about the divinity of Christ which Scripture attests to.

C. S. LEWIS—THE WORK OF CHRIST REVEALED

i. The Gospels

All questions relating to Jesus of Nazareth, the Christ, are grounded in this one proposition—who is this man and why does he say and do the things he does? There are many accounts recorded in the Gospels of all kinds of people speculating as to who Jesus was—the one conclusion that people did not come to was that he was just an ordinary man. Early in his ministry some of the Romans regarded him as eccentric but harmless. However, the Jewish religious authorities began to see him as a troublemaker, and then as a heretic; many of the ordinary Jews who met him wondered if he was Elijah, some even question if he was John the Baptist returned from the dead.[1] As his works and reputation develop people are forced to make a decision. Many decide he is *malus*: evil, wicked. For example, "All the people were astonished and said, 'Could this be the Son of David?' But when the Pharisees heard this, they said, 'It is only by Beelzebub, the prince of demons, that this fellow drives out demons.'"[2] Or, "Again the Jews were divided because of these words. Many of them were saying, 'He has a demon and is out of his mind. Why listen to him?' Others were saying, 'These are not the words of one who has a demon. Can a demon open the eyes of the blind?'"[3] Also,

> And the teachers of the law who came down from Jerusalem said, "He is possessed by Beelzebub! By the prince of demons he is driving out demons." So Jesus called them and spoke to them in parables: "How can Satan drive out Satan? If a kingdom is divided against itself, that kingdom cannot stand. If a house is divided against itself, that house cannot stand. And if Satan opposes himself and is divided, he cannot stand; his end has come. In fact, no one can enter a strong man's house and carry off his possessions unless he first ties up the strong man. Then he can rob his house. I tell you the truth, all the sins and blasphemies of men will be forgiven them. But whoever blasphemes against the Holy Spirit will never be forgiven; he is guilty of an eternal sin." He said this because they were saying, "He has an evil spirit."[4]

Therefore, there is disagreement; some claim he is evil, possessed, presumably because Jesus' words and actions do not conform to their religious expectations. But whoever came into contact with Jesus *had to decide*. And if they made the wrong decision they were putting their eternal salvation at risk. In this instance the Scribes, the teachers of the Torah, are *deluded* into believing he is possessed when logically he cannot be: one possessed by demons cannot drive out demons. Faced with his miracles and his controversial sayings the Scribes dismiss his as evil: "The Jews answered him, 'Are we not right in saying that you are a Samaritan and have a demon?' Jesus answered, 'I do not have a demon; but I honor my Father, and you dishonor me.'"[5] It is this question of religious conformity that sets Jesus apart, according to the Jewish religious elite: "Some of the Pharisees said, 'This man is not from God, for he does not observe the

---

1. Matt 14:2; Mark 6:14.
2. Matt 12:23–24.
3. John 10:19–21.
4. Mark 3:22–30.
5. John 8:48–50.

5. aut Deus aut malus homo II: The Theological Tradition

Sabbath.' But others said, 'How can a man who is a sinner perform such signs?' And they were divided."[6] There is division: no one is recorded as regarding him to be of no consequence: "When they heard these words, some in the crowd said, 'This is really the prophet.' Others said, 'This is the Messiah.' But some asked, 'Surely the Messiah does not come from Galilee, does he? Has not the Scripture said that the Messiah is descended from David and comes from Bethlehem, the village where David lived?' So there was a division in the crowd because of him. Some of them wanted to arrest him, but no one laid hands on him."[7] During his ministry, addressing the disciples, Jesus asks who do people say that the Son of Man is. Simon Peter reiterates what people are saying—speculating—about him; but Jesus presses Peter—

> Now when Jesus came into the district of Caesarea Philippi, he asked his disciples, "Who do people say that the Son of Man is?" And they said, "Some say John the Baptist, but others Elijah, and still others Jeremiah or one of the prophets." He said to them, "But who do you say that I am?" Simon Peter answered, "You are the Messiah, the Son of the living God." And Jesus answered him, "Blessed are you, Simon son of Jonah! For flesh and blood has not revealed this to you, but my Father in heaven" . . . Then he sternly ordered the disciples not to tell anyone that he was the Messiah.[8]

Peter utters a profound christological statement: this man Jesus of Nazareth is the Messiah, the Son of the Living God, the one sent to save Israel (therefore, for Peter incarnation and messiahship go hand-in-hand). Jesus does not force his true identity onto the people he meets; it is important for people to come to a realization of who Jesus really is. Jesus doesn't simply declare who he is and demand that people accept it—that is how Herod and Pilate expect the people to respond. Jesus of Nazareth is God *incognito*. Neither Peter, nor the other disciples, nor those in authority who exercised power and judgment over Jesus, doubted that this man was not ordinary, further that he was a challenge to their power even though he wielded no power himself. Peter understood the truth of who Jesus was; but on the night of Jesus's arrest he denies that he ever knew him.

Therefore, the origin of *aut Deus aut malus homo* lies in Jesus's encounters with the people he met, but essentially in his question to Peter. Jesus is not saying, "Who would you like me to be?" The option is not to make up what we want to believe about Jesus: he is not a plasticine idol to mould and conform to our needs and desires. What is important is that through faith each and every one Jesus met had the opportunity to perceive the truth about him. This related to their salvation, and echoes with Lewis's own conversion experience.

---

6   John 9:16–17.
7   John 7:40–43.
8   Matt 16:13–17, 20, cf. See also Mark 8:27, 30; Luke 9:20, 21.

ii. The Apostle Paul

The apostle Paul develops this question into an either-or dialectic: either Jesus was God incarnate and he was raised from the dead (when no ordinary mortal could be resurrected) or he was not. If not then our faith is of no discernable value

> If there is no resurrection of the dead, then Christ has not been raised; and if Christ has not been raised, then our proclamation has been in vain and your faith has been in vain. We are even found to be misrepresenting God, because we testified of God that he raised Christ—whom he did not raise if it is true that the dead are not raised. For if the dead are not raised, then Christ has not been raised. If Christ has not been raised, your faith is futile and you are still in your sins.[9]

Paul takes the question of Jesus's identity and turns it round and looks at the implications for the human situation. If Jesus was not the Christ and was not resurrected then we are of all people to be pitied for such a hopeless delusion. Jesus is *aut Deus*, or we are still irretrievably lost in our sins—we are *malus*. Hiding in religion will not help; but it is important that we come to realize the truth about Jesus's identity for ourselves.

iii. Patristic Roots?

This either-or distinction is therefore rooted in the Gospel accounts. Nothing humanity can do or say can close the dialectic: people have to come to a decision when they encounter Jesus, either through reading the Bible or through the witness of the churches. In the early church and the patristic church the arguments were about the precise nature of Jesus Christ as perfect God and perfect man: "Was he an apparition?" "Just how real was he?" "How did divinity and humanity co-exist?" The, "What do we make of him if he is not divine?" question did not really arise until the fourth century. With the acceptance of Christianity as the official religion by the Roman Emperor Constantine, following the Battle of the Milvian Bridge in 312AD, there is a period of relative calm, certainly following on from the early centuries of persecution. However, under the Emperor Julian (355–63AD)—often called Julian the Apostate, or Julian the Philosopher—the church was on the defensive. Although raised as a Christian, Julian converted to paganism. He sought to return the Roman Empire to its pagan roots through the restoration of Hellenic paganism as the state religion. During his reign many theologians and churchmen were pressed to justify Christ's divinity. It is at this time that the "What if?" question begins to be fielded: "What or who is Jesus if he was not divine, what can we say about him if he was only an ordinary person?"

The Victorian churchman Charles Gore[10] attributes the origin of the either-or decision—with the qualifier that if Jesus was merely a man then he cannot be

---

9   1 Cor 15:13–18.
10.   Charles Gore (1853–1932) was an Anglican bishop and theologian, vice-principal of Cuddesdon Theological College (1880–83), and principal of the newly founded Pusey House (1884); in 1892 had founded a religious order—a clerical fraternity—the Community of the Resurrection (CR), at Pusey House, an Anglican order of monk-priests, whose permanent home became Mirfield in Yorkshire.

5. aut Deus aut malus homo II: The Theological Tradition

considered good and wise[11]—specifically to the Emperor Julian's contemporary, the patristic theologian Gaius Marius Victorinus; The rejection of Christianity and the revival of the Roman pagan religion by the Emperor Julian (331–63) fuelled Victorinus' writing.[12] He published many treatises on the Trinity (in particular the incarnation), several defenses of the Nicene Creed, and several commentaries of Paul's Epistles.[13] As a Christian philosopher Victorinus focused on the either-or question of Jesus Christ's nature that could not be ignored: no ordinary man would have said and done the things attributed to Jesus. It is, therefore, clear from the sayings of Jesus that he was God. In a short treatise to his friend Candidus the Arian entitled, *de generatione verbi divini* (*From the Generation of the Divine Word*), written around 385AD, Victorinus writes, referring to the sayings of Jesus, that, "Saying these things he was God, if he did not lie; if however he lied, he was not the work of God perfect in all ways."[14] Victorinus is writing about the theology of the divine Word (Jesus Christ); he often uses and invokes the word existential (*exsistentialis, exsistentialitas, exsistentialiter*) to describe the relationship between the Christian and Christ, and writes of the eternal generation of the divine word. Jesus was not *made*, as such, into God's Son; there never was a time when the second person of the Trinity was not divine; hence, Victorinus can write that if Jesus only pretended to be God then he was not completely in every way the perfect work of God. He does not go as far as to say, in so many words, that if he is not God he is a bad man, but the implication is that if he pretended, feigned or lied, then he was not a good man, he was not perfection.

iv. Pope Innocent III—aut Deus es aut homo

The Lewis scholar Walter Hooper notes that the phrase *aut Deus aut malus homo* is probably from Lewis's reading of the treatise of Pope Innocent III, *On the Misery of the Human Condition*, in which the king encounters a philosopher who comments: "*Aut Deus es aut homo: si Deus es, debui te adorari; si homo, potui iuxta te sedere.*"[15] This is translated as, "You are either a god or a man: if you are a god, I ought to worship you; if a man, I should be able to sit beside you." There is, therefore, this distinction between

---

11. Gore, *The Incarnation of the Son of God: Being the Bampton Lectures for the Year 1891*, 257–58. See also, Gore, *Dissertations on Subjects Connected with the Incarnation*.

12. Gaius Marius Victorinus, born late third century (c. 297–300AD) in North Africa, was a Roman grammarian, rhetorician and neo-Platonic philosopher, who converted to Christianity around the year 355; he was disenfranchised as a professor under Julian because he was a Christian, he died in c. 370.

13. See, Roberts, Alexander; James Donaldson; Philip Schaff and Henry Wace, *Ante-Nicene Fathers* Vol. 7, 339–60.

14. "*Haec dicens Deus fuit, si mentitus non est: si autem mentitus est, non opus Dei omnimodis perfectum*": Victorinus, "*De Generatione Verbi Divini*," cols. 1019c–36c, ref. col. 1020. See, for details of this work, Bruce, "Marius Victorinus and his Works," 132–53. Hanson, *The Search for the Christian Doctrine of God. The Arian Controversies 318–81AD*, Ch. 17 "The Western Pro-Nicenes III," §1 "Marius Victorinus Introduction," and, §2 "Marius Victorinus' Christology," especially 533–56.

15. Walter Hooper notes this at the end of Lewis's letter to Owen Barfield. See, Lewis to Owen Barfield, August* 1939. *Collected Letters*, Vol. II, 269, n.99. Lotario de Conti (1160-1216) was Pope Innocent III from 1198–1216. See: Pope Innocent III, *De miseria humane conditionis. On the misery of the human condition*. *: no specific date is given.

God and man in Lewis's thinking, though it does not relate directly to Jesus Christ's ontology or the question of the nature of the moral character of Jesus if merely human.

v. Thomas Aquinas—Pride and Humility

Philosophers and theologians generally accepted the divinity of Christ in Western Europe during the Middle Ages—deism, theism, and "modern" atheism had yet to rear their Lernaean-Hydra-like heads. This does not imply that in the Middle Ages, the age for many of the church, that these questions were ignored. Theologians and philosophers would examine the questions and deduce from the scriptural record, applying the skill of reason, in much the same way as Lewis did—*aut Deus aut malus homo*. For example, Thomas Aquinas (1225–74) writes not of madness, lunacy, or evil if Jesus is not divine; Aquinas writes of pride—pride being the root of all sin. "The man Christ, speaking of himself, says many divine and supernatural things, as, 'I will raise him up at the last day' (John 6:40), 'I give them life everlasting' (John 10:28). Such language would be the height of pride, if the speaker were not himself God, but only had God dwelling in him. And still Christ says of himself: 'Learn of me, because I am meek and humble of heart' (Matt. 9:29)."[16] What has pride to do with Jesus' ontology? Aquinas notes, quoting the book of Sirach (Ecclesiasticus)[17] that pride is the root of all sin: "We must therefore say that pride, even as denoting a special sin, is the beginning of every sin . . . Therefore, from this point of view, pride, which is the desire to excel, is said to be the 'beginning' of every sin."[18] If we reject Jesus' claims, whether explicit or implicit, then we pride ourselves on superior knowledge. Intellectual pride is expressed in our judging Jesus to be merely human and deluded. If Jesus was merely human then he exhibited the height of pride, which does not tally with what we know of the man. Therefore, we cannot take seriously Jesus as an ordinary man. Putting aside questions of sanity, if pride is the antithesis—amongst other attributes—of normality, anyone who consistently says and does the things Jesus does time and time again cannot be considered a normal human being. If he is not God then, for Aquinas, pride is the only explanation for the arrogant overbearing manner, the superiority manifested in

---

16. Aquinas, *Summa contra Gentiles*, Bk. 4, Ch. 34, §.27: "*Amplius. Manifestum est quod homo Christus, loquens de se, multa divina dicit et supernaturalia: ut est illud Ioan. 6-40, ego resuscitabo illum in novissimo die; et Ioan. 10-28, ego vitam aeternam do eis. Quod quidem esset summae superbiae, si ille homo loquens non esset secundum hypostasim ipse Deus, sed solum haberet Deum inhabitantem. Hoc autem homini Christo non competit, qui de se dicit, Matt. 11-29: discite a me quia mitis sum et humilis corde. Est igitur eadem persona hominis illius et Dei.*" My acknowledgement is to Brendan N. Wolfe, a patristic scholar from Oxford, for introducing me to this source/reference.

17. The understanding that pride is at the root of all sin originated, to a degree, in the Bible Apocrypha: "How can dust and ashes be proud? . . . The beginning of human pride is to forsake the Lord; For the beginning of pride is sin . . . Pride was not created for human beings . . . The fear of the Lord is the beginning of acceptance; obduracy and pride are the beginning of rejection." The Book of Sirach (Sir 10:9, 12–13, 15, 18, 21). See also: Prov 8:13 & 16:18–9; Ps 10:4; Amos 6:8; Prov 29:23; Mark 7:20–23; 1 Cor 8:1–2; 4:7; 1 Tim 3:6 & 6:17; 1 Pet 5:5; and Jas 4:6.

18. On pride and its relation to all other sins, see, Aquinas, *Summa Theologiae* Pt. I–II (*Prima Secundae*), Treatise on Habits, in particular Q.84 Of the Cause of Sin, Article 2 Whether Pride is the Beginning of every Sin?.

5. aut Deus aut malus homo II: The Theological Tradition

his presumptuous claims. This becomes a problem when we consider the man Jesus's humility: this is no ordinary human being. And if we reject Jesus's divinity we are guilty of pride.

vi. Sir Thomas More: "If Christ were not God, he would be no Good Man either"

The English lawyer, statesman, and writer Sir Thomas More (1478–1535), a leading Renaissance humanist scholar, published many works on the church and the Christian life. His last work, *Dialogue of Comfort against Tribulation*, written while in prison in the Tower of London awaiting execution for refusing to acknowledge Henry VIII as supreme head of the Church in England, is a dialogue between two characters— Vincent, a young man seeking spiritual guidance from his uncle, Anthony.[19] Although this work is often criticized for appearing to be formless and without structure there are profound moments of clarity (particularly given the appalling conditions of Mores imprisonment). Thomas More painted a picture, a word portrait, in the *Dialogue* of a society collapsing. The dialogue is set in Hungary in the late 1520s, just before the Turkish occupation by Suleiman the Magnificent following the defeat of the Hungarian forces; the analogy More was creating was with the chaos unleashed by Henry VIII's reformation—for better or for worse. In Book 3, chapter 14, Anthony warns of the consequences for Christians of the belief systems of the Turks—Islam—and how what is at the heart of the Christian faith is at stake, namely, the divinity of Christ. Anthony speaks against dialogue with "the Turk," i.e., with Islam. Gradually, warns Anthony, the Turk will seek your conversion through your denial of Christ.

> But he would, little by little, ere he left you, make you deny Christ altogether and take Mohamed in his stead. And so doth he in the beginning, when he will not have you believe him to be God. For surely, if he Christ were not God, he would be no good man either, since he plainly said he was God. But through he would go never so far forth with you, yet Christ will, as I said, not take your service by halves, but will that you shall love him with all your whole heart . . . You cannot serve both God and your riches together.[20]

Christ's demand is wholehearted; lukewarm neutrality over the question of the divinity of Christ is not acceptable. More is writing in the context of the Muslim invasion of parts of Eastern Europe in the early sixteenth century and the demands of Islam on Christians. In this context, More asserts that if Christ is not God he could not be considered a good man, because "he plainly said he was God." It is the evidence from Scripture that condemns Jesus's moral character if he was only a mere human. No good man, no one considered morally upright and true, would have said the things Jesus said or did the things he did if he was not God incarnate.

---

19. Written during his imprisonment in the Tower of London from April 17, 1534 until his execution on July 6, 1535, the *Dialogue of Comfort* is part of his "Tower Works"; it was first published during Queen Mary's reign in 1553 by Richard Tottel. See, Sir Thomas More, *Dialogue of Comfort against Tribulation*.
20. Ibid., Book 3, Ch. XIV, 179.

2. "GOD . . . OR A BAD MAN":
THE POST-REFORMATION THEOLOGICAL TRADITION

Pushing the question of Jesus's identity to, in relative terms, a dialectical extreme became popular amongst Protestant and Reformed ministers and preachers from the time of the Age of Reason (it can be argued that the intellectual climate in the eighteenth and nineteenth centuries was similar in many ways to that encountered by Gaius Marius Victorinus under the Emperor Julian in the fourth century). Questions about Jesus's identity, if he was but a mere man, were not always uppermost in the mind of churchman in the early church, nor in the medieval period—the testimony of the church was sufficient, built as it was on apostolic witness. If the human intellect is to try to define what Jesus was from its own resources then the witness of Scripture comes into prime importance. Therefore, apologists draw on their reading of the Gospels and the examples we noted earlier of how Jesus engendered such an either-or decision with regards to his ontological identity amongst those who encountered him.

i. Protestant and Reformed Developments: John Calvin

Calvin's *Institutes* is grounded in Scripture. He does not tackle the question "What do we say about Jesus if he was not God incarnate?" directly. Christ's divinity is taken for granted[21]—there are numerous theological justifications relating to sacrifice and salvation as to why he must be perfect God and perfect man, Son of God and Son of Man; however, he does comment that those who doubt the incarnation make God out to be a liar.[22] So if Jesus is not God incarnate then the account is a lie—God, Jesus, or the Evangelists are deceiving us. However, Calvin asserts that, "Little dependence could be placed on these statements, were it not proved by numerous passages throughout the sacred volume that none of them is of man's devising."[23]

ii. Protestant and Reformed Developments: John Duncan

The Scottish preacher John Duncan[24] used just such an argument for Christ's divinity. In discussions with William Knight, published in 1870, Duncan commented that, "Christ either deceived mankind by conscious fraud, or he was himself deluded and self-deceived, or he was divine. There is no getting out of this trilemma. It is inexorable."[25] So, Jesus is a fraudster, or self-deceived, or he is divine. Duncan's comments are in a sub-section entitled "Christ's Trilemma," and conclude discussions—undertaken

---

21. Calvin, *Institutes of the Christian Religion*, Vol. 1, Bk. II. ch. XIII. §.1, 474.
22. Ibid., Bk. II. ch. XII. §.7, 471.
23. Ibid., Bk. II. ch. XIV. §.2, 483.
24. John Duncan (1796–1870), minister of the Free Church of Scotland, preacher, Professor of Hebrew and Oriental Languages at New College, Edinburgh, and missionary to Hungarian Jews, graduated from the University of Aberdeen. As a young man Duncan was an atheist who, like Lewis, became a theist in his twenties, then a Christian confessing Christ's divinity.
25. Duncan and Knight, *Colloquia Peripatetica (Deep-Sea Soundings): Being Notes of Conversations*, 109.

in October 1861—about the incarnation, and lead into material on the doctrine of ignorance, and Western concepts of justification.[26]

Lewis is not unique in his use of an argument to force a decision on Christ's identity. [27] Therefore, from the time of the Age of Reason and the Enlightenment orthodox churchmen and theologians were, in effect, on the defensive. There was a much greater demand to prove the divinity of Christ. In consequence there is a greater emphasis on the either-or nature to apologetic propositions about Jesus, a tradition that Lewis is clearly a part of. There are several examples of the type of reasoning that undergirds a bipartite dialectical proposition being used to demonstrate Jesus's divinity, especially within the last two hundred years. It would help if we examine three in relative depth: Mark Hopkins, H. P. Liddon and G. K. Chesterton

3. MARK HOPKINS—CONDITION, CLAIMS, AND CHARACTER

The American theologian, educator, and preacher Mark Hopkins[28] used this argument often in lectures.[29] In Lecture VIII of the series delivered before the Lowell Institute in January 1844, Hopkins examines the condition, character, and claims of Christ. Of necessity Hopkins has to consider whether this man was an imposter, or does he have what he terms the true insignia of office. The question revolves around a decision: was Jesus a good or a bad man—"if we were simply to withdraw his character and acts, the whole [Christian] system would collapse at once."[30] Hopkins accepts that "In general, he claimed to be the Messiah, the Son of God, and the Saviour of men."[31] Hopkins does not go into the question of what it is to be a truly divine person, or to be the Lamb of God, and what is implied by taking away the sins of the world (he also assumes that "messiahship" and "incarnation" are part of the same identity); however, he does examine two crucial questions—what did it mean to be a perfectly sinless being and what does it tell us that he was—or more pertinently is—to be the final judge of the world. Jesus did not simply fulfill the stereotypical idea of a Messiah common amongst the Jews living under the yoke of Rome. Jesus was not the militaristic liberator they

26. Duncan and Knight, *Colloquia Peripatetica*, 96–112.
27. For example: "*Aut Christus Deus, aut homo non bonus est,*" in, Van Dyke, *The Gospel for an Age of Doubt*, 62; also, "*Christus aut Deus aut homo non bonus,*" in, Eck, *The Incarnation*, 28; and, "*Christus aut Deus aut non bonus,*" in, Ottley, *The Doctrine of the Incarnation*, Vol. 1, 69.
28. Mark Hopkins (1802–87), a graduate of Williams College, was Professor of Moral Philosophy and Rhetoric, and, from 1833, a Congregational preacher. *Lectures on Evidences of Christianity* (1846) became a popular book of Christian apologetics. Hopkin's argument in the *Lectures* drew often from legal language grounded in the importance of the eyewitness accounts in the Gospels. Hopkins apologetics are similar in their use of argument (and a mild, almost hidden, dialectic) to the work of William Paley (1743–1805) apologist, philosopher of religion and utilitarian, and Thomas Hartwell Horne (1780–1862), a librarian, clerk and theologian.
29. Mark Hopkins, *Lectures on the Evidences of Christianity*, before the Lowell Institute, January. See, Lecture VIII, "The Condition, Character and Claims of Christ," 227–57. An online edition can be accessed at the Making of America library of the University of Michigan: http://quod.lib.umich.edu/cgi/t/text/text-idx?c=moa;cc=moa;idno=ajf6183.0001.001;frm=frameset;view=toc.
30. Ibid., 229.
31. Ibid., 235.

expected; he came declaring himself to be not just a light, but the light of the world, while declaring his relationship to the whole human race. Whatever understanding the Jews who knew Jesus had of God, whatever concept of God Jesus the human spoke of, there can be no higher conception, "He taught them as one having authority, and not as the scribes, or as the philosophers who ran into subtle distinctions, and deduced everything from the nature of things . . . He spoke with the calmness, and dignity, and decision, of one who bore credentials that challenged entire deference."[32] And this, asserts Hopkins, before we even contemplate the depth and weight of his sayings and parables. The greatest amount of human activity (ideas that parallel comments by Lewis in the *Broadcast Talks*,[33] though there is no direct evidence that Lewis had read Hopkins lectures), the human efforts to be civilized and progressive has failed to actually advance the cause of humanity, or, in contemporary terms, change the human condition, the human predicament. Only conforming ourselves to the model that is Christ would change humanity.[34] And Jesus expounded the Scriptures and honored them as the word of God—he didn't dismiss the Jewish Bible as a human construct. Jesus is an admirable, altruistic, wise, and human character, yet he spoke of himself and acted in messianic terms:

> [He displayed the] qualities, and that deportment, which were appropriate to him as the Messiah and Saviour of the world. Is it possible that he who claimed to be greater than Solomon, to command legions of angels, to raise the dead, who spoke of himself as the Son of God, and as the final Judge of the world— should so move, and speak, and act, as to sustain a character compatible with these high pretensions, and yet have the condescension, and gentleness, and meekness, of Christ? And yet such is the character presented by the evangelists. There is no break, no incongruity. Like his own seamless garment, the character is one. He seems to combine, with perfect ease, these elements, apparently so incompatible.[35]

This is the dilemma at the heart of *aut Deus aut malus homo*; if he was human the messianic pretensions do not fit in with the good and altruistic, the wise and humble character bereft of all human preferment, a character that eschewed authority and power (as displayed and exercised by the Roman rulers or the Jewish priestly elite). Authority and power inevitably go hand in hand with sin, Jesus delivers his people from their sins; therefore he must be free from sin (and not just free from the corruption of worldly authority and power). But this claim—to be sinless and apart from sinners—

---

32. Ibid., 237–38.
33. "That is the key to history. Terrific energy is expended—civilisations are built up—excellent institutions devised ; but each time something goes wrong. Some fatal flaw always brings the selfish and cruel people to the top and it all slides back into misery and ruin. In fact, the machine konks. It seems to start up all right and runs a few yards, and then it breaks down. They're trying to run it on the wrong juice. That's what Satan has done to us humans." Lewis, *Broadcast Talks*, 49.
34. Hopkins, *Lectures on the Evidences of Christianity*, 242.
35. Ibid., 247–48.

has never been made by another sane and rational human being. Such a claim would be impossible for an imposter to maintain. Such a claim must come from the Christ.[36]

Therefore, Hopkins asserts, that the condition, the claims, and the character, of Jesus Christ raise the question—was he either deceived or a deceiver? Was he sincere? If he was, and given his background as a carpenter's son, then we must conclude that anyone who made such claims must be "utterly insane."[37] Such notions are, Hopkins writes, entertained by some of the most disturbed inmates of lunatic asylums—"can we conceive of wider hallucinations."[38] Hopkins concludes that either Jesus's claims were well founded or he was hopelessly unbalanced—

> No wonder those who did not believe said of him, "He hath a devil, and is mad: why hear ye him?" But then, as now, there was the unanswerable reply, "These are not the words of him that hath a devil. Can a devil open the eyes of the blind?" When we look at his discourses, at their calmness, at their deep insight and profound wisdom; when we see that the discoveries of all ages have only shed lustre upon their wisdom . . . we feel that not a voice from heaven could make it more certain that his was not a crazed, or a weak, or an unbalanced intellect.[39]

It is then even harder to believe that if he was of a sound mind that he sought to deceive all around him, and kept up the pretence—faultlessly—even when it led to his torture and death. If this were so then there is no ground of faith in goodness.

4. HENRY PARRY LIDDON

The Victorian theologian, churchman, and preacher Henry Parry Liddon[40] was fully versed in the arguments surrounding the status of Jesus Christ inherent in the statement *aut Deus aut malus homo*. In the 1866 Bampton Lectures at Oxford, which he devoted to the question of Christ's divinity, he commented how Christ's self-assertion was not just embodied in his sayings—statements that would be blasphemy coming from anyone else—but his sayings and actions together "underlie and explains his entire attitude towards his disciples, towards his countrymen, towards the human race, towards the religion of Israel."[41] This witness is found right across the Gospels, where Jesus insists that people accept him as he is, for what he is. And what he is, is revealed not just by what he says but by his actions and the whole demeanor of his attitude towards those around him from the poorest of the poor to the great and powerful in Israel (the high priests, the Scribes, Pharisees, and Sadducees) and Rome (Pilate and the occupying forces).

36. Ibid., 251.
37. Ibid., 254.
38. Ibid.
39. Ibid.
40. Revd. Henry Parry Liddon (1829–90), theologian, graduate of Christ Church, Oxford, Anglican priest, became Vice Principal of Cuddesdon College from 1854. The 1866 Bampton Lectures on the doctrine of the divinity of Christ established his considerable reputation as a preacher. He became a Canon of St Paul's Cathedral in 1870.
41. Liddon, "Preface to the Second Edition." *The Divinity of Our Lord and Saviour Jesus Christ*, xii.

i. Christus, si non Deus, non bonus

If this is not so, and Jesus Christ is not God, then he is by no means good. This man stands or falls by his deeds, actions, and demeanor. Therefore: "A man must either base such self-assertion on its one sufficient justification, by accepting the Church's faith in the Deity of Christ; or he must regard it as fatal to the moral beauty of Christ's Human character—*Christus, si non Deus, non bonus*."[42] We cannot, therefore, admire the moral beauty and wisdom of Jesus if we do not take seriously the divine ontological status that is integral to his moral character. Indeed his status is revealed by his moral character: "*Christus, si non Deus, non bonus*" ("Christ, if not God, is not good"). Therefore any value we may read from the sayings and actions of Jesus is because he is the Son of God and Son of Man. If he is not God then by what evidence, value, or supposition do we consider him good?

Liddon comments that we must not take Christ's divinity for granted. There were among those he was addressing—and still are today—many who refute Jesus's claims. Liddon is well aware of the detractors and their objections. Those denying Christ must be taken seriously. Their objections must be addressed because asserting Jesus's divinity involves grave responsibility. In answer to Jesus's question, "Who do you say that I am?"[43] Liddon asserted that there were essentially three groups: those who unquestioningly saw and accepted Jesus as God incarnate; then there were the vast majority of his countryman, as he put it, who shrank from a rejection of orthodox Christianity, yet were puzzled and skeptical of these assertions associated with Jesus as the Christ; and, third, the relatively large group of intellectuals who rejected the concept of incarnation and revelation. This third group, an intellectual élite, issuing from the Age of Reason and the Enlightenment, would prefer to keep God—if "god" exists—as some impersonal force outside the universe:

> There are others, and, it may be fared, a larger class than is often supposed, who have made up their minds against the claims of divine revelation altogether. They may admit the existence of a Supreme Being, in some shadowy sense, an infinite mind, or as a resistless force. They may deny that there is any satisfactory reason for holding that any such being exists at all. But whether they are theists or atheists, they resent the idea of any interference from on high in the human world, and accordingly they denounce the supernatural, on *àpriori* grounds. The trustworthiness of Scripture as an historical record is to their minds sufficiently disproved by the undoubted fact, that its claim to credit is staked upon the possibility of certain extraordinary miracles. When that possibility is denied, Jesus Christ must either be pronounced to be a charlatan, or a person of whose real words and actions no trustworthy account has been transmitted to us.[44]

Liddon's argument is that Jesus is God incarnate. If we reject his status, the very nature of his being (because of a range of deistic, theistic, or atheistic, viewpoints that issued from the Age of Reason and the Enlightenment), then there are two options open

---

42. Ibid., xii–xiii.
43. Matt 16:15.
44. Liddon, *The Divinity of Our Lord and Saviour Jesus Christ*, xiii.

5. aut Deus aut malus homo II: The Theological Tradition

to us: either Jesus is a charlatan (a pretender who swindled his followers out of the truth—which is a more nuanced way of saying he was *malus*, a liar, bad, or evil), or the biblical account is flawed—a true account of his words and actions has not been conveyed to us. Liddon's bipartite proposition is between truth and untruth: Jesus is God incarnate or he is a liar, or Scripture is a liar. If we do not accept the biblical account as genuine and accurate, despite some mythical elements, then we reject God's revelation to us. And if we reject God's revelation we are left with an infinite number of "gods" of our own making, "gods" and idols that won't interfere with us, won't trouble us, "gods" and idols that are really only a projection of our deepest fears and desires, "gods" and idols that cannot save. The key, certainly for Liddon, is in what he terms the trustworthiness of Scripture.

ii. "Our Lord's Divinity as Witnessed by his Consciousness"

Liddon examines this thesis is some detail in the fourth lecture, which he entitles, "Our Lord's Divinity as Witnessed by his Consciousness."[45] At the heart of the Gospel accounts is the consciousness, the personhood of Jesus; this is what is important in considering the nature of being of Jesus—God or man. Liddon acknowledges that there is, to a degree, a dilemma. This dilemma is between the Christ of dogma and the Christ of history; however, if this appears dialectical then we must see the Christ of history subsumed into the Christ of dogma. We must accept that the dogma of the universal church is correct, and is historical. The incarnation may not be obvious to our innate religious ideas; it may appear at times to be an inaccessible abstraction.[46] However, the incarnation is intimately intertwined with the resurrection, and resurrection is at the heart of the truth of Christianity: reject the resurrection and we reject Christianity.[47] The resurrection is the chief amongst the miracles that relate to Jesus's divinity.[48] Liddon places great emphasis on the relationship between the miracles and Jesus's divinity; however, it is important to remember that other religious individuals during the New Testament era performed miracles and these actions were not necessarily taken as a hallmark of their divinity. The miracles of Jesus are to be seen in the context of his life and the other evidence that points to his divinity. The miracles are part of the mysteries of Christ's life on earth, a life that implied that "his person was superhuman . . . thus the Christ of dogma is the Christ of history . . . as the Gospel narratives stand, they present a block of difficulties to humanitarian theories; and these difficulties can only be removed by mutilations of the narrative so wholesale and radical as to destroy."[49] Therefore, we do not necessarily need to be orthodox believing Christians to see that asserting Christ's divinity is the fairest interpretation of the text if we are going to respect the text and not deconstruct it into oblivion.[50] The problem comes when we

---

45. Ibid., "Lecture IV Our Lord's Divinity as Witnessed by his Consciousness," 153–208.
46. Ibid., 155.
47. Ibid., 156.
48. Ibid., 158.
49. Ibid., 160 & 161–62.
50. Ibid., 162.

try to assert "the perfection of Jesus's moral character, while denying the historical reality of his miracles."[51] Liddon asks why the exponents of a merely human Jesus, a humanitarian prophet and moral teacher, do not question why Jesus never challenged his disciples projecting onto him these miraculous happenings if he was merely human and the miracles did not happen. Was he, Liddon asks, the ignorant victim or the promoter of a crude superstition; was he passive and unresisting or conniving? If either is correct can we still uphold this Jesus as the moral ideal of humanity, a moral paradigm?[52] We cannot be neutral to the miraculous element in the Gospels.

iii. The Moral Character of Jesus?

If Jesus's divinity is witnessed to by his, in Liddon's term, consciousness, then what do we make of his personality, his moral character? What was the state of his being conscious, of his self-awareness in his mind evident from how he interacted with people and with the world? Talk of moral character is very Victorian; today in the postmodern West people typically do not seek a righteous and good moral character—ethics are utilitarian and consequential. Despite the heavy Victorian morality that underpins Liddon's phrasing, there is a serious and important question here: what do we make of Jesus's self-awareness and self-perception, how does he come across to other people? The question then is what we can say about the moral character of Jesus in relation to the question of his divinity. What was Jesus's understanding of himself in relation to and in conversation with his disciples and his followers? What allusions did he make to the subject of his personality, his character?[53] This, for Liddon, is the heart of the matter. Given that the first stage of Christ's teaching is mainly ethical then we are concerned with fundamental moral truth. The Sermon on the Mount lays down the highest law of holiness. Jesus enforces this absolute morality—he demands that those listening be perfect as our Father in heaven is perfect (Matt 5:48). Do we detect any unworthiness, humility, or personal compromise in Jesus? No; he makes no concession to being, like his listeners, human and endowed with the ability to struggle to achieve moral perfection.[54] There is no distance between himself and his message. There is no confession of personal shortcomings; no hint of his own personal unworthiness. Liddon notes that Jesus never once confesses to being sinful; and he never once asks for pardon: "He challenges his enemies to convince him of sin. He declares positively that he does always the will of the Father. Even when speaking of himself as man, he always refers to eternal life as his inalienable possession. It might, so perchance we think, be the illusion of a moral dullness, if only he did not penetrate the sin of others with such relentless analysis."[55] We are forced to conclude that he has a sense of perfect sinlessness; an absolute sinlessness unknown to our human experience—this is a moral being unique in human history. Therefore, there is an authoritative character to

51. Ibid., 162–63.
52. Ibid., 163.
53. Ibid.
54. Ibid., 165–66.
55. Ibid., 167.

5. aut Deus aut malus homo II: The Theological Tradition

Jesus's teaching.[56] Jesus also has the authority to revise the, as Liddon terms it, Sinaitic revelation—the law given to Moses on Mount Sinai. He does, as the Gospels assert, have authority not like that exhibited by the Scribes who reasoned and explained, who balanced argument with argument, who appealed to what Liddon terms the critical and verifying faculties of those who heard them. But what of Jesus?—

> Here is a teacher who sees truth intuitively, and announces it simply, without condescending to recommend it by argument. He is a teacher, moreover, not of truth obvious to all, but of truth which might have seemed to the men who first heard it to be what we should call paradoxical. He condemns in the severest language the doctrine and the practice of the most influential religious authorities among his countrymen. He takes up instinctively a higher position than he assigns to any who had preceded him in Israel.[57]

Therefore, it is not just the explicit claims to divinity that are usually cited from John's Gospel that Liddon relies on but this whole manner, this approach which is uncompromisingly not merely human—that is human in terms of our normal expectations. This demeanor, this approach, would be of moral superiority, even arrogance, but for who he was. This in part is why Jesus provoked such unfriendly scrutiny amongst those of the religious authorities whom he encountered.[58]

In the second stage of Jesus's teaching we are faced with his self-assertion, indeed the persistency of Christ's self-assertion.[59] Jesus persistently asserts the real character of himself, his position in relation to God and humanity, and his claims upon the soul of humanity. He speaks of himself as the light of the world, a world darkened by sin; he claims to be the judge of all mankind (we cannot ignore the force of his claim to be not just a, but *the* universal judge). He encourages people to trust in him in the way they would trust in God. In this context, asserts Liddon, the upper room discourses (John chapters 13–17), the sorrows and perplexities, in the upper room are representative. What are we to make of these words, the length of this discourse? In contrast to the developing "liberal" tradition in biblical studies, which claimed these discourses were fabricated, Liddon comments that, "We cannot deny that he used words which have substantially the same meaning. We cannot deny that he called himself King, Master, and judge of men; that he promised to give rest to the weary and the heavy-laden; that he instructed his followers to hope for life from feeding on his body and his blood."[60] These comments and the demands of Christ upon the human soul would be intolerable if he was only a man. The title Son of Man, relating to his humanity, is because he is more than human, he is to judge us precisely because he is a man. It is, comments Liddon, impossible to reflect on the claims of Jesus in relation to the Last Judgment without feeling that if he was human then these words should never have been spoken; if he is God incarnate then these words "carry us forward irresistibly to

56. Ibid., 169.
57. Ibid.
58. Ibid., 170–71.
59. Ibid., 172–76.
60. Ibid., 175.

a truth beyond and above itself."[61] This is precisely because Jesus regards those who come to him as belonging to him, his own—"in virtue of an existing right."[62] Christ's claims are therefore intolerable if he is only, or merely, even fully, human.

This relationship of judgment and ownership in relation to humanity is confirmed by his relationship with God as Father. Jesus places himself on terms of equality with the Father. This is two-fold: he claims what Liddon terms a parity of working power; and he claims an equal right to the homage of mankind. Therefore Christ reveals his Godhead to the apostles, and simultaneously he reveals his Godhead to the Jewish people—more pertinently to the Jewish religious authorities (it is this religious elite that is referred to in John's Gospel as "the Jews").[63] Therefore, we have the reaction of "the Jews," not only because he broke the Sabbath but because he made himself equal with God by claiming God was his own Father (John 5:18). It is this claim to work on the Sabbath that point to his true identity: the Son is to be honored as the Father.[64]

Jesus's relationship with God the Father goes deeper than this. There is Christ's claim to be one with the Father; this oneness with the Father is essential and indispensible to what we see and know of Jesus.

> Beyond this assertion of an equal operative Power with the Father, and of an equal right to the homage of mankind, is our Lord's revelation of his absolute oneness of essence with the Father. The Jews gathered around him at the Feast of Dedication in the Porch of Solomon, and pressed him to tell them whether he was the Christ or not.* Our Lord referred them to the teaching which they had heard, and to the miracles which they had witnessed in vain.[65]
>
> (* : John 10:22–25.)

Christ's consciousness is of having existed before his human birth—"Before Abraham was 'I Am'"(John 8:58); Christ affirms that he came down from heaven, however, Liddon comments that pre-existence alone, does not confirm divinity.[66]

According to John's Gospel "the Jews" understood Jesus to be assuming divine honors, which is why they went to stone him to death—the capital sentence decreed against blasphemy by the Mosaic law.[67] Jesus merely reasons with them, getting them to see their own "real or assumed grounds, and so to bring them back to a point at which they were forced to draw for themselves the very inference which had just roused their indignation."[68] Therefore, what the Father is to the Son, the Son is to the Father. As Liddon points out, "the Jews (Jewish religious authorities)" did not understand Jesus's claim to be one with the Father, they did not take these claims as implying a relationship in a moral, spiritual, or mystical sense, where he had a heightened sense of the divine which affected all he said and did; no, they believed him to mean that he was

61. Ibid., 177.
62. Ibid.
63. Ibid., 179–81.
64. Ibid., 183.
65. Ibid., 185.
66. Ibid., 188–89.
67. Ibid., 186–87.
68. Ibid., 187.

5. aut Deus aut malus homo II: The Theological Tradition

ontologically at one with the Father, that he was the divine person. Jesus did not seek to contradict them on this assumption, and the accusation of blasphemy issued from it.[69] If the religious authorities condemned him it was not for being a false prophet and false Messiah, as Liddon states, it was because he claimed literal divinity.[70] This is confirmed by Jesus's testimony before the Sanhedrin (Matt 23:63–65).

iv. Christ's Self Assertion and His Character

It is the relationship between Christ's assertion of divinity, the self-disclosure of his being, and his character that compels Liddon to state that if Christ is not God, then he is by no means good: *Christus, si non Deus, non bonus*.[71] To arrive at this point Liddon examines the sincerity of Jesus Christ, the unselfishness of Jesus Christ, and the humility of Jesus Christ; and how this compares with "ordinary" human beings.[72] Therefore, he is compelled to ask three questions—"Is Jesus Christ humble, if he is not God?" "Is Jesus Christ unselfish, if he is not God?" and "Is Jesus Christ sincere, if he is not God?"[73] Liddon is forced to conclude that Christ, if sincere, must be divine. A close analysis of the human life of Jesus reveals a portrait unlike any that has been seen before or since—there is no trace of *malus* about this man, no evil intent, no deception or duplicity, no psychological disorder, we have a harmonious representation of the normal moral nature, yet his actions and speech disclose him as divine.[74] He was sincere; he believed in what he said. In response to accusation of demonic possession or deceit he merely exposes the deception and evil intent in others. Therefore, Liddon asks, what are we to make of these integral features, these character traits, if—in the context of what he said and did—we choose to deny that he is God?[75] "If Christ is God as well as Man, his language falls into its place, and all is intelligible; but if you deny his divinity, you must conclude that some of the most precious sayings in the Gospel are but the outbreak of a preposterous self-laudation; they might well seem to breathe the very spirit of another Lucifer."[76] It is at this point that Liddon gets close to the mad or bad elements in Lewis's trilemma. Liddon writes of Jesus' perpetual self-assertion, which no ordinary human would do in the context of his chosen role as victim and sacrifice. As a man, his death loses its meaning.

Christ's Godhead is warranted by his character; the Christ of history is the Christ of dogma, writes Liddon. The human glory, as he terms it, fades if we deny Jesus's divinity: he is only perfect man if he is truly God.[77] Therefore, in conclusion Liddon asserts that, "The choice really lies between the hypothesis of conscious and culpable insincerity, and the belief that Jesus speaks literal truth and must be taken

---

69. Ibid., 189.
70. Ibid., 193.
71. Ibid., 206.
72. Ibid., 197–99.
73. Ibid., 199–201.
74. Ibid., 195.
75. Ibid., 198.
76. Ibid., 199.
77. Ibid., 205.

at his word . . . It is no hardship to faith that we cannot deny the divinity of Jesus, without casting a slur upon his human character."[78] Christianity as doctrine, creed, and life, as church and as salvation, depends completely upon the personal character of its founder—Jesus of Nazareth, the Christ. And this personal character is not good if he was not God: *aut Deus aut malus homo*.[79]

v. Did Lewis read Liddon?

There are several points Liddon makes that Lewis also offers at some point in his discussion of *aut Deus aut malus homo*. For example, Liddon notes how many atheists or deists "resent the idea of any interference from on high in the human world, and accordingly they denounce the supernatural, on *àpriori* grounds."[80] Lewis makes the same point during his protracted conversion. Lewis concluded, as God drew near to him around 1929–30, that at the centre of Christianity was what he termed a transcendental interferer. Lewis commented that, "there was no region even in the innermost depth of one's soul which one could surround with a barbed wire fence and guard with a notice, 'No Admittance'!"[81] Lewis also lays the same emphasis, as does Liddon, on how Jesus never confesses to being sinful or asking pardon.[82] There are many markers between the two writers that suggest that Lewis very possibly did read Liddon's work. Liddon's reputation and fame as a Victorian writer and preacher—of orthodoxy—was great, particularly given these Bampton Lectures. Plenty of copies would still have been available in the Oxford of Lewis's youth. However, this cannot be proved, and there is little reason to prove a connection other than it does pose an example of Lewis's wide reading and how his theology developed in an orthodox Anglican tradition; furthermore that his understanding of his "Mad, Bad, or God" trilemma was rooted in the tradition of *aut Deus aut malus homo*.

5. G. K. CHESTERTON

Liddon's examination of *aut Deus aut malus homo* is probably the most extensive analysis, however, it is in the work of G. K. Chesterton that we find the source, in many ways, of Lewis's appropriation and argument. Lewis comments in *Surprised by Joy* that in Chesterton's *The Everlasting Man* he had read a version of human history that finally made sense. But as this was during his pre-Christian period, he had to dismiss Chesterton's faith as having no bearing on his worldview.[83] Lewis's view at the time, and this was in 1926, was "that Christianity itself was very sensible, apart from its

---

78. Ibid., 206. (Liddon acknowledges in a footnote that the source for this wording was derived from, Guizot, *Méditations sur l'Essence de la Religjon Chrétienne* (Paris, 1864), 324–26. See, Guizot, *Meditations on the actual state of Christianity and on the attacks which are now being made upon it*.)

79. Ibid., 208.

80. Liddon, *The Divinity of Our Lord and Saviour Jesus Christ*, "Preface to the Second Edition," xiii.

81. Lewis, *Surprised by Joy*, 166.

82. Ibid., 167. Lewis commented that, "he [Jesus] denied all sin of himself." See also, Lewis, *Reflections on the Psalms*, 117.

83. Lewis, *Surprised by Joy*, 216, also, 206.

5. aut Deus aut malus homo II: The Theological Tradition

Christianity."[84] Furthermore, he commented that not long after reading *The Everlasting Man* he was confronted by a fervent atheist within a tutorial who commented "that the evidence for the historicity of the Gospels was really surprisingly good."[85] This was during Lewis's Hegelian period. Later, in 1945, speaking to church youth leaders, Lewis reiterated the importance of Chesterton as the source of his use of *aut Deus aut malus homo*.[86]

Chesterton's *The Everlasting Man*, asserts a creedal Christ without compromise.[87] The material we are interested in is entitled "The Strangest Story in the World." Which immediately invokes paradox and the unbelievable? Chesterton examines the character of Jesus—a Christ who was and is the most merciful of judges, a sympathetic friend; this is beyond the merely philosophical or historical. Chesterton warns against the fact that Jesus has been "swamped in cheap generalizations."[88] But we must be prepared to work through these to find the real Christ, the one who haunts us like a ghost, which we can be informed of from the New Testament account. Chesterton notes how the character of Jesus is the very last for us to associate with the intoxication of megalomania, and yet "such steep and staggering megalomania as might be associated in that claim"[89] causes us to reconsider. Humanity may not like what Jesus says; humanity may think it's not what a normal person would say and yet humanity refuses to accept the veracity of this man's claims. Judging by the sayings and actions of Jesus this is not the sort of man—if he were merely a man—whom we would expect to suffer from such intoxication. Why? For Chesterton Jesus, despite what he said, does not exhibit "the mark of the self-deluding sensationalist in religion."[90] No other prophet or religious teacher of the order of Jesus ever made such a claim, and it would seem impossible and preposterous for such a religious leader, guru or prophet to have such a claim projected onto him: "Even if the Church had mistaken his meaning, it would still be true that no other historical tradition except the Church had ever even made the same mistake. Muslims did not misunderstand Muhammad and suppose he was Allah. Jews did not misinterpret Moses and identify him with Jehovah. Why was this claim alone exaggerated unless this alone was made? Even if Christianity was one vast universal blunder, it is still a blunder as solitary as the incarnation."[91] If all religions are equal, asserts Chesterton, then we may suppose that this is a fixed falsity. But clearly all religions are not equal. The greater a person is, the less likely s/he is to assert such a claim as Jesus does—only secretive or self-centered people do, not someone of the ministry of Jesus, comments Chesterton. Only the Pharaohs and Roman Emperors,

---

84. Ibid., 216.
85. Ibid.
86. Lewis, "Christian Apologetics," 74–75.
87. G. K. Chesterton, *The Everlasting Man* (1925. Reprint. Vancouver: Regent College Publishing, 2006).
88. Chesterton, *The Everlasting Man*, 185.
89. Ibid., 187–88.
90. Ibid., 188.
91. Ibid. N.b. Chesterton uses the archaic medieval spellings/variants of Mahomet and Mahomedans, which I have here changed to the modern spellings/variants of Muhammad and Muslims.

for example, got anywhere near making such a claim and then it was to be one of the "gods," nothing approaching the one true living God, the God above all Gods that the Jews bore witness to, and suffered for at the hands of the nations that surrounded them. Jesus was no solitary narcissistic megalomaniac pseudo-divine autocratic ruler. There are rare cases of such men or women outside of the ranks of the Emperor Caligula but, and here Chesterton moves into the question of sanity-insanity, they are to be found in asylums, "in padded cells possibly in strait waistcoats"; such deluded individuals are locked away "under very crude and clumsy laws about lunacy."[92] Because of the manner in which such individuals are imprisoned within their delusions, writes Chesterton, a genuine delusion of divinity may subsist. However, you do not find this among religious leaders, gurus, great philosophers, and prophets. Was Jesus amongst the former group—the isolated and deluded, the mentally ill—or do we consider him among, at the very least, the wise and profound, compassionate religious leaders?

> For nobody supposes that Jesus of Nazareth was that sort of person. No modern critic in his five wits thinks that the preacher of the Sermon on the Mount was a horrible half-witted imbecile that might be scrawling stars on the walls of a cell. No atheist or blasphemer believes that the author of the Parable of the Prodigal Son was a monster with one mad idea like a Cyclops with one eye. Upon any possible historical criticism, he must be put higher in the scale of human beings than that. Yet by all analogy we have really to put him there or else in the highest place of all.[93]

Chesterton, therefore, uses a sort of common sense logic, an appeal to the reasonableness of what we see and know of Jesus. If we try to balance out the claims and possibilities we are left with a dilemma. We cannot categorize this man as deluded or insane because the wisdom and strength of his teaching and actions, which are above what we would expect from the everyday man or woman. His megalomaniac divine behavior and assertions separate him from the ordinary man or woman. What are we to do? We can accept him for what he was and is, or we can try to invent some other excuse or explanation. The only satisfactory way in which these two characters have been combined is for Chesterton in the creed—as very God and very man.

For Chesterton Jesus is precisely what a deluded person never is—he is wise, he is a good judge, he is compassionate, he does not exhibit the simplicity of a madman, he is clearly a highly complex character on a human level. If God is God, and humanity is humanity then we are left with a paradox: as we approach a point we are receding. Socrates, Chesterton notes, realized that as a wise man he knew nothing—the more he knew the more he did not know. But then, "No two things could possibly be more different than the death of Socrates and the death of Christ."[94]

---

92. Ibid., 189.
93. Ibid., 190.
94. Ibid., 193.

5. aut Deus aut malus homo II: The Theological Tradition

6. CONTEMPORARY DEVELOPMENTS

Variations on *aut Deus aut malus homo* have been used often by Presbyterian or Evangelical ministers and preachers in the nineteenth and twentieth centuries from Reuben Archer Torrey (1856–1928) to the contemporary evangelical preacher Josh McDowell (b. 1939). McDowell has rephrased Lewis's trilemma as, "Lunatic, Liar, or Lord."[95] This has been a successful ploy, it raises the profile of the question when so many seek to believe Jesus was just a good man: "Jesus's distinct claims of being God eliminate the popular ploy of skeptics who regard him as just a good moral man or a prophet who said a lot of profound things."[96] McDowell notes how it is not just the teachings, and for that matter the miracles, that make Jesus so distinct and remarkable, it is the man himself. When faced with the trilemma McDowell asks which is more probable, that Jesus managed somehow to keep up the pretence (the "liar" option) faultlessly; or, given what we know about psychological disorder today, that he genuinely believed himself to be the God of Israel (the "lunatic" option); or that he was what he revealed himself to be (the "Lord" option).

Contemporary theologians and philosophers are generally cautious about such confident assertions; however, the basic proposition is often used but phrased in a more nuanced manner. For example, "Therefore, the question of Jesus identity, role, or relationship to the divine forced itself on those who came in contact with him. Either he was blasphemous, a fool, or he spoke with divine authority."[97] Lewis's "Mad, Bad, or God," is popular amongst contemporary Evangelicals, and is featured as an important part in the Alpha Course, though in most of these instances there is little or no rigorous debate about the pros and cons within the argument, and rarely any acknowledgement of the theological history of the proposition in *aut Deus aut malus homo*.

The Roman Catholic philosopher Peter Kreeft has reiterated the proposition *aut Deus aut malus homo* on many occasions, often in the context of using and defending Lewis's trilemma. Kreeft asserts that if Jesus speaks the truth, then we must fall at his feet and worship him. But if he is not what he said he was then, "a mere man who wants you to worship him as God is not a good man."[98] If he is not God and knows it, then he must be considered morally and/or intellectually bad; if he doesn't know it, then he must be considered deluded, maybe even insane.

> A measure of your insanity is the size of the gap between what you think you are and what you really are. If I think I am the greatest philosopher in America, I am only an arrogant fool; if I think I am Napoleon, I am probably over the edge; if I think I am a butterfly, I am fully embarked from the sunny shores of sanity. But if I think I am God, I am even more insane because the gap between anything finite

---

95. McDowell, *Evidence Demands a Verdict*, 104.
96. McDowell, *A Ready Defence*, Ch. 21 "The Trilemma: Lord, Liar or Lunatic?," 241–45, n. 241. See also, Ch. 22 "Is Jesus both Messiah and God," 246–42.
97. Fuller and Perkins, *Who Is This Christ? Gospel Christology and Contemporary Faith*, 24.
98. Kreeft, *Fundamentals of the Faith: Essays in Christian Apologetics*. See, Ch. 1 Creed: Fundamentals of Christian Belief, §A. Fundamentals of Christian Apologetics, §8. "The Divinity of Christ," 59–63, and ref., 60.

and the infinite God is even greater than the gap between any two finite things, even a man and a butterfly.[99]

Was Jesus deluded or a deceiver? Kreeft notes the wisdom displayed in Jesus's ability to know people deep in their souls, his capacity to know the unspoken behind the outward appearance of people, his gift to heal the hurt and flaws deep in people's souls. This, writes Kreeft, is not what we would expect from a deluded man or a deceiver. Furthermore his love, his compassion, his ability to generate forgiveness in those who followed him, the manner in which he relates to people, this does not reflect the talents, character or abilities of a deluded man or a deceiver. Likewise, Jesus's ability to astonish, to be creative, none of this fits with a picture of Jesus as insane or evil: "No one who knows both the Gospels and human beings can seriously entertain the possibility that Jesus was a liar or a lunatic, a bad man."[100] Peter Kreeft and Ronald Tacelli have expanded Josh McDowell's adaptation ("Lunatic, Liar or Lord") from a trilemma to what they call a *quadrilemma*: "Lunatic, Liar, Lord, or Legend"; however, this element of legend seems to apply more to the nature of the scriptural narrative than to Jesus himself—unless those who propose legend as an explanation are saying that Jesus simply did not ever exist![101] Does a *quadrilemma* really tell us any more about Jesus than the bipartite dilemma inherent in *aut Deus malus homo*?

An exception to the superficial, and sometimes trite, treatment of the "Mad, Bad, or God" argument by those who can be broadly considered to be American Evangelicals, can be found in the work of the American Christian philosopher Stephen T. Davis. Together with Gerald O'Collins SJ and David Kendall SJ, Davis worked on an Interdisciplinary Symposium on the incarnation of the Son of God, Easter 2000, held in New York.[102] Davis spoke on his analysis of the philosophical structure of Lewis's trilemma, which we will consider later. Davis is relatively rare in being an academic philosopher-theologian who takes Lewis's trilemma seriously, regarding it as a demonstration of the rationality of the belief in the incarnation.[103]

7. "UNBALANCED LIAR," "POSSESSED," OR "THE GOD OF ISRAEL": THE JOHANNINE TRILEMMA

Gerald O'Collins SJ has summarized the twentieth-century developments of the bipartite dilemma, *aut Deus aut malus homo*, into a trilemma. O'Collins sees these developments essentially in the work of Chesterton and Lewis, and in the case of the latter, the subsequent American Evangelical developments. However, he has also identified the roots of the Chesterton-Lewis trilemma in John's Gospel:

---

99. Ibid., 59–63.
100. Ibid.
101. Kreeft and Tacelli, *Handbook of Christian Apologetics*, 161–74.
102. Davis, Kendall SJ & O'Collins (eds.), *The Incarnation. An Interdisciplinary Symposium on the Incarnation of the Son of God*.
103. Davis, "Was Jesus Mad, Bad or God?" 2nd ed., 149–71.

5. aut Deus aut malus homo II: The Theological Tradition

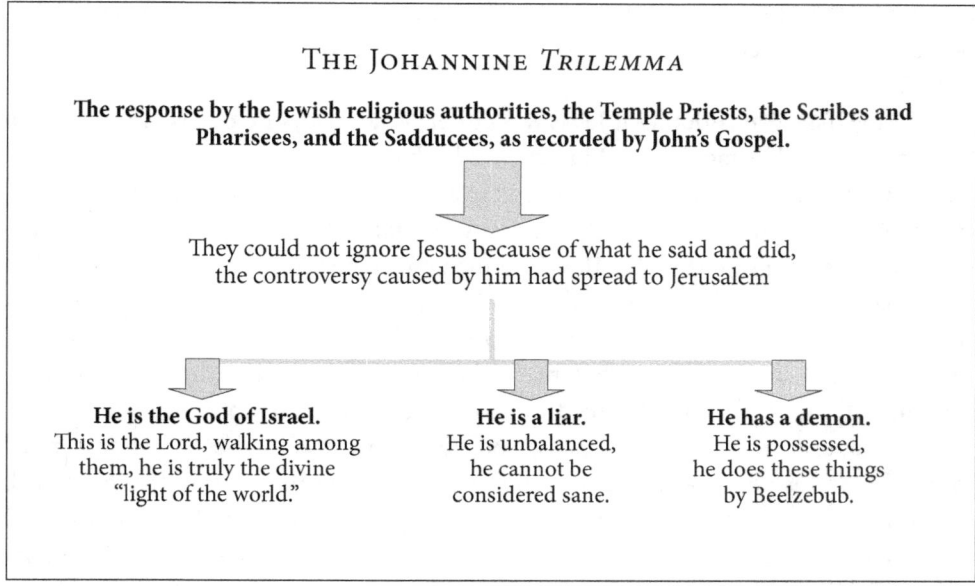

Figure 7: The Johannine Trilemma

In the twentieth century, G. K. Chesterton and, even more clearly C. S. Lewis developed a "bad," "mad" or "(Son of) God" argument. The claims Jesus made to an authority that has to be acknowledged as divine, leaves us with three possibilities: he was morally and religiously wicked; or he was out of his mind; or his claims were true and he genuinely was the Son of God come among us. At the end of the first century AD, John's Gospel presents a similar choice in Jesus's controversy with his critics; either Jesus is a "liar," or he is unbalanced and "has a demon," or else he is truly the divine "Light of the world."[104]

O'Collins ties the idea of a trilemma into John's Gospel: those who wanted to stone Jesus were not motivated by his miraculous signs and healings but because they interpreted his actions and sayings as evidence that he claimed to be God (John 10:31–39)—not just that he claimed to be at one with God, but that he acted as if he was truly the God of Israel. Thus, Jesus is either falsehood of varying degrees or he was demonically possessed (John 8:49 and 10:21); however, it is important to remember that the accusation of demonic possession was also leveled at John the Baptist (Matt 11:18 and Luke 7:33). Therefore, those who represented the Jewish religious authorities who encountered Jesus perceived that they were faced with a dilemma, which was like the Chesterton-Lewis trilemma. There is similar concern in Mark's Gospel: "When his family heard about this, they went to take charge of him, for they said, 'He is out of

---

104. O'Collins SJ, *Incarnation*, see, Ch. 11 "The Credibility of the Incarnation," 125–33, specifically, 130–31.

his mind.' And the teachers of the law who came down from Jerusalem said, 'He is possessed by Beelzebub! By the prince of demons he is driving out demons' " (Mark 3:20–22).

So Lewis's proposition that Jesus was either "Mad, Bad, or God" is grounded in a long theological heritage of *aut Deus aut malus homo* (a dialectical dilemma), which itself is rooted in Scripture: Jesus's question to all of us, "But who do you say that I am?" (Matt 16:15). But more pertinently *aut Deus aut malus homo* is grounded not in the either-or dilemma so characteristic of the theological history we have considered but in a tripartite question in John's Gospel: the Johannine trilemma. John's Gospel records the response by the Jewish religious authorities (the Temple priests, the Scribes, the Pharisees, etc.) and their representatives who regarded Jesus as a threat. They could not ignore him, so they were forced to choose between three options: either he was an "unbalanced liar"; or he was "possessed"; or he was the God of Israel descended to dwell with his people—he was the Son of God and the Son of Man (terms we will define in the next chapter). Many contemporary, including Gerald O'Collins, can perceive what is at the heart of this speculation: the key to the question of the divinity of Jesus lies in what he was and is, and the key to the nature of what and who Jesus was and is (his ontology) lies with John's Gospel. If we accept Christ as God incarnate we must accept John's Gospel; if we reject this man's divinity it is through a rejection of the fourth Gospel.

Therefore, we must now turn to examine the arguments for self-disclosure, that Jesus gave himself away as God incarnate. We must also include an assessment of the value of John's Gospel, but also consider the arguments against divinity, the arguments for seeing Jesus as just an ordinary man. We then need to examine the proposition in its contemporary context. Did Jesus actually make such claims for himself? If not the argument collapses. A review of the scriptural evidence is important, as is the biblical scholarship. Likewise we will examine contemporary philosophical objections to Lewis's proposition. This digression is necessary given the academic opposition to Lewis's trilemma, opposition which we can demonstrate to be consider invalid.

6

aut Deus aut malus homo III:
Divine Self-Disclosure

SYNOPSIS:
What is the theological background to *aut Deus aut malus homo* (either God, or a bad man)? What underpins C. S. Lewis's trilemma? What is the logicality of this proposition? In defence of Lewis's proposition we need to consider what the evidence is that this man Jesus of Nazareth, the carpenter's son, was the God of Israel walking among his chosen people? What are the arguments for divine self-disclosure? What is self-disclosure? Disclosing our identity is a complicated and paradoxical activity, even more so considering the gradual unfolding of revelation in Jesus. Lewis writes of the transposed reality of divine Sonship. This can be understood from the markers for self-disclosure evident in the witness of the New Testament writers, but also the Hebrew expectations within the intertestamental tradition: i. Sonship, identity and becoming; ii. incarnation (he was not aware of being *only* human); iii. the expectation and understanding of messiahship (though the title Messiah did not necessarily imply that he was the second person of the Trinity); iv. the categories of "Son of God" and "Son of Man"; and, v. the "I am" sayings.

What Jesus was and is can only be understood in the context of the first-century Jewish religious categories that Jesus was born into. For the New Testament scholar N. T. Wright these are Torah, Wisdom, and Temple: the "Tabernacling Presence"—the Son of God with his people. Therefore, we need to consider what Lewis understood about the titles "Son of God" and "Son of Man" given the strong assertive proclamation in his trilemma of this man's divinity. What is it about this man Jesus that gives him away as identified with God, from God, as God, at one with God? At the heart of this understanding is incarnation. What do these terms mean in the first-century Jewish religious tradition? For Lewis, Jesus is who he reveals himself to be. Reason and logic are paramount here. It is, therefore, important that we examine the evidence for self-revelation. It is important that we consider the scriptural evidence. This is the biblical testimony, which can be divided in six overlapping groups: i. Jesus's self-disclosure of divinity; ii. the miracles as testimony; iii. the witness of the apostles and disciples; iv. the prefigurements of Christ's divinity in the Old Testament; v. the worship that is offered to him; and finally, vi. the audacity and manner in which Jesus forgave people their sins. Given its status as key evidence for the divinity of Jesus, this leads into an examination of the reliability of the Gospel according to John. According to John, the Jewish religious authorities sought to stone Jesus to death—not for his works, not for the healings and miracles, but for blasphemy because he as a mere man claimed to be the God of Israel. So John's Gospel is at the heart of the proposition, *aut Deus aut malus homo*: can we trust it? Is it reliable?

1. INTRODUCTION

We have examined in relative detail what Lewis wrote on several occasions in his popular apologetics and in his serious philosophical theology on *aut Deus aut malus homo*, and how the mad, bad, or God, proposition is only one approach he took. We have also examined the theological history of this proposition—rooted as it is in Jesus's question to Peter, "But who do you say that I am?" and the tripartite reaction by the Jewish religious authorities to Jesus—for them he was either the God of Israel descended to come among them, or he was unbalanced, or he was possessed. Therefore given Lewis's reliance upon it we may ask what is the evidence for Jesus of Nazareth to be more than merely human? What is the structure of Lewis's proposition? We need to examine what he said in much more depth.

2. SELF-DISCLOSURE—UNDERSTANDING AND IDENTITY?

i. A Declaration of Identity?

It is important to bear in mind that Jesus does not *directly* announce who he is; he does not wear a security tag clipped to his cloak declaring his credentials, with a tamper proof holographic seal from the Father. He does not need to because he is not on the same level as the rest of humanity even though he is fully human; as God incarnate he is bound to relate to people on a different level. Jesus is revealed as who he is: we are talking here about revelation being disclosed. Jesus divulges, unveils, who he is simply by the way he speaks to and relates to people. This is divine self-disclosure: revelation is relational. Jesus's identity is unveiled progressively (John's Gospel is probably best at presenting this); self-disclosure is the gradually revealing of who he is in the form of his purpose. We cannot know, let alone understand, who and what Jesus is outside of his purpose. This is true of many people from teachers to fireman. This is especially pertinent to monarchs and priests: such people are defined by God and before God by their role. In Jesus's case this gradual unveiling is discreet and controlled; moments of revelation operate as unspoken indicators to Jesus's identity, but also to the nature of his being as both fully human and fully divine. This is ontological, it is about the very nature of being that is someone, not just status assumed, or humanely conferred. Self-disclosure consists of moments of veiling and unveiling. At times these moments are relatively obscure indications of Jesus's deity, his oneness with the Father; at other times this is more explicit. Self-disclosure is both the conscious and unconscious act of revealing more about ourselves to others; self-disclosure is often controlled, but it may equally be that through unconscious actions and thoughts, failures and successes, aspirations and goals, fears, dreams and feelings we give away more of who and what we are. This is probably at its truest in how we respond to other people, therefore revelation is relational. However, it is probably impossible for someone to write a perfect account of the identity disclosed about another person because of their own subjective limited understanding, but also because of the veiling-unveiling dialectic we have encountered already. There is, therefore, an incompleteness to the Gospel portraits of Jesus (note the plural—we are meant to have four portraits, not one, of Jesus: four pictures, biographical accounts, by different people). These Gospel portraits of Jesus lack the artificiality and falseness we would expect to see if the Evangelists had simply made up the story of Jesus's divinity.[1] The Gospel portraits are too consistent, yet inconsistent, to be an invention. As Lewis often would argue, if there is not a strong historical-biographical element to the Gospels, if the portraits are false, if we are to dismiss much of the Jesus of the Gospels as a fabrication, if the Evangelists had invented something of the genre of realistic fantasy, then this is entirely without precedent for its time.

ii. The Tabernacle Presence—Signals of Transcendence

If Jesus discloses himself as the God of Israel, as Lord, what can we say about his self-identity, and his self-understanding? Indeed what can any of us say about our identity and self-understanding? How possible is it for us mere mortal humans to have a sound understanding about ourselves after the fall, tainted as we are by the effects and consequences of original sin? What is it, given Jesus's Jewish roots and religious heritage, that discloses his divinity? The New Testament scholar N. T. Wright has worked in the field of the quest for the historical Jesus, but from the perspective of an orthodox high Christology. For Wright it is the first century Jewish categories that Jesus was born into that formed much of his self-identity in his mind, these are pertinent. Wright cites "Torah," "Wisdom" and the "Tabernacle Presence" as important and formative; these are clear indicators that Jesus knew who and what he was, both in his Jewish heritage but also as the Son of God: "My case has been, and remains, that Jesus believed himself called to do and be things which, in the traditions to which he fell heir, only Israel's God, YHWH, was to do and be. I think he held this belief both with passionate and firm conviction and with the knowledge that he could be making a terrible, lunatic mistake. I do not think this in any way downplays the signals of transcendence within the Gospel narratives."[2] Christ's divinity is expressed in the Jewish context of the things that Jesus, for Wright, believed himself called to do and be. Jesus's frail humanity would have struggled with this, but he could not escape this difference in him, between him and the rest of humanity, a difference which given the Jewish religious context was highly problematic and risky: his self-disclosure got him killed. Either Jesus was and is, as Lewis puts it, the God of Israel, identified as only what YHWH could do and be, or he was mistaken—deluded or malicious. For Wright, Jesus's humanity would have doubted the sanity of this enterprise but he continued on because of the soundness of his self-understanding, which displayed a rare conviction.

1. See Burridge, *Four Gospels, One Jesus*? Burridge, whose doctoral work identified that the grammatical structure of the Gospels was the same as Graeco-Roman biography, assesses why we have four different but overlapping portraits and how this relates to revelation, but also how this respects the humanity and freedom of the four Evangelists—what Lewis called the humanity of Scripture. See also, Stanton, *The Gospels and Jesus* and *Gospel Truth: Today's Quest for Jesus of Nazareth*. See also, Adams, *Parallel Lives of Jesus*.
2. Wright, "Jesus' Self-Understanding," 47–61, specifically, 59. See also, Wright, "Jesus and the Identity of God," 42–56. Also available online: http://www.ntwrightpage.com/Wright_JIG.htm.

This self-understanding and conviction was non-existent among those around him bedevilled as they were by original sin.

A key Jewish motif in Jesus's self-identity for Wright is the Jewish understanding about the Temple. In response to critics who assert that the very concept of incarnation was new in Israel Wright comments that this was not so: the Temple was the dwelling of Israel's God in the midst of his people, and the sacrifices assured God's forgiveness—"the Temple has for too long been the forgotten factor in New Testament Christology. Omit it, and you will spend a lifetime in titles, 'figures,' and other unsatisfying by-paths. Make it central, and the whole picture will come into focus."[3] The Tabernacle,[4] as the dwelling place for the divine presence from the time of the exodus from Egypt (Exod 36:8) through to its placing in the first Temple in Jerusalem, was the dwelling-place of God among his chosen people. Jesus is the new Tabernacle because he is God incarnate: the fulfilment of revelation is the dwelling of God with humanity (Rev 21:3). The Temple and Tabernacle can, as Wright asserts, be seen as all that had gone wrong with the Jewish religion, all that opposed the breaking in of the kingdom of God; however, he also notes how, despite its drawbacks, the Temple symbolized the promise and hope of fellowship with God. Jesus then takes on this role by offering all who would believe in him the same forgiveness and fellowship—"He was acting as a one-man Temple-substitute . . . The opening charge at Jesus's 'trial' is that he had spoken against the Temple, threatening it in some way with imminent destruction . . . And John has Jesus say 'destroy this Temple, and in three days I will build it again'."[5] It is difficult for people today to appreciate just what Jesus was doing in aligning himself so much with all that the Temple was to the Jewish people, he could not have made a clearer statement that he was of God and with God—the central sanctuary within the Temple was the holy of holies; it was through the holy of holies that the Jews were forgiven their sin, it was through the Temple sacrifices that they were at-one (i.e., atonement, at-one-ment) again with the one true living God. This, for Wright, is the Tabernacling Presence.

3. C. S. LEWIS: TRANSPOSED REALITY OF DIVINE SONSHIP

Christ will share his Sonship with us, and will make us like himself. This would not be so if he were a mere mortal, deluded, or wicked: "He will share his 'sonship' with us, will make us, like himself, 'Sons of God.'"[6] It is through this uniting with humanity that the divinity of Jesus is revealed; we noted earlier how what is revealed is real "Sonship," the solid reality (Lewis's term), where the transposed human biological "sonship" is but a diagrammatic representation of it. Human familial relationships are validated by the trinitarian relationship, the co-eternal, co-existing, ever-relating, tripartite relationship of the three persons within the Godhead. But what are the markers of

---

3. Ibid., 56.
4. Tabernacle is derived from the Hebrew *mishkan*, "residence" or "dwelling place"; the English word tabernacle is derived from the Latin for tent—*tabernaculum*.
5. Wright, "Jesus' Self-Understanding," 57.
6. Lewis, Mere Christianity, 147.

6. aut Deus aut malus homo III: Divine Self-Disclosure

self-disclosure revealing this, for Lewis, transposed reality of divine Sonship? These markers emanate from the observation of the apostles, and then from the disciples and followers within the early church: first, incarnation, identity and becoming; second, the expectations of the Messiah, and messiahship; third, the titles "Son of God" and "Son of Man"; fourth, the "I am" sayings.

i. Markers of Self-Disclosure I: Sonship—Identity and Becoming

Titles given today to people, certainly in the West, are, to a degree, movable and relative; titles used to be a sound reflection of a person's identity; however, many people appear to change their identity as they change their clothes and lifestyle. The primary element of Lewis's trilemma is the divinity of Jesus of Nazareth; this divinity is at the heart of this man's identity. This is encapsulated in Jesus's Sonship before the Father. In *Beyond Personality* Lewis commented that Jesus, the Christ, "is the Son of God (whatever that means). They say that those who give him their confidence can also become Sons of God (whatever that means). They say that his death saved us from our sins (whatever that means)."[7] This immediately opens up the question of the relationship between ontology, identity, and status, bringing the question pertinently into the human realm—indeed it brings into sharp focus the relationship between the human predicament (original sin) and this Jesus. Furthermore, Lewis comments that "The Son of God became a man to enable men to become sons of God."[8] Sonship is inherent to the second person of the Trinity, yet it is also extended, because of the nature of Jesus, to humanity; more specifically, it issues from Jesus's crucifixion and resurrection. Talk of salvation in relationship to the Son of God-Son of Man raises the question for Lewis of what would have happened had humanity not rebelled (i.e., the relationship between original sin and this Sonship). Putting aside speculation, Lewis questions whether, had we not fallen, we would all have been in Christ and shared in the life of the Son.[9] Is the purpose of Jesus to restore the relationship between humanity and God lost through the fall? Living in Christ changes us, moment by moment through the Son of God/Son of Man who, Lewis confidently asserts, is human like us, yet God, like his Father. Therefore, moment by moment Jesus turns our pretence into a reality: he is beginning to turn us into the same kind of thing that he is.[10] This brings us to the centre of Lewis's trilemma, the key passage we noted earlier, where Lewis graphically pushes the question away from a nuanced mid-grey indecisive compromise to a black-or-white dilemma: "Either this man was, and is, the Son of God: or else a madman or something worse. You can shut him up for a fool, you can spit at him and kill him as a demon; or you can fall at his feet and call him Lord and God. But don't let us come with any patronising nonsense about his being a great human teacher. He hasn't left that open to us. He didn't intend to."[11] However, in maturity, in the later years of his

---

7. Lewis, *Beyond Personality*, 11.
8. Ibid., 28.
9. Ibid.
10. Ibid., 36.
11. Lewis, *Broadcast Talks*, 50–51.

life, and in the context of his philosophical theology Lewis was wise enough to state that when we proclaim that Jesus Christ is the Son of God there is inevitably distance between Jesus and God because we cannot think of the relationship in exactly the same way that we perceive of human relationships between a human father and a son, or between a parent and child. This understanding is by analogy; the relationship is real, not metaphorical or allegorical, there is no one-to-one correspondence but our flawed (transposed) way of receiving revelation means that we must "continue to see human sonship and fatherhood are still merely analogical."[12] Jesus's Sonship is real—it is the best way we can conceptualize the relationships within the Trinity, but we can only intimate any idea of this by analogy. Our relationship with Christ and therefore with the Father is, as we have seen earlier, in Lewis's analogical word picture, God descends to reascend, drawing humanity up with him: the patriarchal relationship is therefore very real, though we can only conceptualize it in the form of the analogy of Father-Son. Therefore, in terms of Lewis's treatment of the transposed reality of divine Sonship this is relational, and relationship is in the form of the drawing-up into God we encountered earlier.[13] Lewis explicitly invokes Paul on the nature of spiritual bodies and the general resurrection—our Sonship in Christ, our drawing up into the divine life is through the resurrection.[14] Lewis does not force the issue of the divinity of Christ into a trilemma lightly; it is for good reason that he provokes in the manner in which he asserts this question: if he is not God incarnate, if the crucifixion is a terrible tragic accident without meaning, if the resurrection did not happen, then it is not only this Jesus who is deluded, but we are equally lost. But we are not deluded and lost on the question of Christ's divinity and our potential salvation. We are bidden, wrote Lewis, to become sons of God, supported by grace this is something we are drawn in to.[15] To do so we must commit ourselves to Christ, we must be drawn up by Christ. Lewis wrote:

> Now the point in Christianity which gives us the greatest shock is the statement that by attaching ourselves to Christ, we can "become Sons of God." One asks "Aren't we Sons of God already? Surely the fatherhood of God is one of the main Christian ideas?" Well, in a certain sense, no doubt we are Sons of God already. I mean, God has brought us into existence and loves us and looks after us, and in that way is like a father. But when the Bible talks of our becoming Sons of God, obviously it must mean something different.[16]

Christ will share his Sonship with us, and will make us like himself. This would not be so if he were a mere mortal man, a deluded or wicked deceiver, a charlatan, or one demonically possessed. Through his divinity we are all drawn up into him to become

---

12. Lewis, "The Language of Religion," 137.
13. See, Lewis, "What Are We to Make of Jesus Christ?," 48–53, in particular, 52. Lewis also uses this doctrine, essentially derived from the work of Athanasius (fourth century) in, Lewis, "Transposition," 2nd ed., 166–82.
14. See, Lewis, *The Great Divorce*, 87. Lewis is drawing on Athanasius' *De Incarnatione Verbi Dei*. See, Athanasius, *The Incarnation of the Word*, Ch. 8, §.54, 93.
15. Lewis, *The Four Loves*, "Introduction," 5.
16. Lewis, *Mere Christianity*, Bk. IV, Ch. 1, 156–57.

6. aut Deus aut malus homo III: Divine Self-Disclosure

sons of God: "He will share his 'sonship' with us, will make us, like himself, 'Sons of God'."[17] In the Lewisian neo-Platonic language of idealism this is, as we saw earlier, *transposition*—a doctrine of transposition. Lewis, therefore, asserts that it is only through the uniting with humanity that the divinity of Jesus is revealed; what is revealed is the real "Sonship," the solid reality (Lewis's term), whereas biological "sonship" is but a diagrammatic representation of it.[18] What we take for the familial and filial relationships between a human father and his daughter or between the mother and her son, these are only valid because first there is the analogous relationships within the Trinity: the co-eternal, co-existing, ever relating tripartite relationship of the three persons within the Godhead. Our familial and filial are a diminuted, transposed, echo in some ways of this communion of love within the trinitarian Godhead, these human relationships are, in Lewis's words, a diagrammatic representation of this eternal co-existence.[19] This relationship in earthly terms is seen at its purest, in intensity, at its best in the relationship between Jesus and his heavenly Father. Hence, he cannot be other than who he discloses himself to be—either this man is the divine Son or else, in the words of Lewis's trilemma, a madman, or worse.

ii. Markers of Self-Disclosure II: Incarnation

The key to this, certainly for Lewis, is in a doctrine of the incarnation. At the heart of Lewis's doctrine of the incarnation is God descending to *become* human (ontologically uniting with us, not merely taking on human status), to *become* one of us, at-one (atonement) with humanity, to draw humanity up into divine selfhood. Platonically this is about us being drawn out of the reality of the pain and suffering of this world and into the *truly* real reality of heaven, eternity: "The incarnation worked not by conversion of the Godhead into flesh, but by taking of the Manhood into God. And it seems to me that there is a real analogy between this and what I have called Transposition: that humanity, still remaining itself, is not merely counted as, but veritably drawn into, Deity."[20] Incarnation is the key to the nature and reality of the Son of God as Son of Man. Incarnation implies divinity. Jesus is not a mere human pretending to be God, or going around as a wandering preacher talking *as if* he was the God of Israel, or deluding people into believing he was more than human, and so on. Therefore, for Lewis, he cannot be merely human because of his purpose and role; he cannot, for Lewis, be other than whom he reveals himself to be; the gradual unfolding of self-disclosure divulges to the Jewish and Roman public that Jesus is either the God of the Hebrews or one we must reject. N. T. Wright adopts the skeptics' position on this and reverses their conclusion, he shows how being rigorously critical approves (if not proves) Jesus's extra-human nature. Wright comments that if Jesus was a mere human being and nothing more, then he would have been aware of being only

---

17. Ibid, Bk. III, Ch. 12, 147.
18. "Divine Sonship is, so to speak, the solid of which biological Sonship is merely a diagrammatic representation on the flat." Lewis, *Miracles*, 1st ed., 111.
19. Lewis, *Mere Christianity*, Bk. IV, Ch. 1, 156–57.
20. Lewis, "Transposition," 2nd ed., 178.

human, in a human context, and nothing more. The insurmountable difficulties lie in Jesus's self-understanding, which is so completely extra human, flawlessly so.[21] This is an incarnated identity. For Wright, it is this self-identity, this self-understanding, accurately reflected by the Gospel writers that are the true markers of Jesus's divinity, perhaps more than the conclusions of the patristic councils and creeds, where the emphasis is on "persons" and "substance." Therefore, it is the markers of Jesus's self-understanding (which are essentially existential and behavioral) that we can trust: "If Jesus was a human being and nothing more, part of the picture will precisely be that he was aware of being a human being and nothing more. Unless we can give some sort of account of Jesus's own self-understanding, I simply don't think it's good enough to talk about two minds (or one), two natures (or one), or about the various combinations and permutations of persons and substances."[22]

iii. Markers of Self-Disclosure III: Messiah

Jesus (Hebrew, *Yeshua*) is generally defined in meaning and use as "God is savior," or "Jehovah is savior"; Christ (Gk) or Messiah (Heb) mean, "anointed one." The notion of a Messiah originated in the Scriptures of Israel (from the early Hebrew *Mashiach*, the anointed one, derived from the ancient Hebrew tradition of anointing the king or a priest with oil). The concept of messiahship developed in the inter-testamental period and in later Judaism with the Messiah being understood as a coming Davidic king (or, for some Jews, a high priest) who would be instrumental in the redemption of Israel. Jesus is taken by some of those around him to be this Davidic king, *the* Messiah; hence the early attribution to him of the title "the Christ." The word Christ was originally a title, not part of a name. As a title for the anointed one, Christ (Greek, *Christos*, χριστός; Latin, *Christus*) is nearly always intended and translated as Messiah; this did not imply that he was the second person of the Trinity. The trinitarian perception is part of the gradual unfolding of revelation, the dawning realization in the early church of what and who Jesus was and is, with ample pointers and examples of Jesus's trinitarian nature in the New Testament (these passages were produced by the early church in the years after the resurrection and ascension). Being the Messiah, the anointed one, carried multiple, though often overlapping, meanings. To some, the coming Messiah would be a political revolutionary, who would save them from the Romans, to others the Messiah would return Israel and the Temple religion back to a happier time. Therefore the coming Messiah could have been seen as a merely human office. Indeed around the time of Jesus of Nazareth there were many, many, false Messiah's, usually men who raised themselves up to fulfill a revolutionary, political, or religious roles required by the people, claiming they were the anointed one come to save Israel. These false Messiahs lapsed into obscurity; many killed by the Romans or the Jewish religious authorities, without even the show trial Jesus of Nazareth had. The Hebrew political overtones associated with the coming Messiah could have made

---

21. Wright, "Jesus' Self-Understanding," 53.
22. Ibid., 53.

6. aut Deus aut malus homo III: Divine Self-Disclosure

the Messiah a high-powered politician (even a celebrity) like the old prophets, but not necessarily God descended to live and walk amongst them. This is about expectations. Jesus's contemporaries had differing expectations of the Messiah, though there was a common thread: salvation; but salvation *from what*, and *to what*? From a purely political perspective this was not necessarily eschatological; yet Jesus's sayings are eschatological, they bypass the local political problems and focus on the individual in judgment before God. As a redeemer figure, expected and foretold, Jesus does not necessarily live up to their expectations. In the Old Testament priests and kings were anointed and were considered messiahs (Exod 30:22–25). Later, particularly in the intertestamental period, messiahship referred to one anointed by God as a leader, with the expectation, often, that he would be a king from the line of David. Jesus of Nazareth was, therefore, in the eyes of many who saw and heard him considered to be *the* long awaited Messiah, with differing expectations as to what his role would be and what he would achieve. However, after the event the early church interpreted this messiahship in the context of Jesus's eschatological role as God descended to earth. Jesus is then the final Messiah of messiahs. Thus Messiah understandably comes to take on richer trinitarian layers of meaning in later Christian theology: God anoints God to descend to save the people and reascend with them into the divine life; in the fullness of the resurrection and ascension messiahship is finally redefined by Jesus's life and ministry, his sayings and actions. Whatever the expectations of messiahship, Jesus is *the Messiah* (therefore, *the Christ*), not *a* Messiah (political or otherwise); the Hebrew expectations are then blown away by God's revelation. The witness of the early church is then a form of revelation equal to the scriptural (specifically Old Testament) tradition. The early church and patristic tradition is therefore superior to all these old Hebrew categories, also the expectations of Jesus's contemporaries, also the interpretation of messiahship the Jewish religious authorities held to in Jerusalem.

iv. Markers of Self-Disclosure IV: "Son of God," "Son of Man"

Jesus of Nazareth is *sent* by God, as God, yet fully human: as "Son of God" and "Son of Man." So what is meant by "Son of God" and "Son of Man"? The two titles are not necessarily interchangeable, though they are closely related. There is a uniqueness intended to each title. As Son of Man Jesus is part of all humanity yet distinct, special, and therefore representational of all humanity; as Son of God he is unique, only begotten uncreated, of the same "substance" as the Father, yet relational. Primarily the terms the "Son of God" and "Son of Man" refer to Jesus's role which cannot be separated from his identity, which is, as we have seen, ontological. Jesus's role and purpose is as the savior of humanity; he is the savior of the world, the redeemer of fallen humanity. But what do the terms mean? Of the three fundamental titles—"Christ/Messiah," "Lord," and, "Son of God/Son of Man"—that emerge from the range of interpretations people came up with in response to meeting Jesus, there is no distinction between the task and the person, between the status or office, and the nature of being that was Jesus. The title Lord could only be used for the God of Israel. The title Son of God immediately connected Jesus with the very being of Israel's God. This relationship is not simply of spiritual closeness—everything that the Father is, is in the Son. This reflected not just Jewish ideas of parenthood but was also reflected in the surrounding peoples and cultures: the first-born son was everything that the father was; the son was always equal to the father, not just in privilege and responsibility but in nature. Son of Man therefore implies that everything that is inherent in humanity is there also in Jesus. The term Son of Man is used fourteen times by Jesus in Mark's Gospel alone.[23] Here the term is used for "the one who is to come," for "the earthly activities of the Son of Man," but also for "the suffering servant and the resurrection of the Son of Man." Although these uses are rooted in Ezekiel and Daniel the term is used as a poetic synonym for the ideal human.[24] The closest to a prefigurement of the Christ is in the book of Daniel—the imagery of the four beasts representing the powers and history of the world, as distinct from the one to come who is different to the evil of this world and can stand in the "presence" of the Ancient of Days, God, YHWH the righteous Lord: "In my vision at night I looked, and there before me was one like a son of man, coming with the clouds of heaven. He approached the Ancient of Days and was led into his presence. He was given authority, glory, and sovereign power; all peoples, nations and men of every language worshiped him. His dominion is an everlasting dominion that will not pass away, and his kingdom is one that will never be destroyed" (Dan 7:13–14).

The Son of Man here represents the coming age of salvation and redemption, this is seen in orthodox terms as a prefigurement of Jesus's identity and role.[25] The title son of god (note, lower case) was widely used amongst the pagan nations and tribes outside of Israel—as in Babylon and Egypt—but here an individual was elevated to become a son of the "gods." In the Old Testament Israel is God's firstborn (Exod 4:22–23), again elevated status, but when we come to Jesus there is something else. The discourses in Luke and Matthew reveal that all things have been given to the Son by the Father, no one but the Son knows the Father, and the Son wills some to know the Father, all that is in the Son is in and from the Father (Luke 10 and Matt 11). This is not elevation and conferment; only the Son truly knows and has seen the Father because he is the only begotten (not created, but begotten from all eternity). The will of the Father is in the Son; this is perfect communion. This is Lewis's analogical language because through transposition this is the closest our mere mortal minds can get to understanding what is happening here in Jesus's Sonship; but it should be clear: Son of God and Son of Man are messianic and divine terms, and reveal and relate to a high Christology.

---

23. Mark 2:10; 2:28; 8:31, 38; 9:9, 12, 31; 10:33, 45; 13:26; 14:21, 41, 62.
24. Num 23:19; Isa 56:2; Ps 79:18; see also Ezek 2:1.
25. See Mark 13:24–27 and 14:62, as to the end of the world, and Jesus before the Jewish religious authorities. In Matt 25, it is the Son of Man who is judge of all at the end of the world, but here the Son of Man as judge is identified with those who have suffered.

6. aut Deus aut malus homo III: Divine Self-Disclosure

ἐγώ εἰμὶ—The "I Am" Sayings

The Absolute Sense	**The Relative Image Sense**	
"I told you that you would die in your sins, for you will die in your sins unless you believe that I am." JOHN 8:24	"I am the bread of life; he who comes to me shall not hunger." JOHN 6:35	"I am the resurrection and the life; he who believes in me shall live even if he dies." JOHN 11:25
"When you have lifted up the Son of Man, then you will realize that I am he, and that I do nothing on my own, but I speak these things as the Father instructed me." JOHN 8:28	"I am the light of the world; he who follows me shall not walk in the darkness, but shall have the light of life." JOHN 8:12	"I am the way, and the truth, and the life; no one comes to the Father, but through me." JOHN 14:6
Jesus said, "Truly, Truly, I say to you, before Abraham was born, I am." JOHN 8:58	"I am the gate; if anyone enters through me, he shall be saved, and shall go in and out, and find pasture." JOHN 10:9	
"I tell you this now, before it occurs, so that when it does occur, you may believe that I am he." JOHN 13:19	"I am the good shepherd; the good shepherd lays down his life for his sheep." JOHN 10:11	"I am the true vine, and My Father is the vinedresser." JOHN 15:1

Figure 8: John's Gospel—The "I am" Sayings

v. Markers of Self-Disclosure V: "I Am"

The "I Am" sayings (NT Greek, ἐγώ εἰμί) are, from the perspective of an Enlightenment-led skepticism, the most controversial markers of Jesus' divinity. Why? Because through them this Jesus of Nazareth, the carpenter's son, is identified as the God of Israel's people, YHWH, come among them; if not and he was a mere man claiming such identity, then this must rank as amongst the most deluded or malicious of deceptions ever undertaken (hence Lewis's either-or logic). What is the connection between YHWH and the "I Am" sayings? Among all of the names in the Old Testament for God it is YHWH that is in many ways the most specific, personal, and revealing (in the *Broadcast Talks* Lewis makes copious use of the name); most often YHWH is translated as Lord, the response of the ancient Hebrews to YHWH was in worship and praise. God was also the raging storm, the violent thunder, the one to whom it was believed pure sacrifice was a daily necessity, the slayer of Israel's enemies, but he was revealed, again a gradual self-disclosure, as the God of his people: El-ohim. For example, Emmanu-el (God with his people, God with us), El-Shallom (God of Peace), Beth-El (House of God), El-Shaddai (God, the Almighty); the God-with-his-people discloses himself as YHWH at its deepest in Exodus: "God said to Moses, 'I Am that I Am.' He said further, 'Thus you shall say to the Israelites, I Am has sent me to you'" (Exod 3:14). As Lewis approached the point of his conversion and acknowledgement of God as Lord he wrote, "It might, as I say, still be true that my 'spirit' differed in some way from 'the God of popular religion'. My adversary waved the point. It sank into utter unimportance. He would not argue about it. He only said 'I am the Lord'; 'I am that I am.'"[26] YHWH is the eternal self-existing one—God's covenant is from God's reality as YHWH, the Lord.

If the value inherent in the use of Son of God and Son of Man is still doubtful to those faced with Lewis's trilemma, the "I am" sayings should make them consider the logic: essentially summarized in John 8:58: "Jesus said, 'Truly, Truly, I say to you, before Abraham was born, *I am*'." The eternal present tense here indicates that the Son is from all eternity to all eternity, uncreated, begotten of the father; the "I am" sayings echo back to God's declaration to Moses (Exod 3:14); therefore, before Abraham was, Jesus is: "I Am." These sayings act as confirmation to all that is integral to the titles Son of God and Son of Man. Although there are many examples in John's Gospel of Jesus using "I am," it is important to separate these sayings into three groups—there are the general use of "I am" with no implied understanding of divinity; then there are those which use the term illustratively, that is, in relation to an image such as "the bread of life," "the gate" or "the light of the world" (i.e., with a predicate); these first two uses must be distinguished from the third group, those instances that use "I am" in what is seen as the absolute sense.[27] The absolute sense of Jesus's use of "I Am" cannot be explained away contextually simply as self-reference. Saying, "I am the gateway to God," or "I am the light of the world," could easily be seen as metaphorical statements by someone who is intensely religious, someone who is one amongst many gates or ways to God, or one who is amongst the lights of the world. The four absolute "I Am" sayings (see figure 8) cannot be dismissed so lightly: the proposition of unity with YHWH the God of Israel, is a proposition of oneness. The implication of this oneness cannot be ignored lightly; hence, we are forced to a position where we must decide—ignoring the question of Jesus's identity is a decision in its own right.

vi. Markers of Self-Disclosure IV: Trinitarian

The New Testament is replete with markers of self-disclosure; the most profound, in many ways, is in the testimony of John's Gospel, particularly the prologue, which in all probability comes from an ultra-early christological hymn. The Word, the Logos, that "resides," and "subsists," "exists" (though do not such localized and spacio-temporal terms do an injustice to God's being?) in the trinitarian communion that is God, became flesh and walked around amongst his people. The Word, that was Jesus of Nazareth, the Christ, was with God, eternally begotten, through whom all things were created, and was the light of the world. There are several examples from the writers of the New Testament of a proto-trinitarian framework; therefore, it is in the early church that revelation continues to unfold, giving rise to Lewis's "mere" core. The letter to the

---

26. Lewis, *Surprised by Joy*, 220.
27. There is a great deal of good orthodox scholarship in this field. For example, see, Brown, *The Gospel according to John*, Appendix IV, Vol. 1. See also, Ball, *"I Am" in John's Gospel: Literary Function, Background and Theological Implications*.

6. aut Deus aut malus homo III: Divine Self-Disclosure

Hebrews, as does the kenotic christological hymn in the second chapter of Philippians, tells us much about the nature of incarnation in Jesus. As Lewis noted, the nature of the transposed reality of divine Sonship is often perceived as being different to most human expectations. But can we rely on this Scriptural testimony and why? What is the Scriptural testimony and evidence?

4. DIVINE SELF-DISCLOSURE—SCRIPTURE

What is the Biblical testimony to divine self-disclosure in Jesus of Nazareth?[28] The Gospels are replete with examples of how Jesus disclosed himself as with and of God: for example, Jesus gives eternal life (John 3:16), he is at one with the Father (John 10:30), he is considered to be omnipotent (Matt 28:18) and omnipresent (Matt 18:20), in addition he accepts worship due to God (Matt 14:33) and he sends the Holy Spirit of God (John 14:25–26). The important factor is what we might call self-disclosure: Jesus gives himself away to be God incarnate, God incognito. Why did he not come clean and declare himself openly from the very beginning of his ministry? If he did, this ministry would not have lasted more than a few days! And there is the importance of individuals coming to know and realize who he was, for themselves. There are broadly six headings under which we may classify the scriptural evidence for Jesus's divinity. All these categories interlock and all the references relate to each other:

First,
Jesus Christ's Self-Disclosure of Divinity
Second
How the Miracles testify to his Divinity
Third,
The Witness of the Apostles and Disciples
Fourth,
The Prefigurements of Christ's Divinity in the Old Testament
Fifth,
The Worship that is Offered to him.
Sixth,
The Audacity and Manner in which Jesus Forgave People their Sins

i. Divinity

First, what is Jesus Christ's self-disclosure of divinity: if we are to rely, as the patristic church did, on the testimony of the writers of Scripture, then what is there in the Gospels that bears witness to Jesus's self-disclosure as being divine? Jesus asserts his true identity to Satan when he is being tempted in the wilderness (Matt 4:7;

---

28. There are numerous sources—books and web pages—which purport to present as complete a picture of the arguments for and against Christ's divinity, likewise the references from the Bible that lead to such conclusions. This section is as fair and comprehensive a summary of the key scriptural references often cited as is possible. In terms of the breadth of scriptural references and the patristic works that analyze and defend the divinity of Christ, the following two websites are to be acknowledged:
Scripture Catholic: http://www.Scripturecatholic.com/
Christian Classics Ethereal Library (Calvin College, Grand Rapids, MI): http://www.ccel.org/

cf. Luke 4:12); Jesus's asserts on many occasions that he is equal before and with God (Matt 5:21–22, 27–28, 31–32, 33–34, 38–39, 43–44); Jesus calls himself Lord, God, (Matt 7:21–22; Luke 6:46). Importantly, Jesus forgives people in the place of God (Matt 9:2; Mark 2:5; Luke 5:20; 7:48); likewise Jesus asserts that he is Lord of the Sabbath, he is the originator and giver of the law, therefore he is the God of the Hebrew people (Matt 12:8; Mark 2:28; Luke 6:5). In terms of prayer, when two or three are gathered in his name, he will be in the centre of them, as God would (Matt 18:20). Jesus refers to himself as Lord; in the Jewish religion and all through the Old Testament God is Lord, and to assert Lordship is to usurp God (Matt 21:3; Luke 19:31, 34); it is in the context of lordship Jesus finally acknowledges that he is the Son of God (Matt 26:64; Mark 14:62; Luke 22:70; John 10:36). In the context of the divine attributes there is the assertion of omnipresence: Jesus will be will us always, till the end of time and into eternity (Matt 28:20). Speaking in the first person Jesus asserts that he has descended from heaven (John 6:38); God is light and no darkness is in God—yet Jesus affirms he is the light of the world (John 8:12, cf. 1 John 1:5).

Beginning and the end: God is the Alpha and the Omega (Rev 1:8); Jesus likewise is Alpha and Omega, the First and the Last (Rev 1:17 and 22:13; cf. Isa 44:6; 41:4; 48:12); this implies equality of Lordship. As the beginning and the end Jesus can announce that he died yet is alive (Rev 1:18), he is the word of the First and the Last, who died and came to life

In terms of trinitarian relationships, Jesus refers to God as "Abba," father in Aramaic, a dangerous precedent unknown in the Hebrew tradition (Mark 14:36); however this is not to invoke human relationships as Jesus distinguishes the relationship he has with the Father from human family bonds when he comments, "My Father and your Father" (John 20:17); it is equally important to remember that Jesus was crucified because of his assertion of identity with the Father, he made himself equal with God, whom he called Father (John 5:18). Jesus gives life; only God gives life; furthermore all authority and judgment has been delegated, given, to him by the Father (John 5:21–22). Therefore, Jesus places himself as equal with and to the Father because whoever fails to honor the Son dishonors the Father who sent him (John 5:23); If you know me, you know my Father, declares Jesus (John 8:19). How else are we to interpret Jesus's comment that, "all things that the Father has are mine" (John 16:15; cf. John 16:28),

Jesus says that, like God, he is not of this world (John 8:23); in terms of eternal existence Jesus says that before Abraham was, "I am" (John 8:58; cf. Exod 3:14). Therefore, as such Jesus has the power to lay down his life and take it up again (cf. John 10:18; Gal 1:1).

In terms of the trinitarian unity and divine oneness, Jesus asserted that he and the Father were one (John 10:30), this was a bone of contention with the Jews, the claim to equality with God. Such messianic assertions were integral to his trial, conviction, and execution. Jesus's statement in John 14:28 refers to his human messianic role as servant and slave, which he, and not the Father or the Holy Spirit, undertook in the flesh. How could an ordinary mere mortal human assert that "the Father is in me and I am in the

6. aut Deus aut malus homo III: Divine Self-Disclosure

Father," without implying equality (John 10:38; 14:10)? If, "He who sees me, sees him who sent me" (John 12:45), then there is implied equality with God.

As a human teacher and equally divine Jesus pronounces that he is both Lord and teacher because he is the divine "I am" (John 13:13). If he is, "The way, the truth and the life" then such a claim must be seen as explicitly messianic (John 14:6).

ii. Miracles

Second, how do the miracles testify to his divinity? Perhaps we need to remind ourselves of what was attributed to this man Jesus by his witnesses, his disciples. Lewis accepted the miracles for he could find no evidence to deny them in principle: "The reason why I can accept as historical a story in which a miracle occurs is that I have never found any philosophical grounds for the universal negative proposition that miracles do not happen."[29] Matthew and Luke testify to the virginal conception (Matt 1:23; Luke 1:27 & 35); the Holy Spirit descends upon Jesus as the Father declares him to be the Son (Matt 3:16–17; Mark 1:10–11; John 1:32). Then there are the healings, cures outside of human expectation and control (Matt 4:23–24; 9:35; 15:30; Mark 1:34; 3:10; 6:5; Luke 4:40; 7:10; 13:13; 14:4; John 4:52), as is the healing of leprosy and speech impediments (Matt 7:35; 8:3; 9:21–22; Mark 1:41; 5:27–34; Luke 5:13; 17:14); and, related, the woman cured of hemorrhage by touching the hem of Jesus's cloak (Luke 8:44; cf. Matt 14:36). Jesus heals the paralyzed (Matt 8:13; 9:7; Mark 2:9; Luke 5:25), he cures Peter's mother-in-law's of fever (Matt 8:15; Mark 1:31; Luke 4:39); restores sight to the blind (Matt 9:30; 12:22; 20:34; 21:14; Mark 8:25; 10:52; Luke 7:21; 18:42; John 9:11) and restores a withered hand (Matt 12:13; Mark 3:5; Luke 6:10). Jesus stills the storm (Matt 8:26; Mark 4:39; Luke 8:24), and has power and authority over demonic spirits (Matt 8:32; 9:33; 12:22; 15:28; 17:18; Mark 1:26,34; 3:11; 5:13; 7:30; 9:26; Luke 4:35, 41; 8:33; 9:42; 11:14); he displays supernatural knowledge through his perception of the thoughts of others (Matt 9:4; 12:25; Luke 6:8; 11:17); it is he who raises the dead to new life (Matt 9:25; Mark 5:24; John 11:44). Jesus multiplies the loaves and fish and feeds the crowd of thousands (Matt 14:19–20; 5:36–37; Mark 6:41–42; 8:7–8; Luke 9:16–17; John 6:11), and walks on water (Matt 14:26; Mark 6:48; John 6:19). He foretells his own end (Matt 15:21; 16:21; 17:9,22; 20:18–19; 26:2; Mark 10:33–34; Luke 9:44; 17:25; 18:32–34) and is transfigured in glory before his disciples (Matt 17:2; Mark 9:2; Luke 9:29). Jesus curses the fig tree, which withers (Matt 21:19; Mark 11:14–20); he prophesies that Jerusalem will be overrun and fall (Matt 24:34; Mark 13:2; Luke 21:32). This is the man who predicts that Peter will deny him (Matt 26:34; Mark 14:30; Luke 22:34; John 13:38) and that Judas will betrayal him (Matt 26:21–25; Mark 14:18–20; Luke 22:21; John 13:21–26). But above all we must acknowledge the miracle of the resurrection (Matt 28:9; Mark 16:9–14; Luke 7:14–15; 8:54–55; 24:5; 31–36; John 20:14–26; 21:1–14).

---

29. See, Lewis, *Reflections on the Psalms*, 94–95.

iii. Witness

Third, the witness of the apostles and disciples. The testimony of the disciples and apostles cannot be lightly dismissed. These men and women risked their lives to bear witness to what they knew and saw at a time when the relationship between the followers of the Way and the religious authorities went from bad to worse; they were stoned to death by their fellow Jews or tortured and crucified by the Romans for bearing witness. The writer of John's Gospel is pre-eminent here: the prologue is in effect a christological hymn to the incarnation, Jesus Christ, very God and very man (John 1:1–14; cf. Isa 43:10). John recounts how Peter confesses that Jesus is the Son of God who has the words of eternal life (John 6:68–69). In the Acts of the Apostles God has made Jesus both Lord and Christ (2:36), the Sovereign Lord of heaven and earth (Acts 4:24); in this context Peter bears witness that the men of Israel slew the author of life (Acts 3:15). The church was founded on the blood of Jesus slain and that of the martyrs (Acts 20:28).

In his letter to the Roman Christians Paul asserts he is an apostle of the gospel of God (Rom 1:1), who preaches the gospel of Christ (Rom 15:19). The Spirit of God and the Spirit of Christ are, for Paul, synonymous (Rom 8:9), as Jesus Christ is God and reigns over all (Rom 9:5), God from God, God in God (Rom 11:36; cf. Col 3:11), as Christ is all in all. In writing to the Corinthians Paul repents that he had persecuted the church of God (as the church of God is the church of Christ, (cf. Matt 16:18 and Rom 16:16). Writing to the Galatians Paul explains how Christ fulfils the law of Christ (Gal 6:2), and he asserts that to God the Father is glory due, as Peter likewise, gives glory and honor to Christ (2 Pet 3:18). In the kenotic christological hymn in Philippians we hear that "Jesus was in the form of God, but instead of asserting his equality with God, emptied himself for our salvation" (Phil 2:6–7). Therefore, Jesus is the image of the invisible God, and is thus the firstborn of all creation (Col 1:15), for in Jesus Christ the whole fullness of deity lived, incarnated, bodily; he is the whole and entire fullness of the indivisible God in the flesh (Col 2:9).

In the Letter of Paul to Titus God has saved us, Christ is our Savior, therefore Jesus Christ is God (1:3–4); Jesus Christ is the grace of God that has appeared to save all men, so we now wait in hope for the appearing in glory of Jesus Christ, God and Savior (Titus 2:13).

In the Letter to the Hebrews all the angels worship the only begotten coming into the world, this is worship reserved only for God (Heb 1:6); God calls the Son God, but of the Son he says, "Thy throne, O God, is forever"; God therefore calls the Son "Lord" (Heb 1:8–10). It is this Jesus for whom and by whom all things are (Heb 2:10). The writer of Hebrews asserts that Jesus sanctifies the people with his blood (Heb 13:12) as the God of peace sanctifies his people (1 Thess 5:23). Peter, in his second letter, comments that those who have faith stand in the righteousness of God, where God is "the savior Jesus Christ" (2 Pet 1:1). In the first letter of John we are told that we may only know him who is true in the Son Jesus Christ (1 John 5:20).

6. aut Deus aut malus homo III: Divine Self-Disclosure

iv. Old Testament Prefigurements

Fourth, we can consider the prefigurements of Christ's divinity in the Old Testament. In terms of the prefigurement of Christ's divinity in the Hebrew Bible, the revelation of the divine "I am" (Exod 3:14 is reiterated by Jesus—John 8:58). The command in Deuteronomy (4:2; 12:32) is reiterated by Jesus in the book of Revelation (Rev 22:18–19) for we must not add or take away from his word. The Old Testament asserts that God as Lord kills and makes alive again, and raises up, this is reiterated in the New Testament (Deut 32:39; 1 Sam 2:6; cf. John 5:21). Therefore, no one can deliver or remove you out of God's/Jesus's hand (Deut 32:39; cf. John 10:28). The worship given in joy and honor to God in the Pentateuch is referred to in Hebrews as accorded to Jesus Christ, the Son (Deut 32:43; cf. Heb 1:6). God in the Old Testament (2 Sam 22:3) and Jesus in the Gospel (Luke 1:68–69) are referred to as "the horn of salvation." Both God and Jesus are referred to as the God of "gods" and the Lord of "lords" (Dan 2:47; Rev 17:14).

Both God and Jesus shepherd the flock (Ezek 34:11–31 and John 10:7–29); God seeks to save that which was lost (Ezek 34:16) as does Jesus (Luke 19:10); God's manifestation is glorious (Ezek 1:26–28, also, Dan 7:9) as is Jesus's (Rev 1:13–16). However, as Jesus judges and separates the sheep from the goats, Ezekiel prophecies how God judges between cattle, rams, sheep, and goats (Matt 25:32; Ezek 34:17).

If we look to the book of the Psalms we find that the law of the Lord is perfect (Ps 19:7). Angels worship the Lord God as they do Jesus (Ps 148:1–2; Heb 1:6); such worship was reserved by the Jews for God and God alone. Christ is the fulfillment of the law (Gal 6:2); both God as the Lord and Jesus are referred to as "the Lord of glory" (Ps 24:10; 1 Cor. 2:8); Jesus, the eternally begotten Son, is anointed by God (Ps 45:7; Heb 1:8–10). The Lord God rewards each according to his/her work (Ps 62:12), as does Jesus (Matt 16:27; Rev 22:12). God as Lord and Jesus Christ as Lord are our only hope (Ps 71:5; 1 Tim 1:1). Jesus is this first-born king, the highest (John 18:36–27, echoing Ps 89:27); likewise the Lord God and Jesus are above all (Ps 97:9; John 3:31). New Testament writers interpreted Psalm 110:1 as God ("the Lord") addressing Jesus ("my [i.e., David's] Lord") as Lord (cf. Acts 2:34–36).

The Book of Isaiah gives us some of the most profound prefigurements relating to Jesus's divinity: a virgin will bear a Son named Emmanuel (Isa 7:14; cf. Matt 1:23); the child to be born shall be called wonderful counselor, mighty God, everlasting, prince of peace (Isa 9:6); for God will swallows up death in victory (Isa 25:8; cf. 2 Tim 1:10) as Jesus bring death to an end. The Word of the Lord shall stand forever as Jesus's words will never be lost (Isa 40:8; cf. Matt 24:35). God gives glory to none other than the eternally begotten Son (Isa 42:8; cf. John 17:5; Heb 1:3); for the Lord God and Jesus are the redeemer (Isa 43:14; Titus 2:14); as the Lord God is the first and the last (Isa 44:6) so too is Jesus (Rev 1:17; 2:8; 22:13). The Lord God did not speak in secret (Isa 45:19; John 18:20) so that "every knee shall bow and every tongue confess" (Isa 45:23; Phil 2:10–11). There are pairings of divine attributes between God and Jesus: for God is the everlasting light (Isa 60:19) as Jesus the Lamb is eternal light (Rev 21:23); God as Lord searches the hearts and knows us according to our actions (Jer 17:10) as Jesus searches the hearts and repays us accordingly (Rev 2:23); for God is the Holy One (Isa 48:17) as Jesus is the Holy One (Acts 3:14).

v. Worship

Fifth, the worship that is offered to Christ is worship that is only rightly given to God, which is why it is given to him, for he is God descended through incarnation. In Matthew's Gospel the magi come to worship him (Matt 2:2–11); likewise the apostles worship Jesus (Matt 14:33; 28:17), as also did a leper (Matt 8:2). In Mark's Gospel the possessed man worshiped Jesus (Mark 5:6). In Luke's Gospel Mary, though somewhat puzzled at first, acknowledges Elizabeth's declaration that she is the mother of her Lord (Luke 1:11) and later the apostles worshiped Jesus as he ascended into heaven (Luke 24:52). In John's Gospel the blind man worships Jesus in response to being cured (John 9:38), though Thomas is more reluctant and needs concrete proof before uttering his famous declaration, "My Lord and my God!" (John 20:28). The book of Revelation explains how Jesus and the Father are worshiped in the same manner (Rev 4:9–11; 5:8, 12–14; 7:11–12)

vi. Forgiving of Sins

Sixth, the audacity and manner in which Jesus forgave people their sins. This, for Lewis, is the overriding evidence for self-disclosure. The patristic church often emphasized the miracles and the evidence of prefigurement for Jesus's divinity in the Old Testament; however, it is Jesus's forgiving of sins that is seen by many in Lewis's day and today as being the most explicit example of divine self-disclosure. This forgiveness often happened not as the primary cause for Jesus healing, but as explanation after the event: "Take heart son, your sins are forgiven" (Matt 9:2–5; cf. 6:14–15; 12:8), "Son your sins are forgiven" (Mark 2:5–9, 28), "Friend, your sins are forgiven" (Luke 5:17–26; cf. 5:31–32; 6:5; 7:36–50). In John's Gospel the context of forgiveness is more precise: if we forgive others God will forgive us, if we judge, we will be judged; and can anyone condemn another when their heart is so deeply stained with sin? Can anyone forgive unless they are sinless? For example, in the context of the woman taken in adultery Jesus asks her, "'Woman, where are they? Has no one condemned you?' 'No one, sir,' she said. 'Then neither do I condemn you,' Jesus declared 'Go now and leave your life of sin'" (John 8:10–11). But more than this, individual encounters are important but we speak of, "the Lamb of God, who takes away the sin of the world!" (John 1:29–30). Can anyone but God truly forgive a sinner? The eternal consequences of sin are seen as worse than any ailment: "See, you are well again. Stop sinning or something worse may happen to you" (John 5:14b). It is the value of the Word alone that can heal and forgive sin. For example, Jesus's encounter with the centurion who believed Jesus's word alone could heal his servant (Matt 8:5–13).

The testimony of the witnesses that underpins Scripture extends into the early church—even though their writings are not canonical—therefore, we may consider

6. aut Deus aut malus homo III: Divine Self-Disclosure

the testimony of the early church fathers (particularly in the pre-Constantinian church, c. 32–312 AD) as important. This is so particularly when the early Christians died asserting Christ's divinity and failing to acknowledge the Emperor as a "god." The price of asserting the divinity of Christ was costly: disenfranchisement, exile, and often martyrdom in the form of crucifixion, or one of the many other tortuous long-draw-out forms of execution the Romans devised.[30]

5. THE RELIABILITY OF THE GOSPEL ACCORDING TO JOHN

> Again the Jews picked up stones to stone him, but Jesus said to them, "I have shown you many great miracles from the Father. For which of these do you stone me?" "We are not stoning you for any of these," replied the Jews, "but for blasphemy, because you, a mere man, claim to be God." Jesus answered them, "Is it not written in your Law, 'I have said you are gods?' If he called them 'gods,' to whom the word of God came—and the Scripture cannot be broken—what about the one whom the Father set apart as his very own and sent into the world? Why then do you accuse me of blasphemy because I said, 'I am God's Son?' Do not believe me unless I do what my Father does. But if I do it, even though you do not believe me, believe the miracles, that you may know and understand that the Father is in me, and I in the Father." Again they tried to seize him, but he escaped their grasp.
>
> (John 10:31–39)

This passage from John's Gospel illustrates the dilemma at the heart of Lewis's trilemma. The Jewish religious authorities seek to stone Jesus. Why? Not for his works, not for healings and miracles, but for blasphemy because he as a mere man claimed to be the God of Israel. So John's Gospel is at the heart of the proposition, *aut Deus aut malus homo*. Can we trust it? Is it reliable? The Fourth Gospel illustrates how people could not disregard Jesus as an ordinary human being; what he said and did forced them to consider what his relationship was with God. This is so in John's Gospel more than in the synoptic Gospels. Hence skeptical "modern/liberal" churchmen and theologians have often dismissed John's Gospel as a fabrication written around sixty years after the events it purports to recall. Lewis was highly critical of the demythologizing, reductive agenda he perceived in the work of such Anglican clerics as Alec Vidler

---

30. For example: Ignatius of Antioch, *To the Ephesians*, 7 (110 AD); Justin Martyr, *Dialogue with Trypho*, 121 (155 AD) and, *First Apology*, 13 (155 AD); *Martyrdom of Polycarp* 14 (157 AD); Tatian the Syrian, *Oration against the Greeks*, 5 & 21 (c. 175 AD); Athenagoras, *Plea for Christians*, 10 (177 AD); Irenaeus, *Against Heresies*, 4,20:1 (180 AD); Theophilus of Antioch, *To Autolycus*, II:10 (c. 181 AD); Tertullian, *Apology*, 21 (197 AD) and *Against Praxeas*, 9 (c. 213 AD); Clement of Alexandria, *The Instructor*, I:8 (202 AD); Hippolytus, *Against the Heresy of One Noetus*, 11 (210 AD) and *Refutation against All Heresies*, 10:29 (220 AD); Origen, *First Principles*, 4:28 (230 AD); Novatian, *Concerning the Trinity*, 11 (235 AD); Cyprian, *Epistle to Jubaianus*, 72[73]:12 (256 AD); Gregory Thaumaturgus, *Sectional Confession of Faith*, 8 (c. 270 AD); Methodius, *Oration on the Palms*, 4 (305 AD); Lactantius, *Divine Institutes*, 4:13 (310 AD). See: Roberts, et al, *The Early Church Fathers: Ante-Nicene Fathers—Translations of the Writings of the Fathers Down to A.D. 325*; *The Nicene and Post-Nicene Fathers of the Christian Church-First and Second Series*. These patristic documents can be consulted online at: Christian Classics Ethereal Library (Calvin College, Grand Rapids, MI): http://www.ccel.org/, listed by author.

and Walter Lock, and also in the German Lutheran theologian and New Testament scholar, Rudolf Bultmann, particular evident in their criticism of the Fourth Gospel. The Christian philosopher and theologian Stephen T. Davis commented on John A. T. Robinson, the "modern/liberal" Anglican bishop who caused something of a storm in a tea cup in the 1960s by challenging the traditional orthodox picture of God and Jesus common amongst ordinary Anglican laity, that even he could see that there was, generally speaking, a sound historical nature to John's Gospel:

> And even J. A. T. Robinson, in the midst of a discussion of the Fourth Gospel in which he argues for the early dating of the book and the general historical reliability of its picture of Jesus, can say: "No sane person goes about saying 'Before Abraham was I am' or 'Whoever eats my flesh and drinks my blood shall live forever.' " These are theological interpretations, not literal utterances. Yet at the deepest level of faith they may indeed be the truth about the eternal Word of life, made flesh in this supremely individual and uniquely moral man of history?[31]

So the sayings of Jesus written down in the Gospel according to John may not be verbatim, word-for-word, courtroom transcribed and verified records of what Jesus said—there is a degree of what Robinson terms theological interpretation to them—but the evidence is too great to dismiss the Fourth Gospel as a fabrication.[32] How do we assess accounts of the holocaust by Jewish survivors today? On television documentaries and in the newspapers men and women who were children or teenagers sixty-five years ago will recount what happened to them in the concentration camps, they will even recount what the SS guards said to them. How accurate are these accounts, these words? Given the passage of years, decades, there will be an element of error, small details confused, that has crept in. Accounts will vary from one survivor to the other, even if they are recounting the same shared experience, the memory will now be more memory of memories, the tale will, subconsciously, be a recounting from memory of the telling to investigators in the 1950s of what happened, but this does not prove that the holocaust did not happen, that they created the memories. In law, in a courtroom, this human fallibility is taken into account. Apparent variances between testimonies given by two or more people are attributed to human frailty; a witness's recollection of another person's words may vary slightly from what happened but the general drift and meaning is accepted as historical. This is especially so when the words and events witnessed to are from the accounts of hundreds of people whose testimony all point to the same conclusion: this is so with the accounts on which the Gospels are based.

The theologian Keith Ward summarizes well the value of Scripture. There may be errors, flaws, and discrepancies in Scripture, but the truths that God reveals to humanity, that which is essential and important for our salvation are "placed there"

---

31. Davis, "Was Jesus Mad, Bad or God?," 2nd ed., 150. Davis is referring to, Robinson, *Can We Trust the New Testament?*, see, 1–3. Robinson in his controversial book, *Honest to God*, was critical of the way Lewis handled the argument for divinity in his trilemma, see, 72. See also, Edwards, *The Honest to God Debate*.

32. See Blomberg, *Historical Reliability of the Gospels*, and Bauckham, *Jesus and the Eyewitnesses*.

6. aut Deus aut malus homo III: Divine Self-Disclosure

without error.[33] This is similar to Lewis's approach to the question of inerrancy: there are no substantial errors; there is no misleading as to the nature of our salvation in Scripture; in the case of what we may call the divinity sayings in John's Gospel these are to be seen as an accurate reflection of what was said, they capture his authentic voice, even if they are not the exact words spoken.[34] It is very easy for skeptics working from an atheistic standpoint to dismiss the evidence as tainted, even fabricated. The Enlightenment's belief in the contingency of history (as evident in Lessing's ugly broad ditch that we noted earlier) dismissed the New Testament accounts as untrue.[35] What Lessing and his adherents do not perceive is that this "ugly broad ditch" is of their own making and should also prevent them from making such sweeping judgments in dismissing the historicity of the Gospels: they must remain undecided or neutral as to the veracity of the Gospel testimony if they truly believe in their "ugly broad ditch." There is a givenness about the Gospel accounts, which is why they are canonical, the decision to give them this status was not arbitrary or accidental; the early church did not consist of uneducated primitive individuals who could not recognize truth when they saw it.

John Redford,[36] a Roman Catholic Bible scholar, has critically demolished the post-eighteenth-century Enlightenment "Quest for the Historical Jesus," in part because of its innate prejudicial ground in believing that incarnation could not happen and that the miraculous never occurred: "[Redford] has lifted the world of rationalistic biblical criticism, starting with Reimarus, Lessing, Strauss, Holtzmann, Wrede, and continuing down through Wellhausen, Schweitzer, Dibelius, and Bultmann, and shaken it to its core. Even more conversant with its basic presuppositions than its most able practitioners, he compares its blinkered Enlightenment methodology to the way we actually make decisions in concrete, historical situations and finds its most sophisticated and widely-accepted conclusions deficient on scientific grounds, or on its own principles."[37] Redford painstakingly lays-out a more acceptable methodology initially asking questions about how we categorize historical evidence and arrive at the relative certainty that something has happened. Redford identifies a seam of high Christology already present in Mark and the Synoptic Gospels, which he asserts becomes a "golden chain" in John's Gospel: what was implicit in the earlier New Testament material becomes explicit in the Johannine dialogues. These dialogues may be phrased, scripted, in the words of the author of John's Gospel, and presented in dramatic situations created from witness recollections, and are therefore not strictly reportage, or tape-recorded evidence, but they are built on an accurate reporting of historical events and sayings. They reflect the same degree of veracity as do the accounts of the miracles, and for that matter the resurrection.

33. Ward, *What the Bible Really Teaches*, see conclusion.
34. See: Lewis to Clyde S. Kilby, May 7, 1959. *Collected Letters, Vol. III*, 1045. See also, Kilby, *The Christian World of C. S. Lewis*, 153; also, Christensen, *C. S. Lewis on Scripture*, 34–35.
35. See: Lessing, *Theological Writings*, 1956.
36. Redford, *Bad, Mad or God? Proving the Divinity of Christ from John's Gospel*, 2004.
37. Madigan, "Review of Bad, Mad or God? Proving the Divinity of Christ from John's Gospel, by John Redford," 631–33.

The Fourth Gospel teaches that Jesus claimed to be the Son of God. Did Jesus really say these things? Lewis is unequivocal here, despite the zeitgeist of "modernist" skepticism that he encountered, the Fourth Gospel is reliable.[38] Redford rightly comments that the primary objection to a high Christology read from John's Gospel is rooted in a rejection of the concept of incarnation.[39] Incarnation is deemed a logical impossibility, though rarely is any sound argument given against God becoming human. Incarnation is one thing; self-disclosure issuing from self-consciousness is another. There is little doubt that Jesus meant to make the connection in the minds of his audience between himself and the God of the Old Testament; furthermore he makes no attempt to deny such a connection, especially when they seek to stone him to death. If there is, as many modern commentators have stated, a lack of self-conscious confusion, even unknowing, in Jesus in terms of the "I Am" sayings, then this, Redford asserts, is in accordance with his human nature and the degree of self-knowing which would have been unique because of his divine nature, while any knowledge the historical Jesus had of his divine nature would have been in accordance with his humanity. Jesus's self-knowledge would have developed and grown in accordance with his humanity.[40] The question then is the degree to which Jesus reveals this self-knowledge as an unfolding self-disclosure. This gradual unfolding fits in with what we have seen already, and also with Lewis's understanding of the divinity of Christ: Jesus in his humanity would have wrestled with this understanding, in much the same way that people today wrestle with a divine-human incarnated identity. Lewis speculated on how the human brain-mind related to the traditional characteristics of God—for example, omniscience—and how this affected Jesus's developing identity and self-understanding.[41] There would have been a struggle to grasp what this identity involved and even errors in his development. In correspondence Lewis commented, "Was Our Lord himself incapable, *qua* Man, of such errors? Would it be a real human incarnation if he was?"[42] For Lewis the incarnation was not primarily a translation of the Godhead into flesh, but was rather humanity being taken up, drawn, into God.[43] Jesus's humanity was gradually drawn into this self-conscious understanding of his divinity; this is in accordance with Lewis's Christology, his doctrine of the incarnation, but also with the patristic tradition.[44]

---

38. See, specifically, Lewis, "Difficulties in Presenting the Christian Faith to Modern Unbelievers," 426. Also, Lewis, "Modern Theology and Biblical Criticism," 166.

39. Redford, *Bad, Mad or God?*, 253. See also, Drumond, *An Inquiry into the Character and Authorship of the Fourth Gospel*.

40. Redford, *Bad, Mad or God?*, 254–58.

41. Lewis, *The Problem of Pain*, 110.

42. Lewis to Lee Turner Jul. 19, 1958. *Collected Letters, Vol. III*, 960–61.

43. Lewis, "Transposition," 2nd ed., 178.

44. See specifically, Athanasius, *The Incarnation of the Word*, Ch. 8, §.54, 93. See also, Justin Martyr, *Dialogue with Trypho*, 121 (155 AD); Irenaeus, *Against Heresies*, 4,20:1 (180 AD); Tertullian, *Apology*, 21 (197 AD); Cyprian, *Epistle to Jubaianus*, 72[73]:12 (256 AD). See also, Roberts, et al, *The Early Church Fathers: Ante-Nicene Fathers—Translations of the Writings of the Fathers Down to A.D. 325*; *The Nicene and Post-Nicene Fathers of the Christian Church-First and Second Series*. Most of the Patristic documents can be consulted online at: Christian Classics Ethereal Library (Calvin College, Grand Rapids, MI): http://www.ccel.org/.

6. aut Deus aut malus homo III: Divine Self-Disclosure

Redford's conclusions develop this: the historical Jesus knew that he was God; his knowledge grew out of his religious understanding as a Jewish man. Jesus knew the Scriptures and recognized that he was the God of Israel, the "I Am" of the Old Testament. What is more if we seriously analyze the Gospels and what we know of how they were written and developed, Jesus revealed this divine identity during his life on earth to those who knew him best. It was not, therefore, possible for his disciples to have fabricated these assertions in so complete and human a way. However, they did draw out the inferences, theologically, of what they saw and knew, especially after the resurrection.[45]

Perhaps it is in the context of *aut Deus aut malus homo*, which we encountered earlier, that H. P. Liddon best extrapolated this. John's Gospel may be a theological extrapolation of what Jesus said and did, but the key is the veracity of the consciousness Jesus has and how this is presented is accurate. This is why "it is undeniable that the most numerous and direct claims to divinity on the part of our Lord are to be found in the Gospel of John."[46] Therefore, it is not surprising that for over one hundred and fifty years John's Gospel has been the battleground of the New Testament. This is why Lewis's trilemma cannot be ignored: "[there is a] deep instinct of our nature which forbids neutrality when we are faced with high religious truth, which forces us to take really, if not avowedly, a side respecting it, which constrains us to hate or to love, to resist or to obey, to accept or reject it."[47] Liddon notes how the problem with taking seriously the skeptics' dismissal of John's Gospel as a mid-second century fabrication is that prior to that time there are sound patristic theologians, rigorous philosophers—from Polycarp to Irenaeus—who take it seriously. It has and always was polemical. It has a direct and dogmatic purpose, but its function is also to chronicle discourses and events omitted in the synoptic Gospels. But what are the arguments, essentially philosophical, for and against divine self-disclosure in Jesus? What do Lewis's opponents have to say? These will be considered next.

---

45 Redford, *Bad, Mad or God?*, 261.
46 Liddon, *The Divinity of Our Lord and Saviour Jesus Christ*, "Lecture V. The Doctrine of Christ's Divinity in the Writings of St John," 209.
47 Ibid., 210.

7

aut Deus aut malus homo IV: Arguments For and Against

SYNOPSIS:
It is now necessary, adopting Lewis's reasoned logic that underpins *aut Deus aut malus homo*, to give attention to the arguments for and against divine self-disclosure through incarnation. First, the theological evidence and arguments for self-disclosure. This is the proposition that Jesus is who he reveals himself to be, which is essentially the argument from orthodoxy: here the work of Peter Kreeft on Lewis's trilemma is considered, followed by an examination of a particular Jewish-Christian model from the scholarship of the American Rabbi Jacob Neusner, in the context of the christological work of Joseph Ratzinger, Pope Benedict XVI. If, like Neusner, we accept the veracity and integrity of the New Testament then what do we conclude? And is it possible to avoid the conclusion for and against becoming a personal decision? Neusner accepts the witness of the New Testament, yet draws back because Jesus is not an orthodox Jew showing absolute respect for "the eternal Israel" and the revelation to Moses on Mount Sinai. Second, a consideration of the arguments against divine self-disclosure—that this man was merely human. These arguments essentially revolve around the dismissal of Scripture as truthful witness, with examples from the work of A. N. Wilson, Gerd Lüdemann, and John Hick. A further objection is in the doctrine, or model, of God subscribed to by those claiming Jesus was not God incarnate: was Jesus just a mystic, guru, or shaman, who sought to make all aware of the divine inside them? This leads us to an objection often termed "the scandal of particularity"; that the incarnation is not universally available as knowledge to all. Philosophers will object, claiming that the Gospel writers cannot square the circle by making an intelligible reasoned claim that the man Jesus was genuinely and unambiguously God. The philosopher John Beversluis objects to Lewis's attempt to try to force a decision, representing those who seek to refuse to make a decision when confronted by the logical choice offered by Lewis in his trilemma. This may be termed, a model of obstinacy. In addition there are still people who would claim that Jesus simply was unhinged, deluded.

1. ARGUMENTS FOR SELF-DISCLOSURE—DIVINE SONSHIP

i. "He is who He Reveals himself To Be"

So how does Jesus reveal through self-disclosure who he is? Why is he considered to be God incarnate? What led to Lewis's decision? Lewis's argument is primarily theological, though these theological arguments are grounded in the scriptural witness. We can summarize Lewis's approach. As we have seen, Lewis's argument for Jesus's divine self-disclosure starts with the proposition *aut Deus aut malus homo*; if he is *malus homo*, he is either deluded or wicked. If we examine what Jesus said then we find that he claims to have always existed, that he has the authority to forgive sins above and beyond the right of the offended, furthermore he will return to judge all people at the end of time. There is an element of universalism about Lewis's perception of Jesus's divinity; that is, universal in the sense of being beyond or above specific human culture. He makes no mention of the Jewish context and heritage (the Tabernacle, etc.) save for the realization that Jesus was revealing himself as being at one with the God of Israel. If we are to consider Lewis's claims encapsulated in *aut Deus aut malus homo* seriously then we need to examine the justifications for divine self-disclosure, but also the arguments against.

ii. The Argument from Orthodoxy

Although "Modern" and "Liberal" biblical study has sought to deconstruct the Gospel narratives and in so doing hope to find the real historical Jesus distinct from the Christ of dogma, more than two hundred years of analysis has failed to find this alternate Jesus. Perhaps the best approach to the scriptural evidence is that though it may contains flaws—what Lewis called, to a degree, the humanity of Scripture—the account and portrait of Jesus is broadly accurate, the actions and claims of Jesus, the deeds and what was disclosed by Jesus are an accurate reflection of what happened. This is what is in many ways at the heart of *aut Deus malus homo*; it is this that turns the proposition into a dilemma (trilemma, for Lewis) because if the Gospels are telling us that the God of Israel descended to earth to redeem us and raise us up them we are faced with the predicament, the quandary, of how to respond. Despite multitudinous attempts to deconstruct the Gospels and find a true model of Christianity that complements and is at one with all other religions and philosophies, that simply presents a Jesus who was a good moral teacher, a religious guru and prophet, this dismantling has not worked.[1]

Peter Kreeft has stressed that the doctrine of Christ's divinity is the ground upon which all belief and dogma is built—"it is like a skeleton key that opens all the others."[2] However hard his sayings may at times be we must trust his authority—because he is divine. Kreeft has shown that the doctrine of Christ's divinity was the focus of concerns by the Jewish religious authorities (who regarded it as scandalous blasphemy) and by the Gentiles (who regarded it as incredulous). Therefore from the earliest time of the church Jesus's followers had to prove that he was what they said he was, and, as Liddon put it, the question about his moral character, his goodness if he was not God incarnate, was often uppermost. Therefore, for Kreeft it is the veracity of the patristic defense of Jesus's divinity that is to be considered uppermost. Many, both outside the church and

---

1. For example, "The gospels give entirely accurate accounts of the actions and claims of Jesus . . . This option represents the most common current explanation of the more spectacular deeds and extravagant claims of Jesus in the gospels," Blomberg, *The Historical Reliability of the Gospels*, xx. See also, Evans, *The Historical Christ and the Jesus of Faith: The Incarnational Narrative as History*.

2. Kreeft, *Fundamentals of the Faith*, 59.

7. aut Deus aut malus homo IV: Arguments For and Against

> **LEWIS—*AUT DEUS AUT MALUS HOMOS***
>
> **First**
> Jesus has always existed.
>
> **Second**
> Jesus has the divine authority to forgive sins;
> he behaves as if he is the person chiefly offended.
>
> **Third**
> Jesus has authority to judge all at the end of time.
>
> **Fourth**
> Jesus is therefore divine; if not he cannot be considered good
> in ordinary human terms.
>
> **Fifth**
> If he is not God he must be deluded or wicked—mad or bad.

Figure 9: C. S. Lewis—Summary of his position on *aut Deus aut malus homo*

within the church wanted to downgrade Jesus's ontology and status, granting him high status as a good and moral religious teacher. The argument against this downgrading uses logic. Either this man was, or was not, what he disclosed himself to be. The early church consisted of men and women who were prepared to die in defense of this central doctrine. Everything hangs together because of the incarnation.

An important argument here is racial—pertinently, religio-cultural. The apostles and the earliest witnesses to Jesus's divinity were Jewish. Would Jews have invented such a story considering they were open to the death penalty for blasphemy? Also asserting Jesus's divinity was a contradiction of the third commandment: "No Jew confuses Creator with creature, God with man. And no man confuses a dead body with a resurrected, living one."[3] For what reason did Jesus's followers invent this hoax, if that is what it is? What did they gain apart from suffering and death? It is a strong apologetic argument to look at the motives and the results particularly given the double risk the early church was exposed to—from the Romans on one hand and the Jewish religious authorities on the other. So, miracles and healings apart, the cultural identity of the Jewish religion asserts that Jesus and his followers would not have claimed divinity without it being so: there was nothing to be gained and the risks were far too great. Self-interest is not a motivating factor in Jesus's behavior or the witness of the earliest Christians. This is in addition to the condition, claims and character

---

3. Ibid., 62. See also, Chesterton, *The Everlasting Man*, 188. Henry Parry Liddon also uses this perspective, to a degree, in Lecture VII: Liddon, *The Divinity of Our Lord and Saviour Jesus Christ*, 360–448, see in particular, 414f.

that, according to Mark Hopkins, Jesus exhibited,[4] or the divinity witnessed to, for H. P. Liddon, by his consciousness, by the moral character of Jesus's self-assertion, and evidenced by his character: hence, *Christus, si non Deus, non bonus*[5]—if he is not God then he can by no means be considered good, by all that is acceptable as good and honest, upright and integrous.

iii. A Jewish-Christian Model

Joseph Ratzinger (since 2005, Pope Benedict XVI), who has published voluminously from the 1960s, is relatively rare amongst Western academic theologians in asserting the dilemma inherent in our response to Jesus's identity; many intellectuals prefer not to have to make a decision, as though they were keeping this Jesus at arm's length where he had no personal claim or effect on them. In his 2007 book *Jesus of Nazareth*, Ratzinger draws often on the work of Jacob Neusner, an American Rabbi and scholar.[6] Ratzinger referred to Neusner's book, *A Rabbi Talks with Jesus*, in his discussion of the identity of Jesus: who or what Jesus was and is, the characteristics determining the nature of his being, that which underpins his authority and nature.[7] Unlike much of the syncretistic "liberal" dialogue between Christians and Jews in the second half of the twentieth century, Neusner was prepared to take seriously the sayings, action, and claims of Jesus the Jew. Ratzinger noted Neusner's profound respect for the faith of Christians, which was in the context of his own faithfulness to Judaism and the Mosaic revelation. This led him into dialogue not with Christians but with Jesus. Neusner does not use any of the methods associated with "Modern" and/or "Liberal" theologians or philosophers, he does not attempt to deconstruct the Gospels to reveal what Bible scholars in the West believe to be the real historical Jesus; rather, he uses analogy and story (a very Lewisian approach!). He imagines himself amid the crowds in Galilee, on the wide grass plains of a shallow hill, hearing Jesus give the Sermon on the Mount. Here, Neusner listens to what Jesus has to say. Neusner then travels to Jerusalem, he converses with Jesus, in particular about how Jesus is leading faithful Jews away from Mosaic commandments (specifically relating to the Sabbath, and family traditions). He decides he cannot become a disciple because what Jesus is saying contradicts the Mosaic Law and revelation: "He remains—as he himself puts it—with the 'eternal Israel.'"[8] Neusner takes seriously the Christian claims about Jesus, he does not reductively deconstruct and therefore obliterate the New Testament—he takes the witness of the Gospel writers seriously and attributes truth to them. Neither does Neusner seek to ignore the great differences between Christianity and Judaism. Neusner does not downgrade Jesus to a social reformer or liberal rabbi, or the teacher

---

4. Hopkins, *Lectures on the Evidences of Christianity*, see, Lecture VIII, 227–57.
5. Liddon, *The Divinity of Our Lord and Saviour Jesus Christ*, Lecture IV, 153–208. See also, Biederwolf, "Yes, He Arose," 21–32.
6. Ratzinger, *Jesus of Nazareth*. See also, Ratzinger, *Introduction to Christianity*.
7. Neusner, *A Rabbi Talks with Jesus*. See also Neusner, *Eternal Israel Endures: Vol. 4, Judaism Transcends Catastrophe—God, Torah, and Israel Beyond the Holocaust*.
8. Ratzinger, *Jesus of Nazareth*, 105.

of a new morality.⁹ However, he does, from the perspective of an orthodox Jew, insist that he cannot follow Jesus:

> If I had been in the land of Israel in the first century, I would not have joined the circle of Jesus's disciples, I would have dissented, I hope courteously. I am sure with solid reason and argument and fact. If I heard what he said in the Sermon on the Mount, for good and substantive reasons I would not have followed him . . . Jews believe in the Torah of Moses and form on earth and in their own flesh God's kingdom of priests and the holy people. And that belief requires faithful Jews to enter a dissent at the teaching of Jesus, on the grounds that the teachings at important points contradict the Torah. Where Jesus diverges from the revelation by God to Moses at Mount Sinai, he is wrong and Moses is right.¹⁰

For Neusner, Jesus asserts himself to be a higher authority than the Jewish Law; if this is so then Jesus was in effect claiming to be God, the God of Israel, the giver of the Law. Neusner doesn't reject the Gospel account as so many academics do today; he accepts the picture of Jesus given by the Gospel writers. Ratzinger considers what Neusner has to say as, in many ways, more important than twentieth-century developments in biblical studies precisely because he accepts what Jesus discloses about his identity in the Gospels, his authority and status, but importantly the nature of his being. Ratzinger concludes that Neusner's debate with Jesus illustrated to him the importance of the choice God puts before each and every one who encounters Jesus—which is why we cannot ignore the question inherent in *aut Deus aut malus homo*, which therefore becomes a dilemma.

Ratzinger and Neusner take seriously the basic orthodox ground of Christian doctrine and Jewish teaching and create a new, yet traditional, model for dialogue. This model takes in part of the theological tradition of *aut Deus aut malus homo*— the dialogue issues from the claims to divinity (and thereby the authority) of Jesus.¹¹ Lisa Fabrizio—an American journalist and columnist, reviewing Ratzinger's *Jesus of Nazareth* for *The American Spectator*—focuses on this basic either-or question (*aut Deus aut malus homo*, though she does not use or identify this theological proposition): "Yet he [Neusner] returns over and over to the main thrust of the question of the identity and mission of Jesus of Nazareth . . . Christian teaching suggests that Jesus Christ was either everything he said he was—most notably the Son of God—or the world's most prolific and pathological liar. Those for whom this question remains unanswered would do well to begin their search anew by sharing in this profound meditation of the 'Servant of the Servants of God.' "¹² Essentially the differences between Ratzinger,

---

9. Ibid., 69–70, 103–11, and 123.
10. Neusner, *A Rabbi Talks with Jesus*, 3–4.
11. See, for example, in a similar field to Ratzinger: Balthazar, *Explorations in Theology: The Word Made Flesh*; Schmaus, *Katholische dogmatik*; Ott, *Introduction to Fundamentals of Catholic Dogma*; de Torre, *The Divinity of Jesus Christ*; Warfield, *The Lord of Glory: a Study of the Designations of Our Lord in the New Testament, with especial reference to His Deity*; Reymond, *Jesus, Divine Messiah: The New Testament Witness*.
12. Fabrizio, "History's Greatest Liar," para 11,
http://spectator.org/archives/2007/06/13/historys-greatest-liar.

as a traditional Roman Catholic Christian, and Neusner, as an orthodox Jew, pale in comparison to the question of decision; religion almost (but not quite) becomes if not irrelevant, second place to the response of each and every single human being to the demands put before them by the man Jesus of Nazareth. The question of identity, divinity, and authority that issues from this dilemma becomes central. Neusner accepts the veracity and validity in the witnesses of the Gospels.

2. ARGUMENTS AGAINST SELF-DISCLOSURE— THE MERELY HUMAN

What are the objections to the divinity of Christ? However nuanced and subtle the objections are, however much they are dressed up in concerns over academic integrity and impartiality, all the objections are grounded in whether the Gospel accounts are reliable. No one really attacks the concept of God or a "god" becoming incarnate, furthermore the idea of such a God/"god" dying to save his creatures from their sins is not attacked. However, the nature of the divinity Jesus claimed is offered as repudiation; likewise, other reasons that are broadly philosophical are put forward to lessen the impact of Jesus's claims. There are even those, admittedly a minority, who claim for insanity.

i. A Model of Scripture

The primary objection to Jesus's claims of divinity is that the scriptural account is wrong. These elements are a fabrication; the disciples elevated Jesus's status after his death out of respect for him, in much the same way that film stars, actors, and popular musicians are "deified": deification is imposed on Jesus who knew nothing of what was claimed on his behalf. The authority of the church, which produced the New Testament, is therefore compromised. However, these critics seem to be working with a concept of authorship, attribution, and truthfulness, that is relativistic and is now dominant in the West today—a concept which allows for individuals to twist the truth, rewrite history, invent (here it is called artistic license) for the sake of the work, or the success of the work.[13] This is a concept of the writer justified by romantic existentialism, the misunderstood genius who, however much others may criticize the re-phrasing and re-writing of truth, must be allowed to do what she or he wants to do. Did the Gospel writers work in this genre? No, such concepts did not exist prior to the late eighteenth century and the Romantic Movement in art and literature.

Philosophers, theologians, and biblical scholars argue endlessly over the historicity of the texts and many dismiss the veracity of the Gospels. The newspaper columnist, media commentator, and biographer A. N. Wilson criticized Lewis because there was no evidence that he respected or accepted the critical Bible scholarship from the nineteenth and twentieth centuries: "Form criticism and redaction criticism of

---

13. One only has to consider how popular television historical drama or dramatizations of novels rewrite the facts or the story for the sake of artistic licence—which means because the ego of the writer of the television programme wanted to see the story that way.

7. aut Deus aut malus homo IV: Arguments For and Against

the New Testament appeared to have passed him by."[14] It may be asserted that from what we have seen already Lewis was right to turn his back on the demythologizing tendency among such Bible scholars. Although they are a relatively small group of academics, it is surprising how the impact of "modern" and "liberal" Bible scholars through the media is out of all proportion to the inherent value of their work. Gerd Lüdemann, a Bible scholar who publically renounced his faith, commented that, "The broad consensus among New Testament scholars is that the proclamation of the divinity of Jesus was a development within the earliest Christian communities."[15] To claim that this is the belief of "Modern" and "Liberal" Bible scholars is something of a circular argument; it can be argued that a disbelief in the divinity of Jesus is, *per se*, fundamental to "Modern" and "Liberal" Bible studies. Many such Bible scholars have decided that the idea that Jesus proclaimed clearly his divinity during his ministry is wrongheaded, ahistorical, and naive. The philosopher of religion John Hick is highly critical of Lewis's trilemma. Hick's unquestioning respect for "Modern" and "Liberal" New Testament studies causes him to believe, like Lüdemann, that such scholars do not today support the view that Jesus claimed to be God: "A further point of broad agreement among New Testament scholars . . . is that the historical Jesus did not make the claim to deity that later Christian thought was to make for him: he did not understand himself to be God, or God the Son, incarnate."[16]

ii. A Model of "God"

A second argument against the divinity claimed by and for Jesus is in the concept of divinity invoked: what do we mean by "God"? There is the argument that Lewis's trilemma presupposes that we know what it is like to be God.[17] Virtually all religions have as a focus some form of a "god," or may acknowledge and invoke God. The later,

---

14. Wilson, *C. S. Lewis: a Biography*, 166. A. N. Wilson was an Anglican and a supporter of Lewis's works, who then became, in his own words, a born-again atheist, writing a deconstructive biography of Lewis. Wilson's initial tirade against Christianity was published two years after his conversion to atheism in 1989—A. N. Wilson, *Against Religion*. Then in 2009 he published an article in the British tabloid newspaper *The Daily Mail* claiming to have "rediscovered" his faith. See: A. N. Wilson, "Religion of hatred: Why we should no longer be cowed by the chattering classes ruling Britain who sneer at Christianity." Online at:
http://www.dailymail.co.uk/news/article-1169145/Religion-hatred-Why-longer-cowed-secular-zealots.html.
See also, Wilson, "Why I Believe Again", *The New Statesman* (Apr. 2, 2009). Online:
http://www.newstatesman.com/religion/2009/04/conversion-experience-atheism.
15. Lüdemann, "An Embarrassing Misrepresentation," 63–64. As a result of his views, Gerd Lüdemann notes on his website that, "The Confederation of Protestant Churches in Lower Saxony has objected to my teaching because in my publications and in my scholarly work I have engaged in critical discussions of the Protestant confession and the results of my research are not acceptable to the Protestant Churches in Lower Saxony and the Administration of the University of Göttingen. Therefore although I am an accredited New Testament scholar the President of the University of Göttingen has forbidden my chair to be designated a Chair of New Testament Studies." http://www.gerdluedemann.de/.
16. Hick, *The Metaphor of God Incarnate*, 27. See also, Hick (ed.), "Preface," The Myth of God Incarnate.
17. Stephen T. Davis notes this point. See, Davis, "Was Jesus Mad, Bad or God?," 2nd ed., 150.

mature, monotheistic religions may lay claim to have identified such a God amongst the "gods" but without revelation the exponents of these monotheistic religions can say little about God. Peter Kreeft notes a particular objection that has developed in the later twentieth century. This is, the ability to "orientalize" Jesus. Here the argument is that Jesus was a mystic or guru who realized his own inner divinity as a Hindu mystic would. In this context everyone is potentially divine: holiness, or intense religiosity, is equated with divinity. In Jesus's case he then went around believing he was the God of Israel, which, of course, is completely different from the Hindu "gods" or the Hindu sense of divinity, or higher consciousness.

> The problem with that theory is simply that Jesus was not a Hindu but a Jew! When he said "God," neither he nor his hearers meant Brahman, the impersonal, pantheistic, immanent all; he meant Yahweh, the personal, theistic, transcendent Creator. It is utterly unhistorical to see Jesus as a mystic, a Jewish guru. He taught prayer, not meditation. His God is a person, not a pudding. He said he was God but not that everyone was. He taught sin and forgiveness, as no guru does. He said nothing about the "illusion" of individuality, as the mystics do.[18]

Lewis was clear on this question. God for Jesus, raised in an orthodox Jewish culture, is the God of the Jews, the creator, YHWH the righteous Lord, the one true God outside of the world and beyond all other "gods." Jesus did not claim to be super religious; he was clearly not referring to being divine in the sense that anyone and everyone have the potential for such holiness divinity as intense religiosity. Lewis best understood this: "And when you've grasped that, you will see that what this man said was, quite simply, the most shocking thing that has ever been uttered by human lips."[19] Furthermore, Lewis comments that such a claim in front of and to other Jews has to be different from any claim to divinity amongst all the world's religions; this is different "to anything that happened with Plato, Confucius, Buddha, Mohammed."[20]

There is still the objection, maintained by some who still believe in the "modernist" agenda built on the innate human capacity to reason confidently, that Jesus's higher consciousness, his sense of the divine was (if you'll excuse the anachronism) Hegelian. For Hegelianism mental activity, thought, leads to a higher sense of self-determination, to a higher consciousness—a form of divinity; human thought and culture was discerned in the movement of what was defined as the world spirit. As the human mind confronted and comprehended this world spirit, this higher consciousness granted salvation: salvation through reason, through knowledge. Hegelian idealism believed that the human mind was implicitly divine, therefore everybody is to a greater or lesser degree divine. This is diametric to the Gospel—where *only Jesus* is divine. From a neo-Hegelian perspective, individuals, such as Jesus (the merely historically human Jesus), could participate in the divinely human life of all humanity. This would have appealed to the young Lewis, the atheist Oxford don who claimed to be a Hegelian idealist. Indeed it was difficult for Lewis to wrench himself away from the all-pervasive

18. Kreeft, *Fundamentals of the Faith*, 63. See also, Kreeft, *Between Heaven and Hell*, 84–100.
19. Lewis, *Broadcast Talks*, 50.
20. Lewis, "Christian Apologetics," 74.

influence of Hegel's philosophy, but the existential nature of the Gospel won: our human religiosity (in Hegelian terms, our sharing in a divine higher consciousness) is corrupted through original sin and often religion merely leads us to see our own reflection. If this is true of Jesus, that he was in effect a Hegelian divine, then he was deluded—and did such a delusion really sustain him to a horrible tortuous death on a cross?

iii. The Scandal of Particularity

We identified earlier what philosophers of religion referred to as the scandal of particularity: the incarnation is a single, small, event unknown to people who lived before Christ, and unknown to people who don't hear about this event. Real truth from God, so the philosophers' argument goes, about the human condition would be universal, available to all humanity, not particular. Jesus's divinity, like the incarnation, is enacted in the contingency of history. Operating contingently is (according to human intellectual perceptions) deemed inappropriate behavior for God. The philosopher of religion John Hick is highly critical of Lewis's trilemma because of its exclusivity; that is, the idea that Christianity represents an exclusive understanding about God because of what is contained in the Creed. By asserting that salvation is uniquely through Jesus Christ the implication is that all other religions are wrong. This depends on what relationship is proposed between the universal Christ sitting in judgment and the particular religion of Christianity down the ages. The American philosopher of religion Nicholas F. Gier, in *God, Reason, and the Evangelicals: The Case against Evangelical Rationalism*,[21] questions the divinity of Jesus in the Christian tradition. He argues that neither the patristic christological debates, nor the Council of Chalcedon, through to the Enlightenment christological debates of the nineteenth and twentieth centuries, have succeeded in squaring the circle by making intelligible the claim that the man Jesus was "genuinely and unambiguously God."[22] Gier opens the third chapter of his work with a number of quotations from theologians and philosophers who either endorsed or repudiated the incarnation; however, all these quotations emphasize the paradoxical nature of the doctrine of incarnation; that it is what Lewis would have seen as supra-rational. At times Gier appears to repudiate the very idea of the God-man, at other times he appears to be attempting to repudiate rationalism, *per se*, especially amongst American Evangelicals.[23] Like so many philosophers Gier appears to regard the concept of God becoming a man as a logical impossibility. The scandal of particularity means that the proposition that God could become incarnated human must be rejected; the idea of a mere human claiming divinity must likewise be discarded; the argument that one human being—Jesus—could be the way the truth and the life and the only way to the Father is, likewise, abandoned. Gier comments:

21. Gier, *God, Reason, and the Evangelicals. The Case against Evangelical Rationalism*.
22. Ibid., Ch. 3 "The Myth of God Revisited," 57–78, specifically 67.
23. Ibid., 57.

> My real sympathies, however, lie with the Christian progressives, primarily the authors of *The Myth of God Incarnate*, who partially justify their actions with a little history lesson: in the 17th Century the church survived when it was forced to give up a three-story, geocentric universe; with the rise of textual criticism. Christianity has not only survived but benefited enormously; and most Christians, even some conservative evangelicals, have also managed to come to terms with modern evolutionary theory. With these major historical adjustments in mind, the Christian liberals see no reason why Christianity cannot give up the myth of God incarnate.[24]

The problem here is—as with John Hick's de-Christianized universal religion read from all the world's religions, or more pertinently, what Hick decides to take from all the world's religions that fits in with the *particular* model he has in his mind of what true religion *should* be—that the philosophers of religion reject Jesus's divinity because of this scandal of particularity, having attempted to draw from all the world's religions and philosophies to try to find a *particular* common ground. The incarnation in Christianity therefore sticks out like a sore thumb. Despite the search for a common universal religion, drawn from all human religiosity, the conclusion of the philosophers of religion (who start from the premise that all religions are equal, except the one's they don't like) is a *particular* viewpoint or perspective: Gier's is different from Hick's, which is different yet again from Don Cupitt's. And all of them hold to varying degrees of belief in a "god" or no "god" at all. In seeking to overcome the *scandal of particularity* they merely create, each of them, individual *particularities* that have the appearance of universalism, indeed merely exhibit the pretence of universalism. Postmodernism actually comes to Lewis's aid here: if from a human perspective there can be no overarching universal perspective then the field is left open to God to act as God sees fit in his infinite wisdom—no one human being can solve the problem of humanity, only God can. Theologians and philosophers talk about a metanarrative (an over-arching story) or a worldview. Christianity has always, traditionally, been a worldview. What is outlined in the creed is of global importance to all humanity; it has always been a meta-narrative, we may say it is *the* narrative. By denying the idea of a meta-narrative issuing from a particular event, those who deny Christ's divinity are still asserting a metanarrative of sorts: to say that there is no metanarrative is to assert a metanarrative. John Hick is, in many ways, one of the last "modernists." Postmodernism eschews worldviews; at least it shuns human-generated worldviews and metanarratives.

Philosophers of religion will claim unity in what they term ultimate reality. Further, that this ultimate reality is available to all, except they appear to have a unique and superior knowledge of it. The problem is that this belief in a universal religion, which often marginalizes doctrine, is human-centered and is grounded in pluralism, or the appearance of plurality. So what is pluralism and why does it seem so attractive? Pluralism is defined as a condition or system in which two or more

---

24. Ibid., 77. Gier is referring to Hick, *The Metaphor of God Incarnate*, and to, Hick (ed.), "Preface," in, *The Myth of God Incarnate*.

states, groups, principles coexist (OED); in addition, a political theory or system of power-sharing among a number of political parties, though in this instance pluralism asserts a number of religious systems that occur side-by-side and recognize (as in philosophy) more than one ultimate principle. Such pluralism asserts that all religions are equal and equally valid, yet the proponents of pluralism simultaneously elevate some religions as valid, but not others: the Aztec religion, grounded in human sacrifice, is eschewed: all religions are equal, but some are more equal than others (to paraphrase a famous aphorism from George Orwell). Therefore, philosophers of religion who assert pluralism will, by and large, deny a hierarchical view of religion, the "gods," and the universe. To assert the particularity of the incarnation is to assert a hierarchical structure to religious truth; what is presented in the gospel is superior and a higher truth to other religious claims. This, above all else, *must* be denied by the philosophers of religion that deny the incarnation. By comparison many scholars in the late twentieth century have deconstructed this idea of pluralism by asserting that, for example, John Hick was not identifying a plurality but simply asserting his particular point of view. Gavin D'Costa has argued that *whatever* position one takes it is a *particular* position and, therefore, it is *not pluralistic*. A pluralistic position is just one among several competing supposedly equally valid positions.[25] All viewpoints and positions are exclusive: "To say that 'A' is true, it logically requires you to deny the truth of 'not A', then you are being selective, you are excluding. So any thesis in that sense is exclusive."[26] Therefore, in the end, inclusivity fails because it too is exclusive. For Lewis, we can acknowledge the particularity of the incarnation; this is the only way of avoiding the specific exclusive viewpoint of universal pluralism: revelation is the way out of this dilemma and paradox. If the initiative lies with God, then Christ, the second person of the Trinity, reaches out to and into humanity, whereby the Holy Spirit intimates explicitly or implicitly in varying degrees God's saving purposes to diverse peoples and cultures spread throughout human history across the world, widely dispersed and often isolated. And Matthew 25 (the Parable of the Sheep and the Goats), reveals to us how judgment and salvation is beyond human religion.

3. A MODEL OF OBSTINACY?

The objections we have considered thus far argue against divine self-disclosure. There are, however, those who would avoid making a decision. There are people who while accepting that Jesus was not mad or bad, when faced with the inherent logic in *aut Deus aut malus homo* will still opt to reject Jesus's divinity. Not on grounds of logic or even by refuting the evidence, but because they either delay making a decision or wait for other evidence to come along. This response we may term the model of obstinacy. Such people are inflexible, adamant, and unmoved; their obstinacy is in some ways reminiscent of so-called blind faith. These people do not want Jesus to be divine. To

---

25. See: D'Costa, "The Impossibility of a Pluralist View of Religion," 232. See also: D'Costa, *Christianity and World Religions*, and D'Costa, *Christian Uniqueness Reconsidered*.
26. Gunton, *Revelation and Reason*. 58.

delve further would bring us into the realm of psychology—there may be many reasons and causes in such a person's life to stall decision making; however, it may be that, like Nicodemus's encounter with Jesus, the time is not right for them to face the choice. This may be true of Lewis in his twenties; Tolkien and Dyson's confronting of Lewis was at the right time, but Lewis could still have chosen the other option, turned away.

i. A Post Mortem Socratic Dialogue

Peter Kreeft has presented something of this model of obstinacy in his narrative theology. In *Between Heaven and Hell*, Kreeft postulates a conversation between C. S. Lewis, the American President John F. Kennedy, and the writer Aldous Huxley.[27] The work is in many ways an example of Socratic dialogue. All three died on the same day—November 22, 1963—and meet somewhere after death in a sort of waiting zone. All three had strong opinions and were learned. Kennedy argues for "modern" humanism, Huxley for Eastern pantheistic religion, Lewis for orthodox Christianity. Much of the dialogue centers on Lewis's trilemma and naturally Lewis tries to force the logic of the argument onto the other two. He succeeds in refuting all of Kennedy's objections—there are no false premises, the terms are clear, the logic is valid; however, Kennedy does not want to accept the logical conclusion: Christ's divinity.[28] In the end Kennedy admits he simply does not want to accept Lewis's conclusion; he, in effect, defers the decision hoping for other evidence to come along.[29] This is a fictitious account; however, it illustrates a truism with regard to the psychology of belief, that what we take for truth, what we accept and feel comfortable with in our lives is often not the result of logically reasoned decisions. Our beliefs may be for reasons beyond our control and we may simply refuse, obstinately, to change what we believe. We may, as Kreeft has Lewis say to Kennedy, sometimes prefer happiness to truth, if the truth is challenging and uncomfortable.[30]

ii. Reason and Logic: The "god" of the Philosophers

In terms of a model of obstinacy, there are intellectuals, most often philosophers, who object to Lewis forcing a decision. This relates in terms of philosophy and logic, and Lewis apologetic methodology, to the law of excluded middle: Lewis's trilemma, in its use of a law of excluded middle, is considered too black-and-white, too clear cut; it lacks the nuanced subtlety of multiple choices, overlapping propositions, one might say indecision. The philosopher John Beversluis has criticized Lewis's use of logic and reason, particularly in his trilemma. He regarded the trilemma as Lewis's weakest argument because it is based on the assumption that we have a sound and authoritative account of what Jesus said— i.e., the scriptural record.[31] Beversluis argues that even if Jesus claimed he was God he could simply have been mistaken, which, for Beversluis,

27. Kreeft, *Between Heaven and Hell*.
28. Ibid., 68–69.
29. Ibid., 72.
30. Ibid., 70.
31. Beversluis, *C. S. Lewis and the Search for Rational Religion*, 115.

does not necessarily make him bad or mad.³² There is nothing new in Beversluis' repudiation of the proposition *aut Deus aut malus homo*, he simply rephrases old objections and reiterates them forcefully (ironically, this is, perhaps, similar to the forceful manner with which Lewis is reputed to have tried to press logic onto people). It is Lewis's capacity to try to force a decision through argument which appears most to disturb Beversluis; therefore he comments of Lewis that: "He habitually confronts his readers with the alleged necessity of choosing between two alternatives when there are in fact other options to be considered. One horn of the dilemma typically sets forth Lewis's view in all its apparent forcefulness, while the other horn is a ridiculous straw man."³³ Furthermore, he castigates Lewis's trilemma as "emotionally inflammatory . . . a false strategy," as a false dilemma it is "not a philosophical argument but a psychological spell."³⁴ In criticizing this Stephen T. Davis comments that:

> The major problem with Beversluis' critique is that he does not succeed in explaining how a sane person can be sincerely mistaken in claiming to be God. When Beversluis sets out to explain this point, he inexplicably switches from Jesus's claim to be divine to his claim to be the Messiah. These are two quite different things. Of course there were sane people in ancient Judaism who mistakenly claimed to be the Messiah; indeed, that was almost commonplace. But how can a sane person—especially a first-century Jew—mistakenly claim to be *divine*?³⁵

Beversluis misunderstands Lewis's use of reason and logic: Lewis saw such debate as an appendage, a human tool, in addition to perceiving and accepting the evidence—it was not only intellectuals, or doctors of philosophy, who could believe the gospel. We noted earlier in the context of Lewis's use of *aut Deus aut malus homo* in *The Problem of Pain*, that, "Christianity is not the conclusion of a philosophical debate on the origins of the universe: it is a catastrophic historical event following on the long spiritual preparation of humanity."³⁶ Lewis did not see logic and reason as necessary evidence for the veracity of the gospel. Although Lewis accepted Christianity on the basis of what he saw as convincing evidence, he saw rationality and logic as a means of showing that the faith was inherently rational; the trilemma demonstrated that a rational basis to Christian doctrine and the faith was possible. The why of the gospel remains in many ways beyond human comprehension. Or as the Apostle Paul put it, "Jews demand miraculous signs and Greeks look for wisdom, but we preach Christ crucified: a stumbling block to Jews and foolishness to Gentiles, but to those whom God has called, both Jews and Greeks, Christ the power of God and the wisdom of God" (1 Cor 1:22–25). According the logic of reasonableness³⁷ proposed by philosophers of

---

32. Ibid., 135.
33. Ibid., 43.
34. Ibid., 54.
35. Davis, "Was Jesus Mad, Bad or God?," 2nd ed., 151. For similar criticisms see, Craig, *Reasonable Faith: Christian Truth and Apologetics*, 2008.
36. Lewis, *The Problem of Pain*, 10–11.
37. That is, the "god" of the philosophers: from the Greek, λογικοτης, λογικότητα—logicality, logicalness, ratiocination, reasonability, reasonableness.

religion, the God of the Bible should not exist in the first place, and even if such a "god" can be postulated as worthy of existence (at the discretion and behest of philosophers) then it is illogical for such a "god" to be incarnated human to save the creature from their supposed sins (according to the logicality of reasonableness the problem of humanity, if there is a problem, would be for this "god" to wipe out humanity and start again). According to the Oxford professor, scientist, and media atheist Richard Dawkins "there almost certainly is no God," whereas according to the Oxford professor and philosopher of religion Keith Ward "there almost certainly is a God,"[38] but neither position can say any more without recourse to revelation, without humanity being ready to accept divine self-disclosure. From the capacity and strength of reason alone all we can do is postulate the non-existence/existence of a "god." Therefore, despite Lewis's use of reason and logic to show the rational basis of faith we are coming up against a wall that Lewis came up against: the limits of reason in the face of God's revelation, the inadequacy of reason and logic to *comprehend* God's self-revelation.

iii. Insanity

There are then those, albeit a minority, that conclude from looking at the Gospel record that Jesus was deluded for various reasons into believing he was God, or a "god"; that he was insane. Gerald O'Collins notes that there are still twentieth-century critics prepared to dismiss Jesus as insane. He refers to people such as the British sexologist, physician, and social reformer Henry Havelock Ellis who, "have argued that Jesus was a candidate for a lunatic asylum. In his *Impressions and Comments* Ellis complained that there was no such lunatic asylum in the suburbs of ancient Jerusalem: otherwise Jesus 'would infallibly have been shut up in it at the outset of his public career.'"[39] There are people who are self-confessed atheists who when pressed would certainly consider anyone who is religious as being deluded; however, generally speaking, most commentators today would not classify Jesus as insane or deluded, though some would question whether he really was of sound mind if he was an ordinary human being and still said the things he did. So we are back to the logic of Lewis's trilemma.

---

38. Dawkins, *The God Delusion*. See: Ch. 4 "Why There Almost Certainly is no God" 137–89, see specifically, 157–58. See also, Keith Ward, *Why There Almost Certainly Is a God: Doubting Dawkins*, see, Ch. 8, "Why there is a God," 141–49. Ironically the argumentation of both is spurious: either there is a God or there is not. If Dawkins's "there is almost certainly no God," is quantified, say, at less than a 1% chance—then there is still a God. God's existence is not reduced or inhibited by arguments around the subjunctive (!).

39 O'Collins SJ, *Incarnation*. See, Ch. 11 "The Credibility of the incarnation," 125–33, ref. 131. O'Collins is referring to Ellis, *Impressions and Comments*; Henry Havelock Ellis wrote on such topics as homosexuality, autoeroticism, and narcissism.

8

aut Deus aut malus homo V: Lewis's Trilemma

SYNOPSIS:
What is the structure of Lewis's argument? Is it bipartite or tripartite? As popular apologetics Lewis presents the argument as a 1+2 trilemma specifically using simplistic language: a) mad, b) bad, or c) God (MBG or BMG). How does this compare with other examples of trilemmas—both religious and secular—for example in politics and economics, or the Munchhausen-Trilemma? It is important for us to consider the conclusions of the philosophers Stephen T. Davis and Peter Kreeft, who analyzed the structure and logic of Lewis's argument. Davis presents the argument in essentially eight premises, with four related ancillary premises; he examines the nature of the argument in terms of proof, validity, and soundness and weighs this against the critical objections in relation to what constitutes the implicit claims to Jesus's divinity. Therefore he considers what *value* there is to the argument in relation to rationality and people's reception of the argument. Peter Kreeft's methodology is in the form of a Socratic dialogue concluding that, *aut Deus aut homo malus, et non homo malus, ergo Deus* (either Jesus is God, or a bad man; he is not a bad man, therefore he is God). Kreeft demonstrates deductive proof in the form of trustworthiness and sagacity: how do we compare the wise, sages, and the deluded? How does Kreeft classify Jesus? By logical deduction we can eliminate all of humanity, except one person: Jesus—who was wise and sagacious, yet claimed divinity.

What value in terms of an inherent rationality do they identify in Lewis's work? Is Lewis's trilemma an attempt at a proof of God's existence? What concept or doctrine of God is Lewis working with and how does this compare with the understanding of God in the first century? If Lewis's trilemma, even though it is grounded in *aut Deus aut malus homo*, is not a proof, is it a question? Lewis's trilemma may be seen as a question, a human quandary, a predicament, where each and every person must come to a decision about this man and recognize Jesus for who he is: God incarnated for his/her salvation. The weak point of Lewis's proposition is in his use of "mad"; in invoking insanity, and in separating madness from wickedness, he is on shaky ground and fails to define or take seriously the element of delusion in all of humanity after the fall. In conclusion, we can consider whether Lewis is right to attempt to force an answer to the question *aut Deus aut malus homo* (if it is a question), and in what sense there is the element of pneumatological preparation for a human acknowledgement of Jesus Christ's Lordship. Can any mere human decision give a final victory to either interpretation? For all its perceived faults there are four reasons why Lewis's trilemma was and still is a very successful piece of Christian apologetic: first because it demonstrates that there is a rational basis to Christian doctrine; second, because it does contain the basic either-or question at the heart of the Christian faith; third, because of the attention it has gained—through it Lewis was effectively preaching the gospel; and, fourth, because so many writers of varying persuasions have sought to repudiate it.

1. INTRODUCTION

So, having examined what Lewis said in terms of his trilemma—the thirteen examples over a twenty-four year period—and having considered the theological history of Lewis's proposition in the form of *aut Deus aut malus homo*, from its biblical and patristic roots through to the either-or proposal in such theologians as Mark Hopkins and Henry Parry Liddon, furthermore having considered what we mean by divine-self disclosure (having taken into account the scriptural evidence and the reliability of John's Gospel) along with the arguments for and against self-disclosure, then we can now turn to Lewis's trilemma and consider its structure and value.

2. THE STRUCTURE OF LEWIS'S ARGUMENT

The argument, or question, for Christ's divinity we have been considering, which has occurred in one form or another in varying degrees through much of the Christian tradition for two thousand years, is in form bipartite: either-or. So if individuals are forced to make a choice then the decision making process is a dilemma. Because of the seriousness of the issue in question—is this man really God, which effects our salvation—then we must make a decision: he is one or the other. Either this man was God incarnate, or he was merely human. Lewis nearly always—certainly when presenting this proposition as popular apologetics—presents not a dilemma but a trilemma: a three option tripartite argument: a trilemma or *triumvirate*.

According to the Oxford English Dictionary, a *triumvirate* is a group of three powerful or notable people or things (originally relating to the office of *triumver* in ancient Rome); a trilemma is a choice between three distinct options, one of which must be selected. Trilemmas can be defined as three-way forced choices; each item represents a choice that is informative, stark, and as contradictory as possible. In political terms Western liberal democracies must choose—their governments cannot be simultaneously free, fair, and equal in their treatment of citizens. In economic terms for Western liberal democracies (or more pertinently Western-style capitalist economies grounded in perpetual economic growth) there is not so much a dilemma but a trilemma: national debt, cutbacks on public spending, or increased taxes; the three are not compatible, but a choice must be made. In environmental consideration we are faced with a trilemma where not making a decision simply makes the problem of pollution and planetary degradation worse: the "trilemma of the earth," or "3E trilemma," is invoked by environmentalist when trying to balance the needs of people with the needs of the planet.[1] The three components are economy, energy

1. Hamakawa, "New Energy Option for 21st Century," 30–35.

8. aut Deus aut malus homo V: Lewis's Trilemma

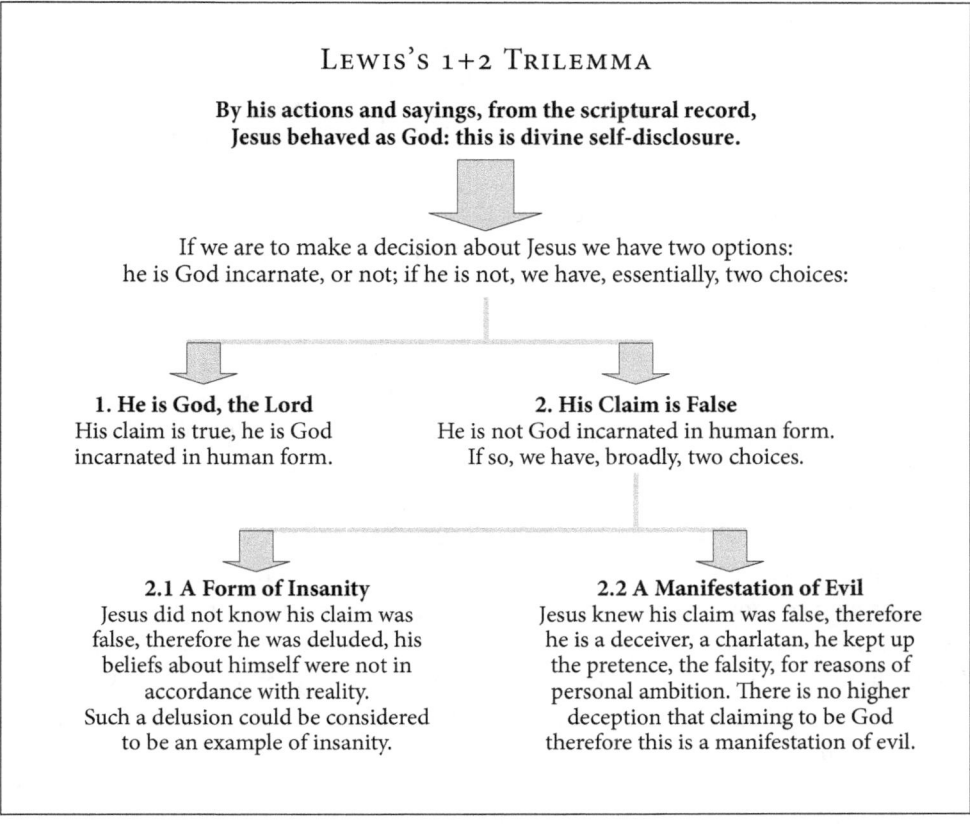

Figure 10: C. S. Lewis—a 1+2 trilemma

and environment, and how these three conflict. Economic development needs an increase in the expenditure of energy, but this increases pollution and environmental degradation; improving the environment will inevitably reduce the use of energy and thus stifle economic development.

In philosophy there is the so-called Munchhausen-Trilemma. In terms of knowledge this stresses the impossibility of proving certain truths. There are three ways of proving certain propositions, but all are incompatible, hence the trilemma.

First, Infinite Regress
Any assertion of truth must justify the means whereby a conclusion was arrived at; and the means of justification must also be justified—and so on. We are faced with what is termed infinite regression, justification is unending.

Second, Dogmatism
We can say the truth is self-evident, it is axiomatic, we may even appeal to common sense, and we can assert authority—as in the Pope asserting infallible statements, *ex cathedra*—but all this does is abandon the demand for justification (though according to the first proposition the demand for justification is, in any case, unending).

Third, Circularity
There is the potential for circularity, or what is called a circular argument, where the proof is assumed in the question. This is the case of using the premise for a question to prove a conclusion, and then using the conclusion to prove the premise—this is an attempt to prove two statements reciprocally from each other.

In the Munchhausen-Trilemma we have three stark and impossible ways of proving certain truths. In other words, from a human perspective, proof becomes impossible to prove, which leaves us open to revelation; reason cannot survive by itself or justify itself without God, without revelation. You cannot prove God; only accept how God communicates, how he imparts understanding to humanity through revelation. And revelation, as we have seen for Lewis, is transposed. So, on the question of Christ's divinity Lewis's argument is where we must choose between three notable and powerful propositions; in this case each is distinct and incompatible with each other, and we must decide on one: hence this *triumvirate* is a trilemma. From a secular humanist perspective all three propositions are wrong: Jesus cannot be God because for secular liberal humanists there is no God (which, of course, has an element of circularity in it). And this man cannot be mad because his statements clearly do not point to insanity, or psychological disorder. And this man cannot be bad because, for Lewis, such secular liberal humanists praise Jesus as a good moral teacher. Therefore Lewis's tripartite structure of the proposition *aut Deus aut malus homo* is how he presents the question of Christ's divinity to such secular liberal humanists in his popular apologetics; this is as a stark three-way forced choice, informative, yet contradictory. However, his comments in the address "Christian Apologetics" where he quotes *aut Deus aut malus homo*s, indicates that the root of this proposition is essentially bipartite: God (*Deus*) or bad-wicked man (*malus homo*); the second element is then divided into two—deluded or evil, hence the trilemma, the three components. Therefore, to be more accurate Lewis's trilemma is a 1+2 trilemma where either of the components must be chosen, all cannot stand.

In bipartite terms either Jesus was speaking truth: he was Son of God (God incarnate) and Son of Man (a messianic term), he was divine; or Jesus exaggerated what he was, his story was a sham, a pretence; he was, as Liddon termed it a charlatan, and importantly, he knew what he was doing and consciously maintained the pretence. Therefore, he was a liar and can be considered evil because he was in effect opposing God by claiming to be God. If, however, Jesus was not divine but fully believed the delusion then there are questions that must be raised about his sanity. People, upon reading the Gospel, can ignore this; they can avoid or delay making a decision, they can sit on the fence and simply ignore the question of the nature of Jesus's being, but they cannot then hold an authoritative opinion about Jesus. However, having read the Gospel they will, perhaps sub-consciously form an opinion. In so doing they are deciding—they are responding to Jesus's question to Peter, "But who do you say that I am?" By the very enigmatic nature of this man Jesus people do make a decision. In forcing the proposition into a trilemma Lewis is showing that there are two options, but that there is a distinction within the second (madness or badness); therefore people's opinion of Jesus will fall broadly into one of these three options. This is why Lewis is so scornful of the idea that the question can be answered by asserting that Jesus was just a good moral teacher.

Aut Deus aut malus homo does not demonstrate one element to be true, it presents the options, the alternatives, and therefore echoes Jesus's question to Peter—the reader is invited to decide, to make up his/her mind. The reader is free to ignore the proposition and not decide; but that in itself is a decision and they take responsibility for that decision.

3. A PHILOSOPHICAL ANALYSIS: STEPHEN T. DAVIS

Stephen T. Davis,[2] the American Christian philosopher, has analyzed in relative depth Lewis's trilemma, or, as he refers to it, the "Mad, Bad, or God" argument.[3] Davis points out that Jesus's being truly human is without doubt, that his bodily resurrection may be difficult for some to accept, though it can be considered reasonable to accept, but that his claimed divinity is another matter. It is therefore the *divinity* of Christ that is the great stumbling block for many and it is this that is at the heart of Lewis's trilemma. But what does it mean to be divine and human? If we are to tackle the detractors who for various reasons question Lewis's argument (for example, because it presupposes what it is to be God, or because it excludes the critical basis of "modern" philosophy, or because the scriptural record is dismissed as a fabrication, or even because it is claimed that Jesus simply did not know what he was talking about), and if we are to use Lewis's trilemma as a piece of assertive Christian apologetic then we need to analyze its veracity and value as philosophical theology. This Davis does. However, we need to place the trilemma in context:

> Is it a good argument, or not? Probably no central issue of Christian belief depends on the argument. Orthodox Christians could go on believing in the divinity of Jesus even if the argument fails. (On the other hand, if the argument succeeds, those who deny the incarnation at the very least have some explaining to do.) But the frequency with which the argument appears in popular defenses of the divinity of Jesus, and its almost total absence from discussions about the status of Jesus by professional theologians and biblical scholars, makes one curious what to make of the argument.[4]

Davis proposes that Lewis's trilemma properly understood can be used to establish the rationality of belief in the incarnation, though it is important to remember that the post-resurrection encounters and sightings are equally important: it is not just what

---

2. A graduate of Princeton Theological Seminary and Claremont Graduate University (PhD), Stephen T. Davis specializes in philosophy of religion, philosophical theology, and Christian thought. See: Davis, *Faith, Scepticism, and Evidence*; Davis, *Logic and the Nature of God*; and, Davis, *Risen Indeed: Making Sense of the Resurrection*.
3. Davis, "Was Jesus Mad, Bad or God?," 2nd edition, 149–71.
4. Ibid., 151.

Jesus said and did that exhibited divine self-disclosure. Davis therefore sets-out an analysis of the argument in what is its logical form.

i. The Nature of the Argument: Proof, Validity, Soundness

For Davis the first premise is crucial; it is the root of the argument—that is, Jesus's claims of divinity (see figure 11). The second premise is, for Davis, an example of substitution-instance, an example of the law of excluded middle. Despite the criticism of its use by academics who do not like cut-and-dried, either-or, arguments, Davis does assert that it is a perfectly valid technique to use. As a premise it is correct: either Jesus was correct in claiming to be divine, or he was incorrect—the trilemma cannot be challenged here. However, Davis asserts, the third premise can be questioned. For example, Jesus may not have been mad or bad, "but was merely sincerely mistaken about the matter, just as it is possible for a person to be sincerely mistaken about who her true parents are."[5] But is it possible for someone to be sincerely mistaken on such a question as self-divinity and still be sane and/or good? Therefore, Davis asks the question (premise 9), "Is it probable that any good person who mistakenly claims to be divine is mad?" Is such a premise innately false? Or, for that matter, is it probable that (premise 10), "any sane person who mistakenly claims to be divine is bad," is likewise false? Davis comments that these are difficult questions, but that he is inclined to accept both premise 9 and premise 10, and therefore premise 3 also.[6] "It is hard to see how a sane and good person could be sincerely mistaken in holding the extremely bizarre belief that he or she is divine (assuming he or she uses the word "divine" as Christians normally do in this context, i.e., as indicating a robust identity with the omnipotent, omniscient, loving creator of the world). There is something extremely odd about the notion of a sincere, good, and sane person mistakenly claiming to be God."[7] So where does that leave us? However questionable the third premise is to "modern" and "liberal" minds, we must accept that if Jesus was wrong to claim such divinity then this was because he was not a good person, or worse, because of delusions bordering on insanity: he was, to put it in simplistic terms, bad or mad! Premises 4 and 5 are generally unchallenged even by the most hardened anti-religious, anti-God atheist: Jesus, they will argue, cannot be regarded as mad or bad: "Virtually everyone who reads the Gospels—whether committed to Christianity or not—comes away with the conviction that Jesus was a wise and good man. He was loving, compassionate, and caring; hardly the sort who tells lies for reasons of self-interest."[8] However, it is important to remember, as we have noted already, that Jesus was accused of being demonically possessed or even out-of-his-mind during his lifetime.[9] Davis does ask the question, did Jesus show what is termed a divinity complex characterized by traits

5. Ibid., 152.
6. Ibid., 153.
7. Ibid.
8. Ibid., 152.
9. For example: Matt 14:2 & Mark 6:14; Matt 12:23–24; John 10:19–21; Mark 3:22–30; John 8:49 and 10:21.

8. aut Deus aut malus homo V: Lewis's Trilemma

> ### Stephen T. Davis: the Logical Form of C. S. Lewis's Trilemma (the MBG Argument)
>
> **The logical progression of the argument is:**
>
> (1) Jesus claimed, either explicitly or implicitly, to be divine.
> (2) Jesus was either right or wrong in claiming to be divine.
> (3) If Jesus was wrong in claiming to be divine, Jesus was either mad or bad.
> (4) Jesus was not bad.
> (5) Jesus was not mad.
> (6) Therefore, Jesus was not wrong in claiming to be divine.
> (7) Therefore Jesus was right in claiming to be divine.
> (8) Therefore, Jesus was divine.
>
> **Four related premises that need to be considered are:**
>
> *Is it probable that–*
>
> (9) Any good person who mistakenly claims to be divine is mad is false?
>
> *Or is it probable that–*
>
> (10) Any sane person who mistakenly claims to be divine is bad is false?
>
> *It may be argued that–*
>
> (11) If Jesus mistakenly claimed to be divine and wasn't mad, then, improbable as it seems, he must have been bad or else,
> (12) If Jesus mistakenly claimed to be divine and wasn't bad, then, improbable as it seems, he must have been mad.
>
> Stephen T. Davis, "Was Jesus Mad, Bad or God?" *Christian Philosophical Theology* (2006).

Figure 11: Stephen T. Davis—The Logical Form of C. S. Lewis's Trilemma

of narcissism, egocentricity, inflexibility, and so forth? In this context he notes that messianic divinity complexes usually lead to death, even mass-suicide: "The Reverend Jim Jones, whose cult followers committed mass suicide in Guyana in 1978, is reported to have said to them: 'I'm the closest thing to God you'll ever see.' "[10]

The difficulty for many secular philosophers comes with premise 6: if he was not deluded or malicious then Jesus cannot have been wrong in claiming to be divine (that is, given what we know about the Judaic understanding of divinity). Therefore, if we accept Jesus was not deluded, insane, or a malicious charlatan, then we must accept that in relation to the God of Israel Jesus was divine.[11] "But," asks Davis, "is the argument also sound? Let us say that a sound argument is a valid argument whose premises are all true. It appears thus far that while premises 3, 4, and 5 can be criticized, a plausible case can be made for their truth. Clearly the premise that will seem most vulnerable to

---

10. Davis, "Was Jesus Mad, Bad or God?," 2nd ed., 153.
11. Ibid., 154.

criticism is premise 1."[12] Davis then seeks to defend the scriptural record in much the same way that we have.

ii. Critical Objections

Did Jesus claim either explicitly or implicitly to be divine? Davis groups the objections to premise 1 under four headings, objections which we have examined already though it is interesting to note the emphasis he gives. First, such claims presuppose that humanity can "know" what it is like to be God; second it assumes the legitimacy of special divine acts in history (what is often dismissed as a naive worldview); third, it misinterprets what Jesus implied by the assertions about himself that we find in the Gospels; fourthly, it presupposes a pre-critical view of the Gospels—especially the Gospel according to John—assuming that certain elements are historical.

iii. Claims of Divinity

In defense of Lewis's trilemma Davis is not "claiming that Jesus went about saying 'I am God' or making any sort of explicit claim to status as deity."[13] He notes how the radical monotheism, as he terms it, of first-century Judaism made this impossible. Likewise Davis is not claiming that Jesus expressed his divinity in the language of creedal orthodoxy, the language of the church fathers and the creeds. Any claim or evidence of Jesus's divinity is implicit: given the words and deeds of Jesus it is, in Davis's words, highly probable that he experienced himself as divine; this divinity is in the form of the unique relationship of divine Sonship to God the Father.[14] Jesus did not intentionally confuse himself with the Father because of his human form; but this relationship revealed in him divine prerogatives, which placed him on a par with God. Deciding how someone exhibits implicit claims (in this case of divinity in an explicitly Jewish context) is fraught with difficulties.

This raises the question: did Jesus teach those around him *about* his divinity? We examined this in the previous chapter; however, it is pertinent to see, considering his analysis of Lewis's trilemma, how Davis approaches this question. He approaches Jesus's self-consciousness in five categories; that is, markers of self-disclosure:[15]

First,
Jesus assumed for himself the divine prerogative to forgive sins

Secondly,
The intimate, almost blasphemous way, Jesus addressed God

Third,
Jesus spoke "with authority," not citing sources or precedents of famous rabbis.

---

12. Ibid.
13. Ibid., 159.
14. Ibid., 160.
15. Ibid., 166–69.

8. aut Deus aut malus homo V: Lewis's Trilemma

Fourth,

Even in the Synoptic Gospels, Jesus said things that can sensibly be interpreted as implicit claims to divinity.

Fifth,

Jesus implicitly made two dramatic claims: first, that our relationship to him would determine our final status before God; secondly, that he himself would be the judge of all human beings at the end of history.

iv. The Value of the Argument

Davis concludes that the argument, according to a systematic philosophical analysis, can be shown to be valid. However, is the argument sound? Generally speaking it is, though its weakest premise (figure 11), Davis acknowledges, is the first premise—that Jesus claimed, either explicitly or implicitly, to be divine. Here the weakness is simply defined by the self-generated criteria of Enlightenment-led "Modern"/"Liberal" academics (indeed this is what is often seen as an almost irrational rejection and prejudice towards Scripture, the belief that the Bible must be automatically rejected, *per se*). Does Davis consider Lewis's trilemma to be a success? This depends on what is perceived to be the goal and purpose of the argument. Is the aim of the trilemma to convince all non-believers in the divinity of Jesus? Davis comments that if the aim of "the MBG argument were to convince all non-believers in the incarnation of Jesus . . . then one must doubt that the MBG argument can count as successful. Few non-believers will be converted by it; no matter how hard we argue for the truth of premise 1."[16] Why? Because, as Davis demonstrates, people who do not want to believe will always find some reason, or construct an argument in their minds, to reject the claims to Jesus's divinity. Thus Davis comments that, "I do not hold that the MBG argument establishes the irrationality of unbelief in the incarnation of Jesus."[17]

Is the aim of the argument to demonstrate the truth of the incarnation? This is related to the first aim; that is, to convince unbelievers, because if something is demonstrated to be true beyond human construct then surely all should accept the truth? If the aim is to demonstrate the truth of the incarnation but crucially to demonstrate the rationality of belief in the incarnation of Jesus, then we are on stronger grounds: "If one of these constitutes the true aim or goal of the MBG argument, then it will not matter whether nonbelievers in the incarnation can rationally reject one or another of the argument's premises."[18] Davis's conclusion is that "[to] demonstrate the rationality of belief in the incarnation of Jesus is the proper goal or aim of the MBG argument. And given what we have concluded . . . I believe it succeeds in doing that very thing. Accordingly, the MBG argument can constitute a powerful piece of Christian apologetics."[19]

16. Ibid., 170.
17. Ibid.
18. Ibid.
19. Ibid., 171.

4. A PHILOSOPHICAL ANALYSIS: PETER KREEFT

We noted the work of Peter Kreeft earlier. In his work *Between Heaven and Earth* he analyses the structure of Lewis's trilemma; Kreeft concentrates on a logical analysis of the question of anthropology—that is, the nature of Jesus as fully human yet fully divine. Kreeft initially identifies five objections to Christ's divinity, all of which can be dismissed in ways similar to the manner in which we have overcome objections: first, a "Modern" and/or "Liberal" Christianity can be found to dismiss the claims of an ancient or patristic Christianity, which asserted the divinity of Jesus; this relates to a second objection, a post-Enlightenment proposition that humans become "gods" in their own mind, but not in what we take to be reality; third, objections often hinge on an out-right dismissal of the miraculous and the supernatural, which is assumed to be at the heart of the idea of Christ as very God and very man; fourth, objectors will often dismiss a traditional concept of church authority; fifth, epistemological issues—objectors question a belief in objective truth, and the relationship between reason and idealism. If these five objections are seen as spurious then we must accept as sound the ground of any argument for the divinity of Christ

i. aut Deus aut homo malus, et non homo malus, ergo Deus

Kreeft's method is that of a Socratic dialogue between three people (Lewis, Aldous Huxley, and John F. Kennedy), as such it is fictitious; however, it is a form of analogical narrative theology, that is, it presents objective christologically-orientated truth though a story of a conversation between three people who have died on the same day (November 22, 1963) and who find themselves in a waiting room, *post mortem*. Kreeft presents Lewis as a Christian apologist defending the incarnation and therefore Jesus's divinity as very God and very man. Within the dialogue, Lewis counters Kennedy's objections to Jesus's divinity by a use of logic and idealism. Kennedy questions whether Lewis can prove anything about someone who died two thousand years ago; Lewis counters that methodological issues are second order questions; however, he asserts that proof is the only proof available: "The only way to show that anything is possible and how it is possible, is to show that it is actual. The only way to prove that a thing can be proved is to prove it."[20] (So actuality, the existing conditions or facts, and therefore the state of existing in reality, breaks the Munchhausen-trilemma!)

The argument, the apologetic defense, for Kreeft is, *aut Deus aut homo malus, et non homo malus, ergo Deus* (either Jesus is God, or a bad man; he is not a bad man, therefore he is God).[21] A mere man who claimed to be God would not be considered to be a good man. The basis of Lewis's trilemma is expressed, for Kreeft in four premises (see figure 12): those who do not claim to be God, nor are they remarkably wise (the vast majority of people); there are then those who do not claim to be God and are wise sages; however, there are then those who claim to be God and are not remarkably wise or sagacious, and are usually categorized as deluded or insane; however, a fourth and

---

20. Kreeft, *Between Heaven and Hell*, 2nd ed., 38.
21. Ibid, 38–39, & 67.

PETER KREEFT: THE LOGICAL FORM OF C. S. LEWIS'S TRILEMMA (THE LLL ARGUMENT)1

The logical deduction of Jesus' Divinity:

(1) Those who neither claim to be God nor are remarkably sagacious: the vast majority of people.

(2) Those who do not claim to be God and are remarkably sagacious: people like Buddha. Socrates, Confucius, Lao-Tin, Moses. Muhammad and the rest.

(3) Those who claim to be God and are not remarkably sagacious: the insane.

(4) Those who both claim to be God and are remarkably sagacious: in this category there is only one—Jesus.

Peter Kreeft, *Between Heaven and Hell* (2006).

Figure 12: Peter Kreeft—The Logical Form of C. S. Lewis's Trilemma 1

PETER KREEFT: THE LOGICAL FORM OF C. S. LEWIS'S TRILEMMA (THE LLL ARGUMENT)2

Jesus is *aut deus aut homo malus*:

(1) He is not a bad man.

(2) Therefore he is God.

(3) Proof of the first premise: A mere man who claims to be God is a bad man, not a good man. He is either a liar (if he doesn't believe his claim) or a lunatic (if he does).

(4) Thus Jesus is either "Lord, Liar or Lunatic".

The Nature of Jesus as a wise sage:

(5) Sages (the wise) are trustable.

(6) Jesus is a sage. Therefore Jesus is trustable. Trustable people are not subject to self-deception, especially with regard to themselves.

(7) Jesus tells the truth, especially about himself.

(8) Jesus says be is God; therefore it is true that he is God.

Peter Kreeft, *Between Heaven and Hell* (2006).

Figure 13: Peter Kreeft—The Logical Form of C. S. Lewis's Trilemma 2

final group identifies those who both claim to be God and are remarkably wise and sagacious: in this last category there is only one—Jesus.

ii. Deductive Proof—Trustworthiness and Sagacity

Kreeft focuses on the trustworthiness of Jesus as compared to those who inhabit two other groups—the wise and sagacious, on the one hand, as compared to the deluded, on the other. How does Kreeft classify Jesus? Jesus as a sage demonstrates practical wisdom, insight into the human heart, and practical love—altruism, compassion, selflessness, and charity; in addition he demonstrates creativity, unpredictability, and, what Kreeft terms, a multidimensionality to his character that renders him essentially unclassifiable.[22] When human beings exhibit a divinity complex they are generally diagnosed as deluded, or suffering from some sort of insanity; that is, except for one—Jesus of Nazareth. A generally accepted principle is that sages, the wise, and prophetic do not claim divinity.[23] Therefore, as we have noted already for Kreeft, a person's sanity is measured by the distance, or lack of, between what you claim for yourself (your self-perception and self-disclosure) and reality: that is, the truth that is external to yourself and what others think about you.[24] Kreeft notes, "The psychological state of a person with a divinity complex is exactly opposite of that of the sage."[25] Therefore, by logical deduction we can eliminate all of humanity, except one: Jesus (see figure 13). Therefore, in terms of deductive proof—from a general principle to a particular case—Jesus cannot be regarded as an ordinary person, nor a sage because of his claims to divinity; therefore the logic is valid: *aut Deus aut homo malus, et non homo malus, ergo Deus*—if he is generally, even universally, not regarded as bad, evil, or deluded, then he must be accepted as God, because of the implicit evidence.

5. PROOF . . . OR A QUESTION, A HUMAN DILEMMA?

Lewis knew that there was a long theological heritage to his trilemma, that this proposition was rooted in the Latin theological phrase, *aut Deus aut malus homo*. However, as a Christian apologist he, to a degree, forced the argument; he popularized the issue. Readers had to come to a decision, and it was no good hiding in a character judgment that said this Jesus was a good moral teacher. In forcing the issue Lewis weakens the argument because there are several loosely defined details in his presentation, which upon examination cast doubts about the way Lewis phrased his trilemma. These concerns are three-fold: the concept of God underpinning his argument, the question of the nature of the proof he is working with, and precisely what he means by and how he uses, invokes, the term insanity (referring—implicitly—to the delusion of a divinity complex in ordinary mortals). These concerns form the next three sections.

22. Ibid., 54–62, & 140.
23. Ibid., 140.
24. Kreeft, *Fundamentals of the Faith: Essays in Christian Apologetics*, Ch. 1 Creed: Fundamentals of Christian Belief, §A. Fundamentals of Christian Apologetics, §8, 60.
25. Kreeft, *Between Heaven and Hell*, 2nd ed., 63.

8. aut Deus aut malus homo V: Lewis's Trilemma

i. A Concept of God

Aut Deus aut malus homo—was Lewis trying to formulate a proof of God's existence, or was he merely extending Jesus's question to Peter, to his readers. Was Lewis therefore presenting a question that needed to be addressed; was this a human dilemma (trilemma according to Lewis's definition)?

First, what do we mean by "God"? What did Lewis mean by God? Or more pertinently, what was meant by God in the first century; what understanding or definition in socio-cultural terms did the human Jesus operate with and what expectation of "God" did he have of those who heard him? For the Romans there were a multiplicity of "gods," and the Emperor was considered to be divine (it was for refusing to acknowledge this supposed divinity that many of the early Christians were martyred). The apostles, following on from the resurrection, were monotheists who had grown up with the Jewish concept of God. For them, in proclaiming Jesus's divinity, they were not regarding him as a "god" amongst the pagan "gods" of Rome, ancient Greece or the surrounding nations, but were invoking the religious history of the perception of God that had grown up amongst the ancient Hebrews as a result of God's self-revealing. What did this model of God contain or invoke? Although there was evidence of a conception of God as anthropomorphic, exhibiting human characteristics, in the Old Testament (often associated with the ancient Hebrews in the southern kingdom of Judah), the developed understanding of the God that had covenanted with his people was of a transcendent God, a being that required obedience, a God who generated terror and dread in his chosen people (by comparison this model of God was often associated with the northern kingdom of Israel). An important understanding to this developing proto doctrine of God was that the Jews knew that they could never look at God, let alone pronounce his full name; hence he appeared in cloud or fire, and in visions and dreams. By the first century Jews often saw God as intertwined with wisdom: God was the authoritative judge, infinitely wise, immeasurably forgiving, and eternally merciful, and this God would, they believed, save them from foreign oppression—he had done so before—but also he would redeem them from themselves. Hence, only God can truly forgive sins; human repentance was everything.

The understanding of God in the New Testament, in Jesus's preaching, is an immense topic in its own right. In the Gospels "God is the enveloping presence, the overarching character in the narratives";[26] in the Gospels there are three terms used: God, Lord, and Father. *Theos* (Θεός—God) in the Gospels was the deity of the ancient Hebrews, the God that was at the heart of the exclusive monotheistic religion of the Jews, a fundamental tenet of which was the rejection of all other "gods." This is the doctrine of God that underpins the devotion of early the church. This God is identical to and identified with Jesus; this God is the definitive authority and the final good. *Theos* is the foundation of the authority of Jesus. The Gospels present Jesus as the Christ, as God; this is revelation. The term *kyrios* (κύριος—Lord) is used in relation to God and

---

26. Green, et al. (eds.), *Dictionary of Jesus and the Gospels*, 271.

Jesus, and in the context of the Old Testament witness. Lordship implies relationship and responsibility, but above all authority. The New Testament Greek word is derived from *kuros* (κυρος—supremacy) and was used for one in authority, the controller: the Lord, God, master, sir! It is the use of *pater* (πατήρ—father), which is unique to the New Testament and is perhaps a departure from the distant authoritarian perception of some of the ancient Hebrews; fathership, in the use of the New Testament Greek word, involved literal and figurative remoteness. All three New Testament words therefore complement and develop the Old Testament concept of God.

We cannot know what God is. Often we are unsure as to what we mean when we use the word "God." We do not come across something that we analyze, dissect, and then label "God." Innately we do not have a clear idea of what God *is*. The Jewish and Christian use developed out of an already rich—though equally vague—use of the word. God was certainly not a "god." Therefore, we can assume that the disciples and those who heard Jesus knew what God was not: "We use the word God to point us towards a darkness, a mystery that is revealed by our question, revealed by our inability to answer the question."[27] Although we need to recognize this distance and separateness as a characteristic of God it is important that we recognize God as he is in the life and words of Jesus, this is something that is beyond reason. We noted earlier how this concept of God had affected the early work of the Swiss theologian Karl Barth: "That 'Father in heaven', to whom Jesus points us is no Ideality . . . but rather the reality, out of which our entire world has fallen. That God is our creator and origin in the other world is entirely new for us . . . All our other speaking of God is a stammering, or it must if it should count seriously, exist in pure negation."[28] What has this to do with asserting or undermining Lewis's trilemma? The New Testament scholar and Anglican bishop N. T. Wright has often emphasized that the champions of Lewis's proposition (and also those who deny that Jesus disclosed himself as God) have been challenged by scholarship that has exposed a much more nuanced, composite and multifarious understanding of the idea and concept of God amongst the earliest Christians, and amongst Jews in the first century.[29] Lewis's trilemma could have been better worded but Wright points out that this was not necessarily Lewis's aim. What Lewis wrote may have been imperfect but it brought people to the subject of Christ's divinity.[30] Wright, even though an orthodox creedal Christian, has criticized Lewis's approach because he shows little understanding of the incarnational principle in Judaism. This doesn't undermine his claim but its absence does weaken his defense; it also weakens the arguments of Lewis's followers when they mount a defense of his trilemma. Wright correctly asserts that an understanding of the incarnational principle does place an understanding of Christ's divinity in an historical context: "It places it in its proper

27. McCabe, *God Still Matters*, 55.
28. Karl Barth, "Kriegszeit und Gottesreich," an unpublished lecture given in Basle, Switzerland, 15 November 1915. All but the first 12 of 31 pages survive in the Karl Barth archive in Basle. Parts of the text are published in Anzinger, *Glaube und kommunikative Praxis*. Quote: 121–22.
29. Wright, *The Challenge of Jesus*, 98.
30. Wright, "Simply Lewis: Reflections on a Master Apologist After 60," 39–40. Online: http://www.touchstonemag.com/archives/article.php?id=20-02-028-f.

> ### Anselm and Lewis—Faith and Understanding
>
> | ANSELM OF CANTERBURY | C. S. LEWIS |
> |---|---|
> | *"Faith Seeking Understanding"* | *"Jesus is what he said he was"* |
> | Anselm accepts that God has revealed of God, he looks to the witness of scripture and the Church; however, he seeks *intelligere* (understanding). Anselm does not start with an idea of a god in his mind, but he arrives at the perfect conceptualization: God is that than which no greater can be conceived. | Lewis does not start from nothing. as the "moderns" do. He looks at the evidence and negates the alternatives; what is left is God, evidenced by the divine self-disclosure read from the sayings and actions of Jesus. This does not abolish faith; however absurd the alternatives are, we still have to come to this realization ourselves. |

Figure 14: Anselm of Canterbury and C. S. Lewis—Faith and Understanding

historical context and enables it to be at once nuanced into a proto-Trinitarian framework, employing and appropriately transcending the messianic category 'son of God,' which simultaneously settles down into first-century Judaism and explodes beyond it. Lewis's overconfident argument, by contrast, does the opposite: It doesn't work as history, and it backfires dangerously when historical critics question his reading of the Gospels."[31]

ii. Proof?

Is Lewis attempting a proof of the divinity of Christ in his trilemma? Is a proof possible? Emerging in and through the Age of Reason and endorsed by philosophers during the Enlightenment the "modern" method of proving the existence of God is to start from nothing, to start from what today is generally believed to be a position of atheism, and arrive at what will be accepted as evidence. During the eighteenth century the position of starting from nothing was considered to be impartial, disinterested, and free from religious dogma and bigotry. This view became more and more widely accepted. Therefore, the dominant view, certainly within the academic circles that Lewis worked within, was in this "modern" concept of proof where the argument for God moves from unbelief to belief (or stays with unbelief). The patristic and medieval approach was different. Anselm of Canterbury (1033–1109) philosopher, theologian, and Benedictine monk, worked from faith, which then sought understanding. Anselm accepted in faith the existence of God, that God was and is, but sought to understand. The modern system of proof works from unbelief to belief; Anselm, whose heritage was patristic, worked from faith to understanding. That God was, is a given, it

---

31. Ibid., 38f. See also, Craig, *Reasonable Faith: Christian Truth and Apologetics*. Craig criticizes Lewis for forcing the issue in his trilemma and not leaving other alternatives open.

was revealed. Working from nothing, from unbelief, to evidence was not Anselm's approach, nor was it Lewis's approach. Lewis sets out the alternatives and dismissed them, using the faculty of reason; so that what you had left—the self-disclosure of divinity by Jesus—was God. Like Anselm, Lewis is generating understanding, he is working *from* revelation (the scriptural evidence from the sayings and actions of Jesus) to reason; reasoning this out is all important for Lewis as he is defending the faith against unbelief. Lewis does not use the methods of his opponents, whereby they would start with nothing and reason out a "god" from what is within the human mind. Lewis's understanding issues from his trilemma; but it does not eliminate faith, we still need to "see" that this person was God incarnate. Therefore, Lewis is, to a degree, establishing the ground for faith. This ground is not absolute knowledge; the evidence from Jesus for divine self-disclosure can, as we have seen, be dismissed. God has revealed God's self, but we still have to work our way into understanding what has been revealed. This is not absolute proof giving absolute knowledge—that is, if such absolutism is possible for the human to perceive and conceptualize. Lewis does not sacrifice his intellect to faith, but neither does he accept the "modern" starting point of working from unbelief, from nothing, because this leads to a false "god" being invented, or projected. Lewis is not necessarily extrapolating a proof of God through Jesus's divinity. Like Anselm, he seeks understanding.

Proof or dilemma? The question only makes sense in the context of a doctrine of God—that is, what we know and understand about God and how God interacts in reality. So what was Lewis's doctrine of God within his trilemma? The doctrine of God in the Jewish religion differed considerably from that behind the religious practices of the numerous tribes and nations that surrounded Israel (including the ancient Greeks). Lewis understood that God was a being of pure spirit and otherness, a being that even defied the use of terms like "being" and "existence" and was therefore outside of, beyond, all that we perceive as reality. YWHW was the creator who was outside the world, and was infinitely different from anything else. This is the doctrine of God that underpins Lewis's invocation of *aut Deus aut malus homo*, it is the doctrine of God that the Jews were grounded in, particularly the Jews that knew Jesus and listened to him, and this is the understanding of God that Jesus himself had—with the proviso that calling God his Father was new because it established a personal relationship which was higher that the relationship between YWHW, the Lord, and his chosen people. This understanding of God is fundamental to what Jesus said, and how he related to people. This is what underpins Jesus's self-disclosure that he was this God come down to earth. Invoking words like "YWHW" or even "God" fall short of the reality of a being that defies being, that exists, yet is beyond existence in terms of what we understand to be existence. The eternal "I am" is infinitely different from all else. What did Lewis say? "God, in their language, meant the Being outside the world that had made it and was infinitely different from anything else. And when you've grasped that, you will see that what this man said was, quite simply, the most shocking thing that has ever been uttered by human lips."[32] For Lewis the actions and words disclose that this man, born among these Jews "claimed to be, or to be the son of, or to be 'one with,' the Something which is at once the awful haunter of nature and the giver of the moral law."[33] We should therefore be shocked at this; we cannot be lulled into treating it lightly. So Lewis was well acquainted with the doctrine of God.

iii. Insanity?

What do we mean by insanity? How do we define mental illness? What was the prevailing understanding of madness in the culture and society that generated Lewis and Chesterton's comments? In the first half of the twentieth century teenage girls who became pregnant were shut away in so-called "lunatic" asylums because of the moral offence they had caused; even as late as the 1960s introverted sexually abused children were locked away in so-called "lunatic" asylums by experts who were oblivious to the sins of the abuser. The Victorians proudly built many such asylums. Contemporaneous with Lewis's apologetic writing, Soviet apparatchiks would incarcerate their political opponents in mental hospitals for life, and the Nazi's defined the Jews as innately deranged simply because they were the Jews. Castigating someone as insane is a dangerous and flawed thing to do. Did Lewis and Chesterton really understand what they were saying? One man's lunatic is another man's seer; wisdom and madness may often be cultural stereotypes issuing from highly subjective and ill-founded opinions. Insanity is defined as being in or relating to an unsound state of mind, this may be because someone is deemed extremely foolish or irrational, however, it is also used to describe someone who is seriously mentally ill (from the sixteenth-century Latin *insanus*, from *in*, "not" with *sanus*, "healthy"). Many people who in hindsight were considered to be geniuses—from artists and musicians (for example, Mozart and Van Gogh) to scientists and engineers—were often derided as mad in their day. Many who challenged the religious bigotry of some of the Christian churches were executed as insane. Lewis and Chesterton do not attempt a definition of insanity; they simply say that if this man was not God then his confused understanding about himself means he is mad. This is a very lose and dangerous use of sanity-insanity. Can anyone truly say that they understand themselves; that they have no illusions about their identity, no delusions about who and what they are? How do we define ourselves? How does our sense of self-identity develop? What influences us in our self-esteem? Is insanity a social disease that affects the accuser more than the poor individual defined as mad?

To delude is simply to believe something that is false. A delusion is an idiosyncratic belief or impression that is not in accordance with generally accepted beliefs about reality. According to the scientist and media atheist Richard Dawkins any belief in God, or a "god," is delusional, because, he contends, that a supernatural creator almost certainly does not exist and therefore faith qualifies as a delusion—as a fixed false belief.[34] Dawkins sweeping generalization is as broad and flawed as perhaps Lewis's

---

32. Lewis, *Broadcast Talks*, 50.
33. Lewis, *The Problem of Pain*, 10–11.
34. Dawkins, *The God Delusion*, 5.

"mad" or "bad." Can anyone be truly convinced that they are not or never have been deluded in their beliefs about something that was important to them? Many people who are deeply in love, "head over heels" in love as the phrase used to go, can be deluded by their lover, or lose some of their rational thinking as they are swept along by their love? In contradiction to Dawkins' sweeping accusation that religious belief is delusional, is belief in God a guarantee of sanity? Does a Christians ever lose his or her mind? Some of the worst atrocities committed by the churches down the centuries have been in the name of the one true living God by people convinced of their sanity and rightness of mind. Perhaps Lewis's simplification of the question, "Who do you say that I am?" into his mad, bad, or God trilemma, is ham-fisted; it may be as crude and simplistic in its sweeping generalization as Dawkins' bland, all-encompassing proposition that all belief in God/"gods" is delusional. In the context of the ancient Hebrews self-perception as God's chosen people, brought about as a result of revelation from YHWH, the God above all "gods," Lewis wrote, "Once more it may be madness—a madness congenital to man and oddly fortunate in its results—or it may be revelation."[35]

Perhaps Lewis was on safer ground in his use of bad, wicked, evil. Perhaps any one or anything that puts itself up in opposition to God is innately evil. Satan, the fallen angel, attempted to raise himself up as a being to rival God, and in so doing became pure evil. If Jesus really was not God incarnate then, as Liddon wrote, he is by no means good. But even then, perhaps these writers need to define goodness, when, according to the Scriptures, only God is good (Mark 10:18; Luke 18:19; cf. Ps 73:1). But whether Lewis invoked insanity or wickedness in the place of *malus*, the dilemma remains and there hangs eternally a question over humanity since the fall, with the way out opened up by Christ's cross being the only hope. There is no proof, only faith and hope in what God has done for us. In this context, and from an orthodox perspective that can see the "Mad, Bad, or God" trilemma as too easy and neat a declaration, N. T. Wright commented that:

> The stock answer from within the conservative Christianity which had nurtured me through my teens came from C. S. Lewis: Jesus was either mad, or bad, or he was who he claimed to be. Yes, we said, for anyone else to say such things would be either certifiably insane or at least wicked; but, since it was true in Jesus's case, it was neither. There is a sense in which I still believe this, but it is a heavily revised sense and must be struggled for, not lightly won. There are no short-circuited arguments in the kingdom of God.[36]

6. *AUT DEUS AUT MALUS HOMO*

"Who do you say that I am?" (Matt 16:15) This question echoes down the centuries and because of who and what Jesus of Nazareth, the Christ, was it is a question that

---

35. Lewis, *The Problem of Pain*, 10.
36. Wright, "Jesus and the Identity of God," 42.
   Online: http://www.ntwrightpage.com/Wright_JIG.htm.

8. aut Deus aut malus homo V: Lewis's Trilemma

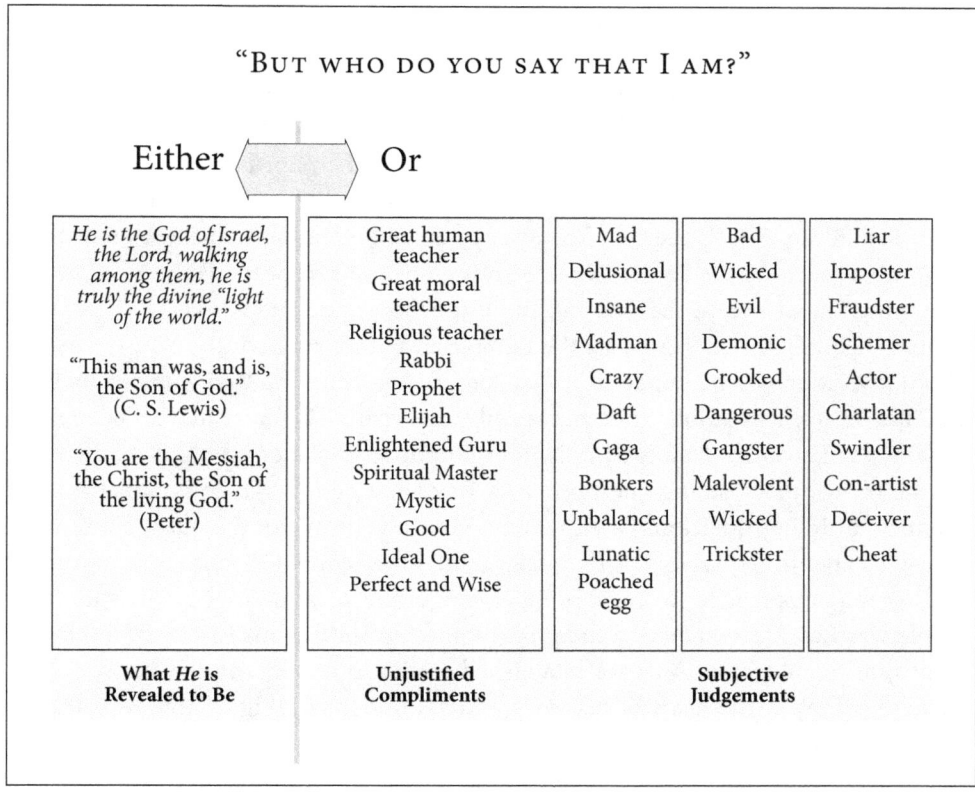

Figure 15: "But Who do you Say that I Am?"—Answers

is highly pertinent to all. However, there is an element in the question where Jesus deliberately leaves the answer open for people to come to their decision. People must come to understand who he is for themselves—hence his pleasure in Peter's response (Matt 16:17). This was so when Jesus encountered people when he walked the earth, but it is also true nowadays when people encounter him through the Scriptures, in the churches, and in other manifold ways in which the Holy Spirit engenders an encounter: this is existential, primarily because a response is demanded, and that response issues from a crisis in humanity—what are we doing, who are we, why are we here, and what is to become of us? Each individual must decide and respond to the ontological reality that is and was Jesus of Nazareth, the Christ. To ignore the question, to ignore Jesus, if confronted by him, is still a response, a decision. If we choose not to decide, then this is a response for which we take responsibility.

i. Pneumatological Preparation

Recognizing Jesus for the Son of God can be argued for through logic, this we have seen, and Lewis excelled and enjoyed pressing the case onto people through his trilemma, but does not the recognition come down ultimately to the will of God? If someone is not ready, if they have not been prepared, so to speak, by the Holy Spirit, then Lewis's appeal to logic will fall on stony ground, on deaf ears: "All things have been handed over to me by my Father; and no one knows who the Son is except the Father, or who the Father is except the Son and anyone to whom the Son chooses to reveal him" (Luke 10:22). Also, "At that time Jesus said, I praise you, Father, Lord of heaven and earth, because you have hidden these things from the wise and learned, and revealed them to little children. Yes, Father, for this was your good pleasure. All things have been committed to me by my Father. No one knows the Son except the Father, and no one knows the Father except the Son and those to whom the Son chooses to reveal him" (Matt 11:25–27). The Son reveals the trinitarian nature of God; the Son chooses to whom revelation will be imparted. What is more, it is little children who can perceive this, not necessarily adults, not necessarily academics, in particular philosophers. So why did Lewis try to force the issue by framing Jesus's question as a trilemma? Did he try to foreclose the question? In a way what he did was to complement the openness of Jesus's question. Lewis merely raised the profile of the question, brought it people's attention, perhaps made them see that they cannot dismiss this man as yet another religious teacher or sage, prophet, or guru. But in forcing the question onto people was Lewis contradicting the philosophical ground of his theory of revelation, a transpositional ground that we established earlier in his doctrine of transposition, the key that lay at the heart of his work and his understanding of how revelation is imparted? In a way, the answer must be yes. We noted earlier that there was no old or new evidence that would foreclose the question: Lewis commented how we can ignore what he termed the "up-grading" that humanity is subject to as a direct result of the incarnation, we can always concentrate on the lower. Therefore, "Men can read the life of our Lord (because it is a human life) as nothing but a human life . . . Just in the same way Scripture can be read as merely human literature. No new discovery, no new method, will ever give a final victory to either interpretation."[37] How does this affect our decision and our salvation? Does Lewis leave the question open in his more serious philosophical theology? In the context of his essay "Transposition" we concluded that there were three reasons why revelation is transposed: first, the *communicatio idiomatum* (the communication of attributes or idioms), where not everything of God is communicated in Jesus Christ, there was a diminution voluntarily enacted by God out of love for humanity, but not out of any need or weakness in God, whereby Jesus was the humble servant, lowly, submitting himself to his destiny (the communication of attributes is characterized by restraint and self-denial by God); second, veiling-unveiling, the knowability of God, where there is an element of veiling in the revealing of God in and through Jesus Christ because when the apostles saw Jesus Christ it was a hidden God, it was not *obvious* it was God; it was a man, a young itinerant religious teacher; third, human fallibility—the misreading of the transposition. Perhaps these three elements that account for the essential and inherently flawed perception of revelation account for why some people just cannot see that Jesus was God incarnate.[38]

37. Lewis, *Reflections on the Psalms*, 100.
38. Lewis, "Transposition," 2nd ed., 123–27.

8. aut Deus aut malus homo V: Lewis's Trilemma

Therefore, the evidence for self-disclosure is all we have to fall back on. There is, therefore, something of a dichotomy between Lewis's popular apologetic and his serious philosophical theology. This dichotomy is between what Lewis says with subtlety and consideration, reflecting the nuanced wisdom in his academic theological papers about our perception and understanding of revelation on the one hand, as compared to what he then confidently asserts in his popular apologetics where he confronts his readers with the need to make a decision relating to their existence, their life and their relationship with God. Ironically, Lewis commented at the end of his life that he had been decided upon and that this was more important than any decision he made: "What I wrote in *Surprised by Joy* was that before God closed in on me, I was in fact offered what now appears a moment of wholly free choice. But I feel my decision was not so important. I was the object rather than the subject in this affair. I was decided upon."[39] So despite what he presents in his various popular apologetics with regard to whether Jesus was mad, bad, or God, and how we need to confront this trilemma and make a decision, we may speculate on what it is that affects our decisions? Also, where is freedom of the will after the fall? Is it actually possible for humanity to make decisions any longer unaffected or unswayed by external influences, whether good or bad? In which case we may ask, "What role does the Holy Spirit have in bringing us to the point of realization as to who this Jesus was and is?" If this is so then we may ask if those who can see that Jesus is God incarnate, who acknowledge and recognize his divinity, are these people brought to this decision by the Holy Spirit? Scripture would seem to say so judging, again, by Jesus's response to Peter's recognition: "Flesh and blood has not revealed this to you, but my Father in heaven" (Matt 16:17b). Is this an instance of what Lewis terms "being decided upon"?

ii. Trilemma or Dilemma?

Is Lewis's proposition really a trilemma, or a simply a dilemma? Does he really advance the proposition beyond a dilemma given that the second (mad) and third (bad) components are only judgments about the merely human. If we take seriously the question posed by this person Jesus then the proposition is a dilemma because our life and salvation depends on what we make of this man. Many atheists today are not bothered with the question and certainly do not see it as a dilemma because if there is, according to their closed belief system, no God or "gods" then it is just an irrelevant observation to speculate on whether Jesus was mad or bad. "Evangelical" atheists—in particular today's media and celebrity New Atheists who seek to convert Christians to their "religious" atheism—do not necessarily see the question as irrelevant. To them— like Screwtape—it is essential that the Christian is converted away from orthodoxy to come to a "right" (in Screwtape's inverted thinking) judgment about Jesus and declare him a man, a *mere* man; perhaps a little deluded and eccentric, but certainly

---

39. Lewis, "Cross-Examination," 215–21.

not a "god."[40] If Lewis's adaptation of *aut Deus aut malus homo* into a trilemma creates unnecessary confusion, then perhaps it would have been better phrased as a dilemma, an either or question. Does this make his apologetics irrelevant or wrong? Either someone who is presented with Lewis's trilemma accepts the divinity of Christ or they do not. On one level then, yes; phrasing as a dilemma would have been better because this is a personal question addressed to all by Jesus, and when presented as a trilemma people can get embroiled in arguments about the merely human (was he mad or bad, and where do we draw the line, and if bad was he evil . . .). This draws them away from the stark existential demands of the question about Jesus's divinity. If someone decides Jesus was merely human then it doesn't matter whether they decide if this ordinary human from two thousand years ago was delusional and insane, or wicked and evil (especially given that our understanding of humanity and the line between wickedness and insanity is blurred by the fall). If Jesus is not God incarnate then our subjective opinion doesn't change what he was: was Peter mad or bad when he denied Christ three times? Any decision is subjective and, to a degree, irrelevant. If Jesus was, and is, God incarnate then what we decide about his human nature verges on blasphemy, and perhaps constitutes a contradiction of the third commandment (i.e., taking the Lord's name in vain): worship is more important than speculation.

7. CONCLUSION

So, was Lewis's trilemma a failure, an irrelevance as compared to the basic proposition, *aut Deus aut malus homo* ? No, because it generated speculation, got people talking; it was—in its controversy—a successful piece of apologetic. Indeed for sixty years it has had people questioning who and what this man Jesus was and is. It has got people questioning the very core of their beliefs. Is this not what was at the heart of Jesus's question to Peter—"But who do you say that I am?" There are many who will accept the divinity of Christ unquestioningly, who can see without the pain of agnosticism, without the intellectual wrestling, that he was and is divine; there are many, however, who reject Jesus's self-disclosure and struggle with the very notion of God coming down to earth to be incarnated in human form. There are many academics of various disciplines and persuasions who—as Lewis noted in his day—want to avoid the question, who want to try to be impartial, disinterested and seemingly neutral about Jesus's status and ontology; these are academics and people who, as we have seen,

---

40. The so-called New Atheists (a title many of them apparently repudiate) are unofficially led by the Oxford scientist and media atheist Richard Dawkins, author of *The God Delusion*; the title of Dawkins' book builds on Lewis's preparedness to invoke insanity in the form of delusion to criticize and denigrate one's opponents. Other New Atheists include the children's novelist Philip Pullman, the journalist and literary critic Christopher Hitchens (who described himself as an "anti-theist"), the philosopher A. C. Grayling, the journalist-writer Sam Harris, the novelist Martin Amis, and the author and screen writer Ian McEwan. All are united, to a greater or lesser degree, in an attempt to raise the public profile of atheism, and, as many see it, to convert people to their particular form of anti-theistic "religion," and often to, in effect, declare war on God. Pullman commented, in an interview for *The Sydney Morning Herald*, "My books are about killing God." See, Meacham, "The Shed where God Died," 8.
Online: http://www.smh.com.au/articles/2003/12/12/1071125644900.html.

objected to Lewis forcing the issue, of presenting the question as a trilemma. Some, in particular today's New Atheists, regard Lewis as the one who was deluded because of his orthodox Christian beliefs. Sir Thomas More's phrasing of *aut Deus aut malus homo* may have been a more accurate reflection of the question Jesus posed to Peter, likewise Liddon's phrasing of the question as *Christus, si non Deus, non bonus* is more subtle and nuanced, and falls short of making any subjective, specifically discriminatory, all-encompassing character judgments, but as an apologist Lewis's "soundbite" or "slogan" has faced people with the question in a way that the fine distinctions and more academically restrained and understated propositions from More, Liddon, Hopkins, *et al.*, have not. However, there is the perennial danger of trivializing, thereby reducing the trilemma to something resembling a pop song or an advertising slogan: "mad, bad, or God" has, amongst some American Evangelicals, become "Lord, Liar, or Lunatic" as if the three "Ls" are somehow important. We might just as well say that he is "Crazy, Crooked, or Christ," or, "Daft, Dangerous, or Divine," or, "Bonkers, Bad, or Beatified," or "Gaga, Gangster, or God," or "Mad, Malevolent, or Messiah." This is all in the field of media culture trivia and should be avoided: we may say mad or lunatic, liar or bad, but we might equally label him—if merely human—as an imposter, a fraudster, a wicked schemer, an actor, trickster or charlatan, a swindler, con-artist or a deceiver; considering the death it led him to then foolhardy, reckless and imprudent, even impulsive, and so on, and so forth.

Ironically, despite two thousand years of theological tradition where the question is phrased as a dilemma, we saw how it was Gerald O'Collins who demonstrated that Jesus's question generated a trilemma in John's Gospel. Lewis was, therefore, justified in developing *aut Deus aut malus homo* into a trilemma: "At the end of the first century AD, John's Gospel presents a similar choice in Jesus's controversy with his critics; either Jesus is a 'liar', or he is unbalanced and 'has a demon', or else he is truly the divine 'Light of the world.'"[41] There is, therefore, good scriptural precedent for phrasing the question about Jesus of Nazareth's identity as a trilemma rather than the dilemma it has been for two millennia of church history, but we must always be wary—as Lewis most certainly was—of trivializing the question. As Lewis noted in the context of his trilemma, our response is relative: "The real question is not what are we to make of Christ, but what is he to make of us?"[42] The pertinent issue is, therefore, the action of the resurrected and ascended Christ towards humanity. Whatever our humble opinion about him when he walked the earth consists of, what is of primary importance and precedent will be what Jesus Christ makes of us when we come before him in the last judgment. The dilemma, *aut Deus aut malus homo* is thus eschatological. Whatever conclusions we come to regarding Jesus Christ the pertinent question is, "To what extent does our opinion of this man Jesus affect or have any bearing on our salvation?" To answer would move the debate out of the question of Lewis's trilemma, and involve much of the anger and frustration, the contradictions of denominationalism, and the dark side of church history: Christians have killed each other over the answer to this question in the past!

41. O'Collins SJ, *Incarnation*, 131.
42. Lewis, "What Are We to Make of Jesus Christ?," 123.

Lewis is correct, what is important is what Jesus Christ makes of us, but what we assert before our neighbor does have some value for it may assist them in their path before God. They like Lewis, and like us, have been decided upon.

For all its perceived faults there are four reasons why Lewis's trilemma was and still is a very successful piece of Christian apologetic: first, because it demonstrates that there is a rational basis to Christian doctrine; second, because it does contain the basic either-or question at the heart of the Christian faith; third, because of the attention it has gained—through it Lewis was effectively preaching the gospel; and, fourth, because so many writers of varying persuasions have sought to repudiate it.

Part Three

Christ Prefigured—

Intimations to the Pagans

"The Pattern is there in nature
because it was first there in God."

Lewis, *Miracles* (1st ed., 1947), 118

9

Christ as the Light of the World I: A Doctrine of Christological Prefigurement

SYNOPSIS:
These next three chapters are an examination of the Christology that C. S. Lewis read from the apparent prefiguring of elements of the incarnation-resurrection narrative in non-Christian religious myths. Lewis saw the Spirit of Christ acting throughout human history; this manifestation is not Hegelian but is Trinitarian, it is a form of revelation—through the Holy Spirit, the Son reveals the Father, potentially drawing all to the Father, interceding for humanity to the Father. This is, in effect, what we may term a doctrine of christological prefigurement. Such a doctrine is summarized in two propositions: first: the actuality of the historic event of the incarnation-cross-resurrection was previsioned in pagan religion and myth (i.e., in non-Judaic-Christian religious stories and myths); second: the gospel account, the incarnation-cross-resurrection narrative, acts on us, whether spoken or read, *both* as fact *and* myth. From his teenage years on, Lewis the apostate atheist held the North European pagan myths in very high regard. This was related to his love of Wagner's music, which is rooted in such myths; but he also valued Middle Eastern and Asiatic-Indian-Oceanic myths—in particular ancient Hindu. However, with his conversion he chose not to reject these pagan myths out-of-hand but sought a way to understand how they related to the Christ-event—an event that was an actuality that he had come to realize was central to human history. Initially we need to examine what we mean by myth and reality, by fact and fiction, in particular how theologians of varying persuasions have sought to define myth. Lewis's writings on the myth that became reality (the incarnation-resurrection) are discussed along with examples of prefigurement (in particular the myth of Balder the Beautiful). By examining the relationship between religion and human creativity we can establish a paradigm—that revelation precedes religion. Lewis's understanding of the myth that became reality is therefore tied up with his conversion. In contrast to his earlier deference for the conclusions of the Victorian colonial religionist and social anthropologist Sir James George Frazer (conclusions rooted, as they were, in a Feuerbachian-Freudian interpretation of a Darwinian model of human evolution, which classified religion as a tribal human construct to a hostile world), Lewis came to regard these prefigurements as the work of the Holy Spirit—*intimations* of God's salvific action in Christ.

1. INTRODUCTION: THE WORK OF CHRIST, REVEALED

If the Christ-event is not limited or restricted to the brief lifespan of Jesus of Nazareth two thousand years ago, if, as we have established, the Holy Spirit of God proceeding from the Father and the Son presses on, converts, and redeems people, and if these encounters are part of salvation history then we need to consider the scope of the work of Christ throughout church history, and for that matter how Lewis saw the *Spirit of Christ* acting throughout human history. This is not Hegel's world spirit, for this *work of Christ* is Trinitarian, it is a form of revelation—through the Holy Spirit, the Son reveals the Father, potentially drawing all to the Father, interceding for humanity *to* the Father. This is the work of Christ, revealed. These encounters, when recounted are a form of history; inevitably they will involve culture, story, and, pertinently for Lewis, myth and mythology—fact and fiction. We are, therefore, in a realm that is to a degree beyond reason. Reason takes Lewis thus far. Although not grounded explicitly in logic (through there is a sort of "supposal" logic to them) much of Lewis's theology—his analogical narrative in particular (for example, *The Chronicles of Narnia*)—echoes back to an interest of the pre-Christian Lewis: myth and mythology. After his conversion Lewis's deep love for pagan mythology and pagan religion was reassessed. How did these myths relate to the Christ-event? Why were there similarities between the Christ-event and ideas in some of these pagan myths? Lewis came to see the answer as being pneumatological—they were the work of the Holy Spirit, and therefore part of the work of Christ revealed.

2. A DOCTRINE OF CHRISTOLOGICAL PREFIGUREMENT

On the evening of his conversion from theism to Christianity C. S. Lewis is recorded as having described myths as beautiful and moving, though they were "lies and therefore worthless, even though breathed through silver . . ."[1] Lewis's understanding of myth was to change radically during his life as a result of his adoption and championing through apologetics of an orthodox Christian faith. Myth was, and continued to be, very important to him—primarily the Northern European myths, closely followed by Asiatic-Indian (Hindu) religion and myth, and Greek mythology. Because professionally his work was in medieval and Renaissance literature he had a very good understanding of myth, story, and the effect such narratives have on us.[2] In these three chapters we will examine what we may term Lewis's doctrine of christological prefigurement. What is this? It is encapsulated in two propositions: first: the actual historical event of the incarnation and resurrection was prefigured—previsioned, but not prophesied—in non-Judeo-Christian religious stories and myths; second: the gospel account itself—the incarnation-resurrection narrative—acts and operates on us, whether spoken or read, *both* as fact *and* as myth. A key to Lewis's Christology lies in his understanding of myth and event. Lewis was a classic orthodox theologian in his Christology; however, two propositions distinguish him from the mainstream

---

1. Quoted by Tolkien in his poem Mythopoeia, reflecting Lewis' position up to the point of his conversion: see, Tolkien "Mythopoeia," 85–90. See also, Letter to Arthur Greeves, Oct, 18, 1931, *Collected Letters, Vol. I*, 975–77. See also: Lewis, *They Stand Together: The Letters of C. S. Lewis to Arthur Greeves 1914–1963*.
2. In particular, see: *Studies in Mediaeval and Renaissance Literature*; also, Lewis, *The Discarded Image*. For a good introduction to Lewis's use of story see: Huttar and Schakel, *Word and Story in C. S. Lewis*.

9. Christ as the Light of the World I: A Doctrine of Christological Prefigurement

---

A DOCTRINE OF CHRISTOLOGICAL PREFIGUREMENT

First
The actual historic event of the incarnation and resurrection was prefigured—*previsioned* but not prophesied—in non Judaic-Christian religious stories and myths.

Second
The Gospel account itself—the Incarnation-Resurrection narrative—acts and operates on us, whether spoken or read, both as fact and myth.

Uniting these two propositions
in a doctrine of Christological prefigurement
is an understanding Lewis had of the relationship between revelation and myth,
and how stories—whether fact or fiction—press on us and change us on a deep level
of our personality, they operate on the soul and therefore effect our relationship with God.

The key is Trinitarian and is therefore part of Lewis's modes of revelation

The key is the person of Christ: both the historic figure of Jesus of Nazareth
but also the universal Christ of all eternity, the second person of the Trinity, who,
in and through the Holy Spirit, presses on, operates on, people
throughout history, drawing all, potentially, to the Father.
This is the perceivable action of the Economic Trinity.

Figure 16: A Doctrine of christological Prefigurement

in orthodoxy: he is prepared to tackle the question of narrative prefigurement, which most other theologians either dismiss or shy away from; also, he is prepared to write about the mythical effect the incarnation-resurrection narrative has on us. There is something of a dialectic here (not a method usually associated with Lewis) in his use of myth and event: the former represents the historical event prefigured in religious stories/myths; the latter encompasses the myth derived from the event. Lewis writes of the idea, the content of the story of Jesus (the incarnation-resurrection narrative) being prefigured in pre-Christian myths; he also writes about the effect that the story of Jesus (again the incarnation-resurrection narrative) has on us even if we do not believe in the historical reality. There are therefore two different propositions here, not mutually exclusive, but nonetheless dealing with different concepts. Lewis's doctrine of christological prefigurement proposes the prevision[3] of the incarnation-resurrection narrative in non-Christian religious stories and myths, but it also proposes that the actual gospel story affects us both as an historical account, but also like a myth. These two propositions are united in the person of Jesus Christ and are part of the trinitarian action we perceive in this world (figure 16).

This doctrine of christological prefigurement was derived from his reading of religious myths from outside of the Judaeo-Christian tradition. These myths were

---

3. Prevision: from the verb, to previse—to foresee or predict, from sixteenth-century Latin *praevis-*, *praevidere*, from *prae* "before" and *videre* "to see" (Oxford English Dictionary).

read in relation to the gospel account of the incarnation and the resurrection. The resemblances were tantalizing: similar, yet dissimilar. These stories were what he termed pagan myths, though it is important to remember that the term "pagan" is used here with no derogatory intent, nor as a term of abuse. Lewis used the term simply to refer to those peoples and cultures outside of the Judeo-Christian tradition and revelation (Oriental, Middle Eastern, Asiatic-Indian, and European tribes and nations, particularly in the ancient world). Initially we shall look at some definitions of myth, that is myth in relation to fact, fiction, and reality. The place of religion will lead us to postulate a paradigm—that revelation precedes religion. This will allow us to reappraise Lewis's conversion and what Lewis actually wrote about myth and event. Defining what is meant by the incarnation-resurrection narrative will lead us to appraise examples of prefigurement. Lewis's position will then be examined in the light of his views on revelation (particularly noting the formative proximity of Lewis's thought to that of Plato and Augustine) and his theories about imagination and inspiration, illumination, and revelation.

3. MYTH AND REALITY, FACT AND FICTION

i. Myth

C. Stephen Evans in his work on Christology[4] argues for the historicity of the Gospel accounts as against modern scholarship that calls into question the reliability of the church's versions of the story of Jesus. Evans argues for the historical basis of Christianity, that the religious significance of this story cannot be adequately captured by the category of non-historical myth. Like many others who assert an orthodox trinitarian account he identifies the category of myth as one that has been employed as a means of dealing with the particular genre of the Gospels by a number of theologians (Lewis's "Modern" and/or "Liberals"). To this end he briefly examines C. S. Lewis's proposition that the incarnation-resurrection narrative is both myth and history: a myth that has been historically enacted without ceasing to be a myth. Before turning to Lewis, Stephen Evans, in the third chapter of his work, briefly sets out four definitions of myth, which are pertinent (figure 17).[5] Evans explains that these four definitions are not mutually exclusive. Someone who holds that a particular myth may express metaphysical or psychological truth may also assert that it may be a pre-scientific explanation of some phenomenon. He quotes the work of Joseph Campbell as an example that reflects a Jungian view, that myths can embody both a psychological function as well as metaphysical one.[6] The term "myth" is therefore a rich depository of

---

4. Evans, *The Historical Christ and the Jesus of Faith: the Incarnational Narrative as History*. See also: Evans, "The Incarnational Narrative as Myth and History," 387–407; also, "Mis-Using Religious Language: something about Kierkegaard and the Myth of God Incarnate," 139–57.

5. Evans, *The Historical Christ and the Jesus of Faith*, ch. 3 "Why the Events Matter: 1. History, Meaning and Myth," 49–51.

6. See: Campbell, *The Hero with a Thousand Faces*; also, Campbell, "Mythological Themes in Creative Literature and Art," 138–75.

9. Christ as the Light of the World I: A Doctrine of Christological Prefigurement

---

C. Stephen Evans: Four Definitions of Myth

First:
Myths can be seen as pre-scientific explanations, bad explanations, of phenomena in the natural world (fanciful stories to explain rainfall, the movement of the sun, etc).

Second:
Myths can be seen as operating a sociological function, for example, to reinforce the identity of a group of people and explain cohesive ritual practices.

Third:
Myths can be seen as embodying psychological truth, which may be crucial to the value of the myth. Pre-scientific explanations are seen as wrong and irrelevant, but psychological truths touch a deeper level of humanity and may give insights that cannot be obtained through other means, for example, the story of Oedipus.

Fourth:
Such mythological stories express in a dramatic fashion some abstract metaphysical truth, even though they may be considered to be historically false.

Figure 17: C. Stephen Evans—Four Definitions of Myth

meanings and nuances—quite different from the way some contemporary theologians have used the term.

In the twentieth century myth was often, simplistically, taken to mean that something is mere fiction, a story with no basis in real events: a misconception, a misrepresentation of the truth. For example, John Hick in the preface to *The Myth of God Incarnate* asserts that the conception of Jesus "as God incarnate, the Second Person of the Holy Trinity living a human life, is a mythological or poetic way of expressing his significance for us."[7] This represents a uniquely modern, Enlightenment approach to Christ based upon a particularly narrow definition of myth (the term "myth" was essentially introduced into theology in the nineteenth century). Hick in *The Myth of God Incarnate* relies heavily on the work of Maurice Wiles.[8] This is a doctrine of the (non)-incarnation, and a definition of myth that is grounded in nineteenth-century theological Liberalism. Wiles asserted that God created the world but does not intervene or interfere with it, therefore there was no possibility of the miraculous. In addition, Wiles held a deep respect for many patristic heresies, in particular Arianism; furthermore he defined prayer as the ability to intuit something of the will of God, but

---

7. Hick, "Preface," in, *The Myth of God Incarnate*, ix. See also, Hick, *The Metaphor of God Incarnate*.
8. Wiles, "Myth in Theology," 149. See also, Wiles, "Christianity without Incarnation," 4–6

not to achieve a change in the natural order.[9] Hick's work is grounded, in many ways, in Wiles "Liberal" redefinition of myth. For example,

> Wiles defended at some length the liberal use of the word myth to describe the incarnation. He appreciated the very imprecision of the term, which some took to indicate deceit but others took to indicate religious truth without regard to historicity. He believed the application of myth to the incarnation allowed for a truer understanding of the possibility of human union with the divine in every man. The particularity of Christ might be lost in the process, but the major positive affirmations of Christianity—openness to God and love towards humans—would be retained.[10]

For both Wiles and Hick the term myth is loosely, pluralistically, defined, and is as such something of a modern definition, open and relativistic, yet is precise in its denial of the historicity of the incarnation: "Moreover, Wiles was not content to question only the doctrine of the incarnation. Among other provocative moves, he also defended the heresiarch Arius, questioned the orthodox doctrine of the immanent Trinity, and queried whether Christology rested on a mistake."[11] Such definitions do not always take into account the full richness of myth—especially from a metaphysical, or more pertinently a pneumatological, perspective. By contrast, Lewis is often critical of progressive Protestant theologians for failing to understand the genre of myth from a literary perspective, particularly given Lewis's professional understanding of story and myth (for example, the criticism we encountered in Lewis's essay "Modern Theology and Biblical Criticism" with its deconstructive censure of Bultmann, Lock, and Vidler for not understanding literary genre when they attempt to approach the Gospels as non-historical records and classify them according to literary genre.[12])

ii. Lewis on Myth

Lewis proposes a definition of myth in an essay on literary criticism published in 1961.[13] He notes that there is a particular kind of story that has a value in itself; a value independent of its embodiment in any literary work. Lewis quotes the story of Orpheus in a summary of a hundred words, showing how it still has an extraordinary power: "it strikes and strikes deep."[14] Lewis then lays out six characteristics of myth (figure 18). Myths cannot be classified along with other forms of literature—they are extra literary; the key element is a sense of inevitability. Mythical characters are different from real human beings but they have a profound relevance to us, they are in effect archetypal. For Lewis Orpheus's plight resonates with all humanity, despite the fantastic element

---

9. Wiles, *God's Action in the World*.
10. Yarnell, *The Formation of Christian Doctrine*, 47. Referring to Wiles, "Myth in Theology."
11. Ibid., Referring to, Wiles, "Does Christology Rest on a Mistake?," 69–76
12. Lewis, "Modern Theology and Biblical Criticism," in particular, 154–57. See also: Christensen, *C. S. Lewis on Scripture*; see also, Harries, *C. S. Lewis: the Man and his God*. In terms of Lewis's criticism of "Modern" and "Liberal" Bible study, see, Lock, *A New Commentary on Holy Scripture, including the Apocrypha*, 241; also: Vidler, *Windsor Sermons*.
13. Lewis, *An Experiment in Criticism*. See ch. 5 "On Myth," 40–49.
14. Ibid.,41

9. Christ as the Light of the World I: A Doctrine of Christological Prefigurement

---

C. S. Lewis on Mythical Stories

First:
Myths are extra literary.

Second:
Myths do not depend upon the usual literary attractions such as suspense or surprise—there is a sense of inevitability about mythical stories.

Third:
Human sympathy is at a minimum, the characters are like shapes moving in another world: they have a profound relevance to our lives, but we do not necessarily identify with them—the story of Orpheus makes us sad, but we are sorry for all men rather than sympathetic with him.

Fourth:
Myth is always fantastic—it deals with impossibilities and preternaturals.

Fifth:
The experience of listening to or reading a myth is always grave.

Sixth:
Importantly we find this experience to be awe-inspiring because we feel a sense of the numinous—it is as if something of great moment has been communicated to us.

Figure 18: C. S. Lewis—Six Elements towards a Definition of Myth

that evokes apparent impossibilities and the supernatural. A key element to myth, for both Tolkien and Lewis, was in hearing rather than reading them—the act of listening is then shared, such communal listening is often grave, awe-inspiring, and evokes the numinous and perhaps a sense of *Sehnsucht*. For Lewis, it is as though something of great moment has been communicated to us. A myth is more than just a fanciful story that did not happen; however, a myth that is also an account of an historical event is something other.[15]

iii. Religion as a Human Construct

As an eighteen year old apostate and atheistic student Lewis, writing to Arthur Greeves, dismissed all religion as mythology and therefore of human invention. These comments could be regarded simply as adolescent rebellion; however, their content and meaning went deeper, and reflected much nineteenth-century "Liberal" scholarship

---

15. Jonathon Miller, scientist, doctor, media celebrity, and self-confessed atheist, has commented of his own piety towards the Christian story: "If there is a God then he could have thought of no more powerful, creative and imaginative way of expressing his presence than through his incarnation in Christ, an 'ordinary' man." Quoted in, Appleyard, "The True Face of Art," 12.

on the philosophy and sociology of religion. Lewis had come to know Arthur Greeves a few years earlier; as teenagers both had realized immediately that this was to be a life-long friendship. Both found they shared a love of Wagner (including Arthur Rackham's illustrations of *The Ring Cycle*), Northernness, pagan mythology, and so forth. Greeves had asked Lewis about his religious views in a previous letter; Lewis's response is relatively detailed for an eighteen-year-old. He comments much about religion in this letter. Greeves is no atheist and so Lewis comments how he needs to be careful over his use of language—words like, exultation, for instance—which had led Greeves to misconstrue meaning and intent. Lewis commented that, "You ask me my religious views: you know, I think, that I believe in no religion. There is absolutely no proof for any of them, and from a philosophical standpoint Christianity is not even the best. All religions, that is, all mythologies to give them their proper name are merely man's own invention—Christ as much as Loki."[16] Lewis then goes on to explain how all these mythologies were generated by primitive humanity to account for elements in the natural world that were frightening and puzzling—"thunder, pestilence, snakes"—thus evil spirits were invented, ritual and sacrifice followed to placate them. Lewis continued:

> Gradually from being mere nature-spirits these supposed beings were elevated into more elaborate ideas, such as the old gods: and when man became more refined he pretended that these spirits were good as well as powerful. Thus religion, that is to say mythology, grew up. Often, too, great men were regarded as gods after their death—such as Heracles or Odin: thus after the death of a Hebrew philosopher Yeshua (whose name we have corrupted into Jesus) he became regarded as a god, a cult sprang up, which was afterwards connected with the ancient Hebrew Jahweh worship, and so Christianity came into being—one mythology among many, but the one that we happen to have been brought up in.[17]

Lewis then claims that this is the recognized scientific account of the growth of religion. He then identifies himself with the elite—the Enlightened elite who are above and beyond such superstition, the educated and thinking ones stand outside it. He then concludes by asserting that ethics and morality are outside of these mythological religions and should be adhered to—honesty, chastity, truthfulness, kindness, "these are things we owe to our own manhood and dignity and not to any imagined god or gods."[18]

---

16. Lewis to Arthur Greeves, Oct. 12, 1916. *Collected Letters, Vol. I*, 230–31.
17. Ibid., 231.
18. Ibid., 231–32.

9. Christ as the Light of the World I: A Doctrine of Christological Prefigurement

4. SIR JAMES GEORGE FRAZER

i. Religion and Anthropology—A Worldview

Lewis is basically expounding a view of religion that was popular amongst academics generally, scientists, and anthropologists specifically, a view culled from the work of the Victorian religionist and social anthropologist Sir James George Frazer. Frazer's massive twelve-volume work, *The Golden Bough*, was the product of an academic life spent travelling the world documenting and analyzing the religious-folk mythology of primitive tribes.[19] He spent decades observing various customs, rituals, beliefs, and myths from the standpoint of the emerging discipline of social anthropology. Like most late Victorian academics he is working in the shadow of Charles Darwin and readily subscribes to an evolutionary framework and ground: thus Frazer is assessing and interpreting these religious mythologies as a social paradigm illustrating three rising stages of human progress. Initially magic gives rise to mythologies, this is codified into religions, polytheism gives way to monotheism, mature monotheistic religions give way to humanity's greatest achievement through progress—science. Frazer's position is also Feuerbachian, and to a degree Freudian: a foundational assumption is that there is no God, religion is a human projection; in terms of cultural anthropology it is a response to a hostile world. Frazer is also a high-Victorian (completing his work as a stereotypical patriarchal Edwardian in the early twentieth century) projecting cultural and racial superiority as he travelled the world, mainly though the British Empire. Frazer rigorously and unsympathetically applied a hermeneutic of suspicion to primitive religion and mythologies, testing and analyzing them to destruction. However, as with the twentieth-century "Liberal" Bible scholars, Frazer and similar academics refused to countenance a hermeneutic of suspicion applied to their methods. Frazer is a "Modern," a late Victorian, convinced that humanity is progressing on and on to superior times; however, this "Modern," predominantly patriarchal, white, European philosophy fell apart during and through the First World War.

It is not just critics of "Modernism"/"Liberalism" like Lewis that see problems with Frazer's approach to religion and humanity, the philosopher Ludwig Wittgenstein is one of Frazer's greatest critics: he wrote that, "Frazer's account of the magical and religious notions is unsatisfactory: it makes these notions appear as mistakes . . . even the idea of trying to explain the practice—say of killing the priest-king—seems to me wrong headed. All that Frazer does is to make this practice plausible to people who think like he does."[20] Frazer's explanations are only hypotheses. What he does is

---

19. Frazer, *The Golden Bough: A Study in Magic and Religion*. Initially published in two volumes in 1890, the work then grew to the final 12 volume, 3rd edition published 1911–15: Vol. 1–2, Part I, The Magic Art; Vol. 3, Part II, Taboo and the Perils of the Soul; Vol. 4, Part III, The Dying God; Vol. 5–6, Part IV, Adonis, Attis, Osiris: Studies in the History of Oriental Religion; Vol. 7–8, Part V, Spirits of the Corn and of the Wild; Vol. 9, Part VI, The Scapegoat; Vol. 10–11, Part VII, Balder the Beautiful the Fire-Festivals of Europe and the Doctrine of the External Soul; Vol. 12, Bibliography and General Index. See also: Frazer, *The Golden Bough* (single volume abridged, 907 pages, edition,).

20. Ludwig Wittgenstein, *Bemerkungen über Frazer's Golden Bough*, 1e.

say, this is what takes place here; you can treat it as primitive, even laughable, risible. Frazer's work replicates itself horizontally; at no point does it advance understanding or offer wisdom beyond these merely religious practices and actions. The problem with Frazer's work is that he tries to offer essentially the same explanation for all of these religious actions and practices, therefore he is trying to explain causation (and Wittgenstein was probably the twentieth-century expert of deconstructive analysis of causation, and the concept of "because"); however, in so doing Frazer merely reinforces the "modernist" cultural stereotype of a Victorian/Edwardian establishment; that is, his own preconceptions of why religious practices are carried out. Postmodernism would offer a much greater caution; likewise, a pre-modern perspective would also cast doubt on the arrogance of his methods. Wittgenstein assesses that Frazer believes that all the recorded actions are to do with confession, repentance, and atonement— "burn an effigy, kissing the picture of a loved one."[21] Whether this is so or not, he does not in the end ask why this is necessary or even consider that such a human practice issues from sublimated guilt over original sin and an unawareness of, or even rejection, of Christ's atoning sacrifice, for only the cross, the death of the Christ, truly atones for all humanity (in potential). Wittgenstein writes, "How impossible for Frazer to understand a different way of life from the English one of his time!"[22]

According to a "modernist" doctrine of religion, all myths, customs, and practices of a religious nature must, according to academic impartiality, be regarded as equal, and in order to enforce this notion of equality, any aspect that relates to a truth claim, especially if it contradicts or upsets the apparent impartially of the academic, must be marginalized or excised.

> Frazer is much more savage than most of his savages, for these savages will not be so far from any understanding of spiritual matters as an Englishman of the twentieth century. His explanations of the primitive observances are much cruder than the sense of the observances themselves. An historical explanation, an explanation as an hypothesis of the development, is only one kind of summary of the data—of their synopsis. We can equally well see the data in their relations to one another and make a summary of them in a general picture without putting it in the form of an hypothesis regarding the temporal development.[23]

Wittgenstein can understand how Frazer's attempt at a worldview (*Weltanschauung*) is historicist[24]—reading more into the data than is there, and projecting his own expectations on to what he studies. Frazer's viewpoint is therefore as particular as any of the so-called primitive tribal religious and mythological customs he presents details of. Frazer also reads too much into the casual folk customs of the British Isles.[25] Perhaps one strength in Frazer's work is that he realizes that much religious manifestation is merely human generated (a viewpoint an orthodox Christian perspective would agree

21. Ibid, 4e.
22. Ibid, 5e.
23. Ibid, 8e.
24. Ibid, 9e, 12e and 16e.
25. Ibid, 16e-18e.

9. Christ as the Light of the World I: A Doctrine of Christological Prefigurement

with, for often these practices are bereft of revelation, where revelation is centered on Jesus Christ as the revelation of God. But Frazer does not appear to believe in divine revelation. Through the Christ, God takes on to God's-self the need for atonement for human sin, marginalizing all these religious attempts at forgiveness and atonement. If Frazer is correct to assert that there is no inherent value in the multifarious attempts by "primitive" religions to atone then is he, ironically, correct?

ii. A Paradigm: Revelation Precedes Religion

Lewis's intellectual starting point is therefore that all religion is a human product, constructed from observing and relating to this aggressive and unsympathetic world. At this time Lewis would have subscribed to a view of theology similar to that of Feuerbach, that God exists only as a psychological projection and hence all theology is a human product, wish fulfillment. Lewis was therefore dismissive of theology because there was no God; further that all our supposed knowledge of God is merely an enlargement of ideas about human experience, because, echoing Feuerbach, the secret of theology is none other than anthropology—the knowledge of God is the knowledge of man.[26] Feuerbach was a profound influence on Frazer; Frazer likewise on Lewis's intellectual development. Was Lewis completely wrong? In many ways this severe criticism of religion provided a ground for his conversion—he was able to see beyond human religion, most of which is a human invention and not divinely inspired, leaving space for him to identify the true revelation amidst a sea of human religiosity. Lewis is writing having spent two years being tutored by Kirkpatrick, whose severe logical atheism had a profound effect on Lewis—Kirkpatrick is probably the source of Lewis's introduction to Frazer's work and all it represents. Ironically Lewis continues in this letter to Arthur Greeves to qualify his comments by asserting that:

> I am not laying down as a certainty that there is nothing outside the material world: considering the discoveries that are always being made, this would be foolish. Anything MAY exist: but until we know that it does, we can't make any assumptions. The universe is an absolute mystery: man has made many guesses at it, but the answer is yet to seek. Whenever any new light can be got as to such matters, I will be glad to welcome it. In the meantime I am not going to go back to the bondage of believing in any old (and already decaying) superstition.[27]

Lewis is right to criticize and dismiss taboo, superstition, and primitive religion (though there is an equal element of "primitiveness" even in the most sophisticated and "Modern" religions and cults). Ironically what Frazer is not criticizing in his work is revelation—though admittedly the Victorian mind-set he was working in, grounded in Darwin, dismissed the concept of revelation, of a God beyond and outside of religion and humanity's manifold projections. Despite the naivety and we may say arrogance of Lewis's earlier remarks, the standpoint he takes in this letter on religion, cult, and

---

26. Feuerbach, *The Essence of Christianity*, 121 & 207.
27. Lewis to Arthur Greeves, Oct. 12, 1916. *Collected Letters, Vol. I*, 231. Lewis's emphasis and capitalization

mythology, is in many ways a relatively healthy position to take, and establishes a paradigm for the mature Christian Lewis: revelation precedes religion; if revelation exists, it precedes religion and stands apart from religion.

5. LEWIS'S CONVERSION—ATONEMENT AND PREFIGUREMENT

i. Natural Theology and Revelation

Having given in to what he perceived to be the God above all gods, and submitted to theism, Lewis's final conversion to the God of the Gospel writers and the creeds was caused by a late-night conversation. Two years after his conversion to theism J. R. R. Tolkien and Hugo Dyson pressed the issue with Lewis as they walked through Addison Walk in Magdalen Meadows, in Oxford on Saturday September 19, 1931.[28] This debate was in part about myth and Christianity. It was this conversation that finally convinced Lewis of the uniqueness of the Gospel account: that Jesus was the Christ, God incarnate, Son of God and Son of Man. The debate was about religious truth, about why Lewis could not accept the unilateral action of God in the Christ-event, in relation to humanity's ideas about God. Therefore, the debate, and Lewis's subsequent theories about christological prefigurement, relate to an understanding of natural theology.

Before we examine what Lewis regarded as prefigurements of the incarnation-resurrection narrative we need to clarify exactly what we are talking about when we speak of natural theology and revelation. Natural theology is to be seen as a branch of philosophy, more pertinently philosophy of religion, because it is based on reason and reflective experience; traditionally it is an attempt to explain the gods rationally, or argue—or not—for the existence of God, or to postulate on the attributes of God. Traditionally natural theology is undertaken without recourse to revelation (i.e., reasoning independent of experience, as in the transcendental philosophy of Immanuel Kant); a common defense is that natural theology is independent of the contingencies and vagaries of history and event. To argue *a priori* is to reason out from a general law to a particular instance, independent of observation. *A priori* reasoning is derived from ideas/propositions existing in the mind prior to and independent of experience, therefore not based on prior study or examination. By comparison *a posteriori* reasoning is reasoning after the event and in the light of experience: Christian theology should be *a posteriori*—after the Christ-event—we cannot simply reason out God, life, the universe, and everything for ourselves without recourse to what happened in Palestine two thousand years ago: this is what was at the heart of the Tolkien-Dyson-Lewis discussion which was the catalyst to Lewis's final conversion to the gospel. A philosophy of natural theology was central to the Enlightenment agenda, where religion and the revelation of the church was marginalized and the endeavor was to find a way to God, or a "god," through philosophical reasoning—this

---

28   This is dealt with in depth in the first book in this series: *C. S. Lewis—Revelation Conversion, and Apologetics*.

9. Christ as the Light of the World I: A Doctrine of Christological Prefigurement

was an attempt to establish the existence of God without recourse to religious belief. Natural theology is not essentially to do with nature, but reasoning in the human mind: the attempt to deduce the existence or otherwise of God/god(s). Nature in the context of the physical world might be invoked simply as evidence for (or against, as Darwin did) the existence of a "god." For the nineteenth-century Russian novelist and prophet Fyodor Mikhailovich Dostoevsky this amounted to a storming of heaven; in effect, the building of a Tower of Babel out of the apparent independence of human reasoning, which for Dostoevsky resonated with the fall—the taking to the human of responsibility for knowledge, for ethics, for decisions about good and evil, and for control and responsibility over humanity.[29] Lewis, like Dostoevsky, is in many ways a prophet speaking out against modernity.

What was Lewis's position, his views, on natural theology? In his twenties the apostate self-confessed atheistic Lewis would have subscribed to a view of natural theology similar to that of Feuerbach; that all theology is of human creation. Lewis came to adopt a diametrically opposite view of natural theology in his thirties after his conversion initially to theism and then to Christianity. Lewis wrote to Arthur Greeves on Tuesday September 22, 1931,[30] two days after the momentous meeting and discussion with Tolkien and Dyson and the impact their argument for Christianity had on him:

> It was really a memorable talk. We began (in Addison's walk just after dinner) on metaphor and myth—interrupted by a rush of wind which came so suddenly on the still, warm evening and sent so many leaves pattering down that we thought it was raining. We all held our breath, the other two appreciating the ecstasy of such a thing almost as you would. We continued (in my room) on Christianity: a good long satisfying talk in which I learned a lot: then discussed the difference between love and friendship—then finally drifted back to poetry and books.[31]

Writing again on October 1—two days after the motorcycle journey with Warnie to Whipsnade Zoo where he finally "knew" that Jesus was the Christ, the incarnate Son of God—Lewis wrote: "How deep I am just now beginning to see: for I have just passed on from believing in God to definitely believing in Christ—in Christianity. I will try to explain this another time. My long night talk with Dyson and Tolkien had a good deal to do with it."[32] In the same letter Lewis also comments about how he has read Paul's Epistle to the Romans, "the first Pauline epistle I have ever seriously read through. It contains many difficult and some horrible things, but the essential idea of Death (the

---

29. See Dostoevsky, *The Notebooks for Crime and Punishment*, 218. See also Dostoevsky, *The Diary of a Writer*, Vol. I, February 1876, ch. 1, "1 On the Subject that we are all Good Fellows," 198–201, and ch. 1, "4 Meditations About Europe," 250–54. See specifically, Dostoevsky, *Demons*, Pt. 2, Ch. 6, "Pyotr Bustles About," 343–87. In commenting on Dostoevsky's use of The Tower of Babel, rooted in Genesis (Gen 11:1–9), see, Kroeker and Ward, *Remembering the End: Dostoevsky as a Prophet of Modernity*, 67; and Sandoz, *Political Apocalypse: A Study of Dostoevsky's Grand Inquisitor*, 137.
30. Letter to Arthur Greeves, Sept. 22, 1931. *Collected Letters*, Vol. I, 969–72.
31. Ibid., 970.
32. Letter to Arthur Greeves, Oct. 1, 1931. *Collected Letters*, Vol. I, 972–75, quote, 974.

Macdonald idea) is there alright."[33] This, in effect, begins to introduce to him a sound understanding of atonement and with it the purpose for the incarnation-resurrection, and therefore the relationship of the Christ-event with the myths of dying and revived "gods."

Writing again to Greeves on the October 18, 1931, he explains how Tolkien and Dyson showed him how redemption was achieved for it was this in many ways that proved the obstacle to Lewis. What had been holding him back from full belief was puzzlement over how the event of the cross and resurrection should achieve salvation for mankind. This was not a question of belief, of faith, but of understanding: knowing what the doctrine meant had been holding him back:

> My puzzle was the whole doctrine of Redemption: in what sense the life and death of Christ "saved" or "opened salvation to" the world. I could see how miraculous salvation might be necessary: one could see from ordinary experience how sin (e.g., the case of a drunkard) could get a man to such a point that he was bound to reach Hell (i.e., complete degradation and misery) in this life unless something quite beyond mere natural help or effort stepped in. And I could well imagine a whole world being in the same state and similarly in need of miracle. What I couldn't see was how the life and death of Someone Else (whoever he was) 2000 years ago could help us here and now—except in so far as his example helped us. And the example business, tho' true and important, is not Christianity: right in the centre of Christianity, in the Gospels and St Paul, you keep on getting something quite different and very mysterious expressed in those phrases I have so often ridiculed (propitiation-sacrifice-the blood of the Lamb)—expressions which I could only interpret in senses that seemed to me either silly or shocking.[34]

Lewis explains how Dyson and Tolkien made him realize how if he met the idea of sacrifice in a pagan story he had no objections—for example, the story of a "god" sacrificing himself to himself. Lewis found such a myth deeply moving, mysteriously moving, as with all the myths of a dying and reviving "god." Dyson and Tolkien made Lewis face his prejudices—that he was content with these stories from all over the world, except when he found it in the Gospels. Lewis explains how he was prepared to feel the myth as profound and suggestive of meanings in pagan stories, provided he was not forced to explain any deeper meaning.

> Now the story of Christ is simply a true myth: a myth working on us in the same way as the others, but with this tremendous difference that it really happened: and one must be content to accept it in the same way, remembering that it is God's myth where the others are men's myths: i.e., the pagan stories are God expressing himself through the minds of poets, using such images as he found there, while Christianity is God expressing himself through what we call "real things." Therefore it is true, not in the sense of being a "description" of God (that no finite mind could take in) but in the sense of being the way in which God chooses to (or can) appear to our faculties.[35]

---

33. Ibid., 975.
34. Letter to Arthur Greeves, Oct. 18, 1931. *Collected Letters, Vol. I*, 975–77, quote, 974.
35. Letter to Arthur Greeves, Oct. 1, 1931. *Collected Letters, Vol. I*, 976–77.

9. Christ as the Light of the World I: A Doctrine of Christological Prefigurement

C. S. Lewis: Christological Prefigurement— The Key Theological and Philosophical Works

1931
C. S. Lewis to Arthur Greeves, Oct. 1, 1931. *Collected Letters, Vol. I*, 2004, 972–975.

1933
Lewis, *The Pilgrim's Regress*.

1940
Lewis, "The Kappa Element in Romance" (paper presented to Merton College Undergraduate Literary Society in 1940), published as, "On Stories", in, Lewis, *Essays Presented to Charles Williams*, 1947, 90–105

1942
Lewis, "Miracles" (a sermon/address preached in St Jude on the Hill Church, London on Nov. 26, 1942, and published in *St Jude's Gazette*, 73, October 1942, 4–7. (A shorter version was published in, *The Guardian*, Oct. 2, 1942, 316). The full sermon was published in Lewis, *Undeceptions: Essays on Theology and Ethics*, 1971, 5–16.

1944
Lewis, "Myth Became Fact" (an essay that first appeared in, *World Dominion* Vol. XXII, September-October 1944, 267–270). Also in Lewis, *Undeceptions: Essays on Theology and Ethics* 1971, 39–43.

1944
Lewis, "Is Theology Poetry?' (a paper read to the Socratic Club in Oxford and first appeared in print in, *The Socratic Digest* 1944). Also in Lewis, *They Asked for a Paper*, 1962, 150–165.

1945
C.S. Lewis, "The Grand Miracle" (a sermon preached in St Jude on the Hill Church, London, and appeared in, *The Guardian* (Anglo-Catholic newspaper), Apr. 27, 1945, 161 & 165). Also in Lewis, *Undeceptions: Essays on Theology and Ethics*, 1971, 56–63.

1946
Lewis, "A Christian Reply to Professor Price" (a paper read to the Socratic Club on 20th May 1946 in answer to a paper of Professor H. H. Price, "The Grounds of Modern Agnosticism", delivered on 20 October 1944; both were later published in, *The Phoenix Quarterly*, Vol. 1, No. 1 Autumn 1946, 31–44; amendments and responses from the floor are in the minutes' book of The Socratic Club, published in, Lewis, *Compelling Reason*, 101–103. "A Christian Reply to Professor Price" was republished as, "Religion Without Dogma?" in Lewis, *Undeceptions: Essays on Theology and Ethics*, 1971, 99–114.

1947
Lewis, "The Grand Miracle" (an expansion on the kernel of material initially presented in 1942 at St Jude on the Hill Church), as Ch. XII "The Grand Miracle" in Lewis, *Miracles* (1st ed.), 1947, 131–158.

1955
Lewis, *Surprised by Joy: the Shape of my Early Life* (Lewis extrapolates how he came to realize how the Pagan myths were a prefiguration of the incarnation), 1955, 59–60.

1958
Lewis, *Reflections on the Psalms*; (how Lewis accounted for the evidence beyond coincidence of Christlikeness in Pagan myths, but in particularly in Greco-Roman), Ch. 10 "Second Meanings".

1959
Lewis, "Modern Theology and Biblical Criticism" (a paper read at Westcott House, Cambridge, 11th May 1959), in Lewis, *Christian Reflections*, 1967, 152–166.

1961
C.S. Lewis, "On Myth", in, *An Experiment on Criticism*, 1961.

Full details can be found in the bibliography

Figure 19 Sources for C. S. Lewis's Christological Prefigurement

The connection, so to speak, the way Lewis reconciled the apparent disparity between the story of the Christ-event and the atonement theories, was by asserting that the story, the "myth," is true, but the doctrines are less true: "they are translations into our concepts and ideas of that which God has already expressed in a language more adequate, namely the actual incarnation, crucifixion, and resurrection."[36] Lewis as a Christian apologist avoided subscribing to one particular theory of atonement (i.e., how Christ's sacrifice works) over another; however, a constant thread in Lewis's apologetic is that he saw atonement theories as inadequate and in many ways inaccurate because they all fell short of the actual reality of what Christ did for us on the cross, they were all wrong yet contained elements of truth because they were transpositions of how redemption was achieved. Myth gives us a more accurate understanding of the truth of an event—myth as Lewis defined in his six elements towards a definition of myth that we cited above. The relationship between these pagan myths and the incarnation-resurrection narrative was not only crucial to Lewis's conversion but also fundamental to his apologetic as a mature Christian.

ii. Myth Became Reality

From this correspondence with Arthur Greeves, and from Tolkien's record of the momentous conversation in Addison walk in the autumn of 1931, Lewis the convert was therefore adopting something approaching a Barthian position in respect to natural theology—God's self-revelation in Christ was the only true story, the actuality. The other stories/myths were to be dismissed as the mere product of humanity striving to perceive a transcendent God—these were only "men's myths," lies breathed through silver. This position was not surprising considering how long and hard it had been to achieve his conversion. Lewis's views at this time are in many ways a reaction to Frazer, hence the idea of the one true (that is, historical) myth. However this Barthian-type position was to soften with maturity. Lewis's christological ideas and his understanding of natural theology and revelation were to undergo change and development over a thirty-year period. His understanding of christological prefigurement and myth developed from 1931 to 1961; the evidence is in his writings (see figure 19). A paper read to an undergraduate literary society in 1940 contains a kernel of his developing ideas, particularly his understanding of the relationship between natural theology and myth, in this case the distinction between story and myth, and how the latter are not dependent upon key words or a cultural context—myths seem to exist, Platonically, outside of a human context, hence they can be a vehicle of truths on a more profound level than mere fact.[37] However, it is in his understanding of miracles that we find the best exposition of his ideas about the mythical-historical nature of the incarnation. Lewis spoke and wrote on several occasions during the 1940s on the subject of the incarnation (the grand miracle as he called it) as well as miracles generally culminating in the essay, "Myth Became Fact."[38] This is the central text to what we may call his

36. Ibid., 977.
37. Lewis, "On Stories," 91 & 101.
38. Lewis, "Myth Became Fact," 39–43.

9. Christ as the Light of the World I: A Doctrine of Christological Prefigurement

proposition of christological prefigurement, though Lewis never gave the proposition a definite title. Lewis opens the essay with a criticism of modern intellectuals, personified by one of his academic colleagues, who though having abandoned the Christian faith persisted in clinging on to something of the form—such modern intellectuals were moved, asserted Lewis, by the mythical qualities of the story. It is the myth, Lewis asserts, that gives life. He then examines the distinction between abstract and concrete experience (which we will come to in the next chapter) and how this allows myths to express something experiential to us, which we could not grasp otherwise:

> Now as myth transcends thought, incarnation transcends myth. The heart of Christianity is a myth which is also a fact. The old myth of the Dying God, *without ceasing to be myth*, comes down from the heaven of legend and imagination to the earth of history. It *happens*: at a particular date, in a particular place, followed by definable historical consequences. We pass from a Balder or an Osiris, dying nobody knows when or where, to a historical Person crucified (it is all in order) *under Pontius Pilate*. By becoming fact it does not cease to be myth: that is the miracle.[39] (Lewis's emphasis)

Lewis continues by showing how many derive sustenance from a story's mythical qualities even if they do not assent to its factuality and historicity. But these mythical qualities in the story of Christ are not equal to the reality:

> Those who do not know that this great myth became Fact when the Virgin conceived are, indeed, to be pitied. But Christians also need to be reminded— we may thank Corineus for reminding us—that what became Fact was a Myth, that it carries with it into the world of fact all the properties of a myth. God is more than a god, not less; Christ is more than Balder, not less. We must not be ashamed of the mythical radiance resting on our theology. We must not be nervous about "parallels" and "pagan Christs": they *ought* to be there—it would be a stumbling block if they weren't.[40] (Lewis's emphasis)

These ideas around prefigured Christology were in part referred to and further developed in a paper read in 1946 to The Socratic Club in Oxford, "Religion Without Dogma?," where Lewis explicitly criticizes Frazer's disinterested anthropological approach to taboo, ritual, superstition, and magic, as though that was all there was to religion; likewise, Frazer's Darwinian evolutionist dismissal of elements in pagan myths of the incarnation-resurrection narrative.[41]

The fullest exposition of the proposition was in an essay initially preached in St Jude on the Hill Church, London in 1942, reworked for publication in 1945, and reworked again to form chapter 14 "The Grand Miracle" of the book *Miracles*, in 1947.[42] It is this chapter that we will draw on in the ensuing analysis. There are also key remarks in his spiritual autobiography, *Surprised by Joy*, published in 1955—chiefly explaining how he came to see the incarnation-resurrection narrative as the one true myth (in this case

---

39. Ibid., 42
40. Ibid., 43
41. Lewis, "Religion Without Dogma?," 99–114, specifically, 101–2.
42. Lewis, *Miracles*, 1st edition, 138–58.

refuting Frazer). For example, how in his youth no one had attempted to show him how pagan myths were fulfilled prophetically in the Christ-event, and therefore how paganism in many ways *prefigured* Christ's redeeming work.[43] In this context Lewis wrote about the importance of the old pagan gods in his time of apostasy, how he was sent back to the old "false" gods to acquire some capacity for worship against the day when the true God should reveal himself to Lewis.

> First, you will misunderstand everything unless you realize that, at the time, Asgard and the Valkyries seemed to me incomparably more important than anything else in my experience . . . More shockingly, they seemed much more important than my steadily growing doubts about Christianity. This may have been—in part, no doubt was—penal blindness; yet that might not be the whole story. If the Northernness seemed then a bigger thing than my religion, that may partly have been because my attitude toward it contained elements which my religion ought to have contained and did not. I came far nearer to feeling this about the Norse gods whom I disbelieved in than I had ever done about the true God while I believed. Sometimes I can almost think that I was sent back to the false gods there to acquire some capacity for worship against the day when the true God should recall me to himself. Not that I might not have learned this sooner and more safely, in ways I shall now never know, without apostasy, but that Divine punishments are also mercies, and particular good is worked out of particular evil, and the penal blindness made sanative.[44]

North European pagan religion was, therefore, what Lewis terms the childhood of religion, a prophetic dream, to awake fully in the gospel.[45] The meaning inherent in these myths changed with the unfolding of salvation history, but the previsions are as important today to apostates as they were prior to the actual incarnation-resurrection. We will also find important considerations about why there are second meanings to ancients sources—both scriptural and pagan—in Lewis's consideration of the Psalms.[46]

6. THE INCARNATION-RESURRECTION NARRATIVE

We now need to address two questions: "What is meant by the phrase, the incarnation-resurrection narrative?" and, "What exactly are these examples of prefigurement that Lewis alludes to?," and therefore, "What do we mean by prefigurement?" Many see the phrase "the incarnational narrative" as encompassing the whole of Christ's life on earth; Lewis refers generally to the Christian story and specifically to either the incarnation or the resurrection. But he is actually quite vague as to what constitutes the subject and object of prefigurement. This will be encountered later when we examine the examples of prefigurement that he cites. At its most concise the incarnation narrative, or story, is encapsulated in John 1:14a: "And the Word became made flesh and lived amongst us." What these few words imply is momentous: God made man; made in the flesh and blood of men and women and children, born a babe. The question then

---

43. Lewis, *Surprised by Joy*, 59–60.
44. Ibid., 73.
45. Ibid., 227.
46. Lewis, *Reflections on the Psalms*, ch. 11, 94–103.

9. Christ as the Light of the World I: A Doctrine of Christological Prefigurement

arises, what exactly is encompassed by the incarnational narrative when Lewis writes of prefigurement. At times he talks of the incarnation and the virginal conception; at other times the idea of a dying and reviving pagan god. For the purposes of this study we will refer to the incarnation-resurrection narrative as the two points in Christ's earthly life that Lewis regarded as critically fundamental to the faith and to God's salvific action with the world and humanity: first, the virginal conception-incarnation and, second, the cross-resurrection. There are numerous allusions pointing towards the incarnation and resurrection in Jewish history and in the Old Testament—the Hebrew Bible previsions and prefigures the incarnation-resurrection. Frazer, in effect, ignores these; Lewis accepts them in faith. What preoccupied Lewis was the evidence of prefigurement in the ancient pagan oral traditions. Therefore, it is pertinent to examine some of the myths that Lewis alludes to.

i. Myths of Prefigurement—Incarnation

Lewis cites specific "gods" from pagan myths; for example, Balder, Adonis, and Osiris. In this Lewis draws on three volumes of Frazer's work.[47] Frazer's work is central to Lewis in his pre-Christian period. He supported the concepts and historicism inherent in Frazer's agenda. After conversion he sought to accommodate Frazer's material; he knew he could not simply dismiss it, so he revised it from a christocentric position. Frazer recorded innumerable examples of stories/myths of what can be considered "gods" in human form, deified humans, and dying and reviving "gods."

Frazer works from the assumption that there is a unified cause and aim amongst all religious traditions when they present or assert examples of incarnation, deification, or possession: an individual is convinced s/he is the "god"; Frazer's superiority is in his conclusion that, from a Western perspective, *we know better*. Lewis, like Frazer, knew his religious history but had extricated himself from this unified Victorian "modernist" mind-set. Lewis wrote of how humanity—characterized by tribal and cultural differences, but essentially amongst the Jews—became conscious of a moral law and the existence of a law-giver as distinct from humanity. He writes of how among the Jews a man turns up talking as if he was God, because he claims to have existed always, he claims to be able to forgive people's sins, further, that he is coming to judge the world at the end of time. Claiming divine status was not unusual amongst pantheists, pagans, and in religious traditions from the Indian sub-continent, or in the numerous religious and mythological traditions Frazer had studied. However, these claims came from a man born and raised a Jew, steeped in the Jewish tradition. These assertions were not the same as deification or possession amongst other world religions. Lewis understood that the understanding of God in the Jewish tradition was in many ways uniquely different from all other world religions and mythologies at that time. Jesus cannot simply be seen as another especially religious person, or as a prophet or guru, or as a wise and mature religious teacher with an enhanced sense of the divine:

---

47. Frazer, *The Golden Bough*, Vol. 4, Part III: The Dying God; Vol. 9, Part VI: The Scapegoat; Vol. 10–11, Part VII, Balder the Beautiful the Fire–Festivals of Europe and the Doctrine of the External Soul.

> Then comes the real shock. Among these Jews there suddenly turns up a man who goes about talking as if he was God. He claims to forgive sins. He says he has always existed. He says he is coming to judge the world at the end of time. Now let us get this clear. Among Pantheists, like the Indians, anyone might say that he was a part of God, or one with God: there'd be nothing very odd about it. But this man, since he was a Jew, couldn't mean that kind of God. God, in their language, meant the Being outside the world Who had made it and was infinitely different from anything else. And when you've grasped that, you will see that what this man said was, quite simply, the most shocking thing that has ever been uttered by human lips.[48]

There are cases cited by Frazer of what he terms "incarnate gods," though these are, in many respects, examples of individuals possessed either temporarily or permanently by a presumed divine source. Often these gods are no more than invisible magicians who work behind the veil of nature using a man or woman as means of temporality. When possessed, the host personality is nearly always in abeyance. There is then another class of incarnate gods where the host is inspired—again temporarily or permanently—acquiring both divine knowledge and divine power, though this stops short of omniscience and omnipotence. Often these incarnate "gods" or possessed individuals assume magical powers over nature and the community and exercise awesome political powers within tribal societies: omnipotence (sociologically, anthropologically), but never omnipresence. In the case of a more organized and mature religion, Hinduism, there are prolific examples of human "gods." For example, the belief in Chinchvad, near Poona in Western India, that since the seventeenth-century there has been an incarnation of the elephant-god Gunputty. The piety, abstinence, mortification, and prayer of a Brahman of Poona was such that the "god" promised a portion of his spirit of holiness to abide with him and each of seven generations thereafter—so that the light of the "god" should be transmitted to a dark world.[49] There are, it can be argued, countless examples of deification of an individual, or possession either wholly or partly, temporarily or permanently, by spirits or divine powers or "gods," but is this the same as the Christian incarnation? Is there anything resembling the incarnation in form or typology?[50] Avatars in Hinduism represent the descent of a "god" to earth in incarnate form.[51] This is often an incarnation or embodiment, or a manifestation (but not the incarnation). For example, Krishna was the eighth avatar of Vishnu, incarnated to help the five brothers regain their kingdom. Sometimes these "gods" appear in human form. Avatar (meaning descent in Hinduism) was usually to counteract some evil

---

48. Lewis, *Broadcast Talks*, 50.
49. See also, Frazer, *The Golden Bough*, Vol. 10–11, Part VII, Balder the Beautiful the Fire–Festivals of Europe and the Doctrine of the External Soul, 121. This and similar material can be found in the abridged single volume: Frazer *The Golden Bough* (abridged edition), ch. VII Incarnate Human Gods I, 109–27.
50. This issue has been dealt with by Scott and Selvanayagam, *Re-visioning India's Religious Traditions*; see also, Ward, *God, Faith and The New Millennium*.
51. From Sanskrit for "descent," and chiefly found in Hinduism, avatars are "gods" in incarnate form, the term is therefore used for a manifestation of a deity or released soul in bodily form on earth, the term also applies to an incarnation or embodiment of a person or idea. (OED)

9. Christ as the Light of the World I: A Doctrine of Christological Prefigurement

in this world. However, "descending," "appearing" or "abiding" is not ontologically synonymous—that is, an avatar is not of the nature of existence, the same sort of being, as with the nature of incarnate being in Jesus of Nazareth. There are similarities but the two are not synonymous: being made flesh with all that is implied in being human is a different concept of ontology altogether. The picture of Jesus in Philippians illustrates this, the apparent self-emptying of God that is kenotic[52] Christology:

> Let the same mind be in you that was in Christ Jesus,
>> who, though he was in the form of God,
>> did not regard equality with God
>> as something to be exploited,
> but emptied himself,
>> taking the form of a slave,
>> being born in human likeness.
> And being found in human form,
>> he humbled himself
>> and became obedient to the point of death–
>> even death on a cross. (Phil 2:5–8)

The Christology that this represents is diametric to the empowerment, the "appearing" and reigning over humanity that is central to avatars and related pagan deities. According to a kenotic Christology God empties himself and is incarnated, humbled and vulnerable in the form of a human baby. Possession or deification imparts divine properties; the Christian incarnation divests! That is, although Jesus of Nazareth was both fully human and fully divine, we can assert that kenosis divests; likewise the adoption of specifically human limitations constitutes disempowerment rather than empowerment.

In many ways a kenotic incarnation is a contradiction of a "god" descending or appearing, whether as a holy person or as of an avatar. So which is right? The Christian incarnation is because God is *infinitum capax finiti*—God is infinite yet capable of being finite. It is precisely because God's transcendence is boundless and infinite, unlimited, endless, that it is fit and competent for god to display the capacity to be contained, finite and restricted, definable. God, therefore, must be finite to be infinite. In the incarnation God is *infinitum capax finiti*; God's freedom is to be immanent and transcendent. God is not so transcendent that he can't be within creation, but this is in ways that are humanely unimaginable. The key is christological: God demonstrates to humanity his transcendence by being incarnated a human being in Jesus. Incarnation does not deny transcendence. According to the prefigurements and previsions in pagan myths the incarnation should be a denial of utter transcendence. God's transcendence implies that he can become finite: *infinitum capax finiti*—the infinite capable of the finite. Colin Gunton explains this in the context of the work of the Congregationalist minister and theologian P. T. Forsyth

---

52. Kenotic, kenosis—the full or partial renunciation of his divine nature by Christ in the incarnation, from the Greek *kenosis* (κενοσις), "an emptying," from *kenoein* (κενοειν) "to empty": (Phil 2:7), "but emptied himself" (ἀλλὰ ἑαυτὸν ἐκένωσεν), God literally emptied himself in the incarnation.

> There is an interesting parallel to this in Forsyth—it is the person in place of Jesus Christ. Forsyth says similar things in conception of God's infinity. If you think of God as infinite he is different from the finite. But says Forsyth, it is greater to be more infinite, so to speak, (unless that is a contradiction to be more infinite than absolute): it is therefore a true infinite to be finite also. If God's infinity means you can't become finite then he is not infinite. Freedom as transcendent freedom comes to a heart in his capacity for the infinite. God therefore does not have to contradict himself to become man in Christ: this is the natural expression of God's *aseitas*.[53]

In asserting that the incarnation is the true myth, God's myth become reality, Lewis is implicitly asserting *infinitum capax finiti*, but he is also asserting the incarnation-resurrection over these other myths, which are as we would expect—they are flawed and do not fully reflect what happened in Palestine two thousand years ago because they are transposed.

John Macquarrie writes that "any revelation of God must be a veiled revelation, for God cannot be revealed directly in a finite earthly medium."[54] Therefore there is a measure of ambiguity, even in the revelation of Christ. Karl Barth writes: "God is always God even in his humiliation. The divine being does not suffer any change, any diminution . . . God cannot cease to be God."[55] Humility and weakness are as much a part of God as are power and transcendence. Incarnation in the Hindu, as well as Oceanic, traditions empowers and gives virtual messianic, dictatorial powers over tribal communities; by comparison the Christian incarnation involves self-restraint: power and authority are marked by humility and forgiveness. The idea of an avatar *appearing* in human form is, to a degree, Docetic—*appearing* involves little risk. Once God is incarnate—not just appearing human or abiding, but born as a human—then there is risk. This idea would seem to have absolutely no precedent in mythology and religion. Examples of pagan incarnational prefigurement regard the indwelling of the divine as empowering; despite the divestment that God undergoes the Gospel writers witness to a glory that is absent in these prefigurement narratives/myths (John 1:14b). Is it fair to Lewis's Christology to speak of kenosis and divestment? Yes. In many of his writings he comments on God's restraint and divestment, likewise humiliation in taking on the human frame.[56] For example, Lewis cites the literary motif of the ruler who disguises himself to go amongst his people, as one of them. Søren Kierkegaard took this further when he extends the analogy to the folk tale of the king who divests himself of his royal regalia to don the clothes of an ordinary citizen to woo the woman he loves, and then having won her heart reveals himself as her Lord and king.[57] This is reminiscent of the courtship of the Hebrew people in the Old Testament; but God does not hide—he is revealed as Yahweh throughout, the one true God, the lord who made heaven and earth (though it is important to remember the principle we examined earlier, that this

---

53. Gunton, *The Barth Lectures*, 102.
54. Macquarrie, *Jesus Christ in Modern Thought*.
55. Barth, *Church Dogmatics*, Vol. IV/1, §59 The Obedience of the Son of God, 179.
56. Lewis, *Miracles*, 1st edition, ch. 14 "The Grand Miracle."
57. Kierkegaard, *Philosophical Fragments*, see ch. 2.

9. Christ as the Light of the World I: A Doctrine of Christological Prefigurement

unveiling also involves a veiling: God is revealed on God's terms only and in freedom: revelation as a vulnerable human baby). The idea of the self-emptying of God in the Christian incarnation is beyond human imagination and comprehension—it is sheer madness from a human perspective. Though if we accept that humility and weakness are as much a part of God as are power and transcendence then we can see how the Christian incarnation transcends the stories/myths quoted by Frazer: *infinitum capax finiti*. Lewis does write in his book *Miracles* about how the incarnation is prefigured in nature—in general revelation—in the sense that there is a descending in the cycle of life: a seed falls to the ground and so forth.[58] This is, however, more of an analogy than a prefigurement and there is still no ontological parallel with the self-emptying and self-restraint seen in the Christian incarnation.

As can be seen from the example quoted in the above paragraph, Kierkegaard has written on the question of christological prefigurement. Whatever the differences are between Lewis and Kierkegaard we can assert that there is no actual parallel of the Christian incarnation in Frazer's evidence specifically, in the work of ethnographers or social anthropologists generally, or even in Lewis's writings. This is another way of reconciling Lewis and Kierkegaard when the latter asserts in the guise of his pseudonym, Johannes Climacus, that: "Christianity is the only historical phenomenon that despite the historical—indeed, precisely by means of the historical—has wanted to be the single individual's point of departure for his eternal consciousness . . . No philosophy (for it is only for thought), no mythology (for it is only for the imagination), no historical knowledge (which is for memory) has ever had this idea—of which in this connection one can say with all multiple meanings that it did not arise in any human heart."[59] We can further assert that there is also no evidence in any of Lewis's writings, correspondence, or papers that he asserted exact one-to-one correspondence between the incarnation narrative and pagan myths, that is, the content, the story and what it represented; the incarnation narrative, *per se*, is, for Lewis, unique. There may be analogies, pointers, but there is no parallel—ontologically, epistemologically or, more important, soteriologically—with the Christian incarnation: none of the examples in Frazer of incarnate "gods" generally or a Hindu avatar specifically take on humanity as God did in Jesus, none can atone and reconcile for original sin, for the fall.[60] What Lewis does is point to analogies, figurative similarities. Why these are there will be considered later when we examine Lewis's concept of imagination. Let us move on to the idea of a dying and reviving god.

ii. Myths of Prefigurement—Resurrection

Generally speaking there is greater evidence of prefigurement in the examples of dying and reviving (not necessarily resurrected) "gods." Lewis was a classicist and knew his Greek myths. For example, the story of Adonis, a beautiful youth beloved by the

---

58. Lewis, *Miracles*, 1st edition, ch. 14 "The Grand Miracle," 117–18.
59. Kierkegaard, *Philosophical Fragments*, 35–36, examined in Evans, *The Historical Christ and the Jesus of Faith*, 53–56.
60. See, Frazer, *The Golden Bough* (abridged edition), ch. VII Incarnate Human Gods, 109–27.

goddesses Aphrodite and Persephone, slain by a wild boar while hunting. Following Aphrodite's pleas the god Zeus restored him so he should spend the winter months with Persephone in Hades and the summer months with Aphrodite. The story was considered symbolic of the natural cycle of death and rebirth. Both Lewis and Frazer place a great emphasis on the myth of Balder.[61] The "god" of light and joy in Norse mythology (son of Odin and Frigga, king and queen of the gods) Balder—or Baldhr—was regarded as beautiful, compassionate, graceful compared to the other gods. An oath was extracted from the forces and objects in nature that they would not harm him, but the mistletoe was overlooked. The "gods," thinking Balder safe, rained blows and objects at him; Loki maliciously placed a twig of mistletoe in the hands of the blind Hoder, god of darkness, and directed his aim against Balder. Balder fell, mortally wounded, pierced to the heart. After his death Odin sent another son the messenger Hermod to the underworld to plead for his return. Balder's release was conditional on everything in the world weeping for him. Everything wept except one old woman in a cave, and so Balder could not return to life. Despite its importance Frazer deals with the myth of Balder in only five pages (this is indicative of *The Golden Bough* because although tens of thousands of myths from all parts of the world are documented none and rigorously and systematically examined and the only method employed is not theological or philosophical but the nominalist reductionist Darwinian dismissal, grounded in Feuerbach and Freud). Frazer opens his account with the comment that, "A deity whose life might in a sense be said to be neither in heaven nor on earth but between the two, was the Norse Balder, the good and beautiful god, the son of the great god Odin, and himself the wisest, mildest, best beloved of all the immortals"[62] Like folk traditions, small details and settings may vary between versions collected from different places across different times—another version of the story of Balder that was collected by the twelfth century Danish historian Saxo Grammaticus was significantly different, though the (pseudo)-christological core remained the same. According to the version Frazer recorded, the death of Balder was in many ways a self-fulfilling prophecy:

> Balder dreamed heavy dreams which seemed to forebode his death. Thereupon the gods held a council and resolved to make him secure against every danger. So the goddess Frigg [Frigga] took an oath from fire and water, iron and all metals, stones and earth, from trees, sicknesses and poisons, and from all four-footed beasts, birds, and creeping things, that they would not hurt Balder. When this was done Balder was deemed invulnerable; so the gods amused themselves by setting him in their midst, while some shot at him, others hewed at him, and others threw stones at him. But whatever they did, nothing could hurt him; and at this they were all glad. Only Loki, the mischief-maker, was displeased, and he went in the guise of an old woman to Frigg, who told him that the weapons of the gods could not wound Balder, since she had made them all swear not to hurt him. Then Loki asked, "Have all things sworn to spare Balder?" She answered, "East of Walhalla grows a plant called mistletoe; it seemed to me too young to

---

61. See, Frazer, *The Golden Bough*, Vols. I and II, specifically Part VII: Balder the Beautiful.
62. Ibid., Vol. I, ch. 3 The Myth of Balder, 101.

9. Christ as the Light of the World I: A Doctrine of Christological Prefigurement

swear." So Loki went and pulled the mistletoe and took it to the assembly of the gods. There he found the blind god Hother standing at the outside of the circle. Loki asked him, "Why do you not shoot at Balder?" Hother answered, "Because I do not see where he stands; besides I have no weapon." Then said Loki, "Do like the rest and show Balder honour, as they all do. I will show you where he stands, and do you shoot at him with this twig." Hother took the mistletoe and threw it at Balder, as Loki directed him. The mistletoe struck Balder and pierced him through and through, and he fell down dead. And that was the greatest misfortune that ever befell gods and men. For a while the gods stood speechless, then they lifted up their voices and wept bitterly.[63]

Frazer notes how, "Whether he was a real or merely a mythical personage, Balder was worshipped in Norway"[64] and he notes how it may be rash to dismiss Balder simply as a

> romantic figure . . . nothing but a creation of the mythical fancy . . . It may be so; yet it is also possible that the myth was founded on the tradition of a hero, popular and beloved in his lifetime, who long survived in the memory of the people, gathering more and more of the marvellous about him as he passed from generation to generation of story-tellers. At all events it is worthwhile to observe that a somewhat similar story is told of another national hero, who may well have been a real man. In his great poem, The Epic of Kings, which is founded on Persian traditions.[65]

Frazer can see that there is more to the myth than mere religious invention, even when faced with similar stories found in widely diverse cultures. Despite the anthropological method no one has produced a satisfactory theory to account for these similarities from widely isolated cultures and places to replace a doctrine of inspiration—the source being outside of the human.

But is Balder the Christ? Balder's characteristics are in many ways similar to those of Christ—love, joy, light, beauty, compassion; there are also similarities with the Logos, the Word. Also the word in Norse, *tivor*, is unquestioningly taken to mean divine, god-like: Balder is the *blaupom tivor*, the bloody victim, the slain god. Furthermore, similarities can be seen with the suffering Christ, though more with the Hebrew concept of the scapegoat. Balder, however, does not take on death voluntarily; he fears death from the prophetic dream, yet the action taken to defend him causes his death. He is tricked by Loki, unaware that he is not immune to mistletoe. Jesus wrestled with his fate in the Garden of Gethsemane but accepted what was to befall him. What is more, there is the potential for Balder being revived or restored but this falls short of resurrection: it does not happen. There is a similar potentiality with the Egyptian god Osiris: he is tricked into death, like Balder, by an evil brother. Because of the love and lamentations for Osiris, the sun god, Ra, initiates the restoration of the broken and fragmented body of the murdered god: Isis fanned the cold clay with her wings, Osiris is revived and thenceforth reigned as king over the dead in the other

63. Ibid., 101–2.
64. Ibid., 104.
65. Ibid., 104–5. See also n. 257 on 105.

world. Again similarities, but does this constitute a parallel? Furthermore, neither in the story of Balder or Osiris (nor the many other stories of dying and reviving "gods") is there an explicit reference to the resurrection of an incarnate god. Such a story is beyond human comprehension or invention (part of Kierkegaard's paradox). Lewis and Kierkegaard are looking at different elements of the incarnation-resurrection narrative—Kierkegaard focuses on the detail, Lewis looking at generalizations. Kierkegaard holds to the uniqueness of the incarnational narrative (the Word became flesh) and in a specific sense he is right—a critical evaluation of the supposed parallels in pagan and Hindu mythology confirm Kierkegaard's reservations. Lewis was talking in terms of generalizations. He uses the term "prefigurement" to indicate foreshadowing. To be more specific, prefigurement indicates a similarity, figuratively or by type; that is, to be like metaphysically, psychologically, and for that matter sociologically *but not in actuality*. In one sense dreams prefigure reality; in another sense the whole of the Old Testament prefigures Christ. This raises the question, "To what extent do these pagan myths prefigure Christ?" Is this an example of natural theology, reasoned human strivings, or is there an element of revelation at play? There is the analogy with death and resurrection in the natural world. That is, the idea of seeds dying to bring forth new crops. Is this an example of general revelation? There are myths the world over of corn gods, but it is difficult to justify the idea of mythological parallels to the incarnation of God or the death and resurrection of Christ. These parallels do not hold when systematically analyzed, epistemologically, ontologically, soteriologically; but there are prefigurements, echoes—indicative, characteristically, of type and form, relating to the one story that was rooted historically in an actuality.

10

Christ as the Light of the World II: Revelation and Meaning—Imagination, Illumination, and Prevenience

SYNOPSIS:
Some may consider there to be a problem with a doctrine of christological prefigurement because it appears to do an injustice to the original aims and intentions of the author of the myth in asserting a second, a subsequent, christological level of meaning? Lewis thought not, and could defend such an interpretation. Is it possible for anyone today to view such myths without considering what has happened in the intervening time? Regardless of concerns over purity, there is an indelible connection that must be explained. For example, the apparent connection between ancient writings—Plato, Socrates, etc.—and what happened to the Christ in *his* passion. Lewis therefore posits an alternative option to prophecy or chance coincidence: to previse may be the result of wisdom.

Questions are raised as to what extent these prefigurements may be considered idolatrous? Again, Lewis could refute accusations of idolatry. Through his understanding of natural theology, revelation, and human imagination (proximately to that of Augustine, but also to the English Romantics, especially the poet, theologian, and philosopher Samuel Taylor Coleridge) Lewis's esteem, prior to his conversion, for pagan myths relating to the appearing (incarnation?) and reviving from death (resurrection?) of pagan gods, avatars, and spirits, led him after his conversion to analyze why and how these religious myths/stories related to the actual Christ-event. Lewis's understanding in this is contiguous with Coleridge and George MacDonald, but also J. R. R. Tolkien (from whom he learns and uses many concepts—for example, sub-creation, mythopoeic/mythopoeia, refractions and splinters of the true light, also eucatastrophe). His cautious respect for these intimations of prefigurement were as a mode of revelation rooted in Augustine's doctrine of illumination and the proposition that there is no un-aided true knowledge of God, knowledge and understanding given through prevenient grace and imbued through the faculty of the imagination.

Is Lewis's doctrine of prefigurement underpinned by a general or special theory of illumination? Lewis's thinking moves more and more to a general theory grounded in the prior—prevenient—action of the Holy Spirit. The relationship between the two realities—heaven and earth—the persistent and consistent consubstantial illumination as Augustine would have phrased it, allows for the prefigured intimations; unlike a Kantian closed universe where there is no commerce between the two realms, Lewis envisages interaction—transposition from the greater, the higher, to the lower, related to the loving purposes of God in seeking humanity's salvation.

1. SECOND MEANINGS

i. Intention and Validity

There is a potential problem with Lewis's doctrine of christological prefigurement. This problem is centered on a number of questions: "Is there a second level of meanings to these pagan myths?" If so, "Are the subsequent interpretations valid?" Also, "Are not the original intentions of the author applicable above subsequent interpretations, particularly given that the author could not have known about the Christ-event and therefore the similarity?," "Is this doctrine of christological prefigurement simply a coincidence?," "Are we projecting our own considerations and conclusions onto ancient texts?"

First, Frazer and other nineteenth-century academics recognized the coincidences in these of stories of incarnate gods and dying and reviving gods and used them as ammunition against Christianity and the church—hence the young apostate and atheistic Lewis's comments that the gospel account was simply one amongst many similar stories; and, of course, recently media celebrity New Atheists have revived Frazer's conclusions to help discredit Christianity.[1] Whether we consider it acceptable or not there is an indelible connection that must be explained. Earlier, in the context of Bultmann, Lock, and Vidler and "modern" biblical criticism, we encountered the concept of *Sitz im Leben*—the attempt to classify the material in its original context, who wrote the text, who heard it? The objective is to attempt to recapture the original setting, meaning, and context of a text, passage, or book. In claiming prefigurement is not Lewis working against the original setting of the myth, ignoring the intentions of the author and audience, how they were conceived to be read and heard? What we are claiming is a second or hidden meaning. Such a doctrine, Lewis claims, generates suspicion; it "arouses deep distrust in a modern mind, because, as we know, almost anything can be read into any book."[2]

What propositions are there to consider?–

- What were the original intention and meaning, the aims and objectives of the author, or authoring community?
- Truth: what truth is there underpinning the text/myth, and does this meaning change with context?
- What aims and objectives, intentions, lie outside of the mind of the author/authoring community?
- How, and in what way, does meaning and truth lie ultimately with God, with divine inspiration?
- What place is there for human freedom in the composition, subject to inspiration (we met this freedom in terms of Lewis's doctrine of Scripture)?

---

1. Dawkins, *The God Delusion*.
2. Lewis, *Reflections on the Psalms*, Ch. 10 "Second Meanings," 85.

10. Christ as the Light of the World II: Revelation and Meaning

Although there is always scope for self-deception because we are human, fallible and fallen, we cannot abandon completely this method of reassigning meaning and intention. Lewis recounts several examples of prophetic prefigurement, though he concedes that in some instances these can be explained simply as coincidence; it is easily possible for someone to make a comment that can be applied to subsequent events: "[it is feasible that] someone says what is truer and more important than he knows; but it does not seem to me that he could have done so by chance. I hasten to add that the alternative to chance that I have in mind is not "prophecy" in the sense of clear prevision, miraculously bestowed.[3] Lewis posits an alternative option to prophecy or chance coincidence: to previse may be the result of wisdom. To foresee, even unselfconsciously, may be caused by wisdom, where wisdom is insight and knowledge, an understanding of how the world works, of what constitutes human existence, which leads to a mature reflection on what is and what is possible.

Lewis being the classicist places great emphasis on examples that confirm a doctrine of prefiguration from Graeco-Roman sources. There are cases where the later truth, which the author or teller was unaware of, is closely related to the truth unknown at the time of composition, a truth which had in many ways underpinned and motivated the composition. Examples of prefigured truths that can be seen after the event they foretell are manifold in relation to the incarnation-resurrection. The sheer number must, Lewis asserts, deny a theory of chance coincidence (here the atheistic anthropologists are in agreement with Lewis). Lewis's preferences are for North European pagan myths, but in defending a doctrine of prefiguration he draws on Graeco-Roman examples.

ii. Plato and the Christ

Writing, in *Reflections on the Psalms*, in relation to the Hebrew perception that after death humanity faced a diminished existence, a disintegration of soul and body, a thin near-to-nothingness existence of the person's continued life after death in the Hebrew Sheol or the Greek Hades, Lewis described this existence as a form of "witless psychic sediment,"[4] furthermore he comments, "If so, Homer's idea that only a drink of sacrificial blood can restore a ghost to rationality would be one of the most striking among many pagan anticipations of the truth."[5] This situation arose from the fall, humanity is infected with death due to original sin; resurrection restores body and soul and life; we are no longer faced with a *post mortem* existence as disembodied souls languishing in Sheol or Hades. It is the blood of Christ's sacrifice that restores; it is this that Homer has an intimation of though he knew not the context of the truth of what was to happen. This is pagan intimation, christological prefiguration. But in terms of classical myth and philosophy this goes further.

Perception, insight, and knowledge will lead to wisdom. This is grounded in reason, but, as Lewis notes, "something more sensitive and personal than scientific

3. Ibid., 87.
4. Ibid., 32.
5. Ibid.

knowledge is involved—what the writer or speaker was, not only what he knew."[6] Lewis draws on Plato's *Republic*. Plato argues that righteousness is often praised for its benefits—honor and popularity—but if we are to truly understand righteousness we must see it without these popular worldly attributes and rewards. Lewis continues, "He [Plato] asks us therefore to imagine a perfectly righteous man treated by all around him as a monster of wickedness. We must picture him, still perfect, while he is bound, scourged, and finally impaled (the Persian equivalent of crucifixion). At this passage a Christian reader starts and rubs his eyes. What is happening? Yet another of these lucky coincidences? But presently he sees that there is something here which cannot be called luck at all."[7] This is not a case of someone who is talking about something else that coincidentally resonates with a subsequent event or person. Lewis correctly asserts that Plato is consciously extrapolating about what happens to goodness in this world, a wicked and misunderstanding world. This understanding is not separate, independent, from what happened to Jesus of Nazareth, the Christ, the only true and good and sinless person: the Passion for Lewis is the supreme example of goodness destroyed by fallen humanity:

> If Plato was in some measure moved to write of it by the recent death—we may almost say the martyrdom—of his master Socrates then that again is not something simply other than the Passion of Christ. The imperfect, yet very venerable, goodness of Socrates led to the easy death of the hemlock, and the perfect goodness of Christ led to the death of the cross, not by chance but for the same reason; because goodness is what it is, and because the fallen world is what it is. If Plato, starting from one example and from his insight into the nature of goodness and the nature of the world, was led on to see the possibility of a perfect example, and thus to depict something extremely like the Passion of Christ, this happened not because he was lucky but because he was wise.[8]

But what exactly did Plato write?–

> As for the choice between the lives we're discussing, we'll be able to make a correct judgment about that only if we separate the most just and the most unjust. Otherwise we won't be able to do it. Here's the separation I have in mind. We'll subtract nothing from the injustice of an unjust person and nothing from the justice of a just one, but we'll take each to be complete in his own way of life . . . let's now in our argument put beside him a just man, who is simple and noble and who, as Aeschylus says, doesn't want to be believed to be good but to be so. We must take away his reputation, for a reputation for justice would bring him honor and rewards, so that it wouldn't be clear whether he is just for the sake of justice itself or for the sake of those honors and rewards. We must strip him of everything except justice and make his situation the opposite of an unjust person's . . . Let him stay like that unchanged until he dies—just, but all his life believed to be unjust . . . remember that it isn't I who speak but those who praise injustice at the expense of justice. They'll say that a just person in such circumstances will be whipped, stretched on a rack, chained, blinded with fire,

6. Ibid., 89.
7. Ibid.
8. Ibid., 90.

10. Christ as the Light of the World II: Revelation and Meaning

and, at the end, when he has suffered every kind of evil, he'll be impaled, and will realize then that one shouldn't want to be just but to be believed to be just.[9]

Lewis concludes that Plato's insight is not simply a prevision, a prophecy. For Christians to recognize something here that resonates with the Passion is not simply retro-projection. Plato's insight issues from wisdom. There is a universal truth. But not all examples are prevision rooted in wisdom. There may be a parallel or comparable perception that resonates with the ultimate sacrifice of goodness that is the Passion, but still rooted in wisdom. For example, Lewis cites an example of a poem written by the Roman poet Virgil, written not long before the birth of Christ, which extols the new age where the Virgin returns, the reign of Saturn returns, and the new child is sent down from high heaven. The poem goes on to describe the paradisal age that this nativity ushers in. Throughout Christian history Virgil's comments were taken to have been prophetic. The question is, "Is this resemblance to the birth of Christ simply an accident?" Although it may be argued that knowledge from the Old Testament prophets might have reached Virgil (though whether there is evidence for this is another matter), there is a resemblance which, as with Plato, can be explained through a common consciousness grounded in knowledge and understanding of humanity, leading to wisdom.

Rooting or grounding prefigurement in a common consciousness leading to wisdom also applies to the numerous examples of prefigurement in pagan myths— whether North European, Asiatic-Indian, or Egyptian, or Oceanic, that is, to a greater or lesser degree, depending on the content and meaning of the prefigurement myth.

iii. Wisdom

Lewis therefore concludes that wisdom is at the heart of prefigurement. But this is not just human cleverness and ingenuity. Wisdom is the connection, the bridge. Wisdom is about inspiration, imagination, and reason. Wisdom in the Bible is real, external, without of the human. Wisdom in the Bible literature proceeds from the Holy Spirit. Lewis commented on several occasions that there is no good work done anywhere without the aid of the Father of Lights.[10] This raises again the question of inspiration and illumination of the human mind. Therefore Lewis can write, "In other words, when we examine things said which take on, in the light of later knowledge, a meaning they could not have had for those who said them, they turn out to be of different sorts."[11] Therefore meaning does, along with truth, exists outside of the human, where the original intentions and aims of the author of the myth, the teller of the tale, are only relative and contribute to a wider meaning and truth that reflects Christ as the way the truth and the life. This is, to a degree, Platonic. So, we may ask, if wisdom is to be equated with light, divine illumination, how does this wisdom relate to revelation?

---

9. Plato, *The Republic*, Bk. II, 1001–2.
10. Lewis, *Reflections on the Psalms*, Ch. 11 "Scripture," 95.
11. Ibid., 92.

Wisdom raises the question of prefigurement in the Old Testament in relation to the sayings of Jesus and the second meanings applied to ancient Hebrew events and stories in The Acts of the Apostles. This is potentially a large area of study—suffice briefly to see what Lewis made of it. Lewis read and studied the Psalms and was aware of the subtle references that could be seen as applying to Jesus of Nazareth, the Passion of the Christ.[12] Further, that from what is recorded both in his ministry and in his words from the cross, Jesus aligned himself with the suffering servant in Isaiah 53.[13] The resurrection narratives—for example, the encounter on the road to Emmaus—have Jesus looking back over the history of the Jews, and the Old Testament, to confirm what has happened.[14] Isaiah 53—referred to explicitly in The Acts of the Apostles—is probably the clearest example of the full meaning of an ancient passage coming out only after an event subsequent to it composition:

> He had no form or majesty that we should look at him, nothing in his appearance that we should desire him. He was despised and rejected by others; a man of suffering and acquainted with infirmity; and as one from whom others hide their faces he was despised, and we held him of no account. Surely he has borne our infirmities and carried our diseases; yet we accounted him stricken, struck down by God, and afflicted. But he was wounded for our transgressions, crushed for our iniquities; upon him was the punishment that made us whole, and by his bruises we are healed . . . He was oppressed, and he was afflicted, yet he did not open his mouth; like a lamb that is led to the slaughter, and like a sheep that before its shearers is silent, so he did not open his mouth. By a perversion of justice he was taken away. Who could have imagined his future? For he was cut off from the land of the living, stricken for the transgression of my people. They made his grave with the wicked and his tomb with the rich, although he had done no violence, and there was no deceit in his mouth. Yet it was the will of the Lord to crush him with pain . . . because he poured out himself to death, and was numbered with the transgressors; yet he bore the sin of many, and made intercession for the transgressors. (Isa 53:2–6, 7–10, 12.)

On the question of second meanings and validity Lewis concludes that when,

> I read that poem of Virgil's . . . such a reading may after all be a mere coincidence (though I am not sure that it is). I may be reading into Virgil what is wholly irrelevant to all he was, and did, and intended . . . But when I meditate on the Passion while reading Plato's picture of the Righteous One, or on the resurrection while reading about Adonis or Balder, the case is altered. There is a real connection between what Plato and the myth-makers most deeply were and meant and what I believe to be the truth.[15]

---

12. Ibid., 102. Lewis in particular notes Mark 15:34 linked to Ps 22.
13. Ibid., 101–2. Lewis in particular notes Acts 8:26–39, Phillip's encounter with the Ethiopian Eunuch over the interpretation of Is 53.
14. Ibid., Lewis in particular notes Jesus's identity as David's Lord (Mark 12:35–36); the use of words from Ps 91:11–12 in Matt 4:6; the explicit appropriation of Ps 118:22 in Mark 12:10; and the linking of Ps 16:11 to the resurrection.
15. Ibid., 92.

Second meanings are therefore valid because there is a God, and this God seeks to impart to humanity something of God's self and God's salvific actions for humanity. This is revelation both in the imparting of understanding, which is relational, and also the event, the action, of the atonement-redemption of humanity. This is a single event that then moves ever and onward towards the final fulfillment in the eschaton. Therefore revelation unfolds. Meaning will therefore change, or be added to. It is a contemporary Western concept that protects and holds sacrosanct the aims, objectives and intentions of the author, leading to the idea that the author is immutable. What was known and led to the inspiration of myths hundreds or even thousands of years ago will inevitably change *in the fullness* of the revelatory event of Jesus of Nazareth, the Christ: meaning is therefore transpositional (our grasp on revelation is, as we saw earlier, tentative) and unfolding towards the final completion in the eschaton—only with death and the Last Judgment when we will know as completely as we are known.

2. IMAGINATION, IDOLATRY, AND THE THEOLOGICAL TRADITION

Lewis places great emphasis on prefigurement in the sense that we have outlined: that these pagan Christs are a foreshadowing, that they relate figuratively to the incarnation-resurrection, that they are rooted in wisdom, but where wisdom is more than human cleverness—it relates to the Logos of God. Lewis's mature beliefs about inspiration and imagination will be examined so as to ascertain what value he placed on prefigurement. It is Lewis's doctrine of the imagination that is fundamental to these beliefs.[16]

For Lewis and George MacDonald, Lewis's self-acknowledged master and teacher,[17] God used people's imagination to get through to them. Through MacDonald Lewis viewed imagination and the intellect as gifted by the Holy Spirit, however, the reception and our subsequent actions are governed by free will and consequently the effects of original sin: humanity is free to reject or accept God on a conscious level, even though God may be pressing on each and every one in their, to a degree, subconscious minds. This is incarnational: the creative-re-creative act of the incarnation validates the created forms of the imagination; what is so important here is a baptized imagination: "It is not surprising that for MacDonald the closer one is to Christ the Creator, the more faithful and vibrant the imagination will be."[18]

If, to summarize what we noted earlier, the imagination is the capacity to create mental images, the ability to generate, spontaneously, illustrations, pictures, or images in the mind, which give meaning to our experience of reality, if this is so then the imagination helps us to understand the world. The imagination is therefore

---

16. For Lewis on imagination see, Schakel, *Reason and Imagination in C. S. Lewis: A Study of Till We Have Faces*; also Lewis, "Psycho-Analysis and Literary Criticism," 123–25. See also, Swinburne, *The Concept of Miracle*; also, Swinburne, *Revelation: from Metaphor to Analogy*.

17. Lewis, *The Great Divorce: A Dream*, 66–67. See also, Lewis, "Introduction," in McDonald, *Phantastes*, v–xii.

18. Dearborn, *Baptized Imagination: The Theology of George MacDonald*, 81.

of fundamental importance, if we are going to *learn*, particularly given the nature of revelation as unfolding. Storytelling is the key to both imaginative creating and also to listening and learning. This is, of course, distinct, from the manner in which our cognitive mental processes work: thoughts appear to happen, the source is often unidentifiable, and is therefore creative, which is why Lewis and MacDonald saw how the imagination should, must, be pneumatologically governed—i.e., under the influence and persuasion of the Holy Spirit.

Walter Hooper[19] notes the importance for Lewis of a distinction between fantasy and imagination where Lewis argued that Freud was incorrect in asserting that all creative art issues from day-dreams, fantasies, and wish-fulfillments generated by the sub-conscious mind. Lewis the literary critic asserts that there are two modes or activities of the imagination: one free and the other enslaved to the will. This will-enslaved imagination conjures up images and ideas primarily, in Lewis's words, to provide imaginary gratifications. Both may be the genesis for creativity, for art: "The former or 'free' activity continues in the works it produces and passes from the status of a dream to that of art by a process which may legitimately be called 'elaboration': it is a motive power which starts the activity and is withdrawn when once the engine is running, or a scaffolding which is knocked away when the building is complete."[20]

If imagination is rooted in creativity, then we may ask, "Where do ideas come from?" Imagination has had a troubled standing in Western philosophy and theology. In the Reformed tradition imagination was considered suspect. Calvin asserted that God rejects without exception all shapes and pictures, and other symbols by which the superstitious believe they can bring *him* near to them. Calvin wrote, "For we know that the Persians worshiped the sun; all the stars they saw in the heavens the stupid pagans also fashioned into gods for themselves. There was almost no animal that for the Egyptians was not the figure of a god. Indeed, the Greeks seemed to be wise above the rest, because they worshiped God in human form."[21] Calvin was writing in the context of the manifold practice within humanity for creating idols out of stone and wood, and in worshipping the sun, the moon, and so forth, inventing religion in humanity's own image, however, his comments in this chapter of *The Institutes*[22] have severely affected the understanding of imagination and its relation to God and God's revelation detrimentally. Calvin quite correctly asserted the censorship of idols and idolatry enshrined in the Ten Commandments, however, there is more to the human faculty of imagination than idolatry. In the Reformed tradition this suspicion of imagination and images influenced not only architecture and decoration but also created a highly conceptualized form of articulation which sought to reduce image-type thinking amongst theologians. Lewis's religious roots were in the Reformed tradition, Ulster Presbyterianism generally (though his parents and grandparents

---

19. Hooper, *C. S. Lewis A Companion and Guide*, 565.
20. Lewis, "Psycho-Analysis and Literary Criticism," 120–38, specifically, 125.
21. Calvin, *Institutes*, Vol. 1, Bk. 1, Ch. 11, §.1, 100.
22. Ibid., Ch. 11 "It is Unlawful to Attribute a Visible Form to God, and Generally Whoever sets up Idols Revolts Against God," 99–116.

were religiously of the Anglican tradition), yet he did not follow this Reformed tradition. When he embraced Christianity it was as an Anglican—pertinently it is his professional work in literature rather than the Anglican or Reformed traditions that influences his ideas about imagination. In sharp contrast to the negative view of imagination in the Reformed tradition, and for that matter amongst Freudian skeptics, there exists a very positive tradition. Lewis's initial contact with this was through J. R. R. Tolkien; following Tolkien's ideas and theories about imagination and creativity, Lewis's understanding is them proximately built upon three streams or veins: George MacDonald we have examined already; the second is in the English Romantic movement of the late eighteenth and early nineteenth centuries; however, the third is much earlier and much more foundational for Lewis's development—the writings of Augustine of Hippo.

3. J. R. R. TOLKIEN

John Ronald Reuel Tolkien was a primary influence on Lewis's development in faith and on his theories with regard to christological prefiguration. Tolkien is important in the pressure put on the theistic Lewis in the walk through the grounds of Magdalen in 1931, which was crucial in Lewis's conversion to being a Christian. It is from Tolkien that Lewis receives four propositions: sub-creation; mythopoeia; refractions and splinters of the true light; and eucatastrophe. Tolkien's thought can be seen proximately in much that Lewis writes on christological prefiguration in the 1940s and 1950s. Tolkien is something of a rock against which Lewis must first be brought to the truth of the gospel story of the incarnation-resurrection, and then against which Lewis's beliefs and theology develop. However, the leading original contribution from Lewis in this area was his doctrine of transposition.

i. Sub-Creation

Sub-creation is the creation of subsequent or secondary worlds within the primary creation—God's creation is primary. God imbues the creation with the ability to create, to *bring forth*. This principle is enshrined early on in the Bible (Genesis 1: where the earth and the waters bring forth). The subsequent or secondary creations will always relate to and derive their ultimate meaning from the primary creation, which in turn derives its legitimacy and ultimate meaning from God and eternity, or ultimate reality. The sub-creator of myths operates in relation to a primary creation that originated and was in existence before his/her creation. Although it is possible for the sub-creator to be original, this uniqueness, this imaginative originality, is in effect an echo from the mind of the creator—God—of the primary creation. The most thorough account of sub-creation is given by Tolkien in the Andrew Lang lecture given at St Andrews University in 1938, which he then developed into an essay: "On Fairy Stories."[23] Tolkien asserted that because there is an infinite potential variety within God and any creation derived from God, the meaning that sub-creations derive from God and

---

23. Tolkien, "On Fairy Stories," 38–89.

from the primary creation is likewise imaginative, creative and wondrous in scope, and not simply a pale shadow of the real. This is legitimate because the sub-creators were first created by God in God's own image—the *imago Dei*—God first creates, then we in God's image create. In reply to a Catholic bookshop owner who questioned the scope and therefore Catholicity of Tolkien's own mythology (*The Lord of the Rings*, etc.) Tolkien asserted that,

> We differ entirely about the nature of the relation of sub-creation to Creation. I should have said that liberation from the channels the creator is known to have used already is the fundamental function of sub-creation, a tribute to the infinity of his potential variety. I am not a metaphysician; but I should have thought it a curious metaphysic—there is not one but many, indeed potentially innumerable ones—that declared the channels known (in such a finite corner as we have any inkling of) to have been used, are the only possible ones, or efficacious, or possibly acceptable to and by him![24]

This proposition that humanity are sub-creators who create alternate realities derived yet distinct from the true form of reality in eternity is potentially dangerous, it is here that Lewis proposition of a baptized imagination, derived as we have seen from George MacDonald, comes in to play. Then sub-creation begins to have immense value: "As a Christian, Tolkien could view sub-creation as a form of worship, a way for creatures to express the divine image in them by becoming creators. As a fantasy writer, Tolkien could affirm his chosen genre as one of the purest of all fictional modes, because it called for the creation not only of characters and incidents, but also of worlds for them to exist in."[25] It is Tolkien's proposition of sub-creation in relation to a baptized imagination that formed the basis, for instance, of Lewis's *The Space Trilogy* and *The Chronicles of Narnia*. However, Lewis questioned the degree of originality in a theory of sub-creation—were not all the elements in these stories derived initially and essentially from and by God. Therefore, we are incapable of creating *ex nihilo* (out of nothing) as has happened with the primary creation.[26] Lewis's response to Tolkien's statement on sub-creation was encapsulated in his essay, "On Stories."[27]

ii. Mythopoeic/Mythopoeia

At the heart of Lewis's understanding of story—whether real or fictitious—is a concept he adopted from Tolkien: mythopoeia. The noun mythopoeia—the creating of myths—was developed from the late nineteenth century by many English speaking writers; however, it is in Tolkien's work (both as Professor of Anglo-Saxon at Oxford and his mythological work in scripting the Middle Earth sagas including *The Lord of the Rings*) that it is imbued with theological meaning and significance, relating to

---

24. Tolkien to Peter Hastings, Letter no 153, 1954. *The Letters of J. R. R. Tolkien*, 187-96.
25. Downing, "Sub-Creation or Smuggled Theology: Tolkien contra Lewis on Christian Fantasy," para. 5.
26. Ibid., para. 25, quoting from Lewis's comments to Sr. Penelope.
27. Lewis, "On Stories," 93f.

divinely gifted, prevenient inspiration.[28] The central principle of mythopoeia is that myths hold fundamental eternal truths that transcend the factual elements of and within the story. A perfect example of mythopoeia for Lewis lay in the story of the fall in Genesis 3: much of the story elements may be mythical, but there is a fundamental truth about the human condition, steeped as we are in original sin, which transcends the mythical elements, yet this truth was best expressed, so God decreed, in mythical form.

The term mythopoeia was used by Tolkien as the title of a poem written in reaction to C. S. Lewis's statement that myths were lies breathed through silver. Lewis's comments, as we have seen, were in conversation with Tolkien and Dyson on the momentous evening where the two of them had to convince Lewis of the truth of the gospel account, the incarnation-resurrection narrative, in relation to myths that prefigured this truth. Tolkien wrote the poem shortly after the conversation in the autumn of 1931, a poem that is addressed from Philomythos (Tolkien, the myth-lover) to Misomythos (Lewis, the myth-hater) and was written to defend myth-making in relation to eternal truths. Tolkien celebrates the power, divinely endorsed, for the myth-maker as sub-creator to create through his/her golden scepter (a slight at Lewis's lies breathed through silver). For Tolkien the eternal ideas/forms, which we can complement through mythopoeic sub-creation are of greater value than illusory human-centered ideas issuing from the rational materialism endemic in the position of Sir James George Frazer on myths, redolent of Freud and Feuerbach, framed in relation to Darwinian human evolution.

iii. Refractions and Splinters of the True Light

The third proposition from Tolkien is the idea that the truths in these myths, the prefigured intimations of what is revealed in its fullest in the incarnational-resurrection narrative in the Gospels, these are in effect splintered fragments of the true light. This is best expressed by Tolkien in the poem "Mythopoeia," again in the context of Lewis's comments about myths being lies breathed through silver:

> The heart of man is not compound of lies,
> but draws some wisdom from the only Wise,
> and still recalls him. Though now long estranged,   line 55
> man is not wholly lost nor wholly changed.
> Dis-graced he may be, yet is not dethroned,
> and keeps the rags of lordship one he owned,
> his world-dominion by creative act:
> not his to worship the great Artefact,   line 60
> man, sub-creator, the refracted light
> through whom is splintered from a single White

28. Mythopoeia, mythopoesis, is derived from the Greek μῦθο (myth) + ποιειν (to make); in Platonic Greek, μῦθοποιός, -όν, (ποιέω), the term is essentially restricted in use to British academics and writers circa 1870–1960. The adjective mythopoetical, from the Greek μυθοποιια, is from the 1950s. Myth is derived from the Greek μῦθος: in New Testament Greek, a myth, fanciful story; in Homeric Greek, a tale, story, narrative, a legend or fable.

> to many hues, and endlessly combined
> in living shapes that move from mind to mind.
> Though all the crannies of the world we filled   line 65
> with elves and goblins, though we dared to build
> gods and their houses out of dark and light,
> and sow the seed of dragons, 'twas our right
> (used or misused). The right has not decayed.
> We make still by the law in which we're made.²⁹   line 70

So what is Tolkien saying? The white light, reminiscent of the pure intensity of God in Dante's *Paradisio*, shines. As the light shines it is "splintered" and "refracted" to use Tolkien's terms—it illuminates human consciousness, it shines in the darkness, in and through men and women, the sub-creators; this light may be broken, split, changed into an infinity of colors and shades, themes, aims and intentions, but it combines into living stories—myths—in the human mind, from mind to mind, to impart intimations of the divine truth. This divine light may inspire, generate, myths but these are not the same as fantasies. Reason is of paramount importance: "Fantasy is a natural human activity. It certainly does not destroy or even insult reason; and it does not either blunt the appetite for, nor obscure the perception of, scientific verity."³⁰ Humanity may be fallen but not irretrievably lost—humanity is not a compound of lies but draws some wisdom from the only Wise (God).

Humphrey Carpenter in his biography of Tolkien phrases this in story. This is biographical fiction, based on fact, but does it accurately reflect both Lewis and Tolkien and what passed between them in conversation that night in the grounds of Magdalen? The answer is yes:

> We have come from God (continued Tolkien), and inevitably the myths woven by us, though they contain error, will also reflect a splintered fragment of the true light, the eternal truth that is with God. Indeed only by myth-making, only by becoming a "sub-creator" and inventing stories, can Man aspire to the state of perfection that he knew before the Fall. Our myths may be misguided, but they steer however shakily towards the true harbour, while materialistic "progress" leads only to a yawning abyss and the Iron Crown of the power of evil.³¹

Many scholars and commentators have noted how this proposition that myths are a splintered fragment of the true light is central to Tolkien's work. Carpenter notes how this is the doctrine at the heart of *The Silmarillion*.³² It is reflected in the story of the two trees that illuminate the creation of the world at the opening of *The Silmarillion*. These two trees are destroyed, but their light is encapsulated in three Silmarils (jewels); the Silmarils are lost and their light refracted, splintered: only memories and fragments endure.³³ The prefigured myths we have been considering are therefore refracted,

---

29. Tolkien, "Mythopoeia," 85–90. Most of this passage was also quoted by Tolkien in "On Fairy Stories," 38–89, see specifically, 71–72.
30. Tolkien, "On Fairy Stories," 38–89.
31. Carpenter, *J. R. R. Tolkien: A Biography*, 197–98.
32. Ibid., 198.
33. Tolkien, *The Silmarillion*, 67.

splintered memories and fragments that endure and point to the incarnation-resurrection narrative.

iv. Eucatastrophe

The term eucatastrophe was explicitly invented by Tolkien to refer to the sudden change in a story, an unpredictable turn of events, usually near the conclusion of a story/myth, resulting in the hero being saved, or the outcome which was disastrous till that moment, resolving itself for the good of all. Though this sounds like a happy-ever-after ending this is not so because of the sheer dark, destructive, nihilistic logical outcome that events are clearly moving towards, which seems like the only possible conclusion. The word was formed by prefacing the word *catastrophe* (commonly used in Classical literature for such events), with the Greek prefix *eu* meaning *good*: this sudden, good catastrophe, leads to the conclusion.[34] The cross and resurrection are probably the most explicit eucatastrophe: the resurrection is the unexpected turn of events following the catastrophic nihilism of the cross, and is unpredictable and unprecedented to the extent that it was not the solution at the end of the Story of Balder—Balder remains dead and all mourn his loss. And yet given all Jesus said and the predictions within the Old Testament, the resurrection of Christ was surely the logical outcome. In Tolkien's *Lords of the Rings*, the sudden unexpected turn of events for the worse, with Frodo claiming the ring for himself just as it is to be hurled into the volcano of Mount Doom to destroy it along with Sauron's evil power is countered with Gollum/Sméagol saving the day. This is unexpected, but the story line that Gollum's lust for the ring leads accidentally to him destroying it is entirely in keeping with the characters and the way the story has developed—eucatastrophe, the world is saved. These events are plausible and fit in with reality, though could not necessarily have been predicted by the reader.

4. SAMUEL TAYLOR COLERIDGE

i. The English Romantics

The English Romantics from the late eighteenth and early nineteenth centuries such as Samuel Taylor Coleridge (1772–1834), William Wordsworth (1770–1850) and John Keats (1795–1821)—and in continental Europe, Friedrich Wilhelm Joseph Schelling (1775–1854)—regarded a form of imagination derived from Immanuel Kant's aesthetic idealism as important. For Coleridge and Keats, in particularly, imagination was to be equated with creation. Imagination here is fused with passion; this is a Romantic concept of the imagination, but—according to Coleridge—all imaginings are not of equal value. Coleridge saw imagination as a three-part faculty: he identified two elements to the imagination, and a third element that is related to the imagination

---

34. Catastrophe was often used in ancient Greek drama. The word is from the Greek (κατα + στροφειν) meaning to overturn, it is an event that causes trauma through its destructive capacity. Tolkien simply added the Greek prefix ευ.

but does not hold the same creative relationship with the divine. Therefore, as poet, philosopher, and theologian, Coleridge distinguished "primary imagination," from "secondary imagination," and/or "fancy." Drawing very much on the continental philosopher Schelling and thereby Kant's transcendental philosophy, Coleridge in his doctrine of the imagination noted how the mind appeared to work. Within the mind a reflective element often seemed to make sense of what was being observed by creating images and models to make sense, reflectively. Coleridge commented on the mind's ability to self-reflect, but also—crucially—to self-experience in the very act of thinking: "There are evidently two powers at work, which relatively to each other are active and passive; and this is not possible without an intermediate faculty, which is at once both active and passive. In philosophical language, we must denominate this intermediate faculty in all its degrees and determinations, the IMAGINATION" [Coleridge's emphasis and capitalization].[35]

ii. *The Categorical Imperative*

According to Kant's transcendental philosophy, particularly in Coleridge's interpretation and application of it, the central role of the imagination is validated through an autonomous principle of the will—Kant's categorical imperative.[36] Contrary to much modern sociological and psychological considerations the will in its purest form is not habituated, changed, or subject to external influence or cultural conditioning. Therefore Schelling, whose writings Coleridge studied and valued, drawing on Kant, could look into the human mind and on reflection deduce something of the transcendental nature of reality: we can see that there is more to reality and to life than what is immediately perceivable and derivable from sense perception, and our actions are not always governed by self-preservation and self-love. These ideas are evident in Lewis's own account of his philosophical development as a student and young don. In *Surprised by Joy* Lewis acknowledges that the will can be influenced, tainted, by external events and people, but he wrote how as the point of conversion came close it was as if he was offered a pure moment of free will, untainted. He recounted how whilst on a bus travelling up Headington Hill he was being presented with a choice—without words or images—where he was not moved by desire, that he saw this as a decisive moment, when he appeared the nearest it is possible to be to a free agent.[37]

---

35. Coleridge, *Biographia Literaria*, 77. The *Biographia Literaria* (first published in 1817) is a discursive philosophical and literary autobiography with important essays on philosophy and aesthetics and as such draws on continental philosophy in the form of Kant and Schelling.

36. The categorical imperative implies a transcendent reality and that morals and ethics that affect and appear to issue from our will, are grounded in this transcendent reality. From Immanuel Kant's *Groundwork for the Metaphysics of Morals* (1785) the categorical imperative is the standard of rationality on which all moral requirements are based; it is a fundamental philosophical concept in Kant's moral philosophy. Morality is derived from an imperative, a commandment grounded in reason. A categorical imperative is an unconditional requirement, it is absolute. Kant so defined the categorical imperative that we should act only according to that maxim whereby we can simultaneously resolve that it should become a universal law—see, Kant, *Grounding for the Metaphysics of Morals*, 30.

37. Lewis, *Surprised by Joy*, 217.

10. Christ as the Light of the World II: Revelation and Meaning

Coleridge and Schelling's theories complement the voluntary basis of human behavior and in consequent Christian ethics: we are responsible for our decisions and actions, and universal laws and values exist. However much we are the product of our nurture and environment, of the culture we grow up in, God, through the Holy Spirit, will grant us moments of what is closest to perfect freedom, close to the human condition prior to the fall—if we so allow the Spirit to act on us. Human freedom, free choice, is no longer innately possible after the fall because of the way we are buffeted to and fro on the winds of fashion, influenced by all around us. Having taken decision-making onto ourselves (Genesis 3), where we are the product of forces outside of us and not of a free will decision, God will still, through grace, grants us a moment closest to, as Lewis termed it, being a free agent, where we may choose God's way, or not (John 3). Art—poetry and stories (fact or fiction doesn't enter into it)—is preeminent in the relationship of the human mind to the transcendent. However much our choices are conditioned from without, freedom is the basis of any philosophical consideration of the human in relation to the transcendent.

iii. Primary and Secondary Imagination

Coleridge wrote in Thesis 7 of the objective basis of his doctrine of the imagination how, "This implies an act, and it follows therefore that intelligence or self-consciousness is impossible, except by and in a will. The self-conscious spirit therefore is a will; and freedom must be assumed as a GROUND of philosophy, and can never be deduced from it."[38] Without this freedom of will, philosophy and science is impossible, and art and poetry is just fanciful yearnings.

Coleridge laid out his doctrine of the imagination systematically at the end of the first volume of the *Biographia Literaria*:

> The IMAGINATION then I consider either as primary, or secondary. The primary IMAGINATION I hold to be the living power and prime Agent of all human perception, and as a repetition in the finite mind of the eternal act of creation in the infinite I AM. The secondary imagination I consider as an echo of the former, coexisting with the conscious will, yet still as identical with the primary in the *kind* of its agency, and differing only in *degree*, and in the *mode* of its operation. It dissolves, diffuses, dissipates, in order to re-create; or where this process is rendered impossible, yet still at all events it struggles to idealise and to unify. It is essentially *vital*, even as all objects (as objects) are essentially fixed and dead ... FANCY, on the contrary, has no other counters to play with but fixities

---

38. Coleridge, *Biographia Literaria*, Ch. 12, Thesis 7, 160–61. Coleridge's emphasis/capitalization. See also, Coleridge's comments in Thesis 9: "This *principium commune essendi et cognoscendi* (common principle of being and knowing), as subsisting in a WILL, or primary ACT of self-duplication, is the mediate or indirect principle of every science; but it is the immediate and direct principle of the ultimate science alone, i.e., of transcendental philosophy alone. For it must be remembered, that all these theses refer solely to one of the two polar sciences, namely, to that which commences with and rigidly confines itself within the subjective, leaving the objective (as far as it is exclusively objective) to natural philosophy, which is its opposite pole. In its very idea therefore as a systematic knowledge of our collective KNOWING (*scientia scientiae*) it involves the necessity of someone highest principle of knowing ..." 161–62. Coleridge's emphasis/capitalization.

> and definites. The fancy is indeed no other than a mode of memory emancipated from the order of time and space; and blended with, and modified by that empirical phenomenon of the will which we express by the word CHOICE. But equally with the ordinary memory it must receive all its materials ready-made from the law of association.[39]

Coleridge's account of the primary imagination is of paramount importance. It states that the living power of God is the primary cause of all human perception—all human perception. This relates to the *imago Dei* (the image of God in humanity—imprinted like an image etched onto stone—Gen 1:26-27). Therefore, through the imagination men and women are made in the image of God, reproducing—but not always—elements, in part, of the mind of God in miniature. It is this that separates us from all other animals, which raises us above nature yet our feet are still embedded in clay! The primary imagination is therefore an echo in the human mind of the eternal I AM. The secondary imagination, which dominates and occupies the human mind most of the time is similar, indeed it is as much an echo etched in our minds, but differs, for Coleridge, only in the degree or mode of its operation. The third level—fancy—can be mistaken for primary or secondary imagination but does not relate to the *imago Dei* or directly to God for it is for Coleridge only a mode of memory emancipated from the order of time and space, for a fleeting moment we think we have originality but this is an illusion. Coleridge's doctrine of the imagination was a profound influence on Lewis. He cites these ideas obliquely as instrumental in his intellectual and religious development on a number of occasions in his spiritual autobiography.[40]

iv. MacDonald on Coleridge

What is the source for Lewis of his contact with Coleridge's doctrine of imagination? George MacDonald. Ever the master of Lewis's understanding of myth, saga, and story, MacDonald wrote a full exposition of Coleridge's ideas in two essays.[41] MacDonald writes that the word imagination means, or evokes, an "imaging," that is, the making of likenesses. Therefore the imagination is a faculty, this gives form to thought: "Not necessarily uttered form, but form capable of being uttered in shape or in sound, or in any mode upon which the senses can lay hold. It is, therefore, that faculty in man which is likest to the prime operation of the power of God, and has, therefore, been called the creative faculty, and its exercise creation."[42] Therefore, drawing on Coleridge's concept of the primary imagination, MacDonald asserts that the imagination in its creativity is analogous to the prime operation of the power of God. In this context for MacDonald, and certainly for Lewis, the role of the poet is

---

39. Coleridge, *Biographia Literaria*, Ch. 13, 175. Coleridge's emphasis/capitalization. See also: Barfield, *What Coleridge Thought*.

40. Lewis, *Surprised by Joy*, 10, 10–11, 25–26, 63, 130, 132, 140, 153, 158, and 164.

41. MacDonald, George, "The Imagination: its Functions and its Culture," 1–28, and, "The Fantastic Imagination," 203–8. See also, related to Lewis, MacDonald and Coleridge's doctrine of the imagination, Barfield, *Poetic Diction: A Study in Meaning*.

42. MacDonald, "The Imagination: its Functions and its Culture," 11.

10. Christ as the Light of the World II: Revelation and Meaning

Figure 20: The Young and Mature Lewis, with George MacDonald in the centre, pen-and-ink drawing by P. H. Brazier

as maker, creator. If Coleridge, MacDonald, and Lewis are correct then the power of an unbaptized imagination in its corruption and its scope for evil is, potentially, truly awesome and demonic in an extreme. The implication of what MacDonald is saying is that the poet or sage, like the prophet, drawing on wisdom in and through the imagination, must be seen as standing aside, in part, from society. This is essential. This does not necessarily make the poet divine. MacDonald continues that we must not forget that there is an unsurpassable gulf between creator and poet. This gulf is "teeming with infinite revelations"; but it is by default a vast space that the poet cannot pass over: "no man can pass to find out God, although God needs not to pass over it to find man."[43] The chasm or abyss is between that which calls (God), and that which is thus called into being (humanity); where humanity is made in God's image (the *imago Dei*—Genesis 1:26–27). Therefore all sub-creation can only be in the context of the primary creation from God: God will call across the gulf, the chasm, and if we respond through the faculty of the imagination, our creative impulse will, to take this beyond Coleridge, echo back to God in love.

MacDonald can see how Coleridge did not divorce the creativity of the poet's imagination from analytic or scientific knowledge and investigation. The scientific region of the imagination complements intellectual truth—this becomes truth in beauty.[44] Therefore MacDonald asserts, "Coleridge says that no one but a poet will make any further great discoveries in mathematics; and Bacon says that 'wonder,' that faculty of the mind especially attendant on the child-like imagination, 'is the seed of knowledge.'"[45] Therefore the scientific imagination is essential for truth and reality; this is where the scientific mind is influenced by the poetic, indeed without the faculty of the imagination scientific mental models could not be constructed. This is most so in the construction of an invisible whole, a model of reality and greater reality, from the intimations given by the visible world: the shadows of this world are guides, "to a multiplex harmony, completeness, and end, which is the whole."[46] It is MacDonald's understanding of Coleridge that is almost certainly the point of contact Lewis had with these concepts. For Lewis and MacDonald, and Coleridge before them, the imagination is the medium by which we enquire into God's creation; hence it is both scientific and poetic.[47] Imagination therefore occupies a central place in enquiry, in hypothesizing, in creating mental-images (for example, mental model-making and conceptualization as practiced by historians, mathematicians and theologians, as well as scientists).[48] Methodologically, from the perspective of the philosophy of theology,

43. Ibid., 11–12.
44. Ibid., 13–14.
45. Ibid., 14.
46. Ibid.
47. MacDonald, "The Fantastic Imagination," 203–8
48. For the role of imagination in historical thinking see, for example, ideas indicative of the time when C. S. Lewis was at the peak of his creative writing, Collinwood, *The Idea of History*, or, Kroner, *The Religious Function of Imagination*. In the field of philosophy of science see, Black, *Models and Metaphors. Studies in Language and Philosophy*; also, indicative of the understanding around the time of Lewis' intellectual formation, see, Lewes, *Comte's Philosophy of the Sciences*.

10. Christ as the Light of the World II: Revelation and Meaning

David Kelsey writes, "At the root of any theological position, there is an imaginative act in which a theologian tries to catch up in a single metaphorical judgment or model the full complexity of God's presence."[49] In this respect, it may be valid to consider that those who composed (or imagined) the stories of incarnational appearing of dying and reviving gods, myths of prefigurement, are methodologically operating in a similar way to contemporary theologians. It has been argued that a theologian of whatever persuasion (for example, Catholic or Calvinistic) undertakes an act of the imagination. S/he will select from the knowledge base within the culture and tradition within which s/he operates, and take those structures that are to form the system behind a theological position. By comparison, Seerveld, writing from the viewpoint of a biblical, Reformed tradition, distinguishes, on the one hand, between imagining which is perceptual error and, on the other hand, imagining that is an oracle of truth.[50]

Lewis absorbed MacDonald and Coleridge's theorizing on the imagination in relation to God's revelation, and thereby how we formulate theology, at an influential time in his life. Lewis wrote, "I think that all things reflect heavenly truth, the imagination not least."[51] Further, "that imagination is distinct from thought; thought may be sound while accompanying images are false."[52] Lewis acknowledges that the mind is illuminated by the divine and that this leads to a degree of understanding—theological activity is not solely the result of human striving and searching. The imagination can, under certain circumstances, be an oracle of truth where general cognitive activities fail.

Therefore for Lewis there is still the possibility of prevenient grace engendering inspiration and intimation, although such revelatory reception is still subject to the effects of the fall. Generally speaking, from a Reformed position, the imagination is indelibly corrupted by original sin. Calvin, as we saw, dismissed images or mental pictures/models, as the product of human imagination, where humanity believed it could bring God near:

> We are forbidden every pictorial representation of God. But as Scripture, having regard for men's rude and stupid wit, customarily speaks in the manner of the common folk, where it would distinguish the true God from the false it particularly contrasts God with idols. It does this, not to approve what is more subtly taught by the philosophers, but the better to expose the world's folly. Therefore, that exclusive definition, encountered everywhere, annihilates all the divinity that men fashion for themselves out of their own opinion: for God himself is the sole and proper witness of himself . . . but God does not compare these images with one another, as if one were more suitable, another less so; but without exception he repudiates all likenesses, pictures, and other signs by which the superstitious have thought he will be near them.[53]

49. Kelsey, *The Use of Scripture in Recent Theology*, 163.
50. Seerveld, "Imaginativity," 43–58.
51. Lewis, *Surprised by Joy*, 167.
52. Lewis, "God in the Dock." These sentiments were also expressed in the first edition of *Miracles* (1947) and Lewis, "The Weight of Glory," 21–33 (an address first delivered at St Mary the Virgin, Oxford, September 13, 1941).
53. Calvin, *Institutes*, Vol. 1, Bk. 1, Ch. 11, §.1, 99–100.

Lewis would not necessarily have disagreed with this. What he did assert was that God used this *fallen* human imagination, images, and mental pictures/models, to communicate some sort of intimation of God's salvific actions: the prefiguring images/myths were for Lewis pneumatologically given, gifted by the Holy Spirit, not humanly invented.

5. AUGUSTINE OF HIPPO

MacDonald and Lewis's reading of Coleridge (and thereby Friedrich Schelling) on imagination was rooted, ironically for Lewis, in the leading philosopher of the Enlightenment—Immanuel Kant—in transcendental philosophy, and, to a degree, the proposition of the categorical imperative. However, these ideas go back much further. The more Lewis read in the years following his conversion, the more this reading drew him back to the patristic church. Hence his seminal use of Vincentius of Lérins' work on the core of Christian doctrine and ethics. But pertinently his thinking approximated more and more to that of the great fifth century patristic church father Augustine of Hippo (340–430 AD). Augustine was a trained philosopher and convert to Christianity who systematized the biblical account of the fall and original sin into a doctrine (which was an essential part of Lewis's theology). Augustine's work was written under the influence of the Neoplatonism of the third-century Greek philosopher Plotinus (204–70 AD). He developed the understanding of the church as the City of God, over and, in many instances, against the City of Man, humanity, the realm of this world. Augustine is also, for many, to be considered the father of Western Christianity, the theological founder of Roman Catholicism, yet was also a focus for and rallying cry for many of the Reformers. Augustine is at his most profound and relevant to Lewis's development in his understanding of the imagination and natural theology.[54]

i. Natural Theology and Revealed Theology

Natural theology is, in effect, philosophical speculation about the existence of a "god," or even *a priori* reasoning about the very nature of God, and God's relation with humanity, from the world, nature and the human mind. The aim of natural theology is to generate knowledge and understanding about God, and therefore to establish truths about God using only our natural cognitive resources. Therefore the method and data for what we may term naturally occurring theology lies with the human mind. The technique of reasoning things out about God are the basis and ground of natural theology. Natural theology is not necessarily reading a theology from nature, from the world about us; that is something other; though, one can do natural theology from the natural world. In the first chapter of Romans, Paul comments that since the creation of

---

54 Lewis first read Augustine's *Confessions* in 1936, then the massive, *de Civitate Dei* (*The City of God*), in 1937, both in the original Latin, he then worked on his own translation of *de Civitate Dei*, which he then often quoted in his correspondence, apologetics and philosophical theology over the coming years. Augustine was for Lewis the authority for his understanding of Christian beliefs. See, Lewis writing to Dom Bede Griffiths, April 24, 1936; and, Lewis writing to Dom Bede Griffiths, May 23 1936. Lewis, *Collected Letters Vol. II*, 187-90 and 191-95.

10. Christ as the Light of the World II: Revelation and Meaning

the world something of God's nature and being can be seen from the world around us, but this will not save us; neither is humanity justified by speculating about God from the world and from nature: humanity is left without excuse (Rom 1:20f.). If natural theology is in effect distinct from revealed theology, theology based on or derived from revelation, involving a supernatural relation with the other, this distinction implies that our understanding of God cannot come unaided from our own strengths of reasoning. Lewis the philosopher exhibited a great respect for reason, and to a degree, for natural theology. He admitted in his spiritual autobiography that he, in many ways, thought his way to faith.[55] However, as we have seen from his conversion and also from his understanding of Scripture, revelation, and reason, Lewis did not necessarily see a hard and fast line dividing revelation on the one hand from reason and natural theology on the other. In maturity Lewis came to see natural theology not merely as intellectual and philosophical argument, speculative gropings for an understanding of God, but rather as bound up with the revelation in Christ: it was of little use to feel about, to search blindly, in one's mind for a basis for a belief in God; we cannot rely solely on our own powers. Therefore a distinction should not necessarily be made between general and specific revelation, but rather the degree to which God reveals himself in a multitude of manners and ways, intimations, whisperings, and instances—transposed—culminating in the specific self-revelation of God in Jesus Christ: event and salvation. Any true and sound understanding of God would not be unaided.

In the years following his conversion Lewis assigned a broader value to natural theology over and against the dismissal he assigned to it immediately after his conversion (the, all myths are lies, comment from 1931); this broadening of and developing respect for natural theology was in keeping with his churchmanship—central Anglican with leanings towards the (Anglo) Catholic. Lewis read and was influenced by the Greek philosophers but also Thomas Aquinas' *Summa Theologiae* (in the 1940s, on a daily basis). Although Aquinas had formulated the distinction between natural and revealed theology (a distinction hardened by theologians in response to the Enlightenment), Lewis subscribed to the older Augustinian view that there is no unaided true knowledge of God. Lewis was therefore profoundly influenced by Augustine in his consideration of, and the value he accorded to, natural theology, also the deep respect he held for Platonic idealism. Hence we find the post-conversion Barthian-type rejection softening as he absorbs this other, older approach to natural theology and revelation.

The central question was, "How do we know anything of value and truth about God?" Lewis's thinking on this question approximated more and more to that of Augustine's on natural theology and revelation. For example, Augustine, writing to Deogratius comments, "Therefore, from the beginning of the human race, whosoever believed in him, and in any way knew him, and lived in a pious and just manner according to his precepts, was undoubtedly saved by him, in whatever time and place

---

55. Lewis, *Surprised by Joy*, 205–21.

he may have lived."⁵⁶ Hence there is Lewis's respect for natural theology and natural law. Augustine continued,

> For as we believe in him both as dwelling with the Father and as having come in the flesh, so the men of the former ages believed in him both as dwelling with the Father and as destined to come in the flesh . . . Wherefore the true religion, although formerly set forth and practiced under other names and with other symbolical rites than it now has, and formerly more obscurely revealed and known to fewer persons than now in the time of clearer light and wider diffusion, is one and the same in both periods.⁵⁷

Therefore, the true religion was perceived in part, or more obscurely revealed prior to the specific revelation of Christ. Christ is a clearer and more widely diffuse light for Augustine. This is the position Lewis came to hold. A number of questions then arise, "What form did these intimations take?" Or, more pertinently, "What is the means whereby such ideas can feature in the thought of men and women?" To answer, it is necessary to delve further into the place of imagination generally in theology, and particularly in Augustine's writings, focusing on his doctrine of illumination, and how this relates to Lewis's understanding of revelation, inspiration, and illumination.

ii. Revelation, Inspiration, and Illumination

We looked briefly at Augustine's doctrine of illumination earlier when we examined Lewis's doctrine of transposition. We need to enquire further into this area of illumination and imagination for it is something that like transposition is at the heart of Lewis's Christology, indeed illumination is at the heart of transposition—that in illuminating the human mind the Holy Spirit intimates ideas about prefigurement to poets and sages, seers and prophets.

The doctrine of divine illumination was commonly accepted and written on up until the post-Reformation, the Age of Reason and the Enlightenment, and the "Modern"/Postmodern era, and as such was seen as an alternative to the metaphysical or ontological naturalism that dominated modern and analytic philosophy. This understanding was central to much ancient Greek philosophy, to Neo-Platonism, and to patristic philosophy, culminating in the writings of Augustine. The doctrine states, at its most basic, that the mind is dependent on illumination in the form of supernatural assistance if the mind is to understand over and beyond the basic mental functions which, like animals, govern our daily lives. Much that our brains and minds can do is created and sustained by God (the ongoing conservation of creation—God does not create, then leave the universe, and humanity, on its own to carry on self-sustained); however, a doctrine of divine illumination is talking about something else, something other than the conservation of creation. Although the doctrine originates with the ancient Greeks—essentially Plato—the Bible consistently speaks of Grace in this context so that divine illumination is equivalent to Grace. As with illumination,

---

56. Augustine, "Letter no 102 to Deogratius, 409," 820.
57. Ibid., 820.

10. Christ as the Light of the World II: Revelation and Meaning

A GENERAL AND SPECIFIC THEORY OF ILLUMINATION

A General Theory of Illumination	**A Special Theory of Illumination**
A general theory of illumination argues that divine grace is always necessary and is ongoing, to a greater or lesser degree. This is independent of whether we are aware or not of the action of God's Holy Spirit on and in our minds. This is separate from and in addition to the conservation of creation. There is, therefore, no unaided knowledge and understanding of God.	A special, or specific, theory of illumination states that divine assistance is needed (though this is not for everything that the human mind does and thinks). Within a special theory of illumination we progress so far in our innate abilities, then God illumines our minds to enable us to perceive and understand truth, as is necessary in relation to God's good purposes.

Figure 21: A General and a Specific Theory of Illumination

Grace is often rare and in addition to our innate creaturely abilities, and must be seen as a form of special divine assistance. The precise relationship between Grace in the Bible, and a philosophical doctrine of illumination is a question of biblical exegesis and interpretation. Grace-illumination relates closely to wisdom (as we have seen above). The basis of this doctrine of illumination is that real and true knowledge is always immutable, fixed, existing outside of us (an obvious example is mathematical knowledge). True knowledge and understanding is, for Augustine, ideas, ideals, and standards, which have a divine basis. If the lower cannot influence, change, or even act on the higher (echoing Coleridge's and MacDonald's views, and elements in Lewis's doctrine of transposition) then we cannot corrupt the divine, we cannot ascend and comprehend the divine ideas. We do not have the power to do this within ourselves (the fall was about believing we had this power and might); therefore, we rely on the higher descending to the lower, in the form of divine illumination, but also ultimately in the incarnation, to draw us up.

A general theory of illumination argues that this divine assistance—grace—is always necessary and is ongoing, to a greater or lesser degree; a special or specific theory of illumination states that this is not always so, but that divine assistance is needed, but not for everything that the human does and thinks. Within a special theory of illumination we progress so far in our creaturely abilities, then God illumines our minds to see in wisdom how, reflectively, these perception come together, and relate to truth. This relates to a concept of free will—how much control and governance we have over our choices and decisions—and how much we can truly know for ourselves. However, there is a much deeper problem because a special theory of illumination evokes a "God of the gaps"—that up to a line we can explain from a purely physical/natural basis how our mind works, how we make decisions and perceive truth (assuming a level of absolute certainty in our scientific observations and decision making), beyond that line is the influence of God: anything that can be explained is not in the realm of God, God is confined to the gaps in science, gaps that are ever shrinking. If there is a hard and fast line between a general and specific theory of illumination then this is where the "God of the gaps" problem comes in (as a basis for a special theory of illumination), but not if there is an element of illumination ongoing, to a greater or lesser degree, all the time, even if we think we have worked things out for ourselves. In contrast to the "God-of-the-gaps" line, which is too rigid and definable, the *actual* range and limits of divine illumination must be seen as far more organic, nebulous (from a human perspective) and subject always to God's will, God's good judgement, in operating on, influencing, the human child: as a mother will care and nurture an infant encouraging it on occasions, controlling it for its own good on others, then leaving it to itself to learn and grow.

iii. Prevenience

A doctrine of divine illumination is of principal importance through all of Augustine's theological and philosophical writings, where he stresses the importance and the place of divine illumination in the human mind. For example, writing in *The Confessions* Augustine comments that "The mind needs to be enlightened by light from outside itself, so that it can participate in truth, because it is not itself the nature of truth."[58] This light and truth exists outside of human perception, particularly when there is agreement as to this light and truth.[59] Because of the way we live, as we are tossed this way and that by social and cultural needs and desires, by fashion and whim, the light is obscured by our actions and the truth is not perceived.[60] Because of the depravity in the human soul we do not realize our true need—"For I did not know that the soul needs to be enlightened by light from outside itself, so that it can participate in truth, because it is not itself the nature of truth."[61] In this context Augustine quotes liberally from the Bible, particularly from the Psalms and from John's Gospel and Epistles. Augustine juxtaposes the illumination from God with the will to sort out life for itself in the human, to go it alone. This illumination is there for all to open themselves to at any time.[62] The light that illumines is unchangeable;[63] this light, infused into the soul, will dispel the gloom of doubt.[64] But, "they wish to be light not in the Lord but in themselves because they hold that the nature of the soul is what God is. They have in fact become a thicker darkness in that by their horrendous arrogance they have

58. Augustine, *Confessions*, Bk. IV.xv (25), 67–68.
59. Ibid., Bk. XII.xxv (35), 265.
60. Ibid., Bk. IV.xiv (22), 65–66.
61. Ibid., Bk. IV.xv (25), 68.
62. Ibid., Bk. IV.xvi (30).
63. Ibid., Bk. VII.x (16).
64. Ibid., Bk. VIII.xii (29).

10. Christ as the Light of the World II: Revelation and Meaning

withdrawn further away from you—from you who are 'the true light illuminating every man coming into this world.'" (John 1:9).[65] So the light shines into human minds and illumines, but we will misinterpret, misrepresent the images given and will—as Lewis affirms—read into the images a false or distorted meaning.[66] The illumination is there for all to open themselves to at any time, asserts Augustine: "I did not know the source of what was true and certain . . . I had my back to the light and my face towards the things which are illuminated. So my face, by which I was enabled to see the things lit up, was not itself illuminated."[67] This raises the question of prevenience—that the grace is prior to the thought, the vision, or *prevision*, the idea, or decision. The degree to which we recognize how the Holy Spirit is illuminating our minds both in these intimations for our good, but also as part of the conservation of creation is then of importance. Prevenient grace (or preceding grace) is a philosophical concept derived from a Christian doctrine of God, which was formulated and rooted in Augustinian theology. Prevenient grace is the divine action of the Holy Spirit that precedes human decision and action, and hence validity. Prevenient grace is prior to and does not rely on anything people do or have done. The Augustinian ground is that because of the corrosive and corrupting effects of original sin where we can no longer make free will decisions unimpeded and not influenced by a wealth of factors around us, prevenient grace allows us to choose salvation and to live for and follow God's will. Prevenient grace precedes our conscious impulses and decisions.

Therefore, the question arises of whether illumination operates always or only in special cases. Partly because of his opposition to the Pelagian heresy, Augustine's thinking moved more and more towards the proposal that illumination in varying degrees operated—potentially—within the human mind all the time. Hence his proposition that there is no unaided knowledge of God, that there is no understanding of God and God's salvific actions that was unaided by divine illumination, though as we have seen this is conditioned by the willful effects of fallen humanity trying to go it alone, humanity turned away from the light (Augustine's comments about how his face was not turned towards the light, how his mind was not illuminated[68]). Augustine argued in a short treatise entitled, *On Free Choice of the Will*, that there are certain kinds of concepts that it appears impossible for us to produce under our own power, likewise certain kinds of judgment.[69] Ideas, for example, do not come from the senses. So where, for Lewis, does the idea of the incarnation-resurrection come from? Augustine's answer to the origin of ideas is that they are generated through divine

---

65. Ibid., Bk. VIII.x (22), 148.
66. Ibid., See specifically, Bk. V.vi (10) 77–78; Bk. X.ii (2) 179; X.xl (65) 217–218. Also, see generally: V.iii (4); VI.i (1); VII.i (2); VII.3 (5); VII.vii (11); VII.ix (13); VIII.iv (9); VIII.v (12); IX.1 (1); IX.iv (7); IX.iv (10); X.xiv (1); X.vi (8); X.xvii (26); X.xxiii (33); X.xxxiv (51);X.xl (65); XI.ii (2).
67. Ibid., Bk. IV.xvi (30), 70. See also, Bk. II.iii (6), 27, where Augustine, in the context of the idolatry of intellectual sins quotes Jeremiah 2:27, "They say to wood, 'You are my father,' and to stone, 'You gave me birth.' They have turned their backs to me and not their faces."
68. πρόσωπον, προσοπον, in Greek the face was more than the physical front of the head but the character, the countenance, the presence, the window to the soul.
69. Augustine, *On Free Choice of the Will*, II,8, 44–46.

illumination in the human soul. In a work aimed at the pagan Roman philosophers and teachers who were skeptical of the claims of the Christians Augustine wrote that only God can teach us.[70] Other people participate in this, they can communicate ideas, and we can choose to believe them, or not, but, writes Augustine, it is not knowledge unless we grasp with our minds the truth of what we are hearing, and this realization of truthfulness is the result of prevenient graceful illumination: "When I speak the truth, I do not teach someone who sees these truths. For he is taught not by my words but by the things themselves made manifest within when God discloses them."[71]

6. C. S. LEWIS: A GENERAL OR SPECIAL THEORY OF ILLUMINATION?

Lewis did not lay-out, systematically, a doctrine of illumination in the way Augustine did though it is important to remember that both Augustine and Lewis were trained philosophers, taught philosophy, and had built up a systematic barrier to God in their minds before their conversion to the Christ. However, this notwithstanding, there are sufficient markers in Lewis's mature Christian apologetic, likewise his acknowledgement as to the importance of Augustine in his life and work, to establish the proximity of his theology generally, and his theory of illumination specifically, to Augustine's (though it is likewise important to remember the place of Platonism in both of them with regards to a doctrine of illumination and the supernatural capacity of the faculty of the imagination).

There are two important propositions we must take on board in relation to the prefigured intimations of the incarnation-resurrection narratives that Lewis valued:

> **First**, the relationship between the two realities—heaven and earth—the persistent and consistent consubstantial illumination as Augustine would have phrased it, allows for the prefigured intimations; this is an understanding of reality that contradicts much of the basis of modern philosophy, pertinently the philosophical and intellectual endeavors of the academy since the Reformation. Unlike a Kantian closed universe where there is no commerce between the two realms (Kant, in effect, invented a glass ceiling, the recognition of which has been imposed unilaterally on all academics since, which—from a human perspective—cuts-off humanity from the graceful influence of God, leastwise, such intellectuals who recognize and acknowledge Kant's glass ceiling cut themselves off from God, and seek to impose this barrier on ordinary people). By contrast Lewis envisages interaction—transposition from the greater, the higher, to the lower.
>
> **Second**, that although the philosophical framework that underpinned this was from Lewis's reading as an undergraduate and a young don at Oxford in the 1920s (his adoption of concepts and propositions from, and the proximity

---

70. Augustine, *Against the Academicians and The Teacher*.
71. Ibid, 12.40. Quoted in Pasnau, "Divine Illumination," online: http://www.science.uva.nl/~seop/entries/illumination/.

of his thought to that of the seventeenth-century Cambridge Platonist Henry More and the eighteenth-century philosopher Bishop George Berkeley, his developing understanding of truth and reason, his Platonic idealism) the synthesis of his beliefs comes from his patristic reading generally, Augustine's doctrine of illumination specifically, itself Platonically derived. Therefore, as we noted in relation to Lewis's doctrine of transposition, the faculties of reason and imagination symbiotically give rise to understanding through illumination by the divine light because we cannot perceive and understand truth from our senses alone.

Lewis, I think it is fair to say, subscribed not completely to an Augustinian general theory of illumination where none of the cognitive and mental activity that leads to our knowing and understanding can be unaided; rather Lewis subscribed to a special theory of illumination, whereby there are special moments of grace which enable our knowledge and understanding, particularly of the ideas/forms and events that transcend our sensory perception. This is so for most of Lewis's theological and philosophical work and thinking in the 1930s and 1940s; however, as he aged and his Christian beliefs matured there is evidence that—like Augustine—he moves more and more towards a general theory of illumination, that there is no unaided knowledge and understanding.[72] This is not just because no one human operates in isolation, but that when we think we are doing things, thinking things, on our own, through our own volition, we are unaware as to just how much God's Holy Spirit underpins our thoughts—and this is not simply the conservation of creation, the ongoing upholding of creation by and through and in God. Therefore, for Lewis, God *continues* to reveal of God's nature and self and his salvific purposes and intentions for humanity in subtle ways that are transposed revealings, essentially through sensations and ideas in our minds, originating in the divine light, that we then reflect on, in, and through, wisdom. However disparate and diverse these hints and intimations are, however transposed, incomplete, and seemingly contradictory to our minds these revealings are, they work together towards the concrete, the particular, the perfect self-revelation in Christ Jesus as do the christological prefigurement myths of ancient and pagan religions.

---

72   For Lewis's developing understanding towards a general theory of illumination, and his understanding of prevenient grace and the work of the Holy Spirit, see, Lewis, *Reflections on the Psalms*. See also the "arguments" he had with God after Joy's death recorded by Lewis in, Clerk, *A Grief Observed* (pseudonym for Clive Staples Lewis), where he explains profoundly how he became aware that grace was not absent—he had excluded God from his mind and therefore his grief. See also, where Lewis, months before his death in 1963, speaks about his conversion (in interview) and how he understands the prevenient action of the Holy Spirit in our minds and lives: Wirt and Lewis, "Cross-Examination," 215–21.

11

Christ as the Light of the World III: Refractions—Splintered Fragments of the True Light

SYNOPSIS:
Following on from what we have established with regard to the prefiguration of the incarnation-resurrection narrative, and in the light of what we have concluded on meaning and revelation, imagination, illumination, and prevenience, Lewis's doctrine of christological prefigurement leads us to ask three groups of questions. First, how do these prefigured ideas come to be in these myths and how do these intimations, splintered fragments of the true light, relate to Lewis's understanding of Christ as the light of the world? Are these intimations the product of mythopoeia or of demonic mimicry? Lewis's orthodoxy accepted that the human imagination was flawed through original sin, but the source of the prefiguring myths was divine and not evil: the pagan imagination had been baptized, to a degree, but such minds continued to be corrupt after the event. We can ask how all these prefigurations (previsions and echoes?) relate to the actuality of Christ Jesus, incarnate and resurrected? This relates to a temporal paradox—i.e., how we perceive time and space as the incarnation-resurrection is at the centre of time in our reality.

The second group of questions centre on how the incarnation-resurrection narrative acts and operates on us as a myth whether spoken or read (a baptized imagination is crucial here for Lewis in both the creation and receiving/hearing of such narratives). The third group of questions relate to the internal evidence for a mythopoeic interpretation within the incarnation-resurrection narrative? Lewis asserted that the incarnation-resurrection narrative operates on us both as fact and myth—was he right? Do these prevision narratives—and the gospel story—act on us in a perlocutionary manner? Why does the incarnation-resurrection narrative appear to resonate with agrarian corn myths the world over? Lewis concluded that, "the pattern is there in nature because it was first there in God," that there is a death-descent/rebirth-reascent paradigm written into creation: Jesus Christ is not another example of this paradigm, he is the Lord of creation, nature's creator, the author of the paradigm.

There is a principle we can read from a doctrine of christological prefigurement, which is an inversion of the Frazer principle (Frazer notes that there are stories in religions and mythologies all over the world about incarnate, dying and rising-up "gods," therefore, he asserts, the incarnation-cross-resurrection narrative is just yet another mythological fiction). We may assert that all stories and myths, whether religious or otherwise, are to be seen teleologically in relation to the Christ-event. Reinterpreting what Plato wrote about the suffering, just, person in the light of the Christ-event is entirely admissible, likewise the ramifications of Balder's death and failed resuscitation is meant to reverberate with the true story of Jesus's death and resurrection when the two are seen together because of the cosmic implications of the one true myth—the Christ-event: christological prefigurements work towards God's loving purposes which are the potential transformation and salvation of all humanity.

1. WHY PREFIGUREMENT?

So, to summarize, many theologians of whatever persuasion may use "secondary imagination" (or Coleridge's "fancy") to create conceptual models relating to christological theories. Likewise, the imagination can, under certain circumstances, be an oracle of truth that may give some understanding or intimation of a revelatory nature. Such revelation, however implicit and ambiguous, must surely be seen as relating to God's salvific redemptive action in Jesus Christ. Often these revealings are amongst prophets and mystics (a word that would need serious qualification). Such revealings may also be subject to the taint and limits imposed on the mind by the fall. Furthermore, all is subject to the specific self-revelation of God in Jesus Christ; all *valid* natural theology is reliant upon grace. If this is all so, then we can cautiously postulate that there is validity in Lewis's general proposition of prevision—his doctrine of christological prefigurement. That is, that throughout many cultures, societies, and religions there have been intimations relating to the specific self-revelation of God in Christ, transpositions of the divine theme of redemption, fragments of the truth that point to Christ whether pre- or post-incarnation-resurrection (the myth of Osiris is pre-incarnation-resurrection and hence a prefigurement; many Hindu avatars are both pre- and post-incarnation-resurrection, and are hence both prefigurements and echoes). In narrative form these intimations can have a power similar to the actual Gospel narratives; however, the fullness of the historic actuality of the incarnation-resurrection is unique and has not, could not, as Kierkegaard asserted, be prefigured or replicated. So if it is accepted that there is a degree of prefigurement relating to the story of Christ's incarnation, death, and resurrection, though there are no direct or indirect parallels ontologically, epistemologically, and soteriologically. If it is also accepted that Lewis had a broad respect for natural theology, in keeping with Augustine, and that his appreciation saw natural theology not merely as intellectual/philosophical speculative gropings for an understanding of God but rather as bound up with the revelation in Christ (because a distinction should not be made between general and specific revelation, but rather the degree to which God reveals himself in a multitude of instances), then it can be accepted that the imagination should not be seen as completely lost because it is intrinsically flawed and evil, but can under certain circumstances be an oracle through which God gives some understanding of a revelatory nature.

We can now proceed to three questions: first, how do these prefigured ideas come to be in the pagan myths and how do these intimations relate to Lewis's understanding of Christ as the light of the world; second, how does the incarnation-resurrection

11. Christ as the Light of the World III: Refractions—Splintered Fragments of the True Light

narrative act/operate on us as a myth, whether spoken or read? And finally, is there internal evidence for a mythopoeic interpretation within the incarnation-resurrection narrative? Along the way we need to examine the perlocutionary effect these stories have and the sanctifying work of the Holy Spirit; also Lewis's Neo-Platonic assertion that where there is light, there is Christ—that as the light of the world, Jesus Christ illumines the minds of those outside cognitive knowledge of the historic actuality of the incarnation-resurrection.

2. SPLINTERED FRAGMENTS OF THE TRUE LIGHT: HOW DO THESE PREFIGURED IDEAS COME TO BE IN PAGAN MYTHS?

i. A Developing Understanding

As an eighteen-year old atheist Lewis viewed all mythology and religion as a human creation. Lewis's dismissal reflected his education and his understanding as an Edwardian young gentleman, formed in English public schools, privately tutored for Oxford; this was a system that had evolved for an elite that ruled an empire that spanned the globe. If this dismissal of any supernatural element in religion reflected a Feuerbachian-Freudian position and, further, if it was grounded in a Darwinian model of human evolution, derived essentially from Sir James George Frazer, it was complemented by his chronological-intellectual snobbery which informed him that his generation had knowledge and understanding superior to any other, to all that had gone before.[1] As he wrestled with his conversion in the autumn of 1931 he labelled myths as lies (the Lewis-Tolkien-Dyson debate). Lewis's position changed as his faith and his theology developed. By the time of his mature writings he believed that such myths, stories and ideas (prefigurement and echoes) were inspired by God: God was the source and ground of the meaning and intention behind the story of Balder or Osiris or the intimations of incarnation in Hindu avatars. In this he draws much on Tolkien's understanding (sub-creation, mythopoeic/mythopoeia, refractions and splinters of the true light, and eucatastrophe) and on Coleridge's definition of imagination, but also on a biblical concept of wisdom, whereby reflection on the human condition leads to a realization of something approximating to God's salvific actions towards humanity. Lewis did not, as we have seen, subscribe to a wholly Reformed position with regard to natural theology and revelation. However, Lewis, progressively, agreed with Augustine that there is no unaided knowledge of God. This is close to a Reformed position but Lewis gave credit to reason in the form of natural theology, and to the imagination that many in the Reformed tradition would not; furthermore he believed that there is value, even intimations of a revelatory nature, in other religious experience, though any value in such a mode of revelation is in relation to and qualified by the specific self-revelation of God in Christ Jesus (again a point of confluence with Augustine).

---

1   See, Lewis, *Surprised by Joy*, Ch. 13, specifically, 206 208

ii. Pagan Mythopoeia and the Shepherds

Unlike Tolkien Lewis argues for a limitation of originality in humanity's mythopoeia; Lewis questioned the degree of originality in Tolkien's theory of sub-creation because any elements in these stories which truly reflected God's salvific actions towards humanity must be derived from God: originality lies truly with the God who can create *ex nihilo*, exactly out of nothing.[2] Lewis explicitly ascribes all inspiration through the faculty of the imagination to God: God is the creator and author of these myths. This reflects Augustine's proposition that there is no unaided true knowledge of God. Lewis and Tolkien agreed that all storytellers and seers, sages and poets, are sub-creators under God the prime-creator, working in a sub-Christian world, and hence "pagan myths are never just lies—there is always something of the truth in them . . . God [was] expressing himself through the minds of poets, and using the images of their "mythopoeia" to express fragments of his eternal truth . . ."[3] Such images are a mode of revelation, that is revelation that is transposed to a greater or lesser degree. Here transposition involves mythopathic images imbued in the minds of the pagan poets and sages inspired by the Holy Spirit, images that are diminuted, changed, transposed, pictures that then become words that are stories that communicate something relating to the Christ-event, the actuality, but without one-to-one correspondence (see figure 22). Lewis argues in "Myth Became Fact" that our only response to God acting mythopoeically is for us to be mythopathic, sympathetic, and empathetic to these intimations: "If God chooses to be mythopoeic—and is not the sky itself a myth?—shall we refuse to be mythopathic? For this is the marriage of heaven and earth: perfect myth and perfect fact."[4]

As we have seen, Lewis often refers to Coleridge's concept of imagination. Human perception of God acting mythopoeically would appear to be an example of Coleridge's "secondary imagination"—like the "primary imagination" but less like it only in degree and operating as an echo of the "primary imagination" in the conscious mind. Such intimations of the incarnation-resurrection, inspired by the Holy Spirit, are one step removed from the actuality of the gospel reality and hence are merely prefigurements or echoes resulting from the illumination of the Logos—the true light that enlightens all, which was to come into the world (John 1:9). In a paper read to The Oxford Socratic Club in 1944 Lewis wrote, "The Divine light, we are told, 'lighteneth every man.' We should, therefore, expect to find in the imagination of great pagan teachers and myth-makers some glimpse of that theme which we believe to be the very plot of the whole cosmic story—the theme of incarnation, death and rebirth. And the differences between the pagan Christs (Balder, Osiris, etc.) and the Christ himself is much what we should expect to find."[5] Therefore, in none of the examples of prefigurement-echoes do we find an actual self-emptying incarnation of God or the dying and actual

2. Downing, "Sub-Creation or Smuggled Theology: Tolkien contra Lewis on Christian Fantasy," Online: http://www.cslewisinstitute.org/node/1207.
3. Carpenter, *The Inklings*, 43–44.
4. Lewis, "Myth Became Fact," 39–43.
5. Lewis, "Is Theology Poetry?," 150–65.

11. Christ as the Light of the World III: Refractions—Splintered Fragments of the True Light

---

ILLUMINATION AND INSPIRATION IN PAGAN MYTHOPOEIA

Image(s) are generated/imparted, transposed, by the Holy Spirit in the mind of a seer or poet.

⬇

The image is a moment outside of time, and is open to free interpretation by the seer or poet.

⬇

The seer/poet responds mythopoeically by creating, forming a story, or myth, or a poem, which encapsulates the image, but this is in time, it is sequential.

⬇

The transposed words of the story, when heard, evoke the original image, which itself was transposed.

⬇

There will be resonances with the Gospel story, which is unknown to the hearers, but this will still affect them.

Figure 22: Illumination-Inspiration in pagan Mythopoeia

resurrection of God incarnate. The incarnation narrative (as expressed in John 1:14a) is rooted in an historical actuality. This can only happen once; any prefigurement-echo is a pointer, a glimpse and will stop short of the true reality; this actuality is not a human invention nor can such prefigurements parallel the Christian incarnation: the paradox, as Kierkegaard would put it. The light that illuminated the pagans, the Greeks and the Hindus may be considered in this context to be the same light that is referred to in the prologue to John's Gospel. Lewis goes as far as to suggest that *ideas* of God's saving purposes were not only foretold in the Hebrew religion but that images or mythical pictures relating to a greater or lesser degree to these *ideas* were given into the minds of myth-makers, shamans, and seers within the North European pagan religion, in the ancient Egyptian religion, and in the Asiatic-Indian (Hindu), to name but three of the instances that Lewis alludes to. As we noted earlier in the context of Lewis's general doctrine of revelation, he balances dialectically the rules and election, the law and prophecy, given to the Hebrews with the pictures infused into the minds of the pagan poets and seers: both must stand as modes of imperfect revelation, both are general and incomplete (in the context of Lewis's modes of revelation these pagan premonitions also relate to the numinous and to *Sehnsucht*). In *Mere Christianity* he asserts that God, "sent the human race what I call good dreams: I mean those queer stories scattered all through the heathen religions about a god who dies and comes to life again and, by his death, has somehow given new life to men . . . [Furthermore God has] selected one particular people and spent several centuries hammering into their heads the sort of God he was—that there was only one of him and that he cared about right conduct."[6] So there is a dialectical relationship between the law and prophecy given to the chosen people of God—the Jews—balanced with the prefiguring myths given to the pagans.

iii. Pagan Prevision

Therefore, for Lewis both the pagan tribes and Israel pointed, to a degree, towards the full and complete revelation in Christ, but neither were complete revelation (that is, as complete as is possible this side of eternity). This is laid out by Lewis in *The Pilgrim's Regress*.[7] He deals with the origins of North European pagan myths in relation to the Jews, but also he address the question of source: divine inspiration or evil lies—what is the supernatural source behind the prefiguring myths, and how does corruption within the human mind affects these intimations? Using allegory Lewis suggests that God gave the Shepherds (the Hebrew people) ideas and rules and set their feet on the road but that he gave pictures, images, to the pagan peoples. Lewis regards the mode of revelation imparted to the ancient Hebrew people—the law, the prophets, integrated as part of the salvation history recorded in the Old Testament—as belonging with the pagan prefiguring myths, because this is all part of the general modes of revelation transposed to what he explicitly names as a sub-Christian world: "Morality is by no means God's only witness in the sub-Christian world, even pagan mythology contained a divine call . . . conscience and sweet desire must come together."[8] The images given generate sweet desire, but they are incomplete, transposed, as is the Jewish law. According to Lewis all peoples will have some degree of intimation whether as morality-law, or the sweet desires of pictures, images that intimate, but the clarity of form (Lewis's term) is affected by the degree of an inherited disease—original sin.[9] When John (the lead character in *The Pilgrim's Regress*, identifiable with an allegorical C. S. Lewis) queries how these modes of revelation hold together, the answer is simple—they come from, in terms of the allegory used, "the Landlord"—God. But herein lies a danger, the danger of incompleteness and corruption caused by the inherited disease (original sin): "The pictures alone are dangerous, and rules alone are dangerous. That is why the best thing of all is to find Mother Kirk [the Church] at the very beginning, and to live from infancy with a third thing which is neither the Rules nor the pictures and which was brought into the country by the Landlord's Son [Christ]."[10] Lewis is not just talking about pre-Christian peoples as the pagans, but this sub-Christian world is also populated by apostates—but as often as people became pagans again God will send pictures accompanied by sweet desire to lead them back

---

6. Lewis, *Mere Christianity*, Bk. 2, Ch. 3, 50–51.
7. Lewis, *The Pilgrim's Regress*, 3rd edition, Bk. VIII "At Bay," Ch. 8 "History's Words," 189–94.
8. Ibid., 189.
9. Ibid., 190.
10. Ibid.

to the church.[11] The danger Lewis talks about is manifold: "They had pictures for their eyes instead of roads for their feet, and that is why most of them could do nothing but desire and then, through starved desire, become corrupt in their imaginations."[12] It is the Shepherds (Israel) who have the road for their feet to travel, but this was not without its pitfalls: the Shepherds rejected the Christ and became over protective about the Hebrew religious tradition and law. The point of the journey is to arrive, whether one is a Shepherd or a pagan, the journey should lead to what the church represents: the Hebrew law and the pagan previsions were not to be seen as ends in themselves: "It is a starting point from which one road leads home and a thousand lead into the wilderness . . . the truth is that a Shepherd is only half a man, and a pagan is only half a man, so that neither people was well without the other, nor could either be healed until the Landlord's Son [Christ] came into the country."[13] Lewis concludes that reconciliation of the Shepherds and the pagans and what they represent, and the incomplete mode of revelation each was subject to, reconciliation can only be achieved in and by the Landlord's Son—Christ. John, in conversation with the hermit: "'It is only a third that can reconcile you.' 'Who is that?' 'The same who reconciled the Shepherds and the pagans. But you must go to Mother Kirk to find him.'"[14] Therefore, the pagan imagination is baptized to a degree, but the freedom given to creation inevitably led to a misinterpretation of the previsions. The mythology of the pagans contained a divine call, however, they mistook the images for what they were not and their imagination became corrupt: only one road led home a thousand led into the wilderness.

iv. Demonic Mimicry and the Fall?

Lewis's views on pagan prevision are remarkably consistent. *The Pilgrim's Regress* (1931) was written shortly after his conversion; however, he takes this further in *Reflections on the Psalms* (1958), written more than a quarter of a century later.[15] Lewis notes how even the anthropologists who are often the most hostile to the faith of Christians will acknowledge that the resemblance between pagan myths and the incarnation-resurrection narrative cannot be accidental. However, they will seek a reductionist explanation, usually rooted in culture. But they are not the only ones who seek to dismiss the previsions, certain groups of Christians will also. Some of the early and church fathers, and for that matter some post Reformation Protestant and Reformed theologians regarded the prefigurements as the work of demonic forces. Lewis comments that these Christians believed that paganism was the work of the devil, so that any coincidence to the story of the incarnation-resurrection was to be classified as an attempt to deceive and mislead humanity with lies; the more closely the myths imitate truth the more effective they will be: because all the devil can do is imitate God. According to this theory, "the resemblance of Adonis to Christ

---

11. Ibid., 191.
12. Ibid., 193.
13. Ibid., 193–94.
14. Ibid., 194.
15. Lewis, *Reflections on the Psalms*, Ch. 10 "Second Meanings," 85–93.

is therefore not at all accidental; it is the resemblance we expect to find between a counterfeit and the real thing, between a parody and the original."[16] Lewis's position on the validity of prefigurement is much more nuanced and multifaceted: for Lewis, there are divine and diabolical elements involved, therefore the resemblance—particularly given that these are agrarian cultures that give rise to these myths—is not accidental. Lewis explains how these myths are therefore grounded in the sequence of night and day, winter and summer, and the lifecycle of plants and crops. Therefore it becomes an intimation that the true course for humanity is for a man or woman to undertake death if s/he is to truly live: "there is already a likeness permitted by God to that truth on which all depends. The resemblance between these myths and the Christian truth is no more accidental than the resemblance between the sun and the sun's reflection in a pond."[17] The question of an agrarian parallel and ground will come up again where we examine whether there is any internal evidence for a mythical interpretation within the incarnation-resurrection narrative.

In *The Pilgrim's Regress* Lewis established a basic proposition regarding the question of an evil or good source for the previsions. John (C. S. Lewis) is in conversation with the hermit. The hermit comments:

> "Oh, a great many deny his existence. But you have to be told a thing before you can deny it. The peculiarity of the pagans was they had not been told: or if they had, it is so long ago that the tradition had died out. You see, the Enemy [the devil] had practically supplanted the Landlord [God], and he kept a sharp watch against any news from that quarter reaching the tenants."
>
> "Did he succeed?"
>
> "No. It is commonly thought that he did, but that is a mistake. It is commonly thought that he fuddled the tenants by circulating a mass of false stories about the Landlord. But I have been through Pagus in my rounds too often to think it was quite so simple. What really happened was this: The Landlord [God] succeeded in getting a lot of messages through."
>
> "What sort of messages?"
>
> "Mostly pictures . . . these pictures awoke desire . . . and then the pagans made mistakes. They kept on trying to get the same picture again, and if it didn't come, they would make copies of it."[18]

Therefore, the source is sound: the previsions are from God. However, the pagan peoples had the creative freedom, in minds diseased by original sin, to make of the pictures/images what they would, and—echoing the young Lewis's invention of a pseudo-religious cult out of his love of Northernness and the experience of *Sehnsucht* he called "Joy"—they became corrupt in their handling of this mode of revelation. Yet, just when their own stories from the previsions had seemed completely corrupted the Landlord would intimate new images and attempt to revive the true meaning. Therefore, Lewis is denying the patristic and Reformer's assertion that the prefigurements were generated by demonic mimicry. The element of evil is still there but on the human side,

16. Ibid., 91.
17. Ibid., 91–92.
18. Lewis, *The Pilgrim's Regress*, Bk. VIII, Ch. 8, 191–92.

11. Christ as the Light of the World III: Refractions—Splintered Fragments of the True Light

because fallen human nature misinterprets, misuses, the images through a corrupt imagination and a fallen will: their interpretation of the transposed images produced a thousand roads leading into the wilderness, but one road still existed to guide them in the right direction.

In terms of pagan religion—defined as essentially any religious system outside of the Judeo-Christian tradition—Lewis distinguishes between the pre-Christian pagan and the Post-Christian. A (pre-Christian) pagan, for Lewis, is simply someone who is *on the way to becoming a Christian*—unless they hold out as the journey becomes an eternity. In post-Christian terms the pagan is a different religious creature. For example, when Lewis heard people complain that England in the 1950s was regressing into paganism he responded that he wished it would. In jest he comments that he did not believe we would see the revival of such practices as "the slaughtering of a garlanded white bull in the House of Lords or Cabinet Ministers leaving sandwiches in Hyde Park as an offering for the Dryads." Why?—because wrong religious ideas are a starting point. He continues, "For a pagan, as history shows, is a man eminently convertible to Christianity. He is essentially, the pre-Christian, or sub-Christian, religious man. The post-Christian man of our own day differs from him as much as a divorcee differs from a virgin."[19] The pagan is, therefore, closer to the truth than the post-Christian. It is a question of movement and direction.

v. A Baptized Imagination

The degree to which the imagination can, on the one hand, be the object of divine inspiration and illumination and, on the other hand, an oracle of truth is debatable. Calvin, as we saw, was dismissive of the imagination; the Reformed tradition regarded both the imagination and natural theology as suspect at best and of little consequence—the emphasis was placed on sin and fallenness. However, Lewis does address the question of sin and fallenness. Lewis, as we have seen, places great emphasis in his spiritual autobiography and in his theological writings on the concept of a baptized imagination,[20] where the imagination through a free and creative ordering of the contents of the mind is governed by the Holy Spirit: because of original sin an unbaptized imagination fails to perceive the intrinsic value and meaning in stories and myths from a God-ward, and hence true, perspective. The hearers (and these stories were nearly always part of an oral tradition) may not "know" the details of the story of when the virgin conceived, when her Son who died on the cross for their/our sins rose from the dead, but something of the profound effect of this true story would have worked on them—and us—and not just on a psychological level: it may be that their/our very being is reordered *to a degree* and reoriented towards the one true living God despite the maze and confusion of religious ideas and "gods." However, Lewis would have concurred with a Reformed position that proposed that

---

19. Lewis, "Is Theism Important?," 138–42, quotes, 138.
20. For instance: Lewis, *Surprised by Joy*. See also, Lewis (ed.) "Preface," in, *George MacDonald: An Anthology*, xxi-xxxiv; Lewis, "Is Theology Poetry"; and, Lewis, *The Pilgrim's Regress*, 1st ed., Bk. X, esp. Ch. 2.

the imagination was fallen and tainted by original sin, but he would have argued that it was not irredeemable in this life. Lewis does not necessarily tie the baptism of the imagination to an explicit liturgical practice: the Spirit blows where it wills (Gen 1:2b and John 3:8). Lewis sees a baptized imagination as an essential key in comprehending ultimate reality; this knowledge of reality is apprehended by acquaintance with and participation in the divine Logos. A person comprehending ultimate reality, a reality illuminated by the Logos (in the sense of an immediate, intuitive and imaginative capacity) has perception of God to the extent that such an acquaintance and perception is considered by Lewis to be revelatory; however, the rational interpretation of such an experience may be subject to distortion whilst communication of the experience may be flawed. Revelation of this kind is mediated through human faculties: it is human to err; to err is to be human. Hence Lewis's assertion that those in receipt of the Northern European myths misinterpreted and misused the images they were given. Lewis assumes that the pagan imagination (individually or collectively) was to a degree baptized when it received/perceived the images; however, we must presume that the imagination of such an individual, and those subsequently hearing the human record of these intimations were, relatively speaking, equally flawed. Lewis does not address whether epistemological baptism is permanent this side of eternity. Human epistemic limitations would seem to dismiss such a proposition; likewise the fact that we are still subject to the vagaries of sin—*simul iustus et peccator* (at the same time a sinner yet justified)—which is confirmed by Lewis's proposition of revelation transposed. Our sinfulness affects the degree of transposition.

3. THE REFRACTED LIGHT OF REVELATION

Is Lewis conceiving of the universal resurrected Christ, the Logos, as working on people's minds regardless of whether they knew what had happened or was to happen for their redemption in Palestine 2,000 years ago? Such illumination, the work of the Spirit, moves and operates where and how it will and we cannot utterly dismiss the salvific effect on—in the case of Lewis's prefigurement theories—the North European pagan tribes who were subject to these myths (the salvation outside of the knowledge of Christ in Matt 25?). But, none of these prefigurements actually replicate what will/did happen on the cross. There is therefore something of a universal Platonic form to Lewis's understanding of the resurrected Christ. Tolkien, as we saw, referred to such intimations as splintered fragments of the true light—"the refracted light . . . splintered from a single white to many hues, and endlessly combined in living shapes that move from mind to mind."[21] For Lewis, where there is enlightenment there is Christ: as the light of the world Jesus Christ illumines the minds of those outside of the cognitive knowledge of the historic actuality of the incarnation-resurrection. Karl Barth worked on the same principle but in a much more systematic way than Lewis. In the fourth volume of his *Church Dogmatics*,[22] he does not assert Jesus Christ as light

---

21. Tolkien, "Mythopoeia," 87.
22. Barth, *Church Dogmatics*, Vol. IV/3i: The Doctrine of Reconciliation Part 3i—Jesus Christ, the True Witness, §69 The Glory of the Mediator, sub-section 2. The Light of Life, 151f.

11. Christ as the Light of the World III: Refractions—Splintered Fragments of the True Light

and truth *from* the one light and truth that is God; rather, he asserts that Jesus Christ simply *is* this light and truth (the one light and truth that God is). He is the light of the world; Jesus is the divine light flooding the world with his light. These other lights must be part of or related to this one true light, they are not independent. As with Lewis, this does move Barth in a universalistic direction: if Jesus Christ is the light of the world then there is a degree to which this light can be recognized anywhere—in the secular world, not necessarily only in the religious. Barth writes:

> Are these truths outside the one? Yes, for the creature has its being and existence outside God. But as lights of the creature these truths are refractions (in this connection there is a real place for the term) of the one light and appearances (this term is also justified at this point) of the one truth. If they have force, value, validity, these are not independent. Primarily and finally, they are not their own. They are merely those which are lent them by the shining of the one light of the one truth. These are lights and truths of the *theatrum of the gloria Dei* ... But as this light rises and shines, it is reflected in the being and existence of the cosmos which is not created accidentally, but with a view to this action and therefore to this revelation.[23]

These refractions (Barth uses *Brechungen*) of the one light and truth are appearances (Barth uses *Erscheinungen*) of God's self-declaration, the self-revelation of God. Lewis and Barth are referring to truths that come from Christ: refractions for Barth; intimations for Lewis; splintered fragments of refracted light, for Tolkien. They are saying that where Christ is not known or recognized, or cognitive knowledge of the event is impossible, the Christ's truth and light has to break in. The incarnation-resurrection is the one real event in this; it is part of the history of this world. Hence for Barth these truths are refractions, because the one light is an expression of the one truth. Apart from Christ there is no light and no truth; but divine light-truth is often distinct from human light-truth, and we may filter this true light though our fallenness (also we must heed to Paul's warning about dark forces parading themselves as the light—2 Cor 4 and 14). As we have seen, Lewis asserted that those receiving or hearing these intimations mistook the images for what they were not and became corrupt in their imaginations—one road led home and a thousand lead into the wilderness.[24] Did this confusion after the fall lead to a multiplicity of gods and religious theories?—eventually to a degree of apophatic denial?

4. A TEMPORAL PARADOX?

There is an issue/question that we alluded to: some of these prefigurations occur in ancient Egyptian myths, or in North European pagan societies and religion prior to the event of the incarnation-resurrection in Palestine 2,000 years ago; others after, for example, in India, perhaps only a few hundred years ago, though they may have been received-composed in ignorance of the Christ-event. There is something of a paradox here, which raises the question of time: we must see the incarnation-resurrection as

---

23. Ibid.,152–53.
24. Lewis, *The Pilgrim's Regress*, 1st edition, Bk. VIII, Ch. 8.

being at the centre of time; therefore any pneumatologically inspired intimations, echoes and/or refractions about or related to the Christ-event are to be seen as derivative from and reliant for meaning upon this central event. Indeed, they must all be seen pertinently as echoes from this single, cataclysmic event. Conventionally we see time in our reality, our universe, starting with the big bang, with creation *ex nihilo*, and leading teleologically to the eschaton. However, christologically we must see time starting and ending in our reality with the incarnation-resurrection; therefore all mythopoeic creations that point to or are narrative echoes of the truth of the incarnation-resurrection relate to this central event, whether they occur before or after the reality of the incarnation-resurrection according to the chronologically linear perception of time. Time is far more organic than this linear clockwork model. Christologically time, in addition to the linear model, must be seen as circular—everything in our reality, everything that has lived, is alive, or will live is a creation ex nihilo related to and radiating out like the ripples on a pool from this central point in our reality: pertinently this point is focused down onto the moment of the death of Christ on the cross. Perhaps the early patristic belief that between his death and resurrection Christ harrowed hell, that is he descended into the depths of hell and the realm of the dead to bring out the righteous, a story that jars with modern sensitivities, perhaps this story might just make sense if we acknowledge the parallel effect a circular eschatological model of time has alongside a biological model of time—the effect of Christ's resurrection redeems the righteous who lived before the Christ-event, the linear model of time is then changed *a posteriori* (though as we have the record of a pre-Christ-event model of time, we will only know the truth of this after death, after all of time and reality has been rolled up, extinguished and judged). The story of the harrowing of hell is an example of transposed analogy.

Temporally the effect of the incarnation-resurrection can be identified like the point of disturbance from a stone touching the surface of a pool, but the shock waves radiate in all directions—rippling the surface of the water, but also radiating into the depths and fanning out as shock waves through the air; this is how the incarnation-resurrection effects our spatio-temporal reality, because the Word was made flesh and dwelt amongst us and we crucified it, and it rose again from the dead. Generally speaking, all of these transposed mythopoeic intimations that illumine the human mind, echoes and/or refractions that point to or are related to God's incarnation-resurrection, are essentially formed in cognitive unawareness, inspired and composed in a lack of knowledge of the historic actuality of the incarnation-resurrection, but the recipients and hearers are profoundly affected by the myths nonetheless. This leads into the question of how the incarnation-resurrection narrative operates on us when we hear it mythopathically.

11. Christ as the Light of the World III: Refractions—Splintered Fragments of the True Light

5. HOW DOES THE INCARNATION-RESURRECTION NARRATIVE ACT/OPERATE ON US AS A MYTH, WHETHER SPOKEN OR READ?

In his essay "Myth Became Fact" Lewis deals with the question of how and why the incarnation-resurrection narrative acts upon us both mythopoeically and as the record of an actuality: an historical event. Lewis writes how the human intellect is incurably abstract yet the only realities we experience are concrete, "this pain, this pleasure, this dog, this man. While we are loving the man, bearing the pain, enjoying the pleasure, we are not intellectually apprehending pleasure, pain or personality." Lewis explains that if and when we begin to intellectualize abstractly the concrete realities are reduced to the level of mere instances or examples:

> We are no longer dealing with them but that which they exemplify. This is our dilemma—either to taste and not to know or to know and not to taste or, more strictly, to lack one kind of knowledge because we are in an experience or to lack another kind because we are outside of it . . . But when else can you really know these things? "If only my toothache would stop, I could write another chapter about pain." But once it stops what do I know about pain?[25]

Lewis cites myth as a partial solution to this dilemma. In listening to and being carried by a myth he asserts that we come nearest to experiencing as concrete what can otherwise be understood only as an abstraction. While we receive a myth as story we experience the principle concretely, though as soon as we translate we get abstraction. To Lewis it is not truth that flows into us from the myth but reality, he notes how "truth is always about something, but reality is that *about which* [Lewis's emphasis] truth is . . . every myth is the father of innumerable truths on the abstract level."[26] Therefore the gospel story generally, and the incarnation-resurrection narrative specifically, operate on us mythopoeically precisely because they convey to us the reality that they represent: whether one believes or not in the reality (the historical actuality of the incarnation and resurrection) the story acts upon us like a myth—many people today will comment about how nice it would be if the story of Jesus were true. The reality is touching them not just the abstract truth which they choose to deny. Lewis writes further,

> Now as myth transcends thought, incarnation transcends myth. The heart of Christianity is a myth which is also a fact . . . I suspect that men have sometimes derived more spiritual sustenance from myths they did not believe than from the religion they professed. To be truly Christian we must both assent to the historical fact and also receive the myth (fact though it has become) with the same imaginative embrace which we accord to all myths. A man who disbelieved the Christian story as fact but continually fed on it as myth would, perhaps, be more spiritually alive than one who assented and did not think much about it.[27]

---

25. Lewis, "Myth Became Fact," 34
26. Ibid., 35
27. Ibid., 36

There is, of course, a heavy dose of Platonic idealism in this, and we must not forget the influence of Classical literature and the theology of the patristic era on Lewis. Thus he could write that the story of the incarnation "comes down from the heaven of legend and the imagination"[28] to us to become reality. Is Lewis talking about a Platonic form? If so, then whether assent is given or not the story/myth works on us concretely—the reality touches us, though we must acknowledge that for some it may not. The incarnation-resurrection narrative acting upon us mythopoeically would seem, therefore, to have a perlocutionary effect. Following Lewis's proposition through, we do not just think abstractly about this narrative and draw conclusions, it acts upon us in a perlocutionary way:[29] in perceiving the reality the words are doing something, like causing someone to blush or when someone suitably authorized declares a couple man and wife. Theologically a marriage ceremony is perlocutionary because the words uttered by the priest/minister change the very nature of being of the couple; or as Jesus said, they become one flesh. They are changed; and as we read the incarnation-resurrection narrative we are changed—for most people this effect cannot be avoided. What is conveyed is monumental. This relates back to Augustine's doctrine of illumination—how the Spirit illumines our minds and hence the text with understanding, how the Spirit enables us to accept the text for what it claims. Hence Lewis's assertion that we examined earlier on Scripture, revelation, and reason, that the biblical text becomes for us the Word of God through our reading of it with minds illuminated by the Holy Spirit. This was so for the tribal warriors who, after a feast in some great forest enclosed Northern chieftain's timbered hall, listened to the story of Balder (though we saw earlier how the story fell short of actual Christ-like resurrection); the story would have had a perlocutionary effect on them (intimations on a deeper level than the conscious mind of God's salvific intentions and actions in relation to human kind) similar to the way the incarnation-resurrection narrative was spoken and received as an oral tradition by the apostles and disciples in Jerusalem, Damascus and Antioch in the immediate months and years after the resurrection: listen to what God has done for you! This leads us into questions about the nature of the incarnation-resurrection narrative.

6. IS THERE INTERNAL EVIDENCE FOR A MYTHOPOEIC INTERPRETATION WITHIN THE INCARNATION-RESURRECTION NARRATIVE?

i. "The Pattern is there in Nature because it was First there in God"

If a mythopathic view of the incarnation-resurrection narrative is to be seen as valid, then the question arises as to whether the gospel narrative itself supports such a

---

28. Ibid.
29. Perlocutionary: perlocution is a noun from philosophy and linguistics referring to an act of speaking or writing which has an action as its aim but which in itself does not effect or constitute the action, for example persuading or convincing.

view. It is not relevant here to analyze both Old and New Testaments to ascertain an answer, especially considering the relationship between many of the stories in the Old Testament and myths from Middle Eastern societies and cultures; however, a brief examination of Lewis's ideas on this subject is possible. In a chapter on the incarnation-resurrection in his work *Miracles*[30] Lewis addresses the problem as he sees it. He writes that although the story of Jesus has remarkable parallels with the principle of descending and ascending within nature myths there is no suggestion in the Gospels of a self-awareness of this parallel in Jesus or his disciples. In the Christian story God descends to reascend. This is a familiar pattern in nature—all life must descend (i.e., a seed) to reascend. Cultures all over the world have death and resurrection myths woven into their perception and understanding of the natural world, many such myths are elevated to the status of corn kings, the king must die in the ground as a seed to reascend, to grow again, to rule again. Lewis writes, "The doctrine of the incarnation, if accepted, puts this principle even more emphatically at the centre. The pattern is there in nature because it was first there in God. All the instances of it which I have mentioned turn out to be but transpositions of the Divine theme into a minor key."[31]

Lewis asserts that many could see Christ as simply another corn-king. Yet although Jesus was addressing an agrarian society, and although the metaphor of a seed falling and dying to rise again is used in his sayings as well as in other parts of the New Testament,[32] there is no conscious parallel drawn between this observable fact of creation and the reality of God descending to reascend taking fallen creation with him. Lewis writes, "The records, in fact, show us a Person who *enacts* [Lewis' emphasis] the part of the Dying God, but whose thoughts and words remain quite outside the circle of religious ideas to which the Dying God belongs . . . It is as if you met the sea-serpent and found that it disbelieved in sea-serpents."[33] Lewis addresses this problem by asserting that the Christians are not simply claiming that God was incarnate in Jesus but that the one true God whom the Hebrews worshipped as Yahweh had descended. On the one hand, this is the God of creation—of nature. On the other hand, this is not a nature-god. This is the God for whom the earth is his foot stool not his vesture—"Yahweh is neither the soul of nature nor her enemy . . ."[34] We can therefore understand why Christ is at once so like the corn-king and so silent about him. He is like the corn-king because the corn-king is a portrait of him. Elements of nature-religion are strikingly absent from the teachings of Jesus and from Hebrew history, in particular the covenant, because of the unique calling of the Hebrew people to testify to the one true God, author and lord of creation, not merely a part of creation:

> In them you have from the very outset got in behind nature-religion and behind nature herself. Where the real God is present the shadows of that God do not

---

30. Lewis, *Miracles*, 1st edition, Ch 14, "The Grand Miracle," 113–38.
31. Ibid., 118.
32. For example, Matt 13; Matt 25; Mark 4; Luke 8; Luke 13; Luke 17; 1 Cor 15; 2 Cor 9:10; 1 Pet 1; 1 John 3.
33. Lewis, *Miracles*, 1st edition, Ch. 14, "The Grand Miracle," 119.
34. Ibid., 121.

> appear, that which the shadows resembled does. The Hebrews throughout their history were being constantly headed off from the worship of nature-gods; not because the nature-gods were in all respects unlike the God of Nature but because, at best, they were merely like, and it was the destiny of that nation to be turned away from likenesses to the thing itself.[35]

Hence, there is no internal evidence within the Gospels; likewise there is no direct parallel between the incarnation-resurrection narrative and these echoes and prefigurements which are merely shadows, because to Lewis the Christ-event is the reality beyond the shadows breaking in to redeem: hence Lewis at his most Platonic. Further, we find that the value he gives to prefiguration, and for that matter natural theology and revelation, is entirely subordinate to the reality of the Christ-event that in many ways transcends religion.

ii. The Death-Descent/Rebirth-Reascent Paradigm

Lewis sees death and rebirth as a key principle in the move towards eternity;[36] this issues from a death-descent/rebirth-reascent paradigm and is inscribed into reality so that in death the secret of secrets is hidden.[37] The death-descent and rebirth-reascent paradigm in nature is for Lewis an echo, the theme transposed into a minor key, whereas we find the real theme, the real text or poem as he terms it, in the gospel;[38] this theme transposed into a minor key is also found in the myth of Adonis[39] Therefore, the theme of death-descent and rebirth-reascent is the imitation of Christ, and is echoed in what is written into the natural world by Christ the creator.[40] At its most explicit it is seen in nature in the myths, folk songs and ballads about the seed dying to be reborn, usually associated with corn/wheat—the seed buried in death to rise up anew the next year.[41] Through the pattern of death and rebirth Christianity transcends the limits of understanding in our conscious minds; the cross-resurrection is a theme unknown to virtually all religious people, especially the significance of it, however, it is the consummation of all religion.[42]

Therefore, there is a pattern of death-descent/rebirth-reascent in paganism, particularly in the North European pagan myths, a transposition, which then prefigures using the imagery innate to the tribal poets and seers, hence prefigured Christianity. It is important for Lewis to assert that the death-descent/rebirth-reascent paradigm is in nature because it was first in nature's creator, Christ, for the cross-

---

35. Ibid., 121
36. Ibid., 112
37. See, Lewis, *Mere Christianity*, 154–55; Lewis, *Miracles*, 1st edition, 125; also, Lewis, *The Screwtape Letters*, 147.
38. Lewis, *Miracles*, 1st edition, 130.
39. Lewis, "The Funeral of a Great Myth," 82–93, specifically, 83.
40. Lewis, "Man or Rabbit," 82–84 and 86. See also, Lewis, *Reflections on the Psalms*, 106–7; also, Lewis, *The Problem of Pain*, 149. Essentially these ideas can be found in, Lewis, *Miracles*, 1st edition, 98, 111–16, 125, 130 and 161.
41. Lewis, *Miracles*, 1st ed., Ch. 14, 113–15.
42. Lewis, "Religion Without Dogma?," 108–12, essentially, 110.

11. Christ as the Light of the World III: Refractions—Splintered Fragments of the True Light

---

C.S. Lewis: Christological Prefigurement— The Death-Descent/Rebirth-Reascent, Paradigm

1940
Lewis, *The Problem of Pain*, 1940, 25.

1944
"Answers to Questions on Christianity", in, *Undeceptions: Essays on Theology and Ethics*, 1971, 26–38, specifically, 33–34.

1944
Lewis, "Myth Became Fact", in, *Undeceptions: Essays on Theology and Ethics*, 1971, 39–43, specifically, 42–43.

1945
Lewis, "The Grand Miracle", in, *Undeceptions: Essays on Theology and Ethics*, 1971, 56–63, with specific references to Adonis, and to Frazer's work, 58–59.

1946
Lewis, "Religion without Dogma?", in, *Undeceptions: Essays on Theology and Ethics*, 1971, 99–114, again with reference and repudiation of Frazer, see, 101–102.

1947
Lewis, *Miracles*, 1st edition, 1947, Ch. 14 "The Grand Miracle", 112–116.

1952
Lewis, "Is Theism Important?", in, *Undeceptions: Essays on Theology and Ethics*, 1971, 138–142, specifically, 140–141.

1952
Lewis, *Mere Christianity*, 54.

1955
Also, set against the development of his thoughts and leading to his conversion, see, *Surprised by Joy*, 1955, 62, 223–224 and 235–236.

1958
Lewis, *Reflections on the Psalms*, 1958, 105–108.

Full details can be found in the bibliography

Figure 23 The Death-Descent/Rebirth-Reascent Paradigm, in C. S. Lewis's Work

resurrection is universal.[43] However, when applied to humanity the previous organism is never restored to its original condition—resurrection is a new life from the old form.[44] The death-descent/rebirth-reascent paradigm can also be seen in the history of human thought—this is for Lewis the juxtaposition, sequentially, of rich, imaginative thought as compared to logical analysis.[45] Therefore, contrary to the anthropologists and Freudians, even though a pattern can be seen this is not accidental: this paradigm is in mythology and nature *because it related to the incarnation-cross-resurrection*—if we are to be truly alive we must first die.[46]

7. WHY? WHY NOT?

There is a principle we can read from a doctrine of christological prefigurement. In effect this is an inversion of the Frazer principle. Frazer notes that there are stories in religions and mythologies all over the world about incarnate, dying and rising-

---

43. Lewis, *Miracles*, 1st edition, 112.
44. Ibid., 151.
45. Ibid., 161.
46. See: Lewis, *Reflections on the Psalms*, 106–7, and, Lewis, *The Problem of Pain*, 149. Essentially these ideas can be found in, Lewis, *Miracles*, 1st edition, 106–7.

up "gods," therefore the incarnation-cross-resurrection narrative is just yet another mythological fiction. Ancient peoples, espousing tribal religions all over the world, would so value a shaman, a prophet or religious leader that they gave that person the status of "god," therefore critics would argue that Jesus was likewise given humanely conferred divine status by the disciples and his followers. Bible scholars note that there was an ancient Greek tradition where unusual events in the heavens—stars, comets, eclipses, etc.—heralded or welcomed a new king, leader, or someone important to the world, therefore the story of the star followed by the three magi in the nativity narrative is a fiction, it is a repetition of this Greek tradition. Stories of Jewish oppression and suffering abound, therefore, critics (for example, the Nazi Holocaust denier David Irving) claim that the story of the holocaust is false because it is a repetition of previous pogroms and anti-Semitic persecutions. However, these criticisms all issue from the hermeneutic of suspicion we encountered earlier. However, if we apply this hermeneutic of suspicion to the skeptics, their arguments begin to fall apart and sound hollow. The truth is that because of the incarnation-cross-resurrection, because of the ontological nature of Jesus as Son of God, because of the Star of Bethlehem, because of the Holocaust, these unique events did happen. Because of the Star of Bethlehem[47] we would expect there to be astrological stories predating the actual Star of Bethlehem, much in the same way that Lewis argued that because of the actual Christ-event we should expect to find echoes and intimations outside of the actual event. If God is and if the Christ-event is the one true event of cosmological importance then we should expect there to be ramifications, seeds, spread throughout human religion and culture. Ancient tribal religion conferred divine status on shamans and prophets because of what was to happen in the incarnation; they were *given* stories of dying and resuscitated "gods" precisely because of the resurrection of Jesus Christ. The Christ-event echoes out from a moment in history to affect all humanity, *in potential*. All stories and myths, whether religious or otherwise, are to be seen teleologically in relation to the Christ-event. That is, they relate to the Christ-event, they promote it—as far as is possible within the confines of the geographic and cognitive limitation of humanity's ability to "know"—they develop out from it and on from it. Reinterpreting what Plato wrote about the suffering person, marginalized and dismissed, who was a completely just person, in the light of the Christ-event is entirely admissible, likewise the ramifications of Balder's death and failed resuscitation is meant to reverberate with the true story of Jesus's death and resurrection when the two are seen together. This is so given the cosmic implications of the incarnation-cross-resurrection for all of humanity, and the action of the Holy Spirit that operates outside and inside of time. All stories and myths, whether religious or otherwise, are characterized by movement—a form of teleology

---

47. Scientists today can track the movements of the planets within the solar system. This predicability means that the position of the planets can be plotted back for thousands of years with accuracy. Approximately every 3000 years there is a conjuction of Jupiter, Saturn and Venus. About the time of the birth of Jesus this conjuction happened, and created a very bright star, which would have been seen at its clearest from Palestine.

11. Christ as the Light of the World III: Refractions—Splintered Fragments of the True Light

that drives them towards the Christ-event; clarity and precision in relation to the incarnation-cross-resurrection is relative, but the movement is concrete.

8. A DOCTRINE OF CHRISTOLOGICAL PREFIGUREMENT—CONCLUSION

The stumbling block that Tolkien and Dyson uncovered on the evening of the momentous conversation in Magdalen grounds in the autumn of 1931 was that Lewis could not believe Christianity if he were forced to dismiss all other religions as wrong, and only the religion he had been raised in was to be the right one.

> But if my religion is true, then these stories may well be a *preparatio evangelica*, a divine hinting in poetic and ritual form at the same central truth which was later focused and (so to speak) historicized in the incarnation . . . On the contrary, I could not believe Christianity if I were forced to say that there were a thousand religions in the world of which nine-hundred and ninety-nine were pure nonsense and the thousandth (fortunately) true. My conversion, very largely, depended on recognizing Christianity as the completion, the actualization, the entelechy, of something that had never been wholly absent from the mind of man.[48]

This was, in part, because, as Lewis admits, he had "loved Balder before Christ and Plato, before St Augustine."[49] Therefore Lewis's initial justification for these prefiguring myths was in reaction to Frazer's work; this was because of the importance and value he had given to these pagan myths but also to Frazer's agenda and conclusions as a young atheist and apostate. With his conversion he believed he could not just dismiss the evidence, and could no longer accept the anthropologist's reductionist dismissal of these prefigurements. As we have seen, however, Lewis's Christology soon developed a justification and role for these myths beyond the context of Frazer's work. What does this tell us about God's salvific actions towards humanity? Lewis is setting out as a principle of salvation that whether we are religious or not our salvation lies not in *our* actions-beliefs, but in what *the Lord* has done for us. The most we can do is acknowledge, repent, and allow the Lord's Spirit to change us, reconcile and redeem us. In the case of those who have consciously heard the Gospel narrative, the very story of the incarnation, passion, and resurrection should operate on us in a perlocutionary way: awareness of the narrative is important because of the event it represents. It is because of the importance of the incarnation-resurrection narrative that the prefiguring myths should be seen as having a relative value and significance. What of these prefiguring myths? In the case of the pagans and heathens outside of the Judaeo-Christian revelation this was operating on a subliminal level. Such myths point towards something of the reality of the incarnation-resurrection, and may likewise operate in a perlocutionary manner on a subliminal level. However important these mythopoeic echoes, intimations, and refractions appear to be, emanating as they do from the true

---

48. Lewis, "Religion Without Dogma?," 99–114, quotation 102.
49. Ibid., 102.

light, illumined in the minds, the imagination of humanity, their function is to point towards the real event: Jesus Christ, the second person of the Trinity crucified and resurrected for our salvation. If you have access to knowledge of the real story, the real event, then why bother with myths? If because of cultural, geographic, or temporal isolation these intimations come to people who can never know the true story, then the myths have a perlocutionary effect on cultures and societies generally, individuals specifically (subject to the degree of reception or rejection, which is governed by our fallen state) in accordance with the will of the Father, and may or may not work towards God's loving purposes which are the potential salvation and transformation of all humankind.

Conclusion
The Work of Christ—Revealed

Despite the sheer volume of theological and philosophical works, Lewis did not devote the time to a systematic exposition of the faith that would have been necessary for a detailed and coherent doctrinal account. This is of no fault of Lewis's; we have his writings and they do hang together, so to speak; they are coherent, despite minor flaws and inconsistencies (blemishes and imperfections we can find in the work of any theologian). What we have examined here is three relatively distinct doctrines of Lewis's, which he wrote on, proposed, and professed consistently in his middle and mature works: a doctrine of Scripture and revelation; a doctrine of the ontological nature of Jesus of Nazareth, the Christ; and a doctrine of christological prefigurement.

The key, as we have seen, was in Lewis's Platonism: that is, the action within the economic Trinity of God's dealings with humanity. In some ways Lewis's Platonism explains, to a degree, how the Holy Spirit operates in the dialogue between eternity and earth. An intentionally "flawed" doctrine of transposition, itself platonically transposed, is formulated to explain how revelation works, how revelation is communicated, or, more pertinently, how revelation is never fully imparted, revelation is modalistic, but it also extrapolates how Lewis's mind was illuminated and inspired to write theology. Revelation is, and will continue to be, communicated in diminuted, translated, transposed modes. Reason is at the heart of this doctrine for Lewis, but he knows the limits: reason is not simply an abstract faculty presiding over an indeterminate field, analyzing at its will, for we are not God, and our kingdom of reason is not God. At the heart of revelation is Christ, the Word of God, who comes to us often in the form of Scripture as the word of God. If there is a criticism of Lewis's doctrine of Scripture it is that it is perhaps weak on the authority and the givenness of Scripture: it is important to state that it is Christ that is the fullest self-revelation of God, but the Bible holds a unique and elevated place in the church as revelation, which we marginalize at our peril. The balance that Lewis maintained between the freedom of God to inspire yet allow creation to be, while intimating to humanity the truths of eternity, built on and from the mediation of Christ, makes sense of his understanding of Scripture, revelation, and reason. What value is there to Lewis's doctrine of Scripture and revelation? Transposition is the key, because only in eternity will we know as we are known. Lewis's understanding of Scripture was intrinsically tied in with God's revealedness, but how the Word of God was essentially the Christ-event, witnessed to then by Scripture as the word of God.

Lewis is relatively unique in the mid-twentieth century in asking the question, who was Jesus if he was not God incarnate? Although there is a strong theological tradition of *aut Deus aut malus homo*, most of this has been forgotten and it is important to remember, as Gerald O'Collins demonstrated, that Jesus's question to Peter—"But who do you say that I am" (Matt 16:15)—generated a trilemma in John's Gospel. Lewis was thus justified in developing *aut Deus aut malus homo* into a trilemma. Essentially this is about knowing—knowing who and what Jesus is. According to John's Gospel, the reaction of the Jewish religious authorities in Jerusalem and throughout Judea and Galilee was such that they had decided, on the evidence of what they knew from inference and observation, that because of what Jesus said and did, and the manner in which he related to those around him, then this man was either one of three things: either Jesus is a liar, or he is unbalanced and has a demon, or else he is truly the divine light of the world (John 10:31–39, also, 8:49 and 10:21). Though, as Lewis pertinently demonstrates, it is not, in the end, what we make of Jesus Christ that really counts, but rather what *he* is to make of us. The relevant issue is, therefore, the action of the resurrected and ascended Christ towards humanity. For all its perceived faults Lewis's trilemma is still a successful piece of Christian apologetic.

Lewis's deep admiration for pagan myths led him to an understanding of the movement of Christ towards humanity outside of the church that predated the incarnation and continues to this day: this is the pneumatological actions of the economic Trinity, that is, how the Holy Spirit attempts to draw people into preparatory knowledge and understanding for what God does for humanity in the Christ-event. Again, most respectable theologians—both orthodox and liberal—have eschewed any reference to these prefigurements. What do these prefigurements tell us about God's salvific actions towards humanity, the intention to bring about redemption *in potential* for all? Lewis is setting out as a principle of salvation that whether we are Christian or not our salvation lies not in our actions-beliefs but in what the Lord has done for us. In the case of those who have consciously heard the gospel narrative, the very story of the incarnation-cross-resurrection should operate on us in a perlocutionary manner. It is because of the importance of the incarnation-resurrection narrative that the prefiguring myths should be seen as having a relative value and significance.

In the next book in this series we will look in relative depth at Lewis's doctrine of creation and the fall, which though formulated very much in an Augustinian mode, is fundamental to his theology, his philosophy, and his literary works (for example, the Space Trilogy, or, *A Preface to Paradise Lost*). Creation and science lead us to naturalism and the Anscombe-Lewis debate. What was Lewis's philosophical training and development, and how does it affect his doctrine of revelation and reason. Philosophically Lewis is characterized, to a degree, by the all-pervasive influence on his theological development of Platonism, which comes together in the Anscombe-Lewis debate of 1948, which illustrates the methodological development of his mature work. We can then look at Lewis's use of narrative, how this is a precursor in some ways of what may be termed postmodern narrative theology: what do Lewis's word pictures (Narnia, *et al.*) of Christ tell us about his doctrine and understanding of Christ? Finally, we will examine in depth Lewis's understanding of salvation and atonement, heaven and hell, and of the church as the body of Christ, returning to his own personal encounter, late in life, with the Christ.

Select Bibliography

LETTERS AND ARTICLES BY C. S. LEWIS

Lewis, C. S. "Christian Apologetics." Paper read at the Carmarthen Conference for Youth Leaders and Junior Priests, Church of Wales, at Carmarthen, Easter 1945. In *Undeceptions—Essays on Theology and Ethics*, 64–76. London: Bles, 1971.

———. "Cross-Examination." In *Undeceptions—Essays on Theology and Ethics*, 215–21. London: Bles, 1971.

———. "De Descriptione Temporum." In *They Asked for a Paper—Papers and Addresses*, 9–25. London: Bles, 1962.

———. "Difficulties in Presenting the Christian Faith to Modern Unbelievers." *Lumen Vitae II* (September 1948) 421–26.

———. "The Funeral of a Great Myth." In *Christian Reflections*, 82–93. London: Bles, 1967.

———. "God in the Dock." In *Undeceptions—Essays on Theology and Ethics*, 197–201 London: Bles, 1971

———. "The Grand Miracle." A sermon preached in St Jude on the Hill Church, London, April 1945. In *Undeceptions—Essays on Theology and Ethics*, 56–63. London: Bles, 1971.

———. "Introduction. New Learning and New Ignorance." In *English Literature in the Sixteenth Century* 2–65. Oxford: Clarendon, 1954.

———. "Introduction." In J. B. Phillips, *Letters to Young Churches—A Translation of the New Testament Epistles*, vii–x. London: Bles, 1947.

———. "Introduction." In George McDonald, *Phantastes*, v–x. Grand Rapids: Eerdmans, 2000.

———. "Is Theism Important?" In *Undeceptions—Essays on Theology and Ethics*, 138–42. London: Bles, 1971.

———. "Is Theology Poetry." In *They Asked for a Paper—Papers and Addresses*, 150–65. London: Bles, 1962.

———. "The Language of Religion." In *Christian Reflections*, 129–41. London: Fount, 1967.

———. "Letter to Arthur Greeves, Aug. 4, 1917." In *Collected Letters, Vol. I—Family Letters 1905-1931*, edited by Walter Hooper, 333. San Francisco, CA: Harper San Francisco, 2004.

———. "Letter to Arthur Greeves, Feb. 28, 1916." In *Collected Letters, Vol. I—Family Letters 1905-1931*, edited by Walter Hooper, 167. San Francisco, CA: Harper San Francisco, 2004.

———. "Letter to Arthur Greeves, Jan. 30, 1944." In *Collected Letters, Vol. III—Narnia, Cambridge and Joy 1950-1963*, edited by Walter Hooper, 1547–48. San Francisco, CA: Harper San Francisco, 2007.

———. "Letter to Arthur Greeves, Oct. 1, 1931." In *Collected Letters, Vol. I—Family Letters 1905-1931*, edited by Walter Hooper, 972–75. San Francisco, CA: Harper San Francisco, 2004.

———. "Letter to Arthur Greeves, Oct. 12, 1916." In *Collected Letters, Vol. I—Family Letters 1905-1931*, edited by Walter Hooper, 230–33. San Francisco, CA: Harper San Francisco, 2004.

———. "Letter to Arthur Greeves, Oct. 18, 1931." In *Collected Letters, Vol. I—Family Letters 1905-1931*, edited by Walter Hooper, 975–77. San Francisco, CA: Harper San Francisco, 2004.

———. "Letter to Arthur Greeves, Sept. 22 1931." In *Collected Letters, Vol. I—Family Letters 1905-1931*, edited by Walter Hooper, 970. San Francisco, CA: Harper San Francisco, 2004.

———. "Letter to Clyde S. Kilby, Feb. 10, 1957." In *Collected Letters, Vol. III—Narnia, Cambridge and Joy 1950-1963*, edited by Walter Hooper, 830–31. San Francisco, CA: Harper San Francisco, 2007.

———. "Letter to Clyde S. Kilby, May 7, 1959." In *Collected Letters, Vol. III—Narnia, Cambridge and Joy 1950-1963*, 1044–46. San Francisco, CA: Harper San Francisco, 2007.

———. "Letter to Dom Bede Griffiths, May 28 1952." In *Collected Letters, Vol. III—Narnia, Cambridge and Joy 1950-1963*, edited by Walter Hooper, 195. San Francisco, CA: Harper San Francisco, 2007.

———. "Letter to Emily McLay Aug. 3 1953." In *Collected Letters, Vol. III—Narnia, Cambridge and Joy 1950-1963*, 354–55. San Francisco, CA: Harper San Francisco, 2007.

———. "Letter to Emily McLay, Aug. 8 1953." In *Collected Letters, Vol. III—Narnia, Cambridge and Joy 1950-1963*, edited by Walter Hooper, 356–57. San Francisco, CA: Harper San Francisco, 2007.

———. "Letter to Genia Goelz, Jun. 20, 1952." In *Collected Letters, Vol. III—Narnia, Cambridge and Joy 1950-1963*, edited by Walter Hooper, 204–5. San Francisco, CA: Harper San Francisco, 2007.

———. "Letter to Genia Goelz, Mar. 18, 1952." In *Collected Letters, Vol. III—Narnia, Cambridge and Joy 1950-1963*, edited by Walter Hooper, 172. San Francisco, CA: Harper San Francisco, 2007.

———. "Letter to Janet Wise, Oct. 5, 1955." In *Collected Letters, Vol. III—Narnia, Cambridge and Joy 1950-1963*, edited by Walter Hooper, 652–53. San Francisco, CA: Harper San Francisco, 2007.

———. "Letter to Lee Turner Jul. 19, 1958." In *Collected Letters, Vol. III—Narnia, Cambridge and Joy 1950-1963*, edited by Walter Hooper, 960. San Francisco, CA: Harper San Francisco, 2007.

———. "Letter to Mr Allcock, Mar. 24, 1955." In *Collected Letters, Vol. III—Narnia, Cambridge and Joy 1950-1963*, edited by Walter Hooper, 587–89. San Francisco, CA: Harper San Francisco, 2007.

———. "Letter to Mrs Green, Jun. 18, 1962." In *Collected Letters, Vol. III—Narnia, Cambridge and Joy 1950-1963*, edited by Walter Hooper, 1353. San Francisco, CA: Harper San Francisco, 2007.

———. "Letter to Mrs Johnson, Nov. 8, 1952." In *Collected Letters, Vol. III—Narnia, Cambridge and Joy 1950-1963*, edited by Walter Hooper, 245–48. San Francisco, CA: Harper San Francisco, 2007.

———. "Letter to the editor of The Spectator, Dec. 11, 1942." In *Collected Letters, Vol. II—Books, Broadcasts and War 1931-1949*, edited by Walter Hooper, 540. San Francisco, CA: Harper San Francisco, 2004.

———. "Letter to Mrs Mary Neylan, Mar. 26, 1940." In *Collected Letters, Vol. II—Books, Broadcasts and War 1931-1949*, 371–76. San Francisco, CA: Harper San Francisco, 2004.

———. "Letter to Vera Gebbert, Oct. 16, 1960." In *Collected Letters, Vol. III—Narnia, Cambridge and Joy 1950-1963*, edited by Walter Hooper, 1198. San Francisco, CA: Harper San Francisco, 2007.

———. "Lewis to Owen Barfield, Aug. 1939." In *Collected Letters, Vol. II—Books, Broadcasts and War 1931-1949*, edited by Walter Hooper, 266–69. San Francisco, CA: Harper San Francisco, 2004.

———. "Man or Rabbit." In *Undeceptions—Essays on Theology and Ethics*, 82–84. London: Bles, 1971.

———. "Miracles." St Jude's Gazette, 73 (October 1942) 4–7.

———. "Modern Theology and Biblical Criticism." Paper delivered at Westcott House, Cambridge, 11 May 1959. In *Christian Reflections*, 152–66. London: Bles, 1967.

———. "Myth Became Fact." In *Undeceptions—Essays on Theology and Ethics*, 39–43. London: Bles, 1971.

———. "Myth Became Fact." World Dominion, XXII (Sept–Oct 1944) 267–70.

———. "On Stories." In *Essays Presented to Charles Williams*, 90–105. Oxford: Oxford University Press, 1947.

———. "Preface." In *George MacDonald: An Anthology*, edited by C. S. Lewis, xxi–xxxiv. London: Bless, 1946.

———. "Psycho-Analysis and Literary Criticism." In *They Asked for a Paper—Papers and Addresses*, 120–38. London: Bles, 1962.

———. "Rejoinder to Dr Pittenger." In *Christian Century* LXXV (26 November 1958) 1369–71.

———. "Religion Without Dogma?" In *Undeceptions—Essays on Theology and Ethics*, 99–114. London: Bles, 1971.

———. "Transposition." 1st ed. A sermon given in Mansfield College, Oxford on Whit Sunday, 28 May 1944. In *Transposition and Other Addresses*, 9–20. London: Bless, 1949.

———. "Transposition." 2nd ed. In *They Asked for a Paper—Papers and Addresses*, 166–82. London: Bles, 1962.

———. "The Weight of Glory." In *Transposition and Other Addresses*, 21–33. London: Bles, 1949.

———. "What Are We to Make of Jesus Christ?" In *Asking Them Questions* (third series) edited by Ronald Selby Wright, 49–53. Oxford: Oxford University Press, 1950.

———. "The World's Last Night." In *The World's Last Night and Other Essays*, 93–113. New York, NY: Harcourt, Brace and World, 1960.

BOOKS BY C. S. LEWIS

Lewis, C. S. *Beyond Personality: The Christian Idea of God*. London: Centenary, 1944.

———. *Broadcast Talks. Reprinted with Some Alterations from Two Series of Broadcast Talks "Right and Wrong: A Clue to the Meaning of the Universe" and "What Christians Believe" Given in 1941 and 1942*. London: Centenary, 1942.

———. *Christian Behaviour*. London: Centenary, 1943.

———. *Collected Letters, Vol. I—Family Letters 1905–1931*. Edited by Walter Hooper. San Francisco, CA: Harper San Francisco, 2004.

———. *Collected Letters, Vol. II—Books, Broadcasts and War 1931–1949*. Edited by Walter Hooper. San Francisco, CA: Harper San Francisco, 2004.

———. *Collected Letters, Vol. III—Narnia, Cambridge and Joy 1950–1963*. Edited by Walter Hooper. San Francisco, CA: Harper San Francisco, 2007.

———. *An Experiment in Criticism*. Cambridge: Cambridge University Press, 1961.

———. *Mere Christianity—A Revised and Amplified Edition, with a New Introduction, of the Three Books Broadcast Talks, Christian Behaviour and Beyond Personality*. London: Bles, 1952.

———. *Miracles—A Preliminary Study*. 1st ed. London: Bless, 1947.

———. *Miracles*. 2nd ed. London: Bless, 1960.

———. *Reflections on the Psalms*. London: Bles, 1958.

———. *Studies in Mediaeval and Renaissance Literature*. London: Cambridge University Press, 1966.

———. *Surprised by Joy—The Shape of My Early Life*. London: Bles, 1955.

———. *The Chronicles of Narnia—The Last Battle*. London: Bles, 1956.

———. *The Chronicles of Narnia—The Lion, the Witch and the Wardrobe*. London: Bles, 1950.

———. *The Chronicles of Narnia—The Silver Chair*. London: Bles, 1953.

———. *The Chronicles of Narnia—The Voyage of the Dawn Treader*. London: Bless, 1952.

———. *The Discarded Image*. Cambridge: Cambridge University Press, 1964.

———. *The Four Loves*. London: Bles, 1960.

———. *The Great Divorce—A Dream*. London: Macmillan, 1945.

———. *The Pilgrim's Regress—An Allegorical Apology for Christianity, Reason and Romanticism*. 3rd ed. London: Bless, 1944. Note in some American reprints this "Preface" is placed at the end of the book and called an "Afterword."

———. *The Problem of Pain*. London: Centenary, 1940.

———. *The Screwtape Letters*. London: Centenary, 1942.

———. *They Stand Together—The Letters of C. S. Lewis to Arthur Greeves 1914–1963*. Edited by Walter Hooper. New York: Macmillan, 1979.

———. *Undeceptions—Essays on Theology and Ethics*. Edited by Walter Hooper. London: Bles, 1971. (Published in the USA as, *God in the Dock—Essays on Theology and Ethics*. Grand Rapids: Eerdmans, 1970.)

OTHER BOOKS AND ARTICLES

Adams, Edward. *Parallel Lives of Jesus: A Narrative-Critical Guide to the Four Gospels*. London: SPCK, 2011.

Appleyard, Bryan. "The True Face of Art." *The Sunday Times* (London), Feb. 13, 2000, 12.

Aquinas, Thomas. *Summa contra Gentiles*. Translated by Anton C. Pegis. 5 vols. Notre Dame, IN: University of Notre Dame Press, 1975.

———. *Summa Theologiae*. 61 volumes. Cambridge: Cambridge University Press, 2006.

Athanasius. *The Incarnation of the Word: Being the Treatise of St Athanasius, De incarnatione Verbi Dei* Translated Sr Penelope CSMV. London: Centenary, 1944.

Augustine of Hippo. *Against the Academicians and the Teacher*. Translated by P. King. Indianapolis, IN: Hackett, 1995.

———. *Confessions*. Translated by Henry Chadwick. Oxford World's Classics. Oxford: Oxford University Press, 1991.

———. "Letter no 102 to Deogratius, 409." In *The Confessions and Letters of Saint Augustine, in, The Nicene and Post-Nicene Fathers*, Vol. 1(first series). Translated by Revd. J. G. Cunningham, 820. 1886. Reprint. Grand Rapids: Eerdmans, 1979.

———. *On Free Choice of the Will*. Translated and edited by Thomas Williams. Indianapolis, IN: Hackett, 1993.

———. "Sermon No. 185 (Homily 3)." In *Ancient Christian Writers 15. St. Augustine: Sermons for Christmas and Epiphany*, edited by Thomas Comerford, 76–79. Mahwah, NJ: Paulist, 1978.

Ball, D. M. *"I Am" in John's Gospel—Literary Function, Background and Theological Implications*. Sheffield, UK: Sheffield Academic Press, 1996.

Balthazar, Hans Urs von. *Explorations in Theology: The Word Made Flesh*. San Francisco, CA: Ignatius, 1989.

Barfield, Owen, *Poetic Diction—A Study in Meaning*. Middleton, CT: Wesleyan University Press, 1973.

———. *What Coleridge Thought*. London: Oxford University Press, 1972.

Barth, Karl. *The Church Dogmatics*. 14 Vols. Translated and edited G. W. Bromiley and T. F. Torrance. Edinburgh: T. & T. Clark, 1936–77.

———. *Dogmatics in Outline*. Reprint. London: Xpress, 1996.

———. "Kriegszeit und Gottesreich." In *Glaube und kommunikative Praxis*, edited by Herbert Anzinger, 120–22. München: Kaiser, 1991.

———. *Der Römerbrief. Zweite Fassung*, 1922. Zürich: Theologischer Verlag Zürich, 1999.

Bauckham, Richard. *Jesus and the Eyewitnesses: The Gospels as Eyewitness Testimony*. Grand Rapids: Eerdmans, 2006.

Beversluis, John. *C. S. Lewis and the Search for Rational Religion*. Grand Rapids: Eerdmans, 1985.

Biederwolf, W. E. "Yes, He Arose." In *Great Preaching on the Resurrection: Seventeen Messages*, edited by Curtis Hutson, 21–32. Murfreesboro, TN: Sword of the Lord, 1984.

Black, Max. *Models and Metaphors: Studies in Language and Philosophy*. Ithaca, NY: Cornell University Press, 1962.

Blomberg, Craig L. *The Historical Reliability of the Gospels*. Leicester, UK: InterVarsity, 1987.

Brazier, P. H. "Barth and Rome: a Critical Engagement." *The Downside Review* 12.431 (2005) 137–52.

———. "Barth and Rome—II: Socialism, the Church and a Theocratic Illusion." *The Downside Review* 124.434, (2006) 61–78.

———. "C. S. Lewis and Christological Prefigurement." *The Heythrop Journal* 48.5 (2007) 742–75.

———. "C. S. Lewis and the Anscombe Debate: from *analogia entis* to *analogia fidei*." *The Journal of Inklings Studies* 1.2 (2011) 69–123

———. "C. S. Lewis on Revelation & Second Meanings: A Philosophical & Pneumatological Justification." *The Chronicle of the Oxford University C. S. Lewis Society* 7.1 (2010) 18–35.

———. "C. S. Lewis on Scripture and the Christ, the Word of God: Convergence and Divergence with Karl Barth." *Sehnsucht* 4 (2010) 89–109.

———. "C. S. Lewis: A Doctrine of Transposition." *The Heythrop Journal* 50.4 (2009) 669–88.

———. "The Pittenger–Lewis Debate: Fundamentals of an Ontological Christology." *The Chronicle of the Oxford University C. S. Lewis Society*, 6.1 (2009) 7–23.

———. "Why Father Christmas Appears in Narnia." *Sehnsucht* 3 (2009) 61–77.

Brown, Raymond E. *The Gospel according to John*. 2 vols. London: Chapman, 1971.

Bruce, F. F. "Marius Victorinus and His Works." *Evangelical Quarterly* 18 (1946) 132–53.

Bultmann, Rudolf. *Das Evangelium des Johannes*. Göttingen: Vandenhoeck & Ruprecht, 1941.

———. *Existence and Faith: Shorter Writings of Rudolf Bultmann*. San Francisco, CA: Collins, 1987.

———. *History of the Synoptic Tradition*. Translated by J. Marsh. Oxford: Blackwell, 1972.

———. *Jesus Christ and Mythology*. Edinburgh: T. & T. Clark, 1980.

———. *The New Testament and Mythology and Other Basic Writings*. Minneapolis, MN: Augsburg Fortress, 1990.

———. *Theology of the New Testament Vol. 1*. Translated by Kendrick Grobel. London: SCM, 1952.

Burridge, Richard. *Four Gospels, One Jesus?* London: SPCK, 1994.

Calvin, John. *Institutes of the Christian Religion*. Edited by John T. McNeill. Library of Christian Classics. Louisville, KY: Westminster John Knox, 2006.

Campbell, Joseph. "Mythological Themes in Creative Literature and Art." In *Myths, Dreams and Religion*, edited by Joseph Campbell, 138–75. New York : Dutton, 1970.
———. *The Hero with a Thousand Faces*. Princeton: Princeton University Press, 1968.
Carpenter, Humphrey. *The Inklings: C. S. Lewis, J. R. R Tolkien, Charles Williams and Their Friends*. London: Harper Collins, 1978.
———. *J. R. R. Tolkien: A Biography*. London: Allen & Unwin, 1977.
Chesterton, G. K. *The Everlasting Man*. London: Hodder & Stoughton, 1925.
Christensen, Michael J. *C. S. Lewis on Scripture*. London: Hodder & Stoughton, 1980.
Clerk, N. W. *A Grief Observed*. London: Faber and Faber, 1961.
Coleridge, Samuel Taylor. *Biographia Literaria, or, Biographical Sketches of my Literary Life and Opinions*. Edited with an introduction by George Watson. Everyman's library 11. London: Dent, 1997.
Collinwood, R. G. *The Idea of History*. London: Clarendon, 1946.
Como, James T. *Remembering C. S. Lewis*. San Francisco, CA: Ignatius, 2005.
Craig, William Lane. *Reasonable Faith: Christian Truth and Apologetics*. Wheaton, IL: Crossway, 1994.
D'Costa, Gavin. *Christian Uniqueness Reconsidered: The Myth of a Pluralistic Theology of Religions* Maryknoll, NY: Orbis, 1990.
———. *Christianity and World Religion: Disputed Questions in the Theology of Religions*. Chichester, UK Wiley-Blackwell, 2009.
———. "The Impossibility of a Pluralist View of Religion." *Religious Studies* 32 (1996) 223–32.
Davies, Brian. *The Thought of Thomas Aquinas*. Oxford: Clarendon, 1992.
Davis, Stephen T. *Faith, Scepticism, and Evidence*. Lewisburg, PA: Bucknell University Press, 1978.
———. *Logic and the Nature of God*. Grand Rapids: Eerdmans, 1983.
———. *Risen Indeed: Making Sense of the Resurrection*. Grand Rapids: Eerdmans, 1993.
———. "Was Jesus Mad, Bad or God?" 1st ed. In *The Incarnation. An Interdisciplinary Symposium on the Incarnation of the Son of God*, edited by Stephen T. Davis et al., 221–45. Oxford: Oxford University Press, 2002.
———. "Was Jesus Mad, Bad or God?" 2nd ed. In *Christian Philosophical Theology*, 149–71. Oxford: Oxford University Press, 2006.
Dawkins, Richard. *The God Delusion*. London: Transworld, 2006.
de Torre, Joseph M. *The Divinity of Jesus Christ*. Manila: Sinag-Tala, 1984.
Dearborn, Kerry. *Baptized Imagination: The Theology of George MacDonald*. Ashgate Studies in Theology, Imagination, and the Arts. Aldershot UK: Ashgate, 2006.
Dostoevsky, Fyodor Mikhailovich. *Demons*. Translated by Richard Pevear and Larissa Volokhonsky. London: Everyman's Library, 1994.
———. *The Diary of a Writer, Vol. I, February 1876*. Translated and annotated by Boris Brasol. New York: Scribner's & Sons, 1949.
———. *The Notebooks for Crime and Punishment*. Translated by Edward Wasiolek. Chicago: University of Chicago Press, 1967.
Downing, David C. "Sub-Creation or Smuggled Theology: Tolkien contra Lewis on Christian Fantasy." *The C. S. Lewis Institute*. Online: http://www.cslewisinstitute.org/node/1207.
Drumond, James. *An Inquiry into the Character and Authorship of the Fourth Gospel*. London: Williams and Norgate, 1903.
Duncan, John, and William Angus Knight. *Colloquia Peripatetica: Being Notes of Conversations 1870*. Whitefish: MT, Kessinger, 2008.
Eck, Herbert Vincent Shortgrave. *The Incarnation*. London: Longmans, Green, 1901.
Edwards, David L., *The Honest to God Debate: Some Reactions to the Book "Honest to God" with a New Chapter by its Author, J. A. T Robinson, Bishop of Woolwich*. London: SCM, 1963.
Ellis Sandoz. *Political Apocalypse: A Study of Dostoevsky's Grand Inquisitor*. Baton Rouge, LA: Louisiana State University Press, 1971.
Ellis, Henry Havelock. *Impressions and Comments*. Three series. London: Constable, 1926–30.
Evans, C. Stephen. *The Historical Christ and the Jesus of Faith: The Incarnational Narrative as History*. Oxford: Oxford University Press, 1996.
———. "The Incarnational Narrative as Myth and History." *Christian Scholar's Review* 23 (1994) 387–407.

———. "Mis-Using Religious Language: Something about Kierkegaard and the Myth of God Incarnate." *Religious Studies* 15 (1979) 139–57.
Fabrizio, Lisa. "History's Greatest Liar." *The American Spectator*, June 13, 2007. Online: http://spectator.org/archives/2007/06/13/historys-greatest-liar.
Feuerbach, Ludwig. *The Essence of Christianity*. Amherst, NY: Prometheus, 1989.
———. *Das Wesen des Christentums* (1841). Edited by W. Schuffenhauer, Gesammelte Werke, Vol. 5. Berlin: Akademie, 1973.
Frazer, Sir James George, *The Golden Bough*. Abridged edition. London: Macmillan, 1922.
———. *The Golden Bough: A Study in Magic and Religion*. 12 volumes, 3rd ed. London: Macmillan, 1911–15.
Fuller, Reginald H., and Pheme Perkins. *Who Is This Christ? Gospel Christology and Contemporary Faith*. Philadelphia, PA: Fortress, 1983.
Gier, Nicholas F. *God, Reason, and the Evangelicals: The Case against Evangelical Rationalism*. Lanham, MD: University Press of America, 1987.
Gore, Charles. *Dissertations on Subjects Connected with the Incarnation*. 1895. Reprint. Whitefish: MT: Kessinger, 2008.
———. *The Incarnation of the Son of God: Being the Bampton Lectures for the Year 1891*. 1891. Reprint. Whitefish: MT: Kessinger, 2006.
Green, Joel B., Scot McKnight, and I. Howard Marshall, eds. *Dictionary of Jesus and the Gospels: A Compendium of Contemporary Biblical Scholarship*. Downers Grove IL: InterVarsity, 1992.
Griffen, Henry William, ed. *Augustine of Hippo Sermons to the People: Advent, Christmas, New Year, Epiphany*. New York: Doubleday, 2002.
Guizot, M. Francoise. *Meditations on the Actual State of Christianity and on the Attacks which are Now Being Made Upon It*. New York: Scribner, 1866.
Gunton, Colin E. *The Barth Lectures*. Transcribed and edited P. H. Brazier. London: T. & T. Clark, 2007.
———. *Revelation and Reason: Prolegomena to Systematic Theology*. Transcribed and edited by P. H. Brazier. London: T. & T. Clark, 2008.
Hamakawa, Yoshihiro. "New Energy Option for 21st Century: Recent Progress in Solar Photovoltaic Energy Conversion." *Japan Society of Applied Physics International* 5 (2002) 30–35.
Hanson, R. P. C. *The Search for the Christian Doctrine of God: The Arian Controversies 318–381AD*. London: T. & T. Clark, 2006.
Harries, Richard, *C. S. Lewis: The Man and his God*. London: Fount, 1987.
Hick, John. *The Metaphor of God Incarnate*. London: SCM, 1993.
———. "Preface." In *The Myth of God Incarnate*, edited by John Hick. London: SCM, 1977.
Hooper, Walter. *C. S. Lewis: A Companion and Guide*. London: Harper & Collins, 1996.
Hopkins, Mark. *Lectures on the Evidences of Christianity, before the Lowell Institute, January, 1844*. Boston: Marvin, 1856.
Huttar, Charles A., and Peter J. Schakel. *Word and Story in C. S. Lewis*. Columbia, MO: University of Missouri Press 1991.
Kant, Immanuel. *Grounding for the Metaphysics of Morals*. Translated by James W. Ellington. 3rd ed. Indianapolis, IN: Hackett, 1993.
Keith Ward. *God, Faith, and The New Millennium: Christian Belief in an Age Of Science*. Oxford: Oneworld, 1998.
Kelsey, David H. *The Use of Scripture in Recent Theology*. London: SCM, 1975.
Kierkegaard, Søren. *Philosophical Fragments*. Translated by Howard V. and Edna H. Hong. Princeton: Princeton University Press, 1985.
Kilby, Clyde S. *The Christian World of C. S. Lewis*. Grand Rapids: Eerdmans, 1964.
Kreeft, Peter, and Ronald Tacelli. *Handbook of Christian Apologetics*. Downers Grove, IL: InterVarsity, 1994.
Kreeft, Peter. *Between Heaven and Hell: A Dialog Somewhere Beyond Death with John F. Kennedy, C. S. Lewis, and Aldous Huxley*. 2nd ed. Downers Grove, IL: InterVarsity, 2008.
———. *Fundamentals of the Faith: Essays in Christian Apologetics*. San Francisco, CA: Ignatius, 1988.
Kroeker, P. Travis, and Bruce K. Ward. *Remembering the End: Dostoevsky as a Prophet of Modernity*. Oxford: Westview Press Radical Traditions, 2001.

Kroner, Richard. *The Religious Function of Imagination. The Bedell lectures delivered at Kenyon College.* New Haven, CT: Yale University Press, 1941.
Lessing, Gotthold Ephraim. *Theological Writings.* Translated with an introduction by Henry Chadwick. London: Black, 1956.
Lewes, George Henry. *Comte's Philosophy of the Sciences.* London: Bell, 1904.
Liddon, Henry Parry. *The Divinity of Our Lord and Saviour Jesus Christ: Eight Lectures Preached Before the University of Oxford in the Year 1866, on the Foundation of the Late Revd John Bampton.* London: Longmans, Green & Co, 1868.
Lock, Walter. "The Gospel according to St John." In *A New Commentary on Holy Scripture, including the Apocrypha,* edited by Charles Gore, Henry Leighton Goudge, and Alfred Guillame, 240–76. London: SPCK, 1928.
———. "History and Character of the Fourth Gospel." *Interpreter* (July, 1907) 442–50.
———. *The Raising of Lazarus: The Message of the Fourth Gospel for Mourners. A sermon delivered in St Paul's Cathedral, London, 6th June 1915.* London: SPCK, 1915.
Lüdemann, Gerd. "An Embarrassing Misrepresentation." *Free Inquiry* (Oct–Nov 2007) 63–64.
MacDonald, George. "The Fantastic Imagination." In *A Dish of Orts: Chiefly Papers on the Imagination, and on Shakespeare,* 203–8. London: Sampson, Low, Marston, 1867.
———. "The Imagination: Its Functions and its Culture." In *A Dish of Orts: Chiefly Papers on the Imagination, and on Shakespeare,* 1–28. London: Sampson, Low, Marston, 1867.
Macquarrie, John. *Christology Revisited.* Harrisburg, PA: Trinity Press, 1998.
———. *Jesus Christ in Modern Thought.* London: SCM, 1990.
Madigan SJ, Patrick. "Review of Bad, Mad or God? Proving the Divinity of Christ from John's Gospel by John Redford." *The Heythrop Journal* 47 (2006) 631–33.
McCabe, Herbert. *God Still Matters.* London: Continuum, 2002.
McDowell, Josh. *Evidence That Demands a Verdict.* San Bernardino, CA: Campus Crusade for Christ, 1972.
———. *A Ready Defence.* Nashville, TN: Nelson, 1990.
Meacham, Steve. "The Shed where God Died." *Sydney Morning Herald Online, Dec. 13, 2003,* Section: "Spectrum," 8. Online: http://www.smh.com.au/articles/2003/12/12/1071125644900.html.
More, Sir Thomas. *Dialogue of Comfort against Tribulation.* Edited and translated by Leland Miles. Bloomington, IN: Indiana University Press, 1965.
Neusner, Jacob. *Eternal Israel Endures. Vol. 4. Judaism Transcends Catastrophe: God, Torah, and Israel Beyond the Holocaust.* Macon, GA. Mercer University Press, 1996.
———. *A Rabbi Talks with Jesus.* 2nd ed. Ithaca, NY: McGill–Queen's University Press 2000.
O'Collins SJ, Gerald. *Incarnation.* New Century Theology. London: Continuum, 2002.
Ott, Ludwig. *Introduction to Fundamentals of Catholic Dogma.* St. Louis, MO: Herder, 1960.
Ottley, Robert L. *The Doctrine of the Incarnation, Vol. 1.* London: Methuen, 1896.
Pasnau, Robert. "Divine Illumination." In *The Stanford Encyclopedia of Philosophy.* Online: http://www.science.uva.nl/~seop/entries/illumination/.
Plato. "The Republic, Bk. II." In *Plato Complete Works,* edited by John M. Cooper, translated by M. J. Levett, revised by Myles Burnyeat, 1001–2. Indianapolis, IN: Hackett, 1997.
———. "Theaetetus." In *Plato Complete Works,* edited by John M. Cooper, translated by M. J. Levett, revised by Myles Burnyeat, 157–234. Indianapolis, IN: Hackett, 1997.
Pope Innocent III. *De miseria humane conditionis: On the Misery of the Human Condition.* Edited by Donald R. Howard, translated by Margaret Mary Dietz. The Library of Liberal Arts 132. Indianapolis, IN: Bobbs-Merrill, 1969.
Ratzinger, Joseph (Pope Benedict XVI). *Introduction to Christianity.* 2nd ed. San Francisco, CA: Ignatius, 2000.
———. *Jesus of Nazareth.* San Francisco, CA: Ignatius, 2007.
Rayment-Pickard, Hugh. *The Devil's Account: Philip Pullman and Christianity.* London: Darton, Longman and Todd, 2004.
Redford, John. *Bad, Mad or God? Proving the Divinity of Christ from John's Gospel.* London: St Paul's, 2004.
Reymond, Robert L. *Jesus, Divine Messiah: The New Testament Witness.* Phillipsburg, NJ: Presbyterian & Reformed, 1990.

Roberts, Alexander, James Donaldson, Philip Schaff, and Henry Wace. *The Early Church Fathers: Ante-Nicene Fathers: Translations of the Writings of the Fathers Down to A.D. 325; The Nicene and Post-Nicene Fathers of the Christian Church: First and Second Series.* 38 vols. Grand Rapids: Eerdmans, 1979.

Robinson, J. A. T. *Can We Trust the New Testament?* Grand Rapids: Eerdmans, 1977.

———. *Honest to God.* London: SCM, 1963.

Schakel, Peter J. *Reason and Imagination in C. S. Lewis: A Study of Till We Have Faces.* Grand Rapids: Eerdmans, 1984.

Schmaus, Michael. *Katholische dogmatik.* Munich: Hueber, 1960.

Scott, David, and Israel Selvanayagam. *Re-visioning India's Religious Traditions: Essays in Honour of Eric Lott.* Delhi: ISPCK, 1996.

Seerveld, Calvin. "Imaginativity." *Faith and Philosophy* 4 (1987) 43–58.

Sherlock, Thomas. *The Gospels and Jesus.* The Oxford Bible Series. Oxford: Oxford University Press, 1989.

———. *Gospel Truth: Today's Quest for Jesus of Nazareth.* London: Harper Collins, 1995.

———. *The Trial of the Witnesses of the Resurrection of Jesus.* New York: Cosimo Classics, 2005.

Stellars, J. T. *Reasoning Beyond Reason.* Eugene, OR: Pickwick, 2011.

Strauss, David Friedrich. *The Life of Jesus Critically Examined.* London: Continuum, 2006.

Swinburne, Richard. *The Concept of Miracle.* London: Macmillan, 1970.

———. *Revelation: From Metaphor to Analogy.* Oxford: Oxford University Press, 1992.

Tolkien, J. R. R. "Mythopoeia." In *Tree and Leaf,* edited by Christopher Tolkien, 85–90. London: Allen and Unwin, 1978.

———. "On Fairy Stories." In *C. S. Lewis, Essays Presented to Charles Williams,* 38–89. Oxford: Oxford University Press, 1947.

———. "Tolkien to Peter Hastings, Letter no 153, 1954." In *The Letters of J. R. R. Tolkien,* edited by Humphrey Carpenter, 187-96. Boston: Mifflin, 1981.

———. *The Silmarillion.* Edited by Christopher Tolkien. London: Allen & Unwin, 1977.

Van Dyke, Henry. *The Gospel for an Age of Doubt: The Yale Lectures on Preaching.* London: Macmillan, 1896.

Victorinus (Maius Victorinus Afer). "De Generatione Verbi Divini." In *Patrologia Latina* Vol. 8, cols. 1019c–36c, edited by Jacques-Paul Migne. Paris: Apud Garnieri Fratres, 1844.

Vidler, Alec R. *Objections to Christian Belief.* London: Constable, 1963.

———. "The Sign at Cana." In *Windsor Sermons,* 66–71. London: SCM, 1958.

Walker, Andrew. "Scripture, Revelation and Platonism in C. S. Lewis." *Scottish Journal of Theology,* 55 (2002) 19–35.

Ward, Keith. *What the Bible Really Teaches: A Challenge for Fundamentalists.* London: SPCK, 2004.

———. *Why There Almost Certainly Is a God: Doubting Dawkins.* Oxford: Lion Hudson, 2008.

Warfield, Benjamin Breckinridge. *The Lord of Glory: A Study of the Designations of Our Lord in the New Testament, with especial reference to His Deity.* New York: American Tract Society, 1907.

Wiles, Maurice, "Christianity without Incarnation." In *The Myth of God Incarnate,* edited by John Hick, 1–10. London: SCM, 1977.

———. "Does Christology Rest on a Mistake?" *Religious Studies* 6 (1970) 69–76.

———. *God's Action in the World: The Bampton Lectures for 1986.* London: SCM, 1986.

———. "Myth in Theology." In *The Myth of God Incarnate,* edited by John Hick, 148–65. London: SCM, 1977.

Wilson, A. N., *C. S. Lewis: A Biography.* London: Collins, 1990.

Wirt, Sherwood E., and C. S. Lewis. "Heaven, Earth and Outer Space." *Decision* II, October, 1963, 4.

———. "I was Decided Upon." *Decision* II, September, 1963, 3.

Wittgenstein, Ludwig. *Bemerkungen über Frazer's Golden Bough.* Edited by Rush Rees. Bishopstone, UK: Brymill, 1979.

Woolston, Thomas. *Six Discourses on the Miracles of Our Saviour and Defences of his Discourses.* New York: Garland, 1979.

Wright, N. T. *The Challenge of Jesus: Rediscovering who Jesus Was and Is.* Downers Grove, IL: InterVarsity, 1999.

———. "Jesus and the Identity of God." *Ex Auditu* 14 (1998) 42–56.

———. "Jesus' Self-Understanding." In *The Incarnation: An Interdisciplinary Symposium on the Incarnation of the Son of God*, edited by Stephen T. Davis, David Kendall SJ, and Gerald O'Collins, 47–61. Oxford: Oxford University Press, 2002.

———. "Simply Lewis: Reflections on a Master Apologist After 60 Years." In *Touchstone Magazine* 20.2 (March 2007) 39–40. Online: http://www.touchstonemag.com/archives/article.php?id=20-02-028-f.

Yarnell, Malcolm B. *The Formation of Christian Doctrine*. Nashville, TN: Broadman & Holman, 2007.

Index of Names

Abraham (Scripture) 65, 118, 137–38, 140, 146
Adonis 199, 209, 213, 222, 251, 260–61
Aeschylus 220
Anselm of Canterbury 179, 180
Antigone 31, 54
Aphrodite 214
Aquinas, Thomas 83, 108, 237
Asgard 208
Arius 196
Athanasius 78–79, 132, 148
Athenagoras 145
Augustine of Hippo 6, 13, 15, 71–73, 76, 79, 194, 217, 225, 236–48, 258, 263
avatar 210–13

Balder 14, 191, 199, 207, 209–10, 214–16, 222, 229, 246–48, 258, 262–63
    Baldhr 214f.
Barfield, Owen 92, 107, 232
Barth, Karl 12, 22, 32–33, 45, 55–62, 65, 67, 80, 83, 178, 212, 254–55
Bauckham. Richard 146
Baxter, Richard 45
Benedict XVI, Pope (Joseph Ratzinger) 151, 154–55
Berkeley, George, Bishop of Cloyne 13, 71–72, 74, 243
Beversluis, John 151, 162, 163
Blomberg, Craig L. 146, 152
Buddha 96, 158, 175
Bultmann, Rudolf 21, 36, 39, 41, 146–47, 196, 218
Burridge, Richard 51, 129

Calvin, John 110, 139, 145, 148, 224, 235, 253
Campbell, Joseph 194
Candidus 107
Carpenter, Humphrey 228, 248
Chesterton, G. K. 13, 91, 96, 103, 111, 120–22, 124–25, 153, 181

Christ, The 1–10, 12–17, 21–24, 27–28, 30–32, 34, 36, 38–40, 45–46, 48, 50, 52–69, 71, 73, 76–80, 82, 84–85, 87, 89–97, 100–104, 106–23, 126–27, 129–32, 134–36, 138–39, 142–45, 147–49, 152, 153–56, 159–63, 165–66, 168–69, 174, 177–79, 182–84, 186–89, 191–98, 200–204, 206–9, 211–13, 215, 217–23, 229, 237–38, 242–43, 245–48, 250–51, 254, 255–56, 258, 259–60, 262–67
    Jesus 1–10, 13–17, 22–23, 28, 30–40, 48, 51–53, 55–62, 65–69, 74, 76, 79–80, 82, 87, 89–98, 100–124, 127–46, 149–70, 172–80, 182–88, 191, 193, 198, 201–3, 209, 211–15, 220, 222–23, 229, 237, 243, 245–47, 254–55, 257–59, 262
    Jesus Christ 1, 3–5, 6, 8, 10, 15–17, 22–23, 30, 32, 34, 36, 39, 52, 53, 55–57, 59–60, 62, 65–67, 76, 79–80, 82, 89, 91, 95, 97, 101, 106–8, 113–14, 119–20, 132, 139, 142–43, 149, 153–55, 159, 165, 184, 187–88, 193, 201, 212, 237, 245–47, 254–55, 262, 264, 266
    Jesus of Nazareth 1–4, 7, 9, 16, 22, 32, 52, 55, 62, 65, 69, 79, 89–90, 95, 100, 103–5, 120, 122, 127–29, 131, 134–35, 137–39, 154–56, 176, 182–83, 187, 191, 193, 211, 220, 222–23, 265
    Messiah 1–3, 90, 105, 111–12, 119, 123, 127, 131–35, 155, 163, 183, 187
    Son of God 38, 55–56, 65, 67, 90, 94, 101–2, 107, 110–12, 114, 124–27, 129, 131–33, 135–36, 138, 140, 142, 148, 155, 168, 183, 202–3, 212, 262
    Son of Man 65, 79, 90, 105, 110, 114, 117, 126–27, 131, 133, 135–38, 168, 202
    Yeshua 1, 134,198
Christensen, Michael J. 24, 29, 63–64, 147, 196
Chronicles of Narnia, The (Characters)
    Aslan 17, 75, 80
    Digory 74
    Eustace 75, 82
    Jill 75

Kirk, Professor 98, 250, 251
Lucy 98–99
Peter 98–99
Rilian, Prince 75
Susan 98–99
Clement of Alexandria 145
Coleridge, Samuel Taylor 15, 217, 229–32, 234–36, 239, 246–48
Confucius 96, 158, 175
Constantine 106
Cupitt, Don 160
Cyprian 145, 148

Daniel (Scripture) 136, 143
Dante 228
Darwin, Charles 199, 201, 203
David (Scripture) 2, 26, 37, 42, 104–5, 124, 135, 143, 222, 235, 262
Davis, Stephen T. 14, 90, 124, 146, 157, 163, 165, 169–73
Dawkins, Richard 164, 181–82, 186, 218
D'Costa, Gavin 161
devil, the 113, 251–52
    Beelzebub 104, 125–26
    Satan 104, 112, 139, 182
Dostoevsky, Fyodor Mikhailovich 203
Dyson, Hugo 22, 162, 202–4, 227, 247, 263

Evans, C. Stephan 152, 194–95, 213–14
Ezekiel (Scripture) 136, 143

Feuerbach, Ludwig 191, 201, 203, 214, 227
Forsyth, P. T. 211–212
Frazer, Sir James George 14, 191, 199–201, 206–10, 213–15, 218, 227, 245, 247, 261, 263
Freud, Sigmund 14, 191, 214, 224–25, 227, 247, 261

Gabriel (Scripture) 1
Gier Nicholas F. 159–60
God 1–9, 12–17, 19, 21–25, 27–35, 37–38, 45–69, 71–73, 75–85, 87, 89, 90–97, 100–112, 114–15, 117–20, 122–49, 151–66, 168–74, 176–87, 189, 191, 193–99, 201–4, 206–14, 217–18, 222–28, 231–32, 234–43, 245–56, 258–60, 262–65
    Abba 140
    Beth-El 137
    El-ohim 137
    El-Shaddai 137
    El-Shallom 137
    Emmanu-el 137
    Father 11, 16–17, 28, 33, 51, 53, 56, 78, 80, 101, 104–5, 116, 118–19, 128, 131, 132–33, 135–37, 139–42, 144–45, 159, 172, 177–78, 180, 184–85, 191–93, 221, 238, 264
    I Am 103, 118, 137–38, 148–49, 183
    Jahweh 198
    Jehovah 1, 121, 134
    YHWH 93–94, 129, 136–38, 158, 182
Gore, Charles 25, 106–7
Graham, Billy 102
Grayling, A. C. 186
Green, T. H. 27, 42, 72, 177
Greeves, Arthur 25, 192, 197–98, 201, 203–4, 206
Gregory Thaumaturgus 145
Griffiths, Alan Bede 53
Gunton, Colin E. 7, 57–58, 61, 80, 161, 211–12

Hegel, Georg 159, 192
Heracles 198
Herod (Scripture) 105
Hick, John 151, 157, 159–61, 195–96
Hippolytus 145
Hitchens, Christopher 186
Homer 219, 227
Hooper, Walter 107, 224
Hopkins, Mark 13, 103, 111–13, 154, 166, 187
Huxley, Aldous 162, 174

Ignatius of Antioch 78, 145
Irenaeus of Lyons 78–80, 145, 148–49
Irving, David 42–43, 262
Isaac (Scripture) 65
Isaiah (Scripture) 143, 222
Israel 2, 12, 14, 29, 45, 64–68, 76, 103, 105, 113, 117, 123–30, 133–38, 142, 145, 149, 151–52, 154–55, 158, 171, 177, 180, 183, 250–51

Jacob (Scripture) 65, 151, 154
Job (Scripture) 25–26, 29–30, 32
John the Baptist (Scripture) 104–5, 125
John (Scripture: gospel and epistles) 21, 33, 35–41, 53–54, 59, 103, 104, 108, 117–18, 124–28, 130, 136, 138–49, 166, 170, 172, 187, 208, 212, 231, 241, 248–50, 254, 259, 266
Johnson, Mrs 53–54, 62, 67, 84
Julian the Apostate 13, 103, 106–7, 110
Jung, Carl 194
Justin Martyr 145, 148

Kant, Immanuel 202, 229–230, 236, 242

Index of Names

Keats, John 10, 229
Kennedy, John F. 162, 174
Kierkegaard, Søren 194, 212–13, 216
Kilby, Clyde S. 21, 24, 31–33, 50–51, 54, 59, 67, 147
Kirkpatrick, William T. 201
Kreeft, Peter 11, 14, 123–24, 151–52, 158, 162, 165, 174–76

Lactantius 145
Lessing, Gotthold Ephraim 34–36, 42, 147
Liddon, H. P. 13, 103, 111, 113–120, 149, 152–54, 166, 168, 182, 187
Lock, Walter 21, 36–37, 39, 146, 196, 218
Lüdemann, Gerd 151, 157
Luke (Scripture) 13, 32, 103, 105, 125, 136, 140–41, 143–44, 182, 184, 259

MacDonald, George 15, 217, 223–26, 232–36, 239, 253
Mark (Scripture) 13, 28, 41, 103–5, 108, 111, 125–26, 136, 140–41, 144, 147, 154, 166, 170, 182, 222, 259
Mary (Scripture) 1, 38, 48, 81, 92–93, 109, 144, 235
Matthew (Scripture) 13, 29, 32, 52, 87, 103–5, 108, 114–16, 119, 125–26, 136, 139–44, 161, 170, 182–85, 222, 254, 259
McDowell, Josh 123–24
McEwan, Ian 186
McLay, Emily 26, 52
Miller, Jonathon 197
Mohammed 48, 96, 158
More, Henry 72, 243
More, Sir Thomas 13, 103, 108–9, 187
Moses (Scripture) 66, 84, 117, 121, 137–38, 151, 155, 175
Mozart, Wolfgang Amadeus 181

Neusner, Jacob 151, 154–56
New Testament 2–3, 6, 8, 21, 24, 27–28, 30. 34–36, 38–39, 41–42, 74, 81–83, 96, 115–16, 121–22, 127, 129–30, 134, 138, 143, 146–47, 149, 151, 154–55, 156–57, 177, 178
Novatian 145

O'Collins, Gerald 103, 124–26, 164, 187, 266
Odin 198, 214
Old Testament 2, 21, 26, 29–31, 34, 50, 68, 84, 127, 135–37, 139–40, 143–44, 148–49, 177–78, 209, 212, 216, 221–22, 229, 250, 259
Origen of Alexandria 145

Orpheus 196–97
Osiris 199, 207, 209, 215–16, 246–48

Paul (Scripture) 30, 32, 39, 51–52, 59, 78, 106–7, 132, 142, 168, 203–4, 236, 255
paulus 32, 59
Pauline 52, 203
Penelope, Sr. 226
Persephone 214
Peter (Scripture) 11, 13–14, 52, 76, 82–84, 98–99 103, 105, 123–24, 128, 141–42, 151–52, 158 162, 165, 168–69, 174–75, 177, 183, 185–87, 226, 266
Pilate (Scripture) 105, 113, 207
Pittenger, W. Norman, 41–42
Plato 7, 13, 35, 71–75, 96, 158, 194, 217, 219–22, 238, 245, 262–63
Pullman, Philip 49, 186

Rackham, Arthur 198
Ratzinger, Joseph (See: Benedict XVI, Pope)
Redford, John 147, 148, 149
Reimarus, Hermann Samuel 34, 36, 147
Robinson, J. A. T. 146
Ruth (Scripture) 31, 54

Saxo Grammaticus 214
Schelling, Friedrich Wilhelm Joseph 229–31, 236
Sherlock, Thomas 33–35
Socrates 122, 175, 217, 220
Stephen (Scripture) 23
Strauss, David Friedrich 37–38, 147
Suleiman the Magnificent 109

Tacelli, Ronald 124
Tatian the Syrian 145
Tertullian 145, 148
Theophilus of Antioch 145
Tolkien, J. R. R. 15–16, 22, 40, 49, 72, 162, 192, 197, 202–4, 206, 217, 225–29, 247–48, 254–55, 263
Torrey, Reuben Archer 123

Van Gogh, Vincent 181
Victorinus, Gaius Marius 13, 103, 107, 110
Vidler, Alec 21, 36–8, 145, 196, 218
Vincentius of Lérins 45, 236
Virgil 221–22

Walker, Andrew 50–51, 63–66, 78, 80
Ward, Keith 146–47, 164, 203, 210

Wiles, Maurice 195-96
Wilson, A. N. 151, 156-57
Wise, Janet 26, 52
Wittgenstein, Ludwig 199-200
Woolston, Thomas 34

Wright, N. T. (Tom) 3, 11, 41, 127, 129-30, 133-34, 178, 182

Zeus 214

Index of Subjects

academic 11, 27, 29, 36, 42, 74, 89, 124, 126, 154, 156, 179, 185, 199-200, 207
acceptance 4, 6, 16, 22, 36, 77, 106, 108
Age of Reason, The 6-7, 9-10, 13, 34-35, 63, 90, 103, 110-11, 114, 179, 238
agnostic 22, 41
    agnosticism 42, 83, 186
allegory 26, 34, 77, 250
    allegorical 33-34, 132, 250
analogy 22, 34, 75, 79, 102, 109, 122, 132-33, 154, 212-13, 216, 256
    analogical 5, 34, 74, 101-2, 132, 136, 174, 192
anoint(ed) 1-2, 90, 134, 135, 143
    anointing 1, 134
    anoints 2, 135
anthropology 174, 199, 201, 207
    anthropological 207, 215
apocalyptic 28
apologetic(s) 5, 8, 13-14, 16-17, 21, 33, 35, 56, 65-66, 82, 84, 89, 90-91, 94-96, 100, 103, 111, 121, 123-24, 128, 153, 158, 162-63, 165-66, 168-69, 173-74, 176, 179, 181, 185-86, 188, 192, 202, 206, 236, 242, 266
    apologist(s) 5, 8, 10-12, 22-23, 90, 110-11, 174, 176, 178, 187, 206
apostate 13, 14, 62, 103, 106 191, 197, 203, 218, 263
a posteriori 2, 202, 256
apostles 2-3, 7-8, 11, 23, 26, 28, 33-34, 39, 58, 76, 84, 118, 127, 131, 139, 142, 144, 153, 177, 184, 222, 258 (See: disciples)
àpriori 114, 120
argument 12, 14, 34, 40-41, 42, 75, 84, 89-91, 98, 101, 103, 110-11, 114, 117, 120, 123-25, 126, 146, 148, 151-53, 155, 157-58, 159, 162-63, 165-66, 168-71, 173-74, 176, 179, 203, 220, 237
Arianism 195
art 10, 16, 26, 156, 224, 231
ascension 2, 42, 134-35
Asiatic 14, 191-92, 194, 221, 249
atheism 34, 68, 72, 108, 157, 179, 185-86, 201

atonement 17, 32, 55, 66, 79, 130, 133, 200-1, 204-6, 223, 267
atone 8, 201, 213
authority 4, 12, 16, 17, 24, 26, 29, 32, 45-46, 48, 50-51, 53, 55-56, 61-63, 101, 105, 112, 117, 123, 125, 136, 140-41, 152-56, 167, 172, 174, 177-78, 212, 236, 265

baptism 77
    Baptist 3, 104-5, 125
    baptized 15, 48-49, 66-67, 82, 84, 223, 226, 245, 251, 253-54
belief 5-8, 9, 26, 33, 63, 72, 82-84, 90, 94, 99, 109, 119, 124, 129, 147, 152-55, 157, 160, 162, 169, 170, 173-74, 179-82, 185, 203-4, 210, 237, 256
Bible 3, 8, 11-12, 21, 24, 25-35, 37, 40-42, 45-46, 48, 50-55, 58-63, 67, 71-72, 74-76, 82-84, 95, 103, 106-8, 112, 132, 139, 143, 147, 154-57, 164, 173, 196, 199, 209, 221, 225, 238-40, 262, 265 (See: Scripture; *sola scriptura*)
    biblical 8, 12, 21, 22, 25, 26, 31, 32, 35, 36, 37, 38, 39, 40, 41, 42, 48, 50, 51, 55, 59, 60, 82, 89, 96, 115, 117, 126, 127, 139, 147-48, 152, 155, 156, 166, 169, 196, 205, 218, 235, 236, 239, 247, 258
blasphemy 34, 113, 118-19, 127, 145, 152-53, 186
Brechungen 255

Christianity 3-4, 10-11, 19, 22-23, 27, 37, 49, 61, 63-65, 68-69, 89-93, 95, 100-101, 106-7, 111-12, 114-15, 120-21, 130, 132-33, 152, 154, 157, 159-63, 170, 174, 182, 192, 194-96, 198, 201-4, 207-8, 213, 218, 225, 236, 249-50, 253, 257, 260-63
    Christian(s) 1, 3-11, 14, 17, 22-25, 28-29, 35-36, 38, 41, 48, 55, 57, 61-64, 73, 81, 84, 90-92, 94-96, 100-101, 106-7, 109-11, 115, 120-24, 132, 135, 139, 142,

Index of Subjects

145–48, 151, 153–61, 163, 166, 168–71, 173–74, 176–79, 181, 182–85, 187–88, 191–94, 196–97, 200, 202, 205–13, 220–21, 225–26, 231, 236, 241–43, 248–53, 257, 259, 263, 266

Christology 3–5, 14–17, 53, 61, 73, 80, 90, 96, 107, 123, 129–30, 136, 147–48, 191–92, 194–96, 207, 211–12, 238, 263
    christological(ly) 14, 15, 16, 90, 92, 103, 105, 138, 139, 142, 151, 159, 174, 191, 192, 193, 202, 205, 206, 207, 211, 213, 214, 217, 218, 219, 225, 243, 245, 246, 256, 261, 263, 265

c/Church(es) 1–9, 11, 13, 22–23, 25–28, 30, 34–35, 37–38, 45, 51–52, 55–63, 66–67, 71, 77, 81–83, 90, 93, 95, 103, 106, 108–10, 113–15, 120–21, 131, 134–35, 138–39, 142–44, 145–48, 152–53, 156, 160, 172, 174, 177, 179, 181–183, 187, 192, 194, 202, 205, 207, 212, 218, 236, 250–51, 254, 265–67 (See: *ecclesia invisibilis*; *ecclesia visibilis*)
    Anglican 3–4, 21, 23, 36, 106, 113, 120, 145–46, 157, 178, 225, 237
    Church of England 4, 9, 34–35, 38, 82, 95
    churchman 13, 103, 106, 110, 113

communicate(d) 13, 61, 68, 236, 71, 79, 83, 84, 85, 184, 197, 242, 248, 265 (See: revelation)

communicatio idiomatum 13, 71, 79–80, 84, 184 (See: revelation)

communion 77, 133, 136, 138

comprehension 12, 21, 163, 213, 216 (See: revelation)

conversion 4–6, 9, 14–15, 16, 22, 24, 61, 64, 72, 78–79, 89, 91, 95, 102–3, 105, 109, 120, 133, 137, 157, 191–92, 194, 201–3, 206, 209, 217, 225, 230, 236–37, 242–43, 247, 251, 261, 263

covenant 38, 64, 66, 138, 259

creation 8, 12–15, 16, 21, 30, 45–46, 49, 51, 65, 68, 71, 74, 81, 85, 142, 203, 211, 215, 217, 225–29, 231–32, 234, 236, 238–39, 241, 243, 245–248, 251, 256, 259, 265–66
    created 8, 28, 49, 52, 82, 97, 99, 108, 136, 138, 146–47, 195, 223–24, 226, 238, 255, 262
    creative 14, 57, 124, 197, 223–24, 226–27, 230, 232, 234, 252–53
    creativity 14, 176, 191, 224–25, 232–34

Creed(s) 3, 4, 8–9, 11, 16, 22–23, 26, 42, 67, 78–79, 90, 92, 107, 120, 122–23, 134, 159–60, 172, 176, 202
    creedal 3, 9, 42, 121, 172, 178

cross, the 2, 12, 14, 16, 28, 48, 53, 60, 66, 68, 81–82, 159, 182, 191, 200, 204, 206, 209, 211, 220, 222, 229, 245, 253–54, 256, 260–63, 266

crucifixion, the 8, 36, 92, 131–32, 145, 206, 220

crucified 8, 32, 55, 140, 142, 163, 207, 256, 264

passion, the 217, 220–22, 229, 263

Darwinian 14, 191, 207, 214, 227, 247
death–descent 245, 260–61
    (see: rebirth–reascent)
deification 156, 209–11
delusion 28, 98, 99, 106, 122, 159, 165, 167–68, 176, 181, 186
demythologize 12, 21
denomination(s) 4, 6
    denominational 11, 12
    denominationalism 187
Deus dixit 32, 59
dialectic(al) 17, 49, 57, 61–62, 71, 85, 92–95, 100, 106, 110–11, 115, 126, 128, 193, 250
    either–or 89, 91, 93–95, 100, 106–7, 110–11, 126, 137, 155, 166, 170, 188
    dilemma 14, 89, 91, 93–94, 96, 112, 115, 122, 124–26, 131, 145, 152, 154–56, 161, 163, 166, 177, 180, 182, 185, 186–87, 257 (See: trilemma)
diminution 49, 71, 73–74, 76–79, 81, 83, 85, 212
    diminuted 85, 133, 248, 265
disciples 2, 28, 39, 84, 87, 105, 113, 116, 127, 131, 141–42, 149, 155–56, 178, 258–59, 262 (See: apostles)
disclosed 55, 128, 139, 152–53, 178
divinity 9, 16, 36, 89, 90, 92–93, 95–96, 98, 103, 106, 108–9, 110–11, 113–14, 115–16, 117–20, 122–23, 126–27, 129–30, 131–34, 137–39, 141, 143–49, 152–62, 165–66, 168–72, 173–75, 177–78, 179–80, 185–86, 235
    divine 2–3, 14, 16, 21, 24, 27, 29–30, 32–33, 37, 47–48, 53, 56–58, 61–62, 64, 67, 71, 73, 76–77, 79–80, 89–90, 94–95, 102–3, 106–8, 110–11, 114, 118–19, 122–23, 125, 127–33, 135–36, 139–41, 143–44, 148–49, 151–52, 153, 158–59, 161, 163–64, 166–74, 177, 179–80, 183, 186–87, 196, 201, 209–12, 215, 218, 221, 226, 228, 230, 234–35, 238–41, 243, 245–46, 250–55, 262–63, 266
doctrine 3–6, 8, 12–15, 21–23, 25–27–28, 45–46, 51, 56, 58–61, 65, 69, 71–73, 79, 82–85, 92, 111, 113, 117, 120, 132–33, 148, 151–53, 155, 159–60, 163, 165–66, 177, 180–81, 184, 188, 191–93, 195–96, 200, 204, 206, 215, 217–19,

223, 225, 228, 230–32, 236, 238–43, 245–46, 249, 258–59, 261, 265–67
  doctrinal 9, 26, 71, 90, 95, 265

ecclesia invisibilis 61, 62
ecclesia visibilis 61, 62
Emmanuel 143
Enlightenment 6, 7, 9, 13, 22, 34, 63, 90, 103, 111, 114, 137, 147, 159, 173–74, 179, 195, 202, 236–38
eschaton 4, 61, 223, 256
  eschatological 135, 187, 256
eternity 16–17, 48, 53, 56, 60–62, 64, 71–78, 80, 82–85, 101, 133, 136, 138, 140, 193, 225–26, 250, 253–54, 260, 265
  eternal 29, 55–56, 74, 78–79, 80, 83, 104, 107, 116, 130, 133, 138–40, 142–44, 146, 151, 154, 180, 213, 227–28, 231–32, 248
ethics 5, 9, 50, 64, 66, 116, 198, 203, 230–31, 236
Eucatastrophe 229
Eucharist 77
European 10, 14, 34, 37–38, 65, 191–92, 194, 199, 208, 219, 221, 249–50, 254–55, 260
Evangelical(s) 3–7, 11, 13, 46, 48–49, 89, 90, 123–24, 159, 185, 187
  evangelist(s) 28, 37, 112
evil 25, 35, 77, 90, 92, 94, 104, 108, 115, 119, 124, 136, 167–68, 176, 182, 186, 198, 203, 208, 210, 215, 221, 228–29, 234, 245–46, 250, 252–53
existence 14, 16, 36, 57–58, 75, 98, 114, 132–33, 140, 164–65, 177, 179–80, 185, 202–3, 209–10, 219, 225, 236, 252, 255
  existential 60, 107, 134, 159, 183, 186
  exsistentialis, exsistentialitas, exsistentialiter 107
  non–existence 96, 164
  pre–existence 118
ex nihilo 16, 226, 248, 256

faith 3–6, 8, 11, 25–26, 32, 36, 52, 55, 62–63, 73, 82, 91, 93, 99–101, 105–6, 109, 113–14, 120, 142, 146, 154, 157, 161, 163–64, 166, 179–82, 188, 192, 204, 207, 209, 225, 237, 247, 251, 265
  faithfulness 154
fall, the 8, 24, 29, 66, 73, 81, 94, 123, 129, 131, 141, 165, 169, 180, 182, 184–85, 186, 203, 213, 219, 227, 231, 235–36, 239, 246, 255, 262, 266 (see: original sin)
  fallen 12, 45, 47–48, 49–51, 78, 84, 131, 135, 178, 182, 219–20, 228, 236, 241, 253–54, 259, 264

fallibility 13, 47–48, 71, 146, 184
fallible 12, 45–46, 49, 219
forgiveness 17, 65, 97, 124, 130, 144, 158, 201, 212
forgave 139
forgive(s) 2, 17, 19, 69, 94, 100, 140, 144, 152–53, 172, 177, 209–10
freedom 9, 12, 17, 29, 45–47, 49, 51, 56–57, 69, 72, 85, 129, 185, 211–13, 218, 231, 251–52, 265
fundamentalism 26, 31
  fundamentalist 26, 29–30, 46, 54

genre 12, 21, 26, 30–31, 37, 39, 45–48, 50–52, 129, 156, 194, 196, 226
God, or a bad man 89–91, 95, 97, 103, 110, 127, 165, 174
  aut Deus aut homo malus, et non homo malus, ergo Deus 165, 174, 176
  aut Deus aut malus angelus 92
  aut Deus aut malus homo 13, 89–96, 100–105, 107, 113, 120–21, 123–24, 126–28, 145, 149, 151–53, 155, 161, 163, 180, 182, 184, 186–88, 266
  Bad, Mad, or God 13, 89
  BMG 14, 84–91, 165
  Christus, si non Deus, non bonus 13, 103, 114, 119, 154, 187
  incognito 105, 139
  Mad, Bad, or God 89–90, 94, 103, 120, 123–24, 126, 182,
  malus homo 13, 89–97, 100–105, 107–8, 112–13, 120–21, 123–24, 126–28, 145, 149, 151–53, 155, 161, 163, 165–66, 168–69, 176–77, 180, 182, 186–87, 266
  MBG 14, 84–91, 165, 171, 173
  wicked 33, 89–90, 94, 104, 125, 130, 132, 152–53, 168, 182, 186–87, 220, 222
Gnostic 38, 77
gospel 4, 7–8, 11, 13–15, 21, 32–41, 53, 57–59, 62, 76, 82, 84, 95–96, 103, 106, 111, 115, 117–19, 123–29, 134, 136–38, 142–49, 151–52, 154–58, 161–63, 166, 168, 172, 187–88, 191–94, 202, 208, 212, 218, 225, 227, 240, 245, 248, 257–58, 260
grace 25, 50, 54, 57–60, 62, 67, 73, 77, 79, 132, 142, 217, 231, 235, 238–39, 241, 243, 246
Greek 1–2, 6–8, 10, 23, 27, 35, 41, 79, 134, 137, 163, 178, 192, 211, 213, 219, 227, 229, 236–38, 241, 262

heaven 4, 8, 28, 57, 60, 64, 67, 73, 76, 78, 102, 105, 113, 116, 118, 133, 136, 140, 142, 144, 158,

162, 174, 175, 176, 178, 184–85, 203, 207, 212, 214, 217, 221, 242, 248, 258, 267
  heavenly 133, 235
Hegelian(ism) 72, 121, 158–59, 191
hell 8, 75, 78, 256, 267
  Hades 214, 219
  Sheol 219
heresy 15, 241
hermeneutic of suspicion 21, 35–36, 38–40, 90, 199, 262
Hindu(ism) 14, 158, 191, 192, 210, 212, 213, 216, 246, 247, 249
history 3, 5, 10, 12, 14, 17, 21, 23–24, 26, 31, 34, 36–37, 39, 51, 53–54, 60, 62–64, 68, 76, 93, 112, 115–16, 119–20, 123, 126, 128, 136, 146–47, 156, 159–61, 166, 172–73, 177, 179, 187, 191–94, 202, 207–9, 221–22, 250, 253, 255, 259–62 (See: unhistorical)
  historical 3, 5, 12, 21, 24, 29, 31–33, 36–37, 39–41, 50, 54, 65, 67, 93, 96–97, 114–16, 121–22, 129, 141, 146–49, 152, 154, 156–57, 160, 163, 172, 178–79, 192–94, 196–97, 200, 206–7, 213, 234, 249, 257
  historically 32–33, 158, 194–95, 216
  historicity 21, 28–29, 32, 38, 50, 54, 96, 121, 147, 156, 194, 196, 207
holiness 12, 17, 45, 64, 67, 69, 116, 158, 210
holy of holies 130
Holy Spirit 4, 12, 14, 16, 24–25, 30, 33, 45–46, 48–49, 51, 53–55, 57, 60, 62, 64–65, 67, 73–74, 80–81, 83–84, 101, 104, 139–41, 161, 183–85, 191–93, 217, 221, 223–24, 231, 236, 238, 239, 241, 243, 247–49, 253, 258, 262, 265–66 (See: pneumatology)
human 2–4, 6–9, 11–15, 17, 21–22, 24, 28–30, 32–34, 37, 41–42, 45–51, 53–54, 56, 58–66, 68, 71, 73, 76–84, 89–90, 92–98, 100, 102–3, 106–9, 110, 112–14, 116–20, 122, 124, 127–36, 139–41, 145–46, 148–49, 151–53, 156, 158–61, 163–64, 165–69, 172–74, 176–77, 180–81, 183–87, 191–92, 195–97, 199–201, 203, 206, 209–13, 215–19, 221, 223–24, 227–28, 230–32, 235–43, 245, 247, 249, 250, 25–58, 261–62
  humanist 48–49, 97, 109, 168
  humanity 1–3, 5, 7–8, 12–13, 16–17, 21, 27, 29–31, 33–35, 40, 45–46, 49, 51, 56–59, 62–69, 71–73, 77–79, 81, 83, 85, 89–90, 93, 96–97, 103, 106, 112, 116–18, 121–22, 128–36, 146, 148, 152, 158–61, 163–65, 168, 172, 176, 182–87, 191–92, 195–96, 198–203, 206, 209, 211, 213, 217, 219–21, 223–24, 226, 228, 232–38, 241–43, 246–48, 251–52, 261–66

mankind 110, 117, 118, 204
humble 16, 27, 80, 100, 108, 112, 119, 184, 187
  humiliation 79, 212
  humility 17, 27, 83, 100, 108, 109, 116, 119, 212, 213

idealism 71, 72, 73, 82, 85, 95, 133, 158, 174, 229, 237, 243, 258
illumination, doctrine of (See: revelation)
  illuminated 84, 235, 241, 249, 254, 258, 265
  illumination 12, 15, 21, 24, 31, 61, 73, 76, 194, 217, 221, 238–43, 245, 247–49, 253–54, 258
  illumines 239–41, 254, 258
imagination 15, 24, 46, 47–49, 63, 65–67, 73–75, 82, 84, 101, 194, 207, 213, 217, 221, 223–26, 229, 230–32, 234–36, 238, 242–43, 245–48, 251, 253–55, 258, 264 (See: revelation)
  imaginings 76, 80, 229
imago Dei 16, 226, 232, 234
Immanuel 16–17, 202, 229–30, 236
immaterialism 72
immortality 78
imparted 12, 13, 71, 84, 184, 249–50, 265
incarnation 2, 6, 8–9, 13–16, 27, 45, 51, 53, 56, 60, 65–69, 71–73, 78–81, 83, 85, 95–97, 105, 107, 110–11, 114–15, 121, 124–25, 127, 130–33, 139, 142, 144, 147–48, 151, 153, 159–61, 164, 169, 173–74, 184–187, 191–97, 202, 204–213, 216–17, 219, 223, 225, 227, 229, 239, 241–42, 245–49, 251, 252, 254, 255–63, 266
  incarnate 4, 13, 16, 28, 32, 55, 66, 73, 85, 89, 90, 92–93, 97, 102–3, 106, 109–10, 114–15, 117, 126, 128, 130, 132, 139, 151–52, 156–57, 160, 166–68, 180, 182, 184–86, 195, 202, 203, 210–13, 216, 218, 245, 249, 259, 261, 266
  incarnated 8, 28, 53, 62, 66, 69, 90, 92, 134, 142, 148, 159, 164–65, 167, 186, 210–11
  incarnational 178, 208–9, 212, 216, 223, 227, 235
India 210, 255
  Indian 10, 14, 94, 191–92, 194, 209, 221, 249
inerrancy 24, 31–32, 45–46, 48, 50, 54–55, 72, 147
  inerrant 12, 31, 45–46, 50–51
infallibility 24, 45
  infallible 12, 29, 45–47, 49, 167
infinitum capax finiti 211–13
insane 94–95, 113, 122–24, 164, 171, 174–75, 181–82, 186

285

insanity 96, 122–23, 156, 165, 167–68, 170, 176, 181–82, 186
inspiration 21, 24, 31, 33, 45–46, 47, 48–49, 50–51, 53–55, 59, 61, 65, 67, 72, 194, 215, 218, 221, 223, 227, 235, 238, 248, 249, 250, 253
    inspire(d) 12, 21, 24, 32–33, 45–50, 51, 53, 55, 58, 62, 66–67, 84–85, 101, 201, 210, 228, 247, 248, 256, 265
intellectual 11, 22, 27, 34, 36, 72, 110, 114, 159, 186, 201, 232–34, 237, 241–42, 246–47
    intelligible 7, 58, 119, 151, 159
interpretation 3, 7, 14–15, 21, 27, 34–36, 41, 45, 52, 83, 100, 115, 135, 146, 165, 184, 191, 217, 222, 230, 239, 245, 247, 249, 252–54
intertestamental 1–2, 127, 135

Judaism 1, 134, 154, 163, 172, 178–79
    Hebrew 1–3, 29, 30, 65, 110, 127, 130, 133–35, 137, 139–40, 142–43, 177–78, 182, 198, 209, 212, 215, 219, 222, 249–51, 259–60
    Israel 2, 12, 14, 29, 45, 64–68, 76, 103, 105, 113, 117, 123–30, 133–38, 142, 145, 149, 151–52, 154–55, 158, 171, 177, 180, 183, 250–51
    Israelites 137
    Jewish 2, 3, 9–10, 14, 16, 37, 41–42, 96, 103–4, 112, 118, 125–26, 127–30, 133–36, 140, 145–46, 149, 151–55, 158, 172, 177–78, 180, 209, 250, 262, 266
    Jews 2, 19, 65–66, 68, 76, 93–94, 96, 104, 110–12, 118, 121–22, 130, 134, 140, 142–43, 145, 153–55, 158, 163, 177–78, 180–81, 209–10, 222, 250
Judeo-Christian 192, 194, 253
Jungian 194

kenosis 139, 211, 212
    kenotic 79–80, 139, 142, 211
knowledge 1, 15–16, 22, 38, 51, 53–54, 56–57, 58, 66, 68, 83, 108, 129, 141, 148–49, 151, 158, 160, 167, 180, 201, 203, 210, 213, 217, 219–21, 231, 234–37, 239, 241–43, 247–48, 254–57, 264, 266

law 12, 23, 37, 45, 64–66, 73, 89, 93, 96, 104, 116–18, 126, 140–43, 146, 162, 170, 181, 202, 209, 228, 230, 232, 238, 249–52
Liberal (philosophical and theological) 9, 30, 36, 39, 42, 46, 54, 90, 103, 152, 154, 157, 173–74, 196–97, 199

liberal (societal) 4, 9, 40, 96–97, 117, 145–46, 154, 157, 166, 168, 170, 196, 266
Liberalism (philosophical and theological) 9, 195, 199
light 6, 9, 15–16, 29–30, 34, 36, 54, 73, 81, 83, 84, 90, 101, 103, 112, 117, 125, 137–38, 140, 143, 183, 194, 201–2, 210, 214–15, 217, 221, 225, 227–28, 238, 240–41, 243, 245–49, 254–55, 262, 264, 266 (See: illumination)
literary 12, 21, 35–38, 96, 186, 196–97, 206, 212, 224, 230, 266
literature 10, 26, 29–31, 39, 46, 51, 54, 83, 84, 156, 184, 192, 196, 221, 225, 229, 258
logic 14, 51, 60, 75, 89, 90, 94–95, 98–99, 102, 122, 127, 137, 138, 151, 153, 161–65, 174, 176, 183–84, 192 (See: reason)
Logos (λόγος) 60, 78, 138, 215, 223, 248, 254
Lord 4–5, 15, 32, 51–52, 56–57, 76, 83, 94, 96, 108, 113–15, 118, 120, 123–25, 129, 131, 135–38, 140–44, 148–49, 153–55, 158, 167, 175, 177–78, 180, 183–84, 186–87, 212, 222, 226, 240, 245, 263, 266
    Lordship 4, 140, 165, 178
love 4, 14, 16–17, 23, 31, 50, 64–65, 68, 72, 79, 100, 109, 124, 133, 149, 176, 182, 184, 191–92, 196, 198, 203, 215, 230, 234, 252

mediation 45, 58, 66, 71–72, 77, 85, 265
    mediated 71, 73, 79, 82–83, 254
    mediator 13, 45, 66
medieval 13, 38, 46, 72, 90, 103, 110, 121, 179, 192
mentally ill 122, 181 (See: God or a Bad Man)
messiah(s) 1–3, 90, 105, 111–12, 119, 123, 127, 131, 134–35, 155, 163, 183, 187
    messiahship 1–3, 105, 111, 127, 131, 134–35
    messianic 2, 94, 97, 112, 136, 140–41, 168, 171, 179, 212
metanarratives 160 (See: *Weltanschauung*; Worldview)
metaphysical 194–95, 196, 238
Methodist 3
Middle Eastern 10, 14, 191, 194, 259
miracle(s) 21, 29, 33–34, 36–38, 40, 60, 91, 96–97, 104, 114–16, 118, 123, 127, 133, 139, 141, 144–45, 147, 153, 189, 204, 205–7, 212–13, 235, 259–61
    miraculous 12, 21, 29, 34, 37–38, 40–41, 116, 125, 147, 163, 174, 195, 204
modalism 265
    modalistic 265
m/Modern 6, 8, 12, 21–23, 25–26, 30, 35–36, 37–42, 46, 54, 58, 69, 72–73, 77, 82–83, 90, 96, 108, 121–22, 145–46, 148, 152, 154, 157,

160, 162, 169–70, 173–74, 179–80, 194–96, 199–201, 205, 207, 212, 218, 230, 238, 242, 256 (See: Liberal
    modernism 6, 9, 23, 34, 63, 199
    modernist 4, 9, 21, 46, 148, 158, 200, 209
moral(s) 12, 16, 21, 26, 29–30, 45, 51, 62, 64, 67–68, 92–94, 96–97, 103, 108–9, 111, 114, 116–19, 123, 146, 152–54, 168–69, 176, 181, 183, 209, 230 (See: ethics)
    morality 9, 64, 116, 155, 198, 250
myth(s) 9, 14–15, 21, 24, 29–30, 36, 39, 45, 51, 53, 63, 65, 68–69, 157, 159–60, 191–97, 199–200, 202–9, 211–219, 221–29, 232, 235–37, 243, 245–60, 262–64, 266
    mythical 115, 193, 197, 206-7, 215, 227, 249, 252
    mythological 21, 42, 195, 198, 200, 209, 216, 226, 245, 262
    mythology 10, 192, 197–99, 202, 212–214, 216, 226, 247, 250–51, 261
mythopoeia 15, 192, 217, 225–26, 227–28, 245, 247–49, 254–55
    mythopathic 248, 258
    mythopathically 256
    mythopoeic 15, 217, 227, 245, 247–48, 256, 263

narrative(s) 5, 14–15, 17, 21, 23, 32, 37, 39, 65, 75, 82, 115, 124, 129, 152, 160, 162, 174, 177, 191–94, 202, 206, 207–9, 212–13, 216, 222–27, 229, 242, 245–47, 249, 251–52, 256–58, 260, 262–63, 266–67 (See: analogy)
natural theology 15, 195, 202–4, 206, 216–17, 236–38, 246–47, 253–54, 260
nature 2, 3, 7, 15, 17, 24, 26, 27–28, 31, 34, 37–38, 40, 46, 52–54, 56, 60, 62, 66, 71, 76–79, 83–85, 89, 92, 95, 97, 100–3, 106–8, 111–12, 114–15, 119, 124, 126, 128, 131–36, 139, 146, 147–49, 154–56, 159, 165, 168–70, 174–76, 181, 184, 186, 189, 198, 200, 203, 206, 210–11, 213–14, 220, 224, 226, 230, 232, 236–37, 240, 243, 245–47, 253, 258–62, 265
    natural world 10, 13, 45, 66, 68, 77, 85, 195, 198, 216, 236, 259–60
    natural 9, 10, 13, 15, 30, 45, 66, 68, 77, 85, 195–99, 202, 203–4, 206, 212, 214, 216, 217, 228, 231, 236, 237–38, 240, 246, 253, 259–60
negation 178
nihilism 78, 229
    nihilistic 78, 229
Northernness 198, 208, 252
numinous 12, 45, 63–69, 82, 197, 249

Oceanic 14, 94, 191, 212, 221
ontology 92, 100–101, 108, 131, 153, 211, 126
    ontological 98, 100–1, 110, 114, 128, 135, 183, 213, 238, 262, 265
    ontologically 73, 119, 133, 211, 213, 216, 246
Oriental 10, 110, 194, 199
original sin 8, 48, 78, 129–31, 159, 200, 213, 219, 223, 227, 235–236, 241, 245, 250, 252–54 (see: the fall; *simul iustus et peccator*; sin; sinners)
orthodox 1, 3, 5, 7, 9, 11, 17, 41, 59, 82, 101, 111, 114–15, 120, 129, 136, 138, 146, 151, 155–56, 158, 162, 178, 182, 187, 192, 194, 196, 200, 266

pagan(s) 8, 9–10, 13–15, 23–24, 45, 65, 66, 68–69, 106–7, 136, 177, 189, 191–92, 194, 198, 204, 206–9, 211–13, 216–19, 221, 223–24, 242–43, 245–46, 248–49, 250–55, 260, 263, 266
    paganism 9, 10, 23, 106, 208, 251, 253, 260
paradox 28, 30, 78, 80, 93, 121–22, 161, 216, 245, 249, 255 (See: dialectic)
parousia 27
particular 11, 13–14, 26, 31, 34, 39–40, 45–46, 53, 55, 63, 65, 66, 68–69, 73, 79–80, 84, 107–8, 132, 146, 151, 153–54, 158, 159–60, 161, 176, 184–87, 191–92, 194–96, 200, 202, 206–8, 222, 243, 250, 259
    particularity 34, 151, 159–61, 196
paulus dixit 32, 59
Pelagian 241
perception 2, 6, 17, 48–49, 68, 80–83, 116, 134, 141, 152, 176–78, 182, 184–85, 219, 221, 228, 230–32, 239–40, 243, 248, 254, 256, 259
    perceivable 7, 13, 45, 69, 193, 230
perlocution 258, 266
    perlocutionary 15, 245, 247, 258, 263–64, 266
philosophy 5–7, 9–10, 13, 25, 52, 71–72, 79, 84, 111, 159, 161–63, 167, 169, 198–99, 202, 213, 219, 224, 230–31, 234, 236, 238, 242, 258, 266
    philosopher 5–7, 11, 13, 15, 24–25, 35, 50, 71–73, 90, 107, 111, 123–24, 146, 151, 157, 159, 162, 164, 169, 179, 186, 198–99, 217, 230, 236, 237, 243
    philosophical 5, 13–14, 29, 42, 72–73, 82, 89, 91–93, 95, 100, 121, 124, 126, 128, 132, 141, 149, 156, 163, 169, 173, 184–85, 198, 202, 214, 230–31, 236–37, 239, 240–43, 246, 265, 266
Platonic 7, 13, 16, 49, 60, 71–74, 81–82, 84–85, 107, 133, 221, 227, 237, 243, 247, 254, 258, 260

287

platonically 84, 133, 206, 243, 265
Platonism 7, 49–51, 61, 63–65, 72, 78, 84, 238, 242, 265, 266
Platonist(s) 7, 13, 60, 71–72, 74, 243
pluralism 160–61
    pluralistic 161
    plurality 160–61
pneumatology 60, 62 (See: Holy Spirit)
    pneuma 62
    pneumatological 62, 165, 192, 196, 183, 266
    pneumatologically 60–62, 224, 236, 256
postmodernism 6, 34, 63, 160, 200
    postmodern 49, 116, 160, 267
preach 58, 76, 163
preacher 13, 16, 27, 58, 103, 110–11, 113, 120, 122–23, 133
prefigurement(s) 14–15, 127, 136, 143–44, 191–94, 202, 205–9, 211–13, 216–19, 221–23, 225, 235, 238, 243, 245–49, 251–52, 254–55, 260–61, 263, 265, 266 (See: Christology)
    prefigured 14–15, 189, 192–193, 207–8, 213, 217, 219, 227–28, 242, 245–47, 260
    prefiguring 14, 191, 236, 245, 250, 263, 266
Presbyterian 3, 123
prophecy 214, 217, 219, 221, 249, 250
    prophesies 141
    prophetic 40, 57–58, 76, 176, 208, 215, 219, 221
Protestant 7, 11, 110, 157, 196, 251

reason(s) 6–7, 9–10, 13–14, 21, 33–35, 45, 60, 63, 71, 73, 79, 83, 85, 90, 103, 110–11, 114, 118, 127, 155, 156, 159, 161–62, 164, 166–67, 169–70, 179, 184, 188, 192, 205, 223, 228, 238, 265
    rational 34, 64, 94, 99, 113, 159, 163–64, 166, 182, 188, 227, 254
    rationality 99, 124, 163–65, 169, 173, 219, 230
    reasoned 8, 16, 95, 117, 151, 162, 216
    reasoning 16, 111, 180, 202–3, 236–37
rebirth–reascent 15, 245, 260–61
    (see: death–descent)
reconciliation 56, 66, 251–52
redeem 16, 72, 152, 177, 260, 263
    redeemer 2, 135, 143
    redemption 2, 16, 134, 136, 204, 206, 223, 246, 254, 266
reductio ad absurdum 73
Reformation 13, 61, 103, 110, 238, 242, 251
    Reformed 7, 61, 110, 224–25, 235, 247, 251, 253–54
    Reformers 51, 236
refractions 15, 217, 225, 247, 255–56, 263

religio–cultural 153
religion 2–5, 8–10, 13–14, 22, 23, 27, 62, 89–90, 106–7, 111, 113, 121, 130, 134, 138, 140, 153, 156–57, 159–62, 164, 169, 177, 180, 186, 191–92, 194, 197–99, 200, 201–202, 207–8, 210, 212, 224, 238, 247, 249, 253, 255, 257, 259–60, 262–63
religionist 14, 191, 199
religions 8–9, 62, 68, 95, 121, 152, 157, 158–61, 198–99, 201, 209, 243, 245–46, 249, 261–63
religiosity 64, 158–60, 201
religious 1–3, 5, 9–10, 14–17, 22–23, 31, 34, 37–38, 41–42, 54, 61–63, 68, 76–77, 101, 103–4, 106, 115, 117–19, 121–22, 125–29, 134–36, 138, 142, 145, 149, 152–53, 158, 161, 164–65, 170, 177, 179–82, 184–85, 191–94, 196, 198–203, 209, 215, 217, 224, 232, 245, 247, 251–53, 255, 259–60, 262–63, 266
resurrection 2, 7, 8, 9, 12, 14–16, 22, 31, 33–34, 38, 42, 53, 55, 60, 65, 68, 78, 94–95, 106, 115, 131–32, 134–37, 141, 147, 149, 169, 177, 191–94, 202, 204, 206–9, 212–13, 215–17, 219, 222–23, 225, 227, 229, 241–42, 245–49, 251–52, 254–63, 266
    resurrected 8, 32, 55, 59, 78, 106, 153, 187, 213, 245, 254, 264, 266
resuscitation 246, 262
revelation(s) 1, 2, 4–8, 10, 12–16, 19, 21, 24, 45–51, 53–60, 61, 62–69, 71, 73–75, 77–85, 87, 91, 96, 102, 114–15, 117–18, 127–30, 132, 134–35, 138, 143–44, 151, 154–55, 158, 161, 164, 168, 177, 180, 182, 184–85, 191–92, 193–94, 201–2, 206, 212–13, 216–17, 221, 223–24, 234–35, 237–38, 243, 245–252, 254–55, 258, 260, 263, 265–66 (See: Transposition; Prefigurement)
    Christ as the light of the world 6, 15, 191, 217, 245, 246
    intimation(s) 12, 14–15, 23, 45, 49, 64–65, 67–69, 74, 76–77, 80–82, 85, 189, 191, 217, 219, 227–28, 234, 235–36, 237–38, 241–48, 250–52, 254–58, 262–64
    intimated 77, 89
    premonitions 13, 45, 65–66, 68, 249
    presence 28, 30, 59, 69, 130, 136, 177, 197, 235, 241
    prevenience 15, 217, 240–41, 245
    prevenient 217, 227, 235, 241–43
    prevision 14–15, 193, 208, 209, 211, 219, 221, 241, 245–46, 251–52
    previsioned 14, 191–93
    proclamation 55–59, 62, 67, 106, 127, 157

realization 2, 6, 56, 105, 134, 152, 179, 185, 242, 247
reveal 34, 39, 72, 80, 136, 151, 154, 184, 208, 243
    revealed 2, 5, 7, 13, 16, 41, 45, 51, 57, 59, 62–63, 65–66, 67, 71, 79–80, 82, 84, 105, 113–14, 123, 128, 130, 133, 137, 149, 172, 178–80, 184–85, 192, 212–13, 227, 237–38
    revealedness 1, 64–65, 83, 85, 266
    revealings 80, 243, 246
    revelatory 12, 45, 53, 55, 62–63, 77, 81–82, 84, 223, 235, 246–47, 254
self-assertion 113–14, 117, 119, 154
self-disclosure 7, 89, 119, 126–29, 131, 133, 137, 134–35, 137–39, 144, 148–49, 151–52, 156, 161, 164, 166, 167, 170, 172, 176, 179–80, 185–86
righteous 94, 116, 136, 158, 220, 256
    righteousness 136, 142, 220
Roman(s) 2–4, 6, 8, 10, 11, 13, 16, 23, 27, 38, 49, 89, 90, 103, 104, 106–7, 112, 121, 123, 129, 133–34, 142, 145, 147, 153, 156, 177, 203, 205, 219, 221, 236, 242
Roman Catholic(s) 3, 4, 11, 13, 16, 38, 49, 89–90, 103, 123, 147, 156
    Catholic 3–5, 11, 16, 38, 48, 103, 123, 139, 147, 155–56, 205, 226, 235, 237
Romantic 10, 156, 225, 229
    Romanticism 10

sacrament 77
    sacramental 5, 77, 82
sacred 24, 26–27, 31, 50–51, 63, 77, 110
sacrifice 33, 48, 82, 110, 119, 137, 161, 180, 198, 200, 204, 206, 219, 221
    sacrificial 119, 219
salvation 1, 2, 5–6, 12, 17, 27, 54, 60, 62–64, 69, 77, 81, 90, 104–5, 110, 120, 131–32, 135–36, 142–43, 146–47, 158–59, 161, 165–66, 184–85, 187, 192, 204, 208, 217, 237, 241, 246, 250, 254, 263–64, 266–67
    salvific 14, 73, 191, 209, 223, 236, 241, 243, 246–48, 254, 258, 263, 266
    saved 2, 131, 137, 142, 204, 229, 237
    savior 1, 134–35, 142
sanctification 17, 54
scandal of particularity 34, 151, 159–61
s/Scholasticism 13, 72, 103
Scripture 2, 9, 11–13, 19, 21, 23–33, 36, 38, 41, 45–68, 71–73, 76, 78, 83–85, 90, 101, 103, 105, 109, 110, 114–15, 126, 129, 139, 144–47, 151–52, 156, 173, 184–85, 196, 218, 221, 235, 237, 258, 265–66 (See: Bible; *sola scriptura*)

scriptural 31, 47, 48, 52, 54, 89, 97, 108, 124, 127, 135, 139, 151, 152, 156, 162, 166, 167, 169, 172, 180, 187, 126
second coming 8, 27–28, 42, 85
second meanings 101, 208, 222
secular 14, 30, 37, 97, 157, 165, 168, 171, 255
Sehnsucht 12, 25, 45, 63, 64–69, 82, 197, 249, 252
shadowlands 16, 49, 71–73, 82
shadows 17, 84, 234, 259–60 (See: Platonic)
simul iustus et peccator 254
sin(s) 4, 8, 16, 19, 22, 26, 48, 62, 69, 71, 78, 94, 100–101, 104, 106, 108, 111, 112, 116–17, 120, 127, 129–31, 137, 144, 152–53, 156, 158–59, 164, 172, 177, 181, 200–201, 204, 209–10, 213, 219, 222–23, 227, 235–36, 241, 245, 250, 252–53, 254 (See: fall; original sin)
    sinner(s) 100, 104, 112, 144, 254
Sitz im Leben 21, 40–42, 218
skeptic 21
    skeptical 21, 42, 75, 77, 114, 145, 242
    skepticism 13, 33–36, 39, 42, 75, 99, 103, 137, 148
    skeptics 11, 34–35, 75–76, 90, 123, 133, 147, 149, 225, 262
Socratic 35, 95, 162, 165, 174, 205, 207–8, 248
sola scriptura 51
soteriology 216
    soteriologically 213, 216, 246
speech-act 46–48, 50
spiritual 25–26, 30, 36, 39, 53, 74, 77–78, 92–93, 109, 118, 132, 136, 163, 200, 207, 232, 237, 253, 257
splintered fragments of the true light 15, 227, 245, 247, 254-55
status 12, 45–46, 48, 51, 61–62, 73, 94–5, 100–101, 113–14, 127–28, 131, 133, 135–36, 147, 153, 155–56, 169, 172–73, 186, 209, 224, 255, 262
story 8, 15, 21, 26, 29, 31, 33, 34, 36–38, 49, 54, 74–75, 81–82, 94, 97–99, 129, 141, 153–54, 156, 160, 168, 174, 192–97, 204, 206–8, 213–16, 225, 226–29, 232, 245–49, 251, 253, 256–59, 262, 263–64, 266 (See: narrative; analogy)
sub-creation 15, 217, 225–27, 234, 247, 248
    sub-creator(s) 49, 226, 225, 227, 228, 248
supernatural 9, 39, 64, 73, 108, 114, 120, 141, 174, 181, 197, 237–38, 242, 247, 250
symbolism 74, 77

tabernacle 129–30, 152
    tabernacle presence 129
    tabernacling 127–30
teleology 71, 262

teleologically 71, 85, 245, 256, 262
Temple 2, 125–27, 130, 134
testimony 23, 32, 55, 110, 119, 127, 138–39, 142, 144–47
Theism 10, 24, 68, 72, 95, 108, 192, 202–3, 253, 261
theology 3, 5–9, 15, 17, 22–23, 29, 36, 38–39, 58–59, 61, 66, 79–80, 82–83, 89, 91, 107, 120, 128, 132, 135, 162, 169, 174, 184–85, 192, 195, 201–3, 206–7, 216–17, 224–25, 234–38, 241, 242, 246, 247, 253, 258, 260, 265–67
    theologian(s) 3–6, 11–13, 15, 22–24, 30, 33–38, 45, 55–56, 63, 69, 71–73, 79, 90, 95, 96, 100–101, 103, 106–8, 111, 113, 123–24, 145–46, 149, 154, 156, 159, 166, 169, 178–79, 191–96, 211, 217, 224, 230, 234–35, 237, 246, 251, 265, 266
    theological 5, 6, 8–9, 11, 13–14, 23, 26, 31, 38, 45, 54–55, 65, 69, 73, 82, 89–90, 93, 96–97, 100, 103, 110, 123, 126–28, 146, 149, 151, 155, 166, 176, 185, 187, 195, 214, 226, 235–36, 240, 243, 253, 265, 266
theopneustos 24, 45–46, 53
Torah 104, 127, 129, 154–55
tradition 1–3, 13–14, 23, 29, 37, 45, 54, 60–61, 63, 66–67, 71, 89–90, 103, 111, 117, 120–21, 127, 134–35, 140, 148, 155, 159, 166, 187, 193–94, 209, 215, 224–25, 235, 247, 251–53, 258, 262, 266
transcendence 129, 211–213
    transcendent 7, 16, 42, 79, 158, 177, 206, 211–12, 230–31
transfiguration 141
    transfigured 141
translate 52, 72, 257, 265
    translated 53, 74, 85, 107, 134, 137,
    translation 1, 27, 83–84, 148, 236
transposition 13, 71–85, 132–33, 136, 148, 184, 206, 217, 225, 238–39, 242–43, 246, 248, 254, 259, 260, 265
    transposed 12–14, 19, 71, 73–77, 80–85, 127, 130–33, 139, 168, 184, 212, 237, 243, 248–50, 253–54, 256, 260, 265
    transpositional 74, 79, 83–84, 184, 223
trilemma 13–14, 89–91, 93–94, 98, 103, 110, 119–20, 123–27, 131–33, 138, 145–46, 149, 151–52, 157, 159, 162–80, 182–88, 266 (See: dilemma; God or a Bad Man)
Trinity 2, 5, 16, 22, 32, 53, 55, 59, 62, 69, 73, 79, 90, 101, 107, 127, 131–34, 145, 161, 193, 195–96, 264–66 (See: Holy Spirit; pneumatology)
    economic Trinity 59, 193, 265–66
    Trinitarian 2, 5, 63, 79, 101, 130, 133–35, 138, 140, 179, 184, 191–94

triune 14, 62, 79, 84
truth 8, 13, 16, 21–22, 25, 29–31, 33–34, 38, 42, 45, 49–50, 53–55, 57, 63, 72–73, 75, 82–85, 92, 95, 98, 101, 104–6, 115–19, 123, 129, 137, 141, 146–47, 149, 154, 156, 159, 161–63, 167, 168, 171, 173–76, 179, 194–96, 200, 202, 206, 218–19, 221–22, 225, 227–28, 234–35, 237, 239, 240, 242–43, 246, 248, 251–53, 255–57

understanding 1–7, 10, 12, 14–16, 21, 24–25, 28–29, 33–34, 38, 41, 45–46, 48–49, 50, 52–54, 56–57, 63–65, 67, 69, 71–73, 80, 83, 85, 91–92, 96, 98, 101, 108, 112, 116, 120, 127–28, 129–30, 132, 134, 136, 138, 148–49, 159, 165, 168, 171, 177, 178–79, 180–81, 184–86, 191–93, 196, 200, 202, 204, 206, 209, 217, 219, 220–21, 223–26, 232, 234–38, 239, 241–43, 245–47, 254, 258–60, 265–67
unhistorical 21, 29, 158 (See: history)
    unhistoricity 21, 32
universal 3, 11–12, 16, 29, 31, 34, 45, 52–53, 55, 60, 62, 64, 68–69, 115, 117, 121, 141, 152, 159, 160–61, 193, 221, 230–31, 254, 261
    universalism 34, 152, 160
    universalistic 255

veiling–unveiling 79–80, 128, 184
    veiling 13, 71, 79–80, 128, 184, 213
    unveiling 13, 71, 79–80, 128, 184, 213
Verkündung 57–58
Victorian 13–14, 103, 106, 113, 116, 120, 191, 199–201, 209

Weltanschauung 200
    worldview(s) 36, 95, 120, 160, 172, 200
wisdom 12, 21, 29, 52, 97, 113–14, 122, 124, 160, 163, 176–77, 181, 185, 200, 217, 219, 221, 223, 227–28, 234, 239, 243, 247
Wissenschaft 22
witness 2–3, 21, 23, 32, 34, 55–62, 66–67, 71, 90, 106, 110, 113, 122, 127, 135, 139, 142, 146–47, 151, 153–54, 178–79, 212, 235, 250
    witnesses 21, 23, 28, 32, 42, 141, 144, 153, 156
word of God 12, 45–46, 53–55, 60, 62, 66–67, 84–85, 112, 145, 265, 266
Word of God 12–13, 32–33, 45–46, 52–62, 65–67, 79, 85, 258, 265–66
Worship 139, 144

Index of C. S. Lewis's Works
An index of Lewis's works cited or quoted

An Experiment in Criticism 196

Beyond Personality: The Christian Idea of God 61, 131
Broadcast Talks: Reprinted with some alterations from two series of Broadcast Talks "Right and Wrong: A Clue to the Meaning of the Universe" and "What Christians Believe" given in 1941 and 1942 89, 90–91, 94–95, 97, 100, 102, 112, 131, 137, 158, 181, 210

"Christian Apologetics" 91, 95, 121, 123–24, 158, 168, 176
Christian Reflections 205
Collected Letters, Vol. I 25, 192, 198, 201, 203–5
Collected Letters, Vol. II 25, 92, 107
Collected Letters, Vol. III 25–27, 31, 51–54, 59, 62, 67, 84, 147, 148
"Cross–Examination" 91, 102, 185, 243

"De Descriptione Temporum" 10, 41
"Difficulties in Presenting the Christian Faith to Modern Unbelievers" 35, 148

"God in the Dock" 21, 35, 235

"Heaven, Earth and Outer Space" 102

"Introduction," in, *English Literature in the Sixteenth Century* 61
"Is Theism Important?" 10, 24, 253, 261
"Is Theology Poetry?" 91, 95, 205, 248
"I was Decided Upon" 102

Letter to Arthur Greeves, Aug. 4, 1917 25
Letter to Arthur Greeves, Feb. 28, 1916 25
Letter to Arthur Greeves, Jan. 30, 1944 25
Letter to Arthur Greeves, Oct. 1, 1931 203–5
Letter to Arthur Greeves, Oct. 12, 1916 198, 201
Letter to Arthur Greeves, Oct, 18, 1931 192, 204
Letter to Arthur Greeves, Sept. 22, 1931 203
Letter to Clyde S. Kilby, May 7, 1959 21, 24, 31–33, 50–51, 54, 59, 67, 147
Letter to Dom Bede Griffiths, April 24, 1936 236
Letter to Dom Bede Griffiths, May, 28, 1952 25
Letter to Emily McLay, Aug. 3, 1953 52
Letter to Emily McLay, Aug. 8, 1953 26
Letter to Genia Goelz, Jun. 20, 1952 25
Letter to Genia Goelz, Mar. 18, 1952 25
Letter to Janet Wise Oct. 5, 1955 26, 52
Letter to Mr Allcock, Mar. 24, 1955 26
Letter to Mrs Green, Jun. 18, 1962 27
Letter to Mrs Johnson, Nov. 8, 1952 53–54, 62, 67, 84
Letter to Mrs Mary Neylan, Mar. 26, 1940 92
Letter to Owen Barfield, Aug. 1939 92
Letter to Peter Hastings, Letter no 153, 1954 226
Letter to The Church Times, Feb. 8, 1952 8
Letter to the editor of The Spectator, Dec. 11, 1942 25
Letter to Vera Gebbert, Oct. 16, 1960 26
Letters to Young Churches 27

"Man or Rabbit" 260
Mere Christianity 3–4, 19, 22, 61, 63–65, 68–69, 89, 91, 95, 100, 130, 132, 133, 249, 250, 260, 261
Miracles (1st and 2nd editions) 34, 60, 91, 96–97, 133, 139, 141, 189, 205–7, 212–13, 235, 259–61
"Modern Theology and Biblical Criticism" 21, 37–39, 41–42, 82, 148, 196, 205
"Myth Became Fact" 205–6, 248, 257, 261

"On Stories" 205–6, 226

"Preface," in, *George MacDonald: An Anthology* 253
"Psycho–Analysis and Literary Criticism" 223–24

Reflections on the Psalms 21, 29–30, 54, 60, 72, 83, 91, 100–101, 120, 141, 184, 205, 208, 218–21, 243, 251, 260–61
"Rejoinder to Dr Pittenger" 42
"Religion Without Dogma?" 205, 207, 260–61, 263

Surprised by Joy 120, 138, 185, 205, 207–8, 230, 232, 235, 237, 247, 253, 261

The Chronicles of Narnia 17, 74, 75, 82, 98, 192, 226
    The Last Battle 74
    The Lion, the Witch and the Wardrobe 91, 89, 98
    The Silver Chair 75
    The Voyage of the Dawn Treader 82
The Four Loves 132
"The Funeral of a Great Myth" 260
"The Grand Miracle" 205, 207, 212–13, 259–61
The Great Divorce 78, 132, 223
"The Language of Religion" 91, 101, 132
The Pilgrim's Regress 65, 205, 250–53, 255
The Problem of Pain 24, 27, 64, 89, 91, 93–94, 148, 163, 181, 182, 260–61
"The Weight of Glory" 82, 235
"The World's Last Night" 27
They Asked for a Paper —Papers and Addresses 205
"Transposition" 71, 72, 74–75, 77–82, 132–33, 148, 184, 265
Transposition and Other Addresses 71, 72, 74–75, 77–82, 132–33, 148, 184, 265

Undeceptions— Essays on Theology and Ethics 205, 261

"What Are We to Make of Jesus Christ?" 91, 97, 132, 187

Sectional Contents

Foreword | xiii

Introduction C. S. Lewis—The Work of Christ Revealed | 1
1. Who or What is the Christ | 1
2. Why C. S. Lewis | 3
3. Aims and Objectives | 4
4. Explanations, Qualifications | 6
    i. Revelation and Reason | 6
    ii. Patristic | 7
    iii. Platonism | 7
    iv. Apologist/Apologetics | 8
    v. Creation, Fall, Incarnation, Resurrection, Second Coming, and the Four Last Things | 8
    vi. Liberal/Liberal, Modernism | 9
    vii. Pagan | 9
    viii. Romantic | 10
5. ". . . and the Collected Works of C. S. Lewis" | 11
6. Lewis on the Christ: God and Redeemer | 12
    i. Part One: Scripture—Revelation Transposed | 12
    ii. Part Two: The Revelation of Christ—God, or a Bad Man | 13
    iii. Part Three: Christ Prefigured—Intimations to the Pagans | 14
7. Lewis's Christ | 15

PART ONE SCRIPTURE—REVELATION TRANSPOSED

Chapter 1 Scripture, Revelation, and Reason I: Skepticism and Suspicion | 21
1. Person, Act, Event | 22
2. C. S. Lewis on Scripture | 24
    i. Illumination and Revelation | 24
    ii. Genre | 26
    iii. Language | 27
3. The Historicity of Scripture | 27
4. The Humanity of Scripture | 30
    i. Reflections on the Psalms | 30

      ii. The Clyde S. Kilby Letter | 31
          Divine and Human Origin | 32
          Levels of Historicity | 32
          A Human Element | 32
          Mythological Narratives | 32
          Divinely Inspired Writings | 32
          Inspiration and the Purposes of God | 33
5. The Gospel according to John | 33
   i. Skepticism and Suspicion | 33
   ii. Lock, Vidler, and Bultmann | 35
   iii. Modern Theology and Biblical Criticism | 37
      Genre and Types of Literature: Expertise | 38
      Historical Superiority | 39
      The Non-Miraculous | 40
      Sitz im Leben | 40
6. Modern Scholarship and Agnosticism | 42

Chapter 2 Scripture, Revelation, and Reason II: Mediation and the Bible | 45

1. C. S. Lewis: A Doctrine of Scripture? | 46
   i. Doctrine | 46
   ii. Inerrancy and Infallibility | 46
      The Freedom Model | 46
      The Amanuensis Model | 48
      The Automaton Model | 48
      The Humanist Model | 48
   iii. Inspiration | 50
   iv. Interpretation: Local and Universal Genre | 52
2. The "word" of God and the "Word" of God | 52
   i. Scripture (word) in Relation to the Christ (Word) | 52
   ii. C. S. Lewis and Karl Barth—The Word of God in a Threefold Form | 55
      Barth: The Word of God Preached | 57
      Barth: The Word of God Written | 58
      Barth: The Word of God Revealed | 59
      Lewis: The Threefold Form of the w/Word of God | 59
   iii. Lewis and Barth: Convergence and Divergence | 61
3. Revelation and the Christ-Event | 62
   i. Revelation and the Bible | 62
   ii. Christensen-Walker on Revelation in Lewis | 63
      The Experience of the Numinous, God's Holiness | 64
      The Universal Ought: Cosmic Bluff or Moral Responsibility | 64
      Sehnsucht: the Hound of Heaven | 64
      Election: Israel and the Law | 64
      Good Dreams: Pagan Premonitions of Christ | 65
      Incarnation: The Word of God Revealed | 65

4. A Hierarchy of Revelation | 66
   i. Mediation | 66
   ii. Revelation as Supra-Theological Categories | 68

Chapter 3 Scripture, Revelation, and Reason III: Idealism and Transposition | 71

1. Introduction | 72
2. Transposition | 72
   i. Platonic Idealism | 72
   ii. Revelation Transposed | 73
3. Incarnational Transposition | 77
   i. *communicatio idiomatum* | 79
   ii. Veiling-Unveiling: The Knowability of God | 80
   iii. Human Fallibility: the Misreading of the Transposition | 80
4. The Key to Lewis's Work: A "Flawed" Doctrine of Transposition | 82
5. Modes of Revelation Subsumed into Eternity | 84

PART TWO THE REVELATION OF CHRIST—GOD, OR A BAD MAN

Chapter 4 *aut Deus aut malus homo* I: What did Lewis Say? | 89

1. Introduction | 90
2. Lewis: "God . . . or a Bad Man": The Early Works | 91
   i. Correspondence—August 1939 | 92
   ii. Correspondence—March 26, 1940 | 92
   iii. The Problem of Pain (1940) | 93
   iv. Broadcast Talks (1942) | 94
3. Lewis: "God . . . or a Bad Man": The Middle Works | 95
   i. "Is Theology Poetry?" (1944) | 95
   ii. "Christian Apologetics" (1945) | 95
   iii. Miracles (1947) | 96
4. Lewis: "God . . . or a Bad Man": The Later Works | 97
   i. "What Are We to Make of Jesus Christ?" (1950) | 97
   ii. The Lion, the Witch and the Wardrobe (1950) | 98
      The Lucy triumvirate | 98
      The Structure of the Professor's Argument | 98
   iii. Mere Christianity (1952) | 100
   iv. Reflections on the Psalms (1958) | 100
   v. "The Language of Religion" (1960) | 101
   vi. "Cross-Examination" (1963) | 102

Chapter 5 *aut Deus aut malus homo* II: The Theological Tradition | 103

1. "God . . . or a Bad Man": The Patristic and Medieval Theological Tradition | 103
   i. The Gospels | 104
   ii. The Apostle Paul | 106
   iii. Patristic Roots? | 106

    iv. Pope Innocent III—*aut Deus es aut homo* | 107
    v. Thomas Aquinas—Pride and Humility | 108
    vi. Sir Thomas More: "If Christ were not God, he would be no Good Man either" | 109
2. "God . . . or a Bad Man": The Post-Reformation Theological Tradition | 110
    i. Protestant and Reformed Developments: John Calvin | 110
    ii. Protestant and Reformed Developments: John Duncan | 110
3. Mark Hopkins—Condition, Claims, and Character | 111
4. Henry Parry Liddon | 113
    i. *Christus, si non Deus, non bonus* | 114
    ii. "Our Lord's Divinity as Witnessed by his Consciousness" | 115
    iii. The Moral Character of Jesus? | 116
    iv. Christ's Self Assertion and His Character | 119
    v. Did Lewis read Liddon? | 120
5. G. K. Chesterton | 120
6. Contemporary Developments | 123
7. "Unbalanced Liar," "Possessed," or "The God of Israel": The Johannine trilemma | 124

Chapter 6 *aut Deus aut malus homo* III: Divine Self-Disclosure | 127

1. Introduction | 128
2. Self-Disclosure—Understanding and Identity? | 128
    i. A Declaration of Identity? | 128
    ii. The Tabernacle Presence—Signals of Transcendence | 129
3. C. S. Lewis: Transposed Reality of Divine Sonship | 130
    i. Markers of Self-Disclosure I: Sonship—Identity and Becoming | 131
    ii. Markers of Self-Disclosure II: Incarnation | 133
    iii. Markers of Self-Disclosure III: Messiah | 134
    iv. Markers of Self-Disclosure IV: "Son of God," "Son of Man" | 135
    v. Markers of Self-Disclosure V: "I Am" | 137
    vi. Markers of Self-Disclosure IV: Trinitarian | 138
4. Divine Self-Disclosure—Scripture | 139
    i. Divinity | 139
    ii. Miracles | 141
    iii. Witness | 142
    iv. Old Testament Prefigurements | 143
    v. Worship | 144
    vi. Forgiving of Sins | 144
5. The Reliability of The Gospel according to John | 145

Chapter 7 *aut Deus aut malus homo* IV: Arguments For and Against | 151

1. Arguments for Self-Disclosure—Divine Sonship | 151
    i. "He is who He Reveals himself To Be" | 151
    ii. The Argument from Orthodoxy | 152
    iii. A Jewish-Christian Model | 154

Sectional Contents

  2. Arguments against Self-Disclosure—The Merely Human | 156
     i. A Model of Scripture | 156
     ii. A Model of "God" | 157
     iii. The Scandal of Particularity | 159
  3. A Model of Obstinacy? | 161
     i. A Post Mortem Socratic Dialogue | 162
     ii. Reason and Logic: The "god" of the Philosophers | 162
     iii. Insanity | 164

Chapter 8 *aut Deus aut malus homo* V: Lewis's Trilemma | 165

  1. Introduction | 166
  2. The Structure of Lewis's Argument | 166
  3. A Philosophical Analysis: Stephen T. Davis | 169
     i. The Nature of the Argument: Proof, Validity, Soundness | 170
     ii. Critical Objections | 172
     iii. Claims of Divinity | 172
     iv. The Value of the Argument | 173
  4. A Philosophical Analysis: Peter Kreeft | 174
     i. *aut Deus aut homo malus, et non homo malus, ergo Deus* | 174
     ii. Deductive Proof—Trustworthiness and Sagacity | 176
  5. Proof . . . or a Question, a Human Dilemma? | 176
     i. A Concept of God | 177
     ii. Proof? | 179
     iii. Insanity? | 181
  6. *aut Deus aut malus homo* | 182
     i. Pneumatological Preparation | 183
     ii. Trilemma or Dilemma? | 185
  7. Conclusion | 186

PART THREE CHRIST PREFIGURED— INTIMATIONS TO THE PAGANS

Chapter 9 Christ as the Light of the World I: A Doctrine of Christological Prefigurement | 191

  1. Introduction: The Work of Christ, Revealed | 191
  2. A Doctrine of christological Prefigurement | 192
  3. Myth and Reality, Fact and Fiction | 194
     i. Myth | 194
     ii. Lewis on Myth | 196
     iii. Religion as a Human Construct | 197
  4. Sir James George Frazer | 199
     i. Religion and Anthropology—A Worldview | 199
     ii. A Paradigm: Revelation Precedes Religion | 201
  5. Lewis's Conversion—Atonement and Prefigurement | 202
     i. Natural Theology and Revelation | 202

ii. Myth Became Reality | 206
6. The Incarnation-Resurrection Narrative | 208
   i. Myths of Prefigurement—Incarnation | 209
   ii. Myths of Prefigurement—Resurrection | 213

Chapter 10 Christ as the Light of the World II: Revelation and Meaning—Imagination, Illumination, and Prevenience | 217

1. Second Meanings | 218
   i. Intention and Validity | 218
   ii. Plato and the Christ | 219
   iii. Wisdom | 221
2. Imagination, Idolatry, and the Theological Tradition | 223
3. J. R. R. Tolkien | 225
   i. Sub-Creation | 225
   ii. Mythopoeic/Mythopoeia | 226
   iii. Refractions and Splinters of the True Light | 227
   iv. Eucatastrophe | 229
4. Samuel Taylor Coleridge | 229
   i. The English Romantics | 229
   ii. The Categorical Imperative | 230
   iii. Primary and Secondary Imagination | 231
   iv. MacDonald on Coleridge | 232
5. Augustine of Hippo | 236
   i. Natural Theology and Revealed Theology | 236
   ii. Revelation, Inspiration, and Illumination | 238
   iii. Prevenience | 240
6. C. S. Lewis: A General or Special Theory of Illumination? | 242

Chapter 11 Christ as the Light of the World III: Refractions—Splintered Fragments of the True Light | 245

1. Why Prefigurement? | 246
2. Splintered Fragments of the True Light: How do these Prefigured Ideas Come to Be in Pagan Myths? | 247
   i. A Developing Understanding | 247
   ii. Pagan Mythopoeia and the Shepherds | 248
   iii. Pagan Prevision | 250
   iv. Demonic Mimicry and the Fall? | 251
   v. A Baptized Imagination | 253
3. The Refracted Light of Revelation | 254
4. A Temporal Paradox? | 255
5. How Does the Incarnation-Resurrection Narrative Act/Operate on Us as a Myth, Whether Spoken or Read? | 257

6. Is There Internal Evidence for a Mythopoeic Interpretation within the Incarnation-Resurrection Narrative? | 258
      i. "The Pattern is there in Nature because it was First there in God" | 258
      ii. The Death-Descent/Rebirth-Reascent Paradigm | 260
   7. Why? Why Not? | 261
   8. A Doctrine of Christological Prefigurement—Conclusion | 263

Conclusion. The Work of Christ—Revealed | 265

Select Bibliography | 269

   Letters and Articles by C. S. Lewis | 269
   Books by C. S. Lewis | 271
   Other Books and Articles | 271

Indexes

   Index of Names | 279
   Index of Subjects | 282
   Index of C. S. Lewis's Works | 291

www.ingramcontent.com/pod-product-compliance
Lightning Source LLC
Chambersburg PA
CBHW060508300426
44112CB00017B/2587